'Antisemitism has often presented itself as a s̶[ ]what is wrong with the world, and repeatedly of[ ]to improve that world. Do our moral and politi̶c̶ ̶.̶.̶.̶.̶.̶.̶ ̶.̶.̶.̶.̶.̶.̶ ̶.̶.̶.̶.̶.̶ ̶.̶.̶.̶.̶.̶.̶ past prejudice and projection? We cannot know without reflection, and it is difficult to imagine a better stimulus to reflection than the essays gathered in this informative, wide-ranging, and important volume'.

David Nirenberg, *author of Anti-Judaism: The Western Tradition*

'This is an indispensable volume on an unignorable subject'.

Anthony Julius, *author of Trials of the Diaspora: The History of Anti-Semitism in England*

'Written by many of this generation's leading scholars, *Mapping the New Left Antisemitism: The Fathom Essays* is a valuable compilation of learned, deeply insightful analyses of contemporary anti-Jewish hostility prevalent in significant strains of western political thought. An eye-opening, much-needed collection, it offers critically important reflections on a phenomenon too often overlooked or denied: the pernicious links between "anti-Zionism" and antisemitism within the political left'.

Alvin Rosenfeld, *Professor of English and Jewish Studies and Irving M. Glazer Chair, Jewish Studies Director, Center for the Study of Contemporary Antisemitism, Indiana University at Bloomington, USA*

'*Fathom* has played an invaluable role challenging some dangerous myths concerning Jews and Zionism that have corrupted parts of the left. This wide-ranging collection will compel anyone concerned with a future left to worry about intellectually and historically simplistic formulas'.

Mitchell Cohen, *Professor of Political Science at Baruch College of the City University of New York and the CUNY Graduate Center. 1991–2009 co-editor of Dissent, one of the United States' leading intellectual quarterlies, now an Editor Emeritus*

'*Mapping the New Left Antisemitism* is essential reading for anyone interested in one of the most destructive ideologies of the 21st century. It includes essays by some of the most pertinent scholars on antisemitism from the political left and makes the case for the urgency of combating antisemitism in its most modern forms'.

Gunther Jikeli, *Erna B. Rosenfeld Professor in Jewish Studies and Associate Director at the Institute for the Study of Contemporary Antisemitism, Indiana University Bloomington, USA*

MAPPING THE NEW LEFT ANTISEMITISM

Mapping the New Left Antisemitism: The Fathom Essays provides a comprehensive guide to contemporary Left antisemitism.

The rise of a new and largely left-wing form of antisemitism in the era of the Jewish state and the distinction between it and legitimate criticism of Israel are now roiling progressive politics in the West and causing alarming spikes in antisemitic incitement and incidents. *Fathom* journal has examined these questions relentlessly in the first decade of its existence, earning a reputation for careful textual analysis and cogent advocacy. In this book, the *Fathom* essays are contextualised by three new contributions: Lesley Klaff provides a map of contemporary antisemitic forms of antizionism, Dave Rich writes on the oft-neglected lived experience of the Jewish victims of contemporary antisemitism and David Hirsh assesses the intellectual history of the left from which both *Fathom* and his own London Centre for the Study of Contemporary Antisemitism, as well as this book series, have emerged. Topics covered by the contributors include antisemitic antizionism and its underappreciated Soviet roots; the impact of analogies with the Nazis; the rise of antisemitism on the European continent, exploring the hybrid forms emerging from a cross-fertilisation between new left, Christian and Islamist antisemitism; the impact of antizionist activism on higher education; and the bitter debates over the adoption of the oft-misrepresented International Holocaust Remembrance Alliance (IHRA) definition of antisemitism.

This work will be of considerable appeal to scholars and activists with an interest in antisemitism, Jewish studies and the politics of Israel.

Alan Johnson is the founder and editor of *Fathom* journal. A professor of democratic theory and practice, he has served on the editorial boards of *Socialist Organiser*, *Historical Materialism* and the US socialist journals *New Politics* and *Dissent*. His writings on the left, and on antisemitism, include 'Aurum de Stercore: anti-totalitarianism in the thought of Primo Levi', in *Thinking Towards Humanity. Themes From Norman Geras*, edited by Stephen De Wijze and Eve Garrard (2012), and the report *Institutionally Antisemitic: Contemporary Left Antisemitism and the Crisis in the British Labour Party* (2019).

Studies in Contemporary Antisemitism

Series editors

David Hirsch
Senior Lecturer in Sociology, Goldsmiths, University of London and Academic Director of the London Centre for the Study of Contemporary Antisemitism
Rosa Freedman
Professor in the School of Law, University of Reading and Research Fellow at the London Centre for the Study of Contemporary Antisemitism

Published in conjunction with the London Centre for the Study of Contemporary Antisemitism, *Studies in Contemporary Antisemitism* is a timely, multidisciplinary book series, drawing primarily, but not exclusively, on the social sciences and the humanities. The series encourages academically rigorous and critical publications across several disciplines and that are explicit in understanding and opposing the presence and ascendancy of contemporary antisemitism in both its theoretical and empirical manifestations. The series provides a unique opportunity to offer an intellectual home for a diversity of works that, taken together, crystallize around the study of contemporary antisemitism. The series consists of research monographs, edited collections and short form titles.

Nazis, Islamic Antisemitism, and the Middle East
The 1948 Arab war against Israel and the aftershocks of WW II
Matthias Küntzel

Mapping the New Left Antisemitism
The Fathom Essays
Edited by Alan Johnson

For more information about this series, please visit: www.routledge.com/studies-in-contemporary-antisemitism/book-series/SICA

MAPPING THE NEW LEFT ANTISEMITISM

The Fathom Essays

Edited by Alan Johnson

Routledge
Taylor & Francis Group

LONDON AND NEW YORK

Designed cover image: © Getty Images

First published 2024
by Routledge
4 Park Square, Milton Park, Abingdon, Oxon OX14 4RN

and by Routledge
605 Third Avenue, New York, NY 10158

Routledge is an imprint of the Taylor & Francis Group, an informa business

British Library Cataloguing-in-Publication Data
A catalogue record for this book is available from the British Library

Library of Congress Cataloging-in-Publication Data
Names: Johnson, Alan, 1962– editor.
Title: Mapping the new left antisemitism : the Fathom essays / edited by Alan Johnson.
Other titles: Fathom essays | Fathom (Online journal)
Description: Abingdon, Oxon ; New York : Routledge, 2024. | Series: Studies in contemporary antisemitism | Includes bibliographical references and index.
Identifiers: LCCN 2023018657 (print) | LCCN 2023018658 (ebook) | ISBN 9781032344737 (hardback) | ISBN 9781032344713 (paperback) | ISBN 9781003322320 (ebook)
Subjects: LCSH: Antisemitism—History—21st century. | Zionism—Political aspects—History—21st century. | Right and left (Political science) | Socialism and antisemitism. | Communism and Judaism.
Classification: LCC DS145 .M236 2024 (print) | LCC DS145 (ebook) | DDC 323.1192/40905—dc23/eng/20230614
LC record available at https://lccn.loc.gov/2023018657
LC ebook record available at https://lccn.loc.gov/2023018658

ISBN: 978-1-032-34473-7 (hbk)
ISBN: 978-1-032-34471-3 (pbk)
ISBN: 978-1-003-32232-0 (ebk)

DOI: 10.4324/9781003322320

Typeset in Sabon
by Apex CoVantage, LLC

*Dedicated with love to Debbie and our children
Ellie and Michael.*

CONTENTS

CONTRIBUTORS

Russell A. Berman is the Walter A. Haas Professor in the Humanities at Stanford University. He is also Senior Fellow at the Hoover Institution, where he directs the Working Group on the Middle East and the Islamic World. His books include *The Rise of the Modern German Novel: Crisis and Charisma* (1986), *Fiction Sets You Free: Literature, Liberty and Western Culture* (2007) and *Anti-Americanism in Europe: A Cultural Problem* (2008). He is editor emeritus of the quarterly *Telos* and a member of the National Humanities Council.

Paul Bogdanor is an independent researcher in the United Kingdom. He is the co-editor (with Edward Alexander) of *The Jewish Divide Over Israel: Accusers and Defenders* (2006) and the author of *Kasztner's Crime* (2016).

Matthew Bolton is a researcher at the Zentrum für Antisemitismusforschung, TU Berlin. He is the co-author (with Frederick Harry Pitts) of *Corbynism: A Critical Approach* (2018) and has written for journals such as *the Political Quarterly, British Politics* and the *Journal of Contemporary Antisemitism*.

Sarah Annes Brown is Professor of English Literature at Anglia Ruskin University. Her research interests include Ovid's *Metamorphoses* and Shakespeare's influence on science fiction.

Marlene Gallner is the editor of *Jean Améry: Essays on Antisemitism, Anti-Zionism, and the Left* (2022). An independent scholar, she is the editor of *sans phrase. Zeitschrift für Ideologiekritik*, the Vienna-based biannual

German-language journal dedicated to social and cultural analyses in the tradition of Frankfurt School critical theory.

Simon Gansinger is finishing his doctorate on 'Reasons of state as reasons in law' at the Department of Philosophy of the University of Warwick. He has worked on the Frankfurt School, legal philosophy and the psychoanalysis of antisemitism. His most recent publication is (in German) 'Inertia as progress: Neumann and Horkheimer on the normative potential of law', in *Kritische Theorien und zeitliche Dimensionen*, supplement to *Archives for Philosophy of Law and Social Philosophy*, edited by Sonja Heimrath et al., Stuttgart: Franz Steiner Verlag (forthcoming).

Eve Garrard was Senior Lecturer in Philosophy and Professional Ethics at the University of Keele, and latterly Research Fellow in the Department of Philosophy at Manchester University, prior to her retirement. Her research interests are in metaethics and applied ethics, and she has published various papers on the Holocaust and on the concepts of evil and forgiveness. She has also co-edited, with Dr Geoffrey Scarre, *Moral Philosophy and the Holocaust* (Routledge, 2003).

Norman Geras (1943–2013) was Professor Emeritus at the University of Manchester. He was the author of many works, including *The Legacy of Rosa Luxemburg* (1976), *Marx and Human Nature: Refutation of a Legend* (1983) and *The Contract of Mutual Indifference: Political Philosophy After the Holocaust* (1998).

David Gurevich is a research fellow in the University of Haifa, Israel. He studies the material culture of pilgrimage, Israel-Church relations and Jerusalem. He co-edited (with Anat Kidron) *Exploring the Holy Land* (2019).

Bernard Harrison is Emeritus E.E. Ericksen Professor of Philosophy in the University of Utah, and Emeritus Professor in the Faculty of Humanities, University of Sussex, UK. He is the author of *The Resurgence of Antisemitism: Jews, Israel, and Liberal Opinion* (2006) and *Blaming the Jews: Politics and Delusion* (2022).

Kathleen Hayes is an independent writer. She has published in *Fathom* and *Tablet* and lives in California.

Jeffrey Herf is Distinguished University Professor Emeritus at the University of Maryland, College Park, USA. His books include *Israel's Moment: International Support for and Opposition to Establishing the Jewish State, 1945–1949* (2022) and *Undeclared Wars With Israel: East Germany and the West German Far Left, 1967–1989* (2016).

David Hirsh is Senior Lecturer in Sociology at Goldsmiths, University of London, and is the Academic Director and CEO at the London Centre for the Study of Contemporary Antisemitism. In 2005, he founded the Engage Network and website, which co-ordinated the resistance to the campaign to boycott Israeli universities. He is the author of *Contemporary Left Antisemitism* (Routledge, 2018).

Lesley Klaff is Senior Lecturer in Law at Sheffield Hallam University and Research Fellow at the London Centre for the Study of Contemporary Antisemitism. She is Editor-in-Chief of the *Journal of Contemporary Antisemitism* and author of several publications on antisemitism and the law. Her most recent article, 'What Is an English Jew? The Legal Construction of Jewish Identity Under the UK Equality Act of 2010', was published in Vol. 11, Issue 1, of the *Indiana Journal of Law and Social Equality* in January 2023.

Shalom Lappin is Professor of Natural Language Processing at Queen Mary University of London, Professor of Computational Linguistics at the University of Gothenburg and Emeritus Professor of Computational Linguistics at King's College London.

Susie Linfield is the author of *The Cruel Radiance: Photography and Political Violence* (2012) and *The Lions' Den: Zionism and the Left From Hannah Arendt to Noam Chomsky* (2019). She is a professor of journalism at New York University.

Sean Matgamna is a leading member of the Alliance for Workers' Liberty. He is the editor of *The Fate of the Russian Revolution Volume 1: Lost Texts of Critical Marxism* (1998), *The Left in Disarray* (2017) and *The Fate of the Russian Revolution Volume 2: The Two Trotskyisms Confront Stalinism* (2015).

Cary Nelson is Jubilee Professor of Liberal Arts and Sciences Emeritus at the University of Illinois at Urbana-Champaign. His 36 books include *Israel Denial: Anti-Zionism, Anti-Semitism, and the Faculty Campaign Against the Jewish State* (2019) and *Hate Speech and Academic Freedom: The Antisemitic Assault on Basic Values* (forthcoming).

Dave Rich is Director of Policy at the Community Security Trust, a Jewish charity that provides advice and support to the UK Jewish community on matters relating to antisemitism, terrorism and extremism. He is a research fellow at the London Centre for the Study of Contemporary Antisemitism and is on the editorial board of the *Journal of Contemporary Antisemitism*. He is the author of *The Left's Jewish Problem: Jeremy Corbyn, Israel and Antisemitism* (2016 and 2018) and *Everyday Hate: How Antisemitism Is Built Into Our World and How You Can Change It* (2023).

Philip Spencer is Emeritus Professor in Holocaust and Genocide Studies at Kingston University and Visiting Professor in Politics at Birkbeck, University of London. He is the co-author (with Robert Fine) of *Antisemitism and the Left: On the Return of the Jewish Question* (2017).

Karin Stögner is Professor of Sociology at the University of Passau. Her research focuses mainly on the critical theory of the Frankfurt School and on feminist theory, as well as on antisemitism, racism and gender. She has authored *Antisemitismus und Sexismus. Historisch-gesellschaftliche Konstellationen*, a comprehensive volume on the socio-historical constellations of antisemitism and sexism (2014) and co-edited *Kritische Theorie und Feminismus*, a volume on feminist readings of critical theory (2022).

Izabella Tabarovsky is a senior advisor at the Kennan Institute (Wilson Center), a fellow at the Institute for the Study of Global Antisemitism and Policy, a fellow at the London Centre for the Study of Contemporary Antisemitism and a contributing writer at *Tablet Magazine*. Her research expertise includes politics of historical memory, the Holocaust, Stalin's repressions, and Soviet and contemporary antisemitism. Her publications have appeared in *Newsweek*, *the Jewish Daily Forward*, *Tablet*, *Fathom*, *the National Interest* and *the Wilson Quarterly*.

Kenneth Waltzer is Professor of History Emeritus at Michigan State University. His most recent publication is 'Contending With Antisemitism in Its Many Forms on American Campuses', in *Contending With Antisemitism in a Rapidly Changing Political Climate*, edited by Alvin H. Rosenfeld, (2021). He was the founding executive director of the Academic Engagement Network (AEN), which organises American faculty to confront BDS campaigns on American campuses.

Michael Walzer is Professor (Emeritus) of Social Science at the Institute for Advanced Study in Princeton, NJ. He is the author of *Just and Unjust Wars* (1977), and many other books, and was for 20 years the co-editor of *Dissent* magazine.

ACKNOWLEDGEMENTS

I have been helped, criticised and inspired by a number of people in the course of thinking about and fighting against left antisemitism over the last 40 years, editing *Fathom* over the last decade, and assembling this collection over the last year. Among those to whom I should especially like to express my gratitude (sorry for any omissions from this list) are Jane Ashworth, Lorin Bell-Cross, Calev Ben-Dor, Paul Berman, Clive Bradley, Gabriel Noah Brahm, Ben Cohen, Mitchell Cohen, the late Steve Cohen, Stan Crooke, the late Robert Fine, Barry Finger, Ruth Fisher, Eve Garrard, Mark Gardner, the late Norman Geras, Richard Gold, Toby Greene, Bernard Harrison, David Hirsh, Anthony Julius, Dermot Kehoe, Lesley Klaff, Andrei Markovits, Sean Matgamna, Cary Nelson, Sam Nurding, Jack Omer-Jackaman, Richard Pater, Simon Pottinger, Dave Rich, Alvin Rosenfeld, Philip Spencer, John Strawson, Martin Thomas, Michael Walzer, Steve De Wijze and Debbie Williams.

Institutions not only within but also outside academia are vital to sustaining research into and action to combat antisemitism. I would like to thank the students who made teaching the Holocaust and leading the Primo Levi Reading Group at Edge Hill University the experience of a lifetime. Thanks also to the editorial board members of the journals *Democratiya* (2005–2010, incorporated into *Dissent*) and *Fathom* (2012–). *Fathom* was made possible by the board of BICOM who understood that there was a crying need for a journal of expert analysis (often critical), informed opinion, genuine debate and global reach that would combat rising antisemitism, defend the right to exist in security of the world's only Jewish state and make the intellectual case for the 'two states for two peoples' paradigm of peacemaking between Israelis and Palestinians; and do so by publishing creative thinking from a wide spectrum of perspectives, left and right, secular and religious, Israeli and Palestinian. I would like to express my gratitude for the granting of permission to reproduce essays from *Fathom* that first appeared elsewhere: to *Dissent* for the essay by Michael Walzer, to the Alliance for Workers' Liberty for Sean Matgamna's essay and to Indiana University Press for the extract from my own essay 'Denial: Norman Finkelstein and the New Antisemitism'. Thanks for the helpful comments to three anonymous readers and for the encouragement and guidance to Craig Fowlie and Elizabeth Hart at Routledge. I owe a considerable debt to my family for their love, encouragement and unfailing support – to Debbie, Ellie and Michael.

PREFACE: THE CRITIQUE OF THE CRITIQUE

Projects

Fathom

This volume is a testament to the *Fathom* project; to its energy, its clarity and its impact. *Fathom* is an online forum for reality-based discourse about Israel and its conflicts with its neighbours; and for thinking about the antisemitism that associates itself with discourse about Israel.

In January 2001, the Israeli–Palestinian peace process collapsed, at least *that* process did, and for *that* period. The following September, antizionism, for which it is axiomatic that such a peace process could never succeed, reasserted itself in the global left and liberal imagination as the common-sense view at the Durban World Conference against Racism. A week later, planes slammed into the World Trade Center in New York, into the Pentagon and one was prevented by a heroic struggle from slamming into the White House. The Durban programme for 'Boycott, Divestment, Sanctions' (BDS) against Israel was taken up by academics in London, who agitated for the exclusion of Israelis from university campuses. The academic unions in Britain did not adopt a boycott of Israeli universities, but they did allow the boycotters to create a culture in which, by 2009, there were no Jews left in their decision-making structures who were willing and able to argue against antizionism, or the antisemitism that came with it, and which inspired it.

Fathom was created in 2012, in the wake of the University and College Union (UCU) defeat of the activists who were challenging its antisemitic culture and norms; and at a time when antisemitism was spreading from the academic union into the key activist layers of the labour movement and the left. By 2015, the Labour Party had elected Jeremy Corbyn as leader, a man steeped in a lifetime of antizionist politics who not only called Hamas and Hezbollah his 'friends' but claimed that Hamas were 'bringing about long-term peace and social justice and political justice in the whole region' (see Hirsh 2018:43).

Fathom was well established by then and it was in a position to offer an intellectual and political lead to those who wanted to understand the Labour antisemitism storm, and to those who found themselves inside it. *Fathom* offered a space for the resistance to Labour antisemitism to think and to debate, to learn and to teach.

Alan Johnson's own 30,000-word 2019 *Fathom* report, *Institutionally Antisemitic: Contemporary Left Antisemitism and the Crisis in the British Labour Party*, went through 130 examples of Labour antisemitism, giving evidence that they happened, and offering clear explanations of why they were antisemitic (Johnson 2019). It was cited in the damning report of the UK's Equality and Human Rights Commission into antisemitism in the Labour Party (EHRC 2020). The EHRC report also made it clear that one of the key manifestations of the 'unlawful harassment of Jews' in Corbyn's Labour Party was the assumption of bad faith made against those who reported antisemitism. This was the assumption that people were only pretending to think there was antisemitism, but were in reality 'faking' it or 'smearing' Corbyn and his faction in pursuance of an unstated underlying motive. The EHRC was re-describing the phenomenon that I had called 'The Livingstone Formulation' in the language of UK Equality law (Hirsh 2016). The EHRC drew on the evidence and the understanding that had been developed, nurtured and published by Alan Johnson in the *Fathom* project and by me through the Engage project.[1]

Studies in Contemporary Antisemitism and the London Centre for the Study of Contemporary Antisemitism

This *Fathom* collection is one of the first books in a new book series, edited by myself and Rosa Freedman. *Studies in Contemporary Antisemitism* is a collaboration between Routledge and the London Centre for the Study of Contemporary Antisemitism (LCSCA) and is one element of an ambitious programme to establish a suite of platforms to publish academic research and debate on contemporary antisemitism. We are also nurturing the *Journal of Contemporary Antisemitism (JCA)* as a high-quality, peer-reviewed, academic platform for publishing research. We are producing policy papers, journalism, blogs, social media and videos, which play important roles in disseminating academic research more widely. We are growing our network of antisemitism scholarship as an international community of research, of reading and writing, and of peer review. Around that academic core, we are developing wider networks of debate, learning and activism.

Both *Fathom* and the London Centre are responses to late 20th-century developments on the left that have contributed to a resurgence of left antisemitism.

Transformations: The Rise of a 'We Are All Hezbollah Now!' Left

The left-wing anti-Stalinist tradition in which both Alan and I were formed politically took as its target those unjust social structures of power that excluded the majority of people from the full benefits of the Enlightenment. We thought that our project was to *complete* the Enlightenment for all of humanity, rather than to allow it to remain something that worked best for the privileged. So we were aghast as our students were increasingly taught that far from being the solution, the Enlightenment was the problem. A left and intellectual tradition, which was quite different to our own, taught that the injustices of ancient societies were simply reconstituted by the Enlightenment, but on a more totalising and oppressive basis. This tradition taught that ostensibly liberating ideas and practices, like reason, science, equality, democracy, autonomy and rights, all placed in sneer quotes, in fact constituted the heart of a modernity of unimaginably efficient, rationalised and powerful enslavement, which replaced the piecemeal, personalised and explicit oppression of old. In this view, the Enlightenment was the fall into darkness, not the path towards the light; and it was a fall which, more and more, is now being treated in practice as irreversible. The aspiration to create a new and better world was giving way to an incoherent, furious and negative politics of 'resistance'.

Hannah Arendt thought that at the heart of 20th-century totalitarianism was an especially toxic ingredient: the breaking free of utopian thinking from immediate, practical and material concerns. That is not to say there is anything wrong with thinking about how to make the world better, only that such thought must not lose its connection with reality. The politics of common interest, and its consequent structures in the modern state and civil society, she argued, binds people into communities that share limited and obtainable goals but totalitarian politics gains a hold where those communal bonds are already cut. And to the extent that those bonds persist, totalitarianism cuts them anyway (Arendt 1951/1985). It preys on 'masses' of furious, atomised individuals, who have already been spat out of society, who it teaches to obsess only about a far-off and dreamed future of sweet revenge and utopian comfort. The 'masses' that totalitarian politics prey on are people who have no immediate next step forward and no comrades, or even friends or family, to take it with. Totalitarian movements seduce their followers into relating to the world only through the single figure of the strongman leader and the fantasies he sows of revenge and utopia.

In 2001, 'Stop the War' originated as a campaign against a particular proposed war, the one against the Taliban in Afghanistan after 9/11. But the campaign persisted, retaining the same name, when it opposed subsequent wars, in the first place, the 2003 invasion of Iraq. It did not oppose all wars, however; it focused on the wars of the 'imperialist states'. And in the case of Iraq, it even refused support to the free trade unions that emerged there *after* the invasion. When one of the leaders of these unions, Hadi Saleh, a man arrested and put on death row under Saddam, returned to Iraq to build new free trade unions, he was tortured and murdered by Saddamist hold-outs in 2005. One leading British 'anti-war' left-winger, Alex Callinicos of the Socialist Workers Party, sneered at those of us who raised Hadi's case for creating a 'hullabaloo' about a 'collaborator' (see Muhsin and Johnson 2006).

This left current gave the name 'imperialism' to the democratic states of the West and the name 'anti-imperialism' to anyone shooting at those states or their allies. *Anybody* fighting against the imperialist aggressors, or their allies, should be supported. The Trotskyist and Stalinist heritage of many of the Stop the War leaders is relevant here. The old division of the world into two warring camps, one reactionary and one progressive, had meant that even if Stalin was 'betraying the revolution' and instigating a rule of terror, one should still 'defend the Soviet Union' against 'the imperialists'. The two camps world view has been updated for today: even if the 'resistance' to 'Empire' includes antisemitic Islamists, and even if its targets include the 21 Jews, including 16 teenagers, who were murdered by a suicide bomber in 2001 while dancing at the Dolphinarium discotheque, one should never support, but always oppose, any Western attack (or act of self-defence) against that resistance. Stop the War's one-time Vice President Kamal Majid founded The Stalin Society and argued in 2012 that Syria's Assads were rulers 'with a long history of resisting imperialism' who must be supported 'because their defeat will pave the way for a pro-Western and pro-US regime' (Bloodworth 2013).[2]

In this radical transformation of the very meaning of 'left', many left and democratic values were sidelined: equality for women, sexual liberation, the fight against antizionist forms of antisemitism, the rule of law, democracy, human rights, freedom of speech, working-class self-liberation, science and reason, respect for minorities and national self-determination. The political significance of this cannot be overstated. Once a transformed left decided to raise the value of a particular understanding of 'anti-imperialism' – which can seemingly accommodate even the murder of Jews as Jews – to an *absolute*, assigning it more value than any and all of these other left-wing values, the road was opened to the left chanting 'We are all Hezbollah now!'; to giving *de facto* support to the Serbia of Milosevic, the Iraq of Saddam, the Iran of the ayatollahs and the Russia of Putin; and to the left-wing academic Judith Butler insisting that 'understanding Hamas, Hezbollah as social movements that are progressive, that are on the Left, that are part of a global Left, is extremely important' (Butler 2006).

'Imperialism', for this transformed left, does not refer to strong states colonising or controlling weaker states and peoples. It refers to a global system of domination that is said to have arisen in Europe, via the Enlightenment, Colonialism and the Industrial Revolution, which now enslaves the world, is the root cause of bad things that happen to human beings, and at the centre of which, for some left-wingers, sits the only Jewish State in the world. The story of how 'Zionism', or 'Global Zionism', was added into this all-encompassing concept, so that it became either central to, or symbolic of, this single, global machine of domination, is the story of contemporary left antisemitism and this collection.

The Critique of the Critique

Alan and I trace our own critique of this critique to our formation in the heterodox Trotskyist organisation *Socialist Organiser*, later to become *Workers Liberty* in the 1980s when its main leader and theoretician, Sean Matgamna, and others, were persuading the group to move away from the antizionism that had already become standard on the Trotskyist left, to support the 'two states for two peoples' position on the conflict and to recognise, and recognise the significance of, left antisemitism. Though this made the group pari-. ahs on the far-left, Matgamna was influential in the political education of a number of people who later contributed significantly to shaping the response of the Jewish community, and of UK society more generally, to antizionism and its boycott, and to the rise of antisemitism in Corbyn's Labour Party.

In retrospect, perhaps the most important thing we took from our years in the group was the need to combine intellectual work with practical action. The group was concerned with the far-off goal of remaking the world as it might be, as it should be, but it was also, at least in aspiration, anchored to the world as it was, obsessed by the question of how to 'seize the next link in the chain' to make progress towards that new world. That meant the steady work of involvement, hopefully fructifying, in existing organisations. *Socialist Organiser* was, for example, part of the 'Bennite' democracy movement in the Labour Party in the late 1970s and early 1980s, of the resistance to the far-left's drive to ban Jewish Student Societies from UK campuses in the mid-1980s, and of the solidarity networks supporting the strikers and their families in the Notts coalfield during the Great Miners Strike of 1984–1985. It was not our role to substitute for those movements, trading in fantasies of revolutionary violence.

By the early 2000s, we were both increasingly worried by the left-wing movements around us becoming unmoored from the material world and floating off where they fancied. And the scholarly thinking around us no longer seemed to challenge existing inequalities or injustices in any practical way, though it did corrupt ways of thinking about them, co-opting them into crude, Manichean frameworks, of which 'Empire' versus 'Resistance' was only one of the crudest. The scholars seemed not to care, or even to notice; they were not connected to any practical sense in which it *mattered*, other than to their own success in constructing rhetorical criticism. We saw a left that was increasingly no longer satisfied with addressing the oppressive structures of social relations, as we had been; they wanted to smash everything: truth, reason, civil society, state, freedom, law, community, nation, democracy and friendship. These were all denounced as the fake productions of those who benefit from 'the system', facades to hide reality and to fool the majority into consenting to their own subordination.

One of our common mentors, Robert Fine, who also had a *Socialist Organiser* pedigree, worked hard in the realm of social theory to hold on to both the radicalism and the anti-totalitarianism of the tradition. He argued that we should never let go of the critique of existing conditions, with their injustices, inequalities and violence, but he said that we must also keep a tight hold, with our other hand, of the critique of the critique. By 'critique of the critique', he meant a *critical* engagement with those ideas and movements that are oppositional with respect to existing conditions. Perhaps Robert Fine's key observation, the alarm that his work sounds, is that the significance of left authoritarianism and totalitarianism, their deep roots and lasting legacies have *not* been sufficiently registered inside contemporary radical thinking and politics. Those who champion the radical critique have not always understood their own responsibilities to attend to the critique of the critique (Fine 2001). And we have come to believe that failing is one important reason for the contemporary resurgence of the left antisemitism that is addressed in this collection.

I remember Alan Johnson saying that it was becoming impossible to operate in an intellectual and political environment that was increasingly unmoored from truth, reason and the civilisational gains of the democratic and industrial revolutions. His argument was that we needed to build our own journals and institutions. The unusual thing about Alan was that he did not just say it, but he also did it. In 2005, he built *Democratiya*, a journal of rational, Enlightenment-based thought and politics; visions anchored to the world, and he created it out of nothing, with no money, and he published 16 issues. (*Democratiya* was incorporated into *Dissent* magazine in 2010 and is archived at the *Dissent* website.) At just about the same moment, I came face to face with the common-sense notion that Israel was a unique and symbolic evil on the planet and that we should address it by excluding Israeli scholars from our campuses, our journals and our conferences. The antisemitism, oozing out from every crack of the academic boycott campaign, came to find me. At the time, I was just about beginning to feel I belonged in a university sociology department, but I learnt that I was not at all at home. I was transformed by this antisemitic thinking from a sociologist into a *Zionist* sociologist, meaning a dishonest, racist and corrupt sociologist. It was clear to me how my exclusion was antisemitic, but that clarity was rare. I, with others, who not entirely accidentally also shared some political heritage with us, set about building the *Engage* network and website, to organise resistance, in practical, political and intellectual terms, to the antisemitism that had been recycled by 20th-century Stalinism and re-disseminated, after the collapse of the peace process, at the Durban *World Conference against Racism* in 2001.

In an inspired moment in 2011, the British Israel Communications Research Centre (BICOM) employed Alan Johnson to reboot its work of promoting awareness and knowledge about Israel in the UK. And in another inspired moment, Alan built *Fathom*; another project to construct our own journals and institutions within which we could take forward serious political education and debate, this time about Israel. In Britain, and not only in Britain, thinking about Israel is significantly connected to antisemitism, so *Fathom* was necessarily concerned with that too. *Fathom* was necessary because rational and reality-based discussion on these topics was increasingly being locked out of the mainstream academic and political discussion in Britain.

Fathom has kept on going for over a decade, due largely to Alan's will to make that happen, combined with his talent and his experience in knowing how to make it happen; and his political and intellectual judgement about how it should best navigate the boundaries of the discourse that it needs to cover.

I experienced writing in *Fathom* as a liberation from the gaslighting that passes for peer review inside the institutions of the antisemitic hostile environment that is today's academia. In *Fathom*, you could write what you felt needed to be written, and I think that some of my best writings on antisemitism were published there. Alan Johnson's knowledgeable, decisive and sensitive editing helped too. And *Fathom* was also hugely more nimble than the dinosaur academic journals, where it can take two years to publish an article. And it is all open access, not hidden away behind the exclusive dusty paywalls of the ivory tower.

The scholarly study of contemporary antisemitism, as well as the study of any question that is impacted by antisemitic thinking, is becoming more and more difficult to do within the current university system, some parts of which have even been complicit with left antisemitism. We are significantly excluded from processes of research funding, publishing and the allocation of academic jobs and resources. In politics, and culture more widely, radical democratic thinking on antisemitism has difficulty finding its space in the publications and on the platforms where one might expect to find it. The London Centre aims to build institutions, networks and funding streams to substitute for those that we are locked out of in the universities. This is not because we want to replicate them and to complete our separation from them but because we want to fight our way back into the mainstream and to transform its culture and its unwritten rules of exclusion. Ours is a hugely ambitious project, to challenge the intellectual underpinnings of antisemitism in public life. It is to change some of the things that have come to appear as common sense. *Fathom*, as an institution, has been doing this work with great effect; not specifically in the universities but in wider civil society and in political life too, as this collection showcases.

David Hirsh

Notes

1 The Engage network was set up in 2005 in response to the passing of some motions at the Association of University Teachers (AUT) Council to boycott Israeli universities. The initiative included the Engage website, edited by David Hirsh, which was a space for news and discussion, and for bringing together facts and arguments that people might want to use to argue against such boycott proposals and against the antisemitism that was associated with them. Available: https://engageonline. wordpress.com/ (accessed 5 April 2023).
2 The 'two camps' world view of the transformed left was given candid expression by the Stop the War leader John Rees when he wrote that 'Socialists should unconditionally stand with the oppressed against the oppressor, even if the people who run the oppressed country are undemocratic and persecute minorities, like Saddam Hussein' (1994:55). His colleague, the Marxist writer John Molyneux, drew out the logic of this world view to the Israel–Palestine conflict with especial clarity: 'We on the left should not, I suggest, "condemn" Palestinian suicide bombers' (2004).

References

Arendt, Hannah (1951/1985) *The Origins of Totalitarianism*, San Diego: Harcourt Brace.

Bloodworth, James (2013) 'Mother Agnes has pulled out of the stop the War conference. And yet she would have fitted in so well', *The Spectator*, 18 November. Available: www.spectator.co.uk/article/mother-agnes-has-pulled-out-of-the-stop-the-war-conference-and-yet-she-would-have-fitted-in-so-well/ (accessed 3 April 2023).

Butler, Judith (2006) 'Judith Butler on Hamas, Hezbollah & the Israel Lobby', *Radical Archives*. Available: https://radicalarchives.org/2010/03/28/jbutler-on-hamas-hezbollah-israel-lobby/ (accessed 3 April 2023). For a video of her remarks see 'Judith Butler Whitewashes Hamas and Hezbollah'. Available: www.youtube.com/watch?v=amJNIcSNPco (accessed 3 April 2023).

Equality and Human Rights Commission (2020). *Investigation Into Antisemitism in the Labour Party*, EHRC. Available: www.equalityhumanrights.com/en/publica tion-download/investigation-antisemitism-labour-party (accessed 11 April 2023).

Fine, Robert (2001) *Political Investigations: Hegel, Marx, Arendt*, New York: Routledge.

Hirsh, David (2016) 'The Livingstone Formulation', in Eunice G. Pollack (ed.), *Anti-Zionism and Antisemitism: Past & Present*, Boston: Academic Studies Press. Available: https://engageonline.wordpress.com/2016/04/29/the-livingstone-formu lation-david-hirsh-2/ (accessed 6 April 2023).

Hirsh, David (2018) *Contemporary Left Antisemitism*, Abingdon and New York: Routledge.

Johnson, Alan (2019) *Institutionally Antisemitic: Contemporary Left Antisemitism and the Crisis in the British Labour Party. Fathom*, May. Available: https://fath omjournal.org/wp-content/uploads/2019/03/Institutionally-Antisemitic-Report-FINAL-6.pdf (accessed 27 March 2023).

Muhsin, Abdullah and Alan Johnson (2006) *Hadi Never Died: Hadi Saleh and the Iraqi Trade Unions*, London: Trades Union Congress.

Molyneux, John (2004) 'Marxism on Terrorism', *The Socialist Review*, April. Available: https://socialistworker.co.uk/socialist-review-archive/marxism-terrorism/ (accessed 3 April 2023).

Rees, John (1994) *The ABC of Socialism*, London: Bookmarks.

PART 1

Introduction and Contexts

1

INTRODUCTION TO *MAPPING LEFT ANTISEMITISM*

The Fathom Essays

Alan Johnson

Introducing the Journal

Fathom was launched in 2012. In our founding statement, the editors expressed the ambition that our new journal about Israel would offer readers tough-minded and expert intellectual analysis, fusing the rigour and intellectual credibility of the old-school journal with the tremendous potential of new publishing technologies and social networks, and would marry a principled and values-based approach to ends to a real-world and prudential approach to means.

Whether those hopes have been met will be for others to judge. What we can say for certain is that in our first decade we have published around 1,000 articles, interviews, reports and reviews; our readers now count in the millions, hail from over 150 nations and include many opinion-formers and decision-makers in universities, foreign ministries, editorial offices, party headquarters and think tanks around the world. Our writers are experts; academics, yes, but also policy analysts, civil society activists and politicians; Israelis and Palestinians; left-wing, right-wing and everything in between; secular and religious.

Two linked concerns have dominated *Fathom's* pages in our first decade.

Two States for Two Peoples

In 2012, we made this promise: '*Fathom* will be a partisan and artisan of the two-state solution, helping to put some intellectual substance back into the project of mutual recognition and peaceful coexistence between Israelis and Palestinians.' I am not sure we could have tried any harder. With BICOM,

DOI: 10.4324/9781003322320-2

we helped to convene a series of private, track-two dialogues between current and former Israeli and Palestinian officials, academics and activists, designed to generate new ideas to breathe new life into the peace process, writing up the experience as *New Thinking on the Israeli-Palestinian Peace Process: Towards a Hybrid Approach*. We also worked with Ned Lazarus, a vastly experienced grassroots peacebuilder, to produce the major report, *A Future for Israeli-Palestinian Peacebuilding*, something the editors considered central to a revival of the paradigm of mutual recognition that will surely underpin any solution. And in 2021, we collected over 50 *Fathom* essays and interviews to create the eBook *Rescuing Israeli-Palestinian Peace: The Fathom Essays*. At 464 pages, we believe it is one of the most comprehensive collections of expert thinking about the history, present and most importantly the future of the 'two states for two peoples' framework for peace.

Contemporary Left Antisemitism and Israel

In our inaugural issue, writing in response to a rising wave of antisemitism, David Hirsh raised a question – 'What kinds of hostility to Israel may be understood as, or may lead to, or may be caused by antisemitism?' – and this has become the journal's second central concern: the rise of antisemitic anti-Zionism, or contemporary left antisemitism.

We have been insistent that *criticism* of Israeli policy, even sharp criticism, was not to be confused with antisemitism, and we have published much of that criticism ourselves, from Israelis and Palestinians. We focused our attention instead on that darker kind of discourse about Israel that could not be contained by the category of 'criticism'. We characterised this discourse as 'antisemitic anti-Zionism' or left antisemitism. It was, we said, demonising and dehumanising, resurrecting antisemitic tropes in new 'progressive' guises, and was bleeding from the sectarian fringe to the mainstream, infecting parts of politics, the academy and civil society. We defined left antisemitism in the following terms in *Fathom*:

> [This] strand of distinctively *left-wing* hostility to Jews . . . has never been the dominant strand of opinion on the left, and it is not so today; not by a long chalk. But it has always existed, it is growing today, and it must be part of any account of the breakdown in the relationship between Jews and the left. It was called the 'socialism of fools' in the 19th century. It became an 'anti-imperialism of idiots' in the 20th century. And it takes the form of a wild, demented, unhinged form of 'anti-Zionism' – not mere 'criticism of Israeli policy' – that demonises Israel in the 21st century. Antisemitic anti-Zionism bends the meaning of Israel and Zionism out of shape until both become fit receptacles for the tropes, images and ideas of

classical antisemitism. In short, *that which the demonological Jew once was, demonological Israel now is*: uniquely malevolent, full of blood lust, all-controlling, the hidden hand, tricksy, always acting in bad faith, the obstacle to a better, purer, more spiritual world, uniquely deserving of punishment, and so on. This antisemitic anti-Zionism has three components: a programme, a discourse, and a movement. First, a *political programme*: not two states for two peoples, but the abolition of the Jewish homeland; not Palestine alongside Israel, but Palestine instead of Israel. Second, a demonising intellectual discourse about Israel . . . Third, antisemitic anti-Zionism is a presence within the global social movement . . . to exclude one state – and only one state – from the economic, cultural and educational life of humanity: the little Jewish one.

(Johnson 2015)

The very existence of left antisemitism remains widely denied on parts of the left. For example, the influential French Maoist philosopher Alan Badiou angrily dismissed the notion of left antisemitism as an 'oxymoron', threatening to punch in the face anyone who used the term to him. We saw a willed historical amnesia at work in this kind of response. After all, it was as long ago as the late 19th century that the German Marxist August Bebel, with the encouragement of Friedrich Engels, railed against antisemitism on the left, which he called the 'socialism of fools'. In 1984, Steve Cohen's *That's Funny You Don't Look Anti-Semitic: An Anti-racist Analysis of Left Anti-Semitism* confronted the left with a century's worth of examples of left antisemitism. Mining the writings of socialist icon after socialist icon, Cohen excavated a long, shameful and ever-evolving international left-wing *tradition* that had to be seen plain and confronted. He showed that parts of the British left – in this example, the Independent Labour Party – were warning in the 1890s that 'whenever there is trouble in Europe, whenever rumours of war circulate, and men's minds are distraught with fear of change and calamity, you may be sure that a hook-nosed Rothschild is at his games, somewhere near the region of the disturbances' (Cohen 1984:20). We knew that if you jumped forward a century to the mid-1980s you could find parts of the UK far-left trying, to their undying shame, to ban Jewish student societies. And we knew that in the 21st century left antisemitism was on the rise everywhere, not least inside the British Labour Party (Johnson 2019). Hence, the need for the essays collected in this volume.

Introducing the Collection

Mapping Left Antisemitism: the Fathom Essays collects 27 articles and interviews published in *Fathom* between 2013 and 2021 as well as four previously unpublished pieces.

Part 1 introduces the collection and sets the context for the chapters that follow.

Lesley Klaff, editor of *The Journal of Contemporary Antisemitism*, maps contemporary left discourse, arguing that while left antisemitism has a long history it is most likely to be expressed today as anti-Israel hostility centring on a collection of labels and discourses that construct Israel as an illegitimate state and Zionism as a racist ideology. These labels and discourses – Israel is a 'Nazi-like', 'Apartheid', 'Settler-Colonial' and 'Pink-Washing' State, while Jews are 'White', 'Privileged' and 'non-indigenous' – function as continuations or variations of the tropes of classical antisemitism, and are used today to demonise and delegitimise Israel and Zionism. To the degree that those tropes are becoming normalised in progressive American and European circles, the oldest hatred is finding a home there in the form of anti-Zionist antisemitism.

Dave Rich, the Director of Policy at the Community Security Trust (CST), the UK's antisemitism monitoring organisation, focuses on an aspect of contemporary antisemitism that is often neglected in academia, the lived experience of its Jewish victims. Both of these chapters have not been published previously.

Alan Johnson then introduces the terms of the bitter division on the left over the existence, character and appropriate political response to left antisemitism in his essay, 'The Jews and the Left: Time for a Rethink', which has been the most read essay at the *Fathom* site over the journal's first decade.

Part 2 maps contemporary left antisemitism, and explores its manifold forms and its contested relationship to 'anti-Zionism' and to criticism of Israeli policies.

Sean Matgamna, a socialist who has been an articulate critic of left antisemitism since the 1980s, argues that it is first and foremost a denial, extended to no other state, of Israel's right to exist and, as a result, a comprehensive and unique hostility to pro-Israel Jews, that is to most Jews alive, branding them as 'Zionists' and seeing that description as akin to 'racism' or 'imperialism'.

Michael Walzer reviews three historical varieties of Jewish anti-Zionism – Orthodox, Reform and diaspora universalist – before examining the paradox that while the most common leftist version of anti-Zionism claims to derive from an opposition to nationalism and the nation state, the left has *supported* the right to national self-determination the world over, reserving its opposition to the nation state to one people, the Jews, and to one state, Israel. Criticism of the policies of the governments of Israel, several of which he sets out, should not, he insists, involve opposition to the existence of the state. While Walzer acknowledges that there are versions of anti-Zionism on the right and the left that involve antisemitic tropes, he believes the main problem with contemporary left-wing anti-Zionism in the United States and Europe is anti-Zionism itself: it is bad politics.

Norman Geras argues that Israel has been made an *alibi* for a new climate of antisemitism on the left. Israel, so parts of the left argue, is a delinquent state and, for many of those who regard it so, a non-legitimate one, its existence is somehow improper. These themes pitch those who sponsor them out of a genuine, and into a spurious, type of universalism: one where the Jews are special amongst other groups in being obliged to settle for forms of political freedom in which their identity may not be asserted collectively; Jews must be satisfied, instead, merely with the rights available to them as individuals, without the freedom to associate with others of their own kind. He shows that, often, the so-called 'criticism' relies, just as Marx did in Part II of On the Jewish Question, on anti-Jewish stereotypes.

Alan Johnson critiques the claims of the radical left-wing US writer Norman Finkelstein that there is a 'Holocaust Industry' and that all talk of left antisemitism is part of it; in his words, a 'calculated hoax – dare it be said, plot?' Drawing on stinging criticism of Finkelstein by the Italian intellectual historian Enzo Traverso, Johnson argues that Finkelstein's denialism and victim-blaming, and his conspiracist dismissal of the new antisemitism as a fraud, straight off the production line of the 'Holocaust Industry', are themselves important components of the new left antisemitism.

Marlene Gallner excavates the voice of Jean Améry, best known in the anglophone world as a Holocaust survivor and author of the Auschwitz memoir *At The Mind's Limits*. In the 1960s, he was also the outspoken left-wing critic of left-wing antisemitism in West Germany and it is this Améry that Gallner's essay makes available to us as a moral and intellectual resource today.

Matthew Bolton, co-author with Frederick Harry Pitts of *Corbynism: A Critical Approach*, critiques the 'Bad News' model of media analysis developed by Philo and Berry and the Glasgow Media Group, as it has been applied by them to left antisemitism in the British Labour Party. The methodology of the Bad News model is held to be reductive and quasi-conspiracist, the analysis to reduce the messy complexity of the Israeli–Palestinian conflict to a Manichean struggle. The authors, Bolton argues, have failed to register that the antisemitism which spread in the UK Labour Party after 2015 was a significant reality deriving from a specific world view, bordering on conspiracy theory, that has come to dominate parts of the left.

Kathleen Hayes, writing in a different register to the other chapters, offers a candid memoir of her 25 years as an activist in the revolutionary left. She mines her own experience with great honesty to examine how 'unrecognised antisemitism gained a hold over me; the purpose I think it served; and how I came to, at least consciously, recognise and reject it'.

Susie Linfield discusses her book *The Lions' Den: Zionism and the Left from Hannah Arendt to Noam Chomsky*. She argues that some portions of the left have failed to grapple with the complexity, and the facts, of the

Israeli–Palestinian conflict, substituting ideology and wishful thinking for lucid political analysis. All parties to the conflict – including the Palestinians, supposedly the beneficiaries of the left's 'solidarity' – have been grievously injured by the left's analytical abdication.

Part 3 traces the little-understood Soviet roots of contemporary left antisemitism.

Izabella Tabarovsky lays bare the story of Soviet Judeophobia and the massive Soviet antisemitic 'anti-Zionist' campaigns that entered a particularly active stage and had a global reach after 1967. She suggests the discourse of today's far-left is often strikingly similar to the messaging of those ugly Soviet campaigns.

Simon Gallner tells the story of the left-wing 'anti-Zionist' campaign that almost destroyed Poland's Jewish community. In 1968, in Communist Poland, dozens of Jews committed suicide after they had found themselves publicly vilified and socially isolated, denounced as a 'fifth column' by Władysław Gomułka, the first secretary of the Polish United Workers Party. A total of 8,300 members were expelled from the Communist party, nearly all Jewish; 9,000 Jews lost their jobs, some were beaten up and hundreds were thrown out of their apartments.

Jeffrey Herf discusses his book *Undeclared Wars With Israel: East Germany and the West German Far Left 1967–1989.* He reviews the antisemitic purges in the Communist states in the 1940s and 1950s; the motivations for, and the forms taken by, communist East Germany's undeclared war on Israel, and the complicity of the United Nations in that war; and the reasons for the rise of left antisemitism on the West German far-left, and for its turn to terrorism in the shape of the Baader–Meinhof Group and the Revolutionary Cells. He also looks at the routinely ignored experiences of the Jewish people who were the targets of these undeclared wars.

Part 4 is concerned with one of the most astonishing aspects of the new left antisemitism, its fatal attraction to 'Holocaust Inversion' and to spurious historical claims of 'Nazi-Zionist Collaboration'.

Lesley Klaff explains how the discourse of 'Holocaust Inversion' involves an *inversion of reality* (the Israelis are cast as the new Nazis and the Palestinians as the new Jews), and an *inversion of morality* (the Holocaust is presented as a moral lesson for, or even a moral indictment of, 'the Jews'), as well as recklessly spreading accusations of bad faith against all who would invoke Holocaust memory.

Jeffrey Herf, author of *Jewish Enemy: Nazi Propaganda during World War II and the Holocaust*, examines the historical inaccuracies in the former Mayor of London Ken Livingstone's incendiary claim, largely derived from his reading of the books of Lenni Brenner, that 'Hitler was a Zionist'.

Paul Bogdanor, author of *Kasztner's Crime*, meticulously rebuts the claims of Brenner and Livingstone. The former Mayor of London asserted that 'you had, right up until the start of the second world war, real collaboration [between Nazis and Zionists].' Bogdanor lays bare Livingstone's 'mutilations of the historical record and of the very sources he cites' as well as the politically reactionary character of Livingstone's version of history, which 'equates persecutors and rescuers, aggressors and victims, the powerful and the powerless, oppressors and the oppressed'. Bogdanor also identifies a catalogue of factual manipulations and pseudo-scholarship in the works of Lenni Brenner upon which Livingstone's claims rest.

Part 5 examines contemporary left antisemitism in Europe and the United States.

Kenneth Waltzer reflects on the sources of the growth of antisemitism in Europe. Economic crisis and populist response are the overarching context of sharpening antagonisms directed against Jews by disparate political forces. Alongside traditional racist right-wing antisemitism, Israel and its supporters have been attacked as the cornerstone of Western imperialism by both the far-left and Islamist forces that mobilise alienated segments of the growing Muslim population, especially marginal youths. Waltzer maps these developments, traces their antisemitic impacts and explores strategies to counter the rising danger.

Dave Rich examines the phenomenon of the quenelle, an antisemitic gesture associated with the French antisemite Dieudonné M'bala M'bala. He reads the gesture as emblematic of a post-Cold War, post-9/11 form of anti-system politics that seeks to erase traditional political divisions and build a new kind of coalition uniting neo-Fascism, anti-capitalism and revolutionary Islamism against 'Global Zionism'. The quenelle functions, Rich argues, as a cultural meme and political identifier for Dieudonné's politics and the movement he has spawned.

During the medieval epoch, Christian antisemitism spread the libel that Jews engaged in the ritual murder of non-Jews, supposedly mutilating their bodies and draining their blood to make Passover bread (known as 'the blood libel'). Countless antisemitic pogroms were inspired by this myth. **David Gurevich** explores the extraordinary rebirth of this blood libel within the Greek Orthodox Christian Church. He presents the case of Saint Philoumenos, supposedly 'ritualistically' murdered by 'Zionists' in 1979 and canonised by the Greek Orthodox Patriarchate of Jerusalem in 2009. The blood libel is alive today and is taking on new, political, 'anti-Zionist' forms. Gurevich shows this libel has been uncritically absorbed by parts of the left and academic publishing.

Shalom Lappin argues US Jews are caught between a white supremacist threat from the far-right and a hostile anti-Zionist challenge from parts of the far-left. For the latter, Israel exemplifies the evils of Western colonialism and racism. Anyone associated with Israel, whether by recognising it as a Jewish homeland or simply by endorsing its right to exist, is at risk of inheriting its essential criminality. 'Anti-Zionism' thus ceases to be a political view, a set of criticisms of Israeli policy, morphing instead into an instrument for encrypting hostility to Jews by embedding reference to them in an ideological proxy term. This is a variant of the coding technique that racists have long used against people of colour. For the first time, argues Lappin, American Jews are no longer outside of the turbulent flow of Jewish history but have been thrust into its midst.

Part 6 looks at the baleful presence of left antisemitism and 'anti-Zionism' within Western universities and publishing houses.

Cary Nelson highlights concerns about the impact of an increasingly politicised and 'anti-Zionist' academy on academic publishing about Israel.

Sarah Annes Brown examines the astonishing claims made in 2012 by the left-wing academic Oren Ben-Dor, and published by a respectable university press, about what he called 'pathologies pertaining to Jewish being and thinking' which is 'nourished by the desire to be hated' and which 'stems, before all else, from sublimated hatred of, and supremacy towards, all "others"'. It is this 'self-provoked hatred against Jews', he wrote, that 'keeps re-igniting' antisemitism.

David Hirsh looks at an example of how teaching can create a hostile environment for Jewish students on campus. In 2020, Bristol University Professor David Miller claimed, 'Britain is in the grip of an assault on its public sphere by the state of Israel and its advocates', and he indicted his university's Jewish student society as 'an Israel lobby group' and part of 'a campaign of censorship and manufactured hysteria' being 'directed by the state of Israel'. He received fulsome messages of support from parts of the UK academic left for these claims and their associated world view. Hirsh explores the controversy, noting some worrying features of academic life in the UK: the explicit rejection of the Macpherson principles regarding the handling of claims of racism by minorities when it comes to Jews; the mainstreaming of some old conspiracist modes of thinking about Jews, and the corruption of empirical social science by such modes; the casual redefinition of claims of antisemitism as bad faith efforts to protect Israel by Zionists (Miller even assailed a Jewish-Muslim interfaith soup kitchen as a Zionist plot); and, subsequent to all this, the creation of a hostile environment for Jews on campuses. Hirsh also highlights the role of the lecturers' trade union, the UCU, which in his view helped to incubate and normalise the culture which made the Miller controversy possible.

Part 7 assesses the importance of the definition of antisemitism proposed by the International Holocaust Remembrance Alliance (IHRA).

Dave Rich argues that the objections raised against the IHRA by parts of the left rest on mistaken assumptions and popular misrepresentations of what the IHRA definition says and does, unevidenced claims about its impact, and confusions about its legal status and power.

Bernard Harrison and Lesley Klaff argue that the most common objection to the IHRA Definition that no criticism aimed at *Israel* can be antisemitic rests on a reductive account of what antisemitism is, treating it only as a form of subjective and intentional 'racism', an emotional disposition – 'hatred of Jews as Jews' – whereas antisemitism has often taken the form of a delusive pseudo-explanatory political theory based on the fear of Jews, a form of defamation 'designed to explain why national or world politics are failing to move in ways congenial to the antisemite and his friends'.

Part 8 examines three examples of contemporary anti-Zionism and anti-semitism functioning in baleful ways within what we might call left theoretical practice, and explores an alternative tradition of left-wing thought that has opposed left antisemitism.

Russell A. Berman critiques what he sees as Judith Butler's abuse of Hannah Arendt's controversial book *Eichmann in Jerusalem* to support her own anti-Zionist conclusions. He shows how Arendt's reservations about a single judicial act are illegitimately inflated in Butler's diasporist anti-Zionism into a fundamental rejection of the very existence of the Jewish state. He also explores the severe limits of Butler's neo-diasporism as a viable response to either contemporary antisemitism or the future of the Hebrew-speaking Jewish people that is now concentrated on the banks of the Mediterranean.

Moral philosopher **Eve Garrard** argues that contemporary antisemitism involves, much like its predecessor forms, much more than a cognitive error, providing also deep emotional satisfactions. Antisemites, she claims, often prefer their errors, with all they offer – dramatic fears and hatreds, and the excitement of conspiracy stories – to the unremarkable truth. She examines three satisfactions antisemitism can provide and that are 'not easy either to overcome or to replace': the pleasure of hatred, the pleasure of tradition and the pleasure of displaying moral purity.

Karin Stögner, co-ordinator of the Research Network on Racism and Anti-semitism in the European Sociological Association, explains why the influential theory of 'intersectionality' so often fails to include global antisemitism, and suggests a radical new approach to intersectionality that would overcome that deficit.

The collection concludes with a previously unpublished conversation about a very different and better tradition within the left, one that has fought left antisemitism, between *Fathom* editor **Alan Johnson** and **Philip Spencer**, co-author (with the late Robert Fine) of *Antisemitism and the Left*. They explore the roots of left antisemitism in the equivocations of Enlightenment universalism, when antisemitic tropes were rearticulated within a universalist frame of reference, setting up a supposed 'Jewish Question' which has persisted in various forms to this day for a significant section of the left. A left-wing tradition of opposition to antisemitism on the left is excavated and critically assessed, taking in Friedrich Engels, Eleanor Marx, Eduard

Bernstein, Rosa Luxemburg, Leon Trotsky, Max Horkheimer and Theodor Adorno, as well as two exemplary contemporary writers, Moishe Postone and Norman Geras.

Note. While *Fathom* editors use the terms 'antisemitism' and 'antisemite', other writers prefer 'anti-Semitism' and 'anti-Semite'. We do not seek to 'rule' on that ongoing debate and both forms will be found throughout the book.

References

Cohen, Steve (1984) *That's Funny, You Don't Look Anti-Semitic: An Anti-Racist Analysis of Left Anti-Semitism*, Leeds: Beyond the Pale Collective.

Johnson, Alan (2015) 'The Jews and the Left: Time for a Rethink', *Fathom*, Autumn. Available: https://fathomjournal.org/the-left-and-the-jews-time-for-a-rethink/?high light=THe%20Left%20and%20the%20Jews (accessed 21 December 2022).

Johnson, Alan (2019) *Institutionally Antisemitic: Contemporary Left Antisemitism and the Crisis in the British Labour Party*, *Fathom*, March. Available: https://fathomjournal.org/fathom-report-institutionally-antisemitic-contemporary-left-anti semitism-and-the-crisis-in-the-british-labour-party/?highlight=Institutionally (accessed 22 December 2022).

2

A NEW FORM OF THE OLDEST HATRED

Mapping Antisemitism Today

Lesley Klaff

Introduction

This chapter provides a map of one contemporary form of the oldest hatred – antisemitic forms of antizionism, or contemporary left antisemitism – which this collection of *Fathom* essays explores.

Antisemitic forms of antizionism target Israel and Zionism, going well beyond 'criticism of Israel' into the realm of demonisation and dehumanisation by reworking ideas, tropes and stereotypes found in 'traditional' or 'classical' antisemitism (Hirsh 2013). Bernard Harrison argues that antizionist antisemitism is a refurbished version of 'political antisemitism' (Harrison 2020). Political antisemitism takes the form of a system or collection of beliefs about Jews as a collective. It supposes that Jews act as one, in pursuit of goals inimical to the interests of non-Jews (Julius 2011). This is more commonly referred to as 'conspiracy theory'. Examples of conspiracism include the belief that 'the Jews' were behind 9/11, or that 'the Jews' start wars, control Hollywood, the media and finance, or it refers to the supposedly unlimited power of the 'Israel Lobby' to suborn governments to its will.

In relation to Israel, political antisemitism supposes that the 'hand of Israel' is behind everything that is bad in the world. Examples include the claim that the Israeli Secret Service trained the American police in the knee-on-the-neck tactic that killed George Floyd (Pollard 2020) and that former Labour Party leader Jeremy Corbyn was 'forced' to resign due to 'a conspiracy within the party motivated from Israel' (Campaign Against Antisemitism 2020). Political antisemitism also supposes that 'Zionism' is colonialism, apartheid, racism, Nazism, the surveillance state, and everything that good people oppose (Hirsh 2023).

DOI: 10.4324/9781003322320-3

There is a significant increase in the number of people holding antisemitic sentiments in both the classical and contemporary forms in America, the United Kingdom and Europe. The latest Anti-Defamation League (ADL) survey, published on 12 January 2023, finds that the percentage of people in the United States agreeing to six or more classical antisemitic statements has doubled since similar surveys in 2014, 2015 and 2019. The survey also finds a significant increase over time in anti-Israel sentiment among the American population. Forty per cent of Americans agree, at least to some extent, that 'Israel treats the Palestinians like the Nazis treated the Jews'; 24 per cent of Americans believe, at least to some extent, that Israel and its supporters are a bad influence on American democracy; and 23 per cent of Americans agree, at least to some extent, that 'Israel can get away with anything because its supporters control the media' (Anti-Defamation League 2023).

A study of antisemitic prejudice across 16 European countries including the United Kingdom, the largest European antisemitism survey to date, was conducted by the Action and Protection League in 2021 (Action and Protection League 2021). It found that many of those who nurture antisemitic sentiment feel strong pressure not to express traditional anti-Jewish prejudice and therefore express their antisemitic sentiment through antisemitic hostility to Israel because they consider such opinions to be publicly acceptable. Thus, the survey found that in relation to traditional antisemitic sentiment, only 3 per cent strongly agreed, another 3 per cent moderately agreed, 1 per cent was unclassifiable and 93 per cent were not antisemitic. But in relation to antizionist antisemitism, 4 per cent were strongly antisemitic, 27 per cent were moderately antisemitic, 24 per cent were unclassifiable and only 45 per cent were not antisemitic. With respect to the United Kingdom, the report concluded that 4 per cent of the population aged 18–75 were strongly antisemitic and expressed their antisemitic sentiment as traditional antisemitism, while 27 per cent of the UK population were strongly antisemitic and expressed their antisemitism as antisemitic hostility to Israel. There is little doubt that antisemitic attitudes in Europe and the UK are more prevalent in relation to Israel than in any other respect. Interestingly, the UK was found to have the lowest level of antisemitic hostility to Israel among the 16 European countries surveyed (Action and Protection League 2021).

In America, while antizionist antisemitism is most prevalent on the populist left, the recent Anti-Defamation League survey found that it is also seen on the populist right and in Islamist, Christian and Black Nationalist milieus (Anti-Defamation League 2023).

The Relationship Between Classical Antisemitism and Antizionist Antisemitism

It is generally acknowledged by antisemitism scholars that antizionist antisemitism has significant continuities with classical antisemitism. Daniel

Allington and David Hirsh point out that the correlation between negative attitudes towards Jews and negative attitudes towards Israel is one of the most solidly established facts of political psychology because it has been proven by so many experimental and survey-based studies (Allington and Hirsh 2019). Drawing on Staetsky's 2017 Jewish Policy Research (JPR) study of negative attitudes to Jews and to Israel, Allington and Hirsh reason that the correlation is not one of *causation* but one of *identity*. In other words, it's not that certain attitudes towards Jews drive certain attitudes towards Israel, or vice versa, but that there is a single social and psychological construct underlying both. For example, the statements 'Israel exploits Holocaust victimhood for its own purposes' and 'Jews exploit Holocaust victimhood for their own purposes' both express the same antisemitic idea, albeit one in relation to Jews and the other in relation to the Jewish state. The JPR study found that 'Jews exploit Holocaust victimhood for their own purposes' to be the most popular anti-Jewish statement among people with strong anti-Israel attitudes (Staetsky 2017).

David Seymour argues that antisemitism and antizionism should be understood as analogous ideologies. Antizionism, he claims, is an ideology that has matured in the twenty-first century because it fulfils twenty-first-century functions that relate to twenty-first-century society. Just as twentieth-century-totalitarian antisemitism portrayed the 'enemy of the people' as having a Jewish face, so too antizionism portrays racism and oppression as having an Israeli face (Seymour 2019).

Thorsten Fuchshuber argues that antisemitism in the sense in which the word is most commonly understood – that is, the racialised Jew-hate associated with the Holocaust – and twenty-first-century antizionism – that is, the seemingly democratic Jew-hate which today uses the language of human rights to delegitimise, demonise and dehumanise the most visible and important Jewish collectivity, the State of Israel – are simply two successive strategies for (a) inflicting the maximum possible harm to Jews and (b) rationalising such harm in a manner that is acceptable to wider society (Fuschshuber 2019).

Pointing to a 2003 European barometer poll which found that an extraordinarily high proportion of Europeans believe that Israel is a threat to peace in the region and to world peace, Bernard Harrison notes that this is a short step from the classical stereotype that Jews in general are evil or, at the very least, that they place the interests of Jews above the interests of non-Jews. This is no more than a revival of the fear of the 'Jewish conspiracy' (Harrison 2020).

Alan Johnson articulates the relationship between classical antisemitism and antizionist antisemitism when he writes, 'Antisemitic anti-Zionism bends the meaning of Israel and Zionism out of shape until both become fit receptacles for the tropes, images and ideas of classical antisemitism. In short, *that which the demonological Jew once was, demonological Israel now is*: uniquely malevolent, full of blood lust, all-controlling, the hidden-hand, tricksy, always acting in bad faith, the obstacle to a better, purer, more spiritual world, uniquely deserving of punishment, and so on' (Johnson 2015, italics in original). In other words, the same negative attitudes that were applied to Jews qua Jews are now applied to Israel, the Jewish State.

The different ways in which antisemitic antizionism bends the meaning of Israel and Zionism out of shape is the subject of the following sections.

Constructing Israel as a Human Rights Abuser: A Preliminary Note on 'Labelling Theory' and the Malleability of the Concept of 'Human Rights'

The meaning of Israel and Zionism have been bent out of shape to construct Israel as a human rights abuser which is central to, or symbolic of, all that is bad in the world. In this way, the construct of the demonic Jew who is a danger to gentiles has been transferred to Israel which is perceived as a danger to peace in the region, if not the world. Zionism, which to Jews represents a movement for self-determination and a political defence against antisemitism, has been constructed as a racist ideology in its very essence, and with supposedly worldwide reach, sometimes called 'Global Zionism', a term saturated with conspiracism and antisemitism (Gardner 2007). These demonising constructs have been facilitated by a process known as 'labelling theory' and by the extraordinary malleability of the concept of human rights.

The point has been made that language is used for more than the transfer of communication; it has a formative role in constituting people's sense of reality. Donald Ellis uses the term 'labelling theory' to describe the psychological and sociological processes by which linguistic terms serve as the basis for perception and the definition of reality. Citing Lakoff, Ellis explains that communication acquires its meaning by being related to some form of foundational experience. Thus, the repeated labelling of Israel by antizionists as, to give just one example, an 'apartheid state', is enough to produce a body of opinion that sees Israel as an 'apartheid state'. This is because the word 'apartheid' is already associated in people's minds with the characteristics of the South African apartheid regime. When the use of a linguistic term to apply to Israel is part of a persistent, persuasive and repetitive campaign, then the label is easily absorbed by the public (Ellis 2019).

Alex Joffe argues that the concept of 'human rights' is infinitely malleable. Although human rights are assumed to be a timeless and agreed-upon unitary body of beliefs, laws and mechanisms, they in fact encompass a vast and diverse range of concepts and instruments, including treaties, national law, international law, international customary law, international humanitarian law, international human rights law, declarations, and specific human rights instruments, such as the Universal Declaration of Human Rights 1948.

The diversity and unevenness of human rights laws and instruments have facilitated the creation of a 'human rights industry' in which the concept of human rights as applied to Israel deliberately blurs many legal and political categories, justifying the practice of linguistic abuse in the application of the demonising labels that are applied to Israel. Joffe claims that the 'human rights industry' is controlled by activists in charge of NGOs and transnational organisations who regard Israel, a small ethno-national state with a clear and explicit Jewish identity, as a challenge to their idea of transnational progressivism. They therefore take full advantage of their positions to lead the charge in demonising and delegitimising Israel (Joffe 2019). Recent NGO reports demonising Israel includes the Human Rights Watch report, 'A Threshold Crossed: Israeli Authorities and the Crimes of Apartheid and Persecution' (2021) and Amnesty International report, 'Israel's Apartheid Against Palestinians: A Cruel System of Domination and a Crime Against Humanity' (2022) both of which accused Israel of being an apartheid state.

The following sections consider the main labels used by antizionists to demonise and delegitimise Israel and Zionism. These labels are the tropes of the 'new' or 'contemporary' or 'antizionist' antisemitism.

Israel as a 'Nazi-Like' State

The claim is frequently made by antizionists that Israel treats the Palestinians just as the Nazis treated the Jews. Labelling Israel as a Nazi-like state is known as 'Holocaust inversion' (Gerstenfeld 2007, 2009). Johnson notes that Holocaust inversion has become a principal signifier or reference point of contemporary antizionist discourse (Johnson 2018, 2019). This is because Holocaust inversion is a powerful political tool in the fight to deny Israel's legitimacy and to justify her replacement with an Arab majority state. It does this effectively for two reasons: first, in the post-war world, 'Nazism' has become the defining metaphor of absolute evil and Israel is therefore constructed as uniquely evil (Wistrich 2004:29); and second, the claim that Israel is inflicting a kind of Holocaust on the Palestinians involves the implicit accusation that Israel is committing genocide against the Palestinians. Thus, a term that is so commonly associated with the mass murder of European Jews in the Shoah, and a reason for the broad international support for the founding of the State of Israel in 1948 (Herf 2022), is now commonly associated with Israel's treatment of the Palestinians and is a justification for its elimination as a Jewish state.

The 'Nazi-like state' label also condemns Israel and Zionism as racist without the need for evidentiary support. It is thought that the need for evidentiary support is dispensed with because the Holocaust inversion trope has morphed from two classic antisemitic tropes. First, Israel's racism is considered to be inseparable from the nature of Jewish culture and consciousness because of the classical antisemitic trope that Jews consider themselves to be the Chosen People destined to be 'set above others' and thus entitled to write 'discriminatory institutions and practices' into 'the basic legal structure of [their] state' (Chomsky and Avishai 1975, cited in Harrison 2020:152). Second, the claim that the Israelis have become the 'persecutors' of the Palestinian Arabs because of the terrible atrocities they suffered at the hands of the Nazis is a variant of the 'persecuted Jews become the persecutors' trope, which was first popularised by the Bishop of Norwich as long ago as twelfth-century England, and even today retains some popularity with antizionists like Jacqueline Rose (Julius 2011:506).

Thus, despite the lack of supporting evidence, a 2011 study of seven European countries found high levels of agreement with the statement, 'Israel is carrying out a war of extermination against the Palestinians' (Gerstenfeld 2013). A 2019 pilot study, conducted on 340 volunteers from King's College London, found that 34 per cent of respondents agreed with the statement that 'Israel treats the Palestinians like the Nazis treated the Jews' (Allington and Hirsh 2019:48); and more recently, as noted earlier, the 2023 ADL survey found that 40 per cent of Americans agree to some extent with the statement that 'Israel treats the Palestinians like the Nazis treated the Jews.'

Holocaust inversion not only accuses Israelis of being no better than the Nazis who murdered their families, it also whitewashes the heinous Nazi crimes. This amounts to 'soft-core Holocaust denial' (Lipstadt 1994). Far-right antisemitism, on the other hand, denies the Holocaust outright, accusing the Jews of conspiring to fabricate or exaggerate the Holocaust for their own benefit, such as to increase their power. Unlike Holocaust inversion, Holocaust denial is a marginal phenomenon.

Israel as an 'Apartheid' State

Israel is condemned by another false analogy: the label of 'Apartheid State'. As with the Nazi analogy, the apartheid analogy is used to delegitimise Israel by comparing it to Apartheid South Africa with its social and political policy of racial segregation and discrimination against the indigenous Black majority. This makes what Alan Johnson refers to as the 'Apartheid smear', (Johnson 2014, 2022) an effective rhetorical strategy in the campaign to delegitimise Israel. As with the other demonising labels, the strategy of repetition is used with references to 'Apartheid Israel', 'the apartheid system' and 'the apartheid wall' (to refer to the security wall). Harrison claims that the charge of apartheid against Israel is believed without question because Israel is a Jewish state, and the homeland of the long-persecuted Jewish people, and so for good historical reasons give Jews anywhere in the world a legal 'right of return' but does not give the same right to Arabs, thus convincing people that

Israel is apartheid-like (Harrison 2020). The apartheid label has also been strongly reinforced by the UN's 1975 and 2001 resolutions equating Zionism with racism, as well as reports of NGOs, like B'tselem, Human Rights Watch and Amnesty International which, as noted earlier, play a prominent role in the political campaigns to delegitimise Israel, most recently by mounting a full-frontal attack against Israel as an apartheid state.

By labelling Israel an 'apartheid state', anti-Israel activists can justify support for the campaign to boycott Israel by comparing Israel to apartheid-era South Africa. As David Hirsh has noted, this presents the boycott of Israel as a moral obligation (2017:95–99) and is a continuation of the long history of the exclusion and repudiation of Jews which has been adopted by many in the Arab world and on the Western left (Hirsh and Miller 2022:21–36). The labelling of Israel as an apartheid state, like the labelling of Israel as a Nazi state, is a convenient and effective way of designating Israel as a racist, and therefore, an illegitimate state.

A closely related political narrative is one that labels Israel a 'settler-colonial state' and therefore, once again, illegitimate.

Israel as a 'Settler-Colonial' State

The application to Israel of the 'settler-colonial state' label portrays Israel as a historical wrong and suggests the possibility of righting that wrong by dismantling Israel as a Jewish state. The settler-colonialism discourse has therefore become a major part of the antizionist narrative to delegitimise Israel, and is a favoured theme of BDS activists who state:

> The origin of Israel's contemporary regime over Palestinians is found in the racist ideology of late 19th century European colonialism. This ideology was shared by the dominant stream of the Zionist movement, which was founded in Europe and would later establish the state of Israel.
>
> *(BDS, nd)*

As with the 'Nazi-like state' and the 'apartheid state' labels, the 'settler-colonial state' label is without any factual support. First, no nationals were sent to Palestine by a mother country to create a polity and dominate the local population. Moreover, as Johnson points out, the 'Zionist settler-colonialism' paradigm erases 'everything one needs to know in order to properly understand the conflict (and so make a useful contribution to its resolution)', ignoring 'everything that distinguishes the Jewish return to Palestine from White European Settler Colonialism', including the long and intimate Jewish relationship to the land; the exceptional history of Jewish persecution; the fact of Jewish indigeneity – Johnson points out that 'Hundreds of thousands of Jews moved to Israel from Arab lands from the late 1940s, moving within a region they had lived in for millennia, and most were *driven out* of their homelands by Arab and Muslim antisemitism (a huge subject that is routinely ignored or covered over by the advocates of "settler colonialism")' – and the stark fact that it was the international community assembled in the United Nations that accepted Jewish claims in Palestine and birthed the Jewish state, proposing a division of the land between Jews and Arabs, a two-state solution, a proposal the Jews accepted and the Arabs, local and regional rejected, launching a war of annihilation against the Jews only a few years after the Holocaust (Johnson 2021a, Strawson 2019).

The 'Indigeneity' Discourse

The settler-colonialism discourse is strongly supported by the 'indigeneity' discourse. 'Indigenous' is a legal concept used to refer to a culturally distinct ethnic group whose members are directly descended from the earliest known inhabitants of a particular region and who, to some extent, have maintained the same language and culture, such as the Aborigines in Australia. The 'indigeneity' discourse has been co-opted by antizionist activists. They label the Palestinian Arabs as the 'indigenous people of Palestine' descended from the Canaanites and other tribes. As such, the Palestinian Arabs are portrayed as the true inhabitants of the land of Israel with sole rights to it. The rights of indigenous peoples, which include the right to protect their culture, identity, language, ceremonies, access to education, employment, health and natural resources, are recognised by international law. The indigeneity discourse thus constructs the Jews as recent foreign invaders and conquerors, thus supporting the colonialism discourse. It also denies the Jews any historical claim to the land of Israel and thus delegitimises Zionism which is set up as a colonialist project and is therefore racist (Troen and Troen 2019). An example of the indigeneity discourse is the claim sometimes made by anti-Israel activists that 'Jesus was a Palestinian.'

'Jews as White' Discourse

A discourse associated with the perception of Zionists as European colonisers and oppressors of the indigenous people of Palestine, and with a perception of Israelis as practising apartheid, is the labelling of Jews as 'white' and as enjoying 'white privilege'. This practice has become more commonplace in academia and in public debates with the arrival over the past 20 years or so of 'Critical Whiteness Studies' as a field of academic scholarship.

Writers of colour, including Ralph Ellison, Franz Fanon and James Baldwin, advanced the idea that 'whiteness' lies at the centre of the problem of racism, and that by problematising whiteness, racism can be disrupted. Critical Whiteness Studies sets out to reveal the invisible structures that produce and reproduce white supremacy and privilege. Thus, it sees the world in binary terms with 'white' representing domination, oppression and racism, and 'black' representing the downtrodden and oppressed. Within this discourse, 'whiteness' is also used to denote those who enjoy 'white privilege'. In this sense, 'whiteness' is not just used in a descriptive sense but is also used in a critical sense.

Balazs Berkovits argues that attributing 'whiteness' to Jews is more than merely controversial; it assimilates the most persecuted minority in European history to the dominant majority, while downgrading the significance of antisemitism. Because Jews are framed as white, 'there cannot by definition be any discrimination against them, or if there is, it cannot be "systemic", that is, meaningful' (Berkovits 2018:93).

Similarly, Israel is seen as a white colony in the Middle East. Indeed, Berkovits asserts that the 'Jewish whiteness' label is used to characterise a variety of phenomena including 'Jewish hegemony and supremacism' and 'Zionist racism and colonialism', allowing Jews to be perceived as 'not only part of the dominant majority, but also the ruling white elite or "caste" exercising their domination on racist grounds, thereby forming one of the most oppressive majorities in the world' (Berkovits 2018:101).

Berkovits argues that the labelling of Jews as 'white' is essential to understanding why so much contemporary criticism is directed at Israel and Zionism. Because Israel has become a symbol of oppression and privilege, denouncing Israel and Zionism signals one's holding of a 'progressive' ideological world view and one's membership in the camp of the good: 'If anti-Zionism has become probably the most popular critical idiom, it is due to the perception of Jews as white colonizers. Criticism of Israel feeds on criticism of Jews as inchoately "white"' (Berkovits 2021).

Antisemitism has always been able to accommodate mutually incompatible anathemas against Jews. Today, while antizionist antisemitism regards Jews as white colonial oppressors, far-right antisemitism regards Jews as destroying white nations (CST 2019). This conspiracy theory is known as 'white genocide'. It holds that Jews control migration flows and are responsible for the immigration of people regarded as ethnically and culturally inferior, resulting in the destruction of native identity.

'Intersectionality': Discourse and Practice

'Intersectionality' is a discourse that is closely associated with the 'Jews-as-white' discourse. The theory of intersectionality recognises that people are often disadvantaged by multiple sources of prejudice, and it burst onto the academic scene in 1989 when American law professor, Kimberlé Crenshaw wrote a seminal essay explaining that black women are oppressed by dual sources of bias and discrimination.

However, 'intersectionality' has morphed from its original meaning and focus into a fashionable but often crude theory which links together simplistically the identities of all those who claim to be the victims of a common power structure. Palestinians are thus regarded by intersectional theory as suffering from the same kind of structural racism as people of colour, and the same structural oppression as the LGBTQ community and feminist movement. Members of these groups thus identify with the Palestinians as the 'victimised other'.

Because the intersectionality discourse reinforces the narrative of Israel as a colonial power that practices apartheid and implements Nazi-like policies against the Palestinians, proponents of the academic boycott and those who support anti-racist campaigns and other minority causes constantly call for the banning of 'Zionists' from participation in progressive movements and activities. Moreover, during the Israel–Hamas conflict in May 2021, academics and student activists on both sides of the Atlantic signed statements affirming the idea that Israel is an apartheid state that must be boycotted and dismantled, as being foundational to their scholarship and morality. These statements functioned as loyalty tests for Jewish academics and students whose membership in the academic community was made conditional on their endorsement (Hirsh 2023).

'Pinkwashing': Discourse and Practice

Closely associated with 'intersectionality' as a discourse and practice, is 'Pinkwashing'. American academic Corinne Blackmer claims that 'the academic notion of queerness and hostility to the Jewish state are now virtually synonymous' (Blackmer 2023), driven by a group of prominent 'progressive' academic scholars, the most prominent of whom is Judith Butler. The term 'pinkwashing' is used to allege that Israel dishonestly uses its excellent record on LGBTQ rights to cover up human rights abuses against the Palestinians, and to paint its Arab neighbours as homophobic.

'Pinkwashing' is not limited to academic discourse. It was used at the Chicago Dyke March in 2016 and the Washington DC Dyke March in 2019 to justify the banning of the rainbow flag with a blue Star of David in the middle from their parades on the grounds that they were 'antizionist' events. The march organisers thought that displaying the blue Star of David might 'make people feel unsafe' because it resembled the Israeli flag (Blackmer 2023).

Alan Dershowitz argues that the 'pinkwashing' accusation amounts to nothing more than the antisemitic canard that Jews can do no right: 'Nothing the Jew or the Jew among nations does can be praised, because its purpose is always to "manipulate," to "conceal", "to divert attention away from", or to "distort" the evil that inheres in all Jewish actions and inactions.

Everything the Jewish nation does is part of a grand conspiratorial plan' (Dershowitz 2017).

Thus, the 'pinkwashing' allegation is yet another rhetorical strategy used by BDS activists and others to demonise and delegitimise Israel and to exclude Jews from progressive spaces.

Antisemitism Denial and the Livingstone Formulation: Discourse and Practice

As noted earlier, one consequence of the 'Jews as white' discourse is that Jews are not believed to be a marginalised or oppressed group that suffers from structural racism. As a result, when antisemitism is alleged, it is frequently denied by those relied on to adjudicate the issue. Not only is the antisemitism denied, but Berkovits argues that the excessive power and dominance associated with 'white Jews' invites criticism in a way that overemphasises the antisemitic content of the response (Berkovits 2021). Berkovits's claim can be illustrated with two examples: antisemitism was denied by the Employment Tribunal in the case of *Fraser v University and College Union* in 2013 (Courts and Tribunals Judiciary 2013) and by the Labour Party under the leadership of Jeremy Corbyn, and in both cases the denial was accompanied by a counter-allegation that those alleging antisemitism, who were mostly Jews, were doing so dishonestly to prevent Israel from being criticised.

The *Livingstone Formulation* is a term coined by David Hirsh in 2006 to describe the practice of responding to a complaint of antisemitism with a counter-allegation that the complainants are just trying to silence criticism of Israel. In other words, it accuses Jews of bad faith and of 'weaponising antisemitism'. Hirsh notes that the Livingstone Formulation is the key mode of bullying experienced by Jews in left and liberal spaces (2023).

Noting that the use of the Livingstone Formulation had become standard practice in response to claims of antisemitism in the Labour Party, the Report of the Equality and Human Rights Commission into Antisemitism in the Labour Party found that social media comments by Labour Party 'agents' (i.e. aides, staff members, and members of the National Executive Committee) alleging that the complaints of antisemitism had been manufactured by the 'Israel lobby' were evidence of 'antisemitic conduct' and concluded that the denial of antisemitism constituted the unlawful harassment of Jewish members under the Equality Act 2010 (EHRC 2020).

The IHRA Working Definition of Antisemitism

Nowhere has the campaign to reject the IHRA working definition of antisemitism been waged more forcefully than in British universities. The campaign has been led by the academic antizionist left, most of whom are members of the UK's academic union, the University and College Union (UCU), which has a history of promoting an academic boycott of Israel. The UCU voiced official opposition to the Department of Education's 2020 request that the IHRA definition be adopted by the university sector to combat rising campus antisemitism. The UCU's opposition was stated to be on the grounds of 'free speech' and 'academic freedom' (Grady 2020).

Despite these purported objections, it appears likely that many antizionist academics who oppose IHRA do so because the Working Definition stigmatises as possibly antisemitic, 'taking into account the overall context', the very expressions of hostility to Israel which they themselves rely on to demonise and delegitimise the Jewish state. The IHRA lists the following:

- Accusing Jewish citizens of being more loyal to Israel, or to the alleged priorities of Jews worldwide, than to the interests of their own nations.
- Denying the Jewish people their right to self-determination, for example, by claiming that the existence of a State of Israel is a racist endeavour.
- Applying double standards by requiring of it a behaviour not expected or demanded of any other democratic nation.
- Using the symbols and images associated with classic antisemitism (e.g. claims of Jews killing Jesus or blood libel) to characterise Israel or Israelis.
- Drawing comparisons of contemporary Israeli policy to that of the Nazis.
- Holding Jews collectively responsible for the actions of the state of Israel (IHRA 2016).

Antizionist academics also oppose the IHRA definition because, as Hirsh points out, its adoption by their universities affirms that antizionist antisemitism exists and that it is significant. To this end, it refutes their self-serving claim that antizionism and antisemitism are two entirely distinct phenomena, or that antizionist antisemitism is insignificant, or that it is being 'weaponised' by Zionists, all claims advanced by parts of the left (Hirsh 2023, and see the articles collected in Johnson 2021b).

Conclusion

Although left antisemitism has a long history, it is most likely to be expressed today as anti-Israel hostility centring on a collection of labels that construct Israel as an illegitimate state and Zionism as a racist ideology. These labels are continuations or variations of the tropes of classical antisemitism which are used today to demonise and delegitimise Israel and Zionism. To the degree that those tropes become normalised in progressive American and European circles, the oldest hatred finds a home there in the form of antizionist antisemitism.

References

Action and Protection League (2021) *Antisemitic Prejudices in Europe: Survey in 16 European Countries.* Available: https://apleu.org/european-antisemitism-survey/ (accessed 27 February 2023).

Allington, Daniel and David Hirsh (2019) 'The AZAs (Antizionist Antisemitism) Scale: Measuring Antisemitism as Expressed in Relation to Israel and Its Supporters', *Journal of Contemporary Antisemitism*, 2 (2): 43–52.

Amnesty International (2022) 'Israel's apartheid against Palestinians: A cruel system of domination and a crime against humanity'. Available: www.amnesty.org/en/latest/news/2022/02/israels-apartheid-against-palestinians-a-cruel-system-of-domination-and-a-crime-against-humanity/ (accessed 27 February 2023).

Anti-Defamation League (2023) 'Antisemitic attitudes in America: Topline findings', 12 January. Available: www.adl.org/resources/report/antisemitic-attitudes-america-topline-findings (accessed 27 February 2023).

BDS (nd) 'BDS Statement'. Available: https://bdsmovement.net/colonialism-and-apartheid/the-origins-of-israel-zionism-and-settler-colonialism (accessed 27 February 2023).

Berkovits, Balazs (2018) 'Critical whiteness studies and the "Jewish problem"', *Zeitschrift fur kritische Sozlatheorie und Philosophie*, 5 (1): 86–102.

Berkovits, Balazs (2021) 'What color are the Jews? (Part II)?' *K*, 23 June 2021. Available: https://k-larevue.com/en/what-color-are-the-jews-part-ii/ (accessed 28 February 2023).

Blackmer, Corinne (2023) 'The queering of antisemitism', *Tablet*, 3 February. Available: www.tabletmag.com/sections/news/articles/queering-antisemitism (accessed 27 February 2023).

Campaign Against Antisemitism (2020) 'Miriam Margolyes says a conspiracy within the party motivated form Israel forced Jeremy Corbyn to stand down as Labour leader', 13 July. Available: https://antisemitism.uk/miriam/margolyes-says-a-conspiracy-within-party-motivated-from-israel-forced-jeremy-corbyn-to stand-down-as-labour-leader/ (accessed 27 February 2023).

Chomsky, Noam and Bernard Avishai (1975) 'An exchange on the Jewish state', *New York Review of Books*, 17 July. Available: www.nybooks.com/articles/1975/07/17/an-exchange-on-the-jewish-state/ (accessed 27 February 2023).

The Community Security Trust (2019) 'Antisemitic incidents report 2018', 7 February. Available: https://cst.org.uk/news/blog/2019/02/07/antisemitic-incidents-report-2018 (accessed 28 February 2023).

Courts and Tribunals Judiciary (2013) 'Mr. R. Fraser-v-University & College Union', 25 March. Available: www.judiciary.gov.uk/media/judgments/2013/fraser-uni-college-union (accessed 28 February 2023).

Dershowitz, Alan (2017) 'Pinkwashing: Another conspiracy theory', *The Daily Beast*, 12 July. Available: www.thedailybeast.com/pinkwashing-another-conspriacy-theory (accessed 27 February 2023).

Ellis, Donald (2019) 'Apartheid', *Israel Studies*, 24 (2): 63–72.

Equality and Human Rights Commission (2020) *Investigation Into Antisemitism in the Labour Party – Report*. Available: www.equality.humanrights.com/sites/default/files/investigation-into-antisemitism-in-the-labour-party.pdf (accessed 27 February 2023).

Fuschshuber, Thursten (2019) 'From Wilhelm Marr to *Mavi Marmara:* Antisemitism and anti-Zionism as forms of anti-Jewish action', in Alvin H. Rosenfeld (ed.), *Anti-Zionism and Antisemitism: The Dynamics of Delegitimization*, Bloomington: Indiana University Press, 30–52.

Gardner, Mark (2007) ' "The Zionists Are Our Misfortune": On the (not so) New Antisemitism', *Democratiya* 10. Available: www.dissentmagazine.org/wp-content/files_mf/1389737385d10Gardner.pdf (accessed 28 February 2023).

Gerstenfeld, Manfred (2007) *Holocaust Inversion: The Portraying of Israel and Jews as Nazis*, Jerusalem: Jerusalem Center for Public Affairs.

Gerstenfeld, Manfred (2009) *The Abuse of Holocaust Memory: Distortion and Responses*, Jerusalem: Jerusalem Center for Public Affairs, 101–113.

Gerstenfeld, Manfred (2013) 'Are 150 million Europeans anti-Semites or dangerous idiots?' *Times of Israel*, 10 July. Available: https://blogs.timesofisrael.com/are-150-million-europeans-anti-semites-or-dangerous-idiots/ (accessed 27 February 2023).

Grady, Jo (2020) 'General secretary of the UCU, Letter to Gavin Williamson', 9 November. Available: www.ucu.org.uk/media/11272/Letter-to-Gavin-Williamson-re.-adoption-of-IHRA-definition-of-anti-Semitism-by-universities/pdf/ (accessed 27 February 2023).

Harrison, Bernard (2020) *Blaming the Jews: The Persistence of a Delusion*, Bloomington: Indiana University Press.

Herf, Jeffrey (2022) *Israel's Moment: International Support for and Opposition to Establishing the Jewish State, 1945–1949*, New York: Cambridge University Press.

Hirsh, David (2013) 'Defining antisemitism down', *Fathom*, Winter. Available: https://fathomjournal.org/defining-antisemitism-down/ (accessed 27 February 2023).

Hirsh, David (2017) *Contemporary Left Antisemitism*, Abingdon: Routledge.

Hirsh, David (2023) 'Contemporary Antisemitism', in Mark Weitzman, Robert J. Williams and James Wald (eds.), *The Routledge History of Antisemitism*, Abingdon: Routledge.

Hirsh, David and Hilary Miller (2022) 'Durban antizionism: Its Sources, its impact and its relation to older anti-Jewish ideologies', *Journal of Contemporary Antisemitism*, 5 (1): 21–36.

Human Rights Watch (2021) 'A threshold crossed: Israeli authorities and the crimes of persecution'. Available: www.hrw.org/report/2021/04/27/threshold-crossed/Israeli-authorities-and-crimes-apartheid-and-persecution (accessed 27 February 2023).

IHRA (2016) 'Working definition of antisemitism'. Available: www.holocaustremembrance.com/working-definition-antisemitism (accessed 27 February 2023).

Joffe, Alex (2019) 'Human rights', *Israel Studies*, 24 (2): 103–118.

Johnson, Alan (2014) *The Apartheid Smear*, BICOM. Available: www.bicom.org.uk/analysis/18870/ (accessed 27 February 2023).

Johnson, Alan (2015) 'The left and the Jews: Time for a rethink', *Fathom*, Autumn. Available: https://fathomjournal.org/the-left-and-the-jews-time-for-a-rethink/ (accessed 27 February 2023).

Johnson, Alan (2018) 'Why the Nazi analogy and holocaust inversion are antisemitic', *Fathom*, August. Available: https://fathomjournal.org/why-the-nazi-analogy-and-holocaust-inversion-are-antisemitic (accessed 27 February 2023).

Johnson, Alan (2019) 'Antisemitism in the guise of anti-Nazism: Holocaust inversion in the United Kingdom during operation protective edge', in Alvin H. Rosenfeld (ed.), *Anti-Zionism and Antisemitism: The Dynamics of Delegitimization*, Bloomington: Indiana University Press, 175–199.

Johnson, Alan (2021a) ' "Can't you see he's fooled you all?": An Open Letter to Peter Gabriel et al. Explaining why Israel is not a "Settler Colonial" Society', *Fathom*, November. Available: https://fathomjournal.org/cant-you-see-hes-fooled-you-all-an-open-letter-to-peter-gabriel-et-al-explaining-why-israel-is-not-a-settler-colonial-society (accessed 28 February 2023).

Johnson, Alan (2021b) *In Defence of the IHRA Working Definition of Antisemitism*, Fathom eBook Series. Available: https://fathomjournal.org/fathom-ebook-in-defence-of-the-ihra-working-definition-of-antisemitism/ (accessed 28 February 2023).

Johnson, Alan (2022) *The Apartheid Smear 2022 Edition*, BICOM. Available: www.bicom.org.uk/analysis/the-apartheid-smear-2022/ (accessed 27 February 2023).

Julius, Anthony (2011) *Trials of the Diaspora: A History of Antisemitism in England*, Oxford: Oxford University Press.

Lipstadt, Deborah (1994) *Denying the Holocaust: The Growing Assault on Truth and Memory* (2nd edn.), London: Penguin.

Pollard, Alexandra (2020) 'Maxine Peake: "People who couldn't vote Labour because of Corbyn? They voted Tory as far as I'm concerned" ', *The Independent*, 25 June. Available: www.independent.co.uk/arts-entertainment/films/features/maxine-peake-interview-labour-corbyn-keir-starmer-black-lives-matter-a9583206.html (accessed 27 February 2023).

Seymour, David M. (2019) 'Continuity and discontinuity: From antisemitism to antizionism and the reconfiguration of the Jewish question', *Journal of Contemporary Antisemitism*, 2 (2): 11–23.

Staetsky, L. Daniel (2017) *Antisemitism in Contemporary Great Britain: A Study of Attitudes Towards Jews and Israel*, London: Jewish Policy Research. Available: https://cst.org.uk/data/file/7/4/JPR.2017.Antisemitism%20in%20contemporary%20Great%20Britain.1615559606.pdf (accessed 28 February 2023).

Strawson, John (2019) 'Colonialism', *Israel Studies*, 24 (2): 33–44.

Troen, Ilan and Carol Troen (2019) 'Indigeneity', *Israel Studies*, 24 (2): 17–32.

Wistrich, Robert S. (2004) 'Anti-Zionism and antisemitism', *Jewish Political Studies Review*, 16 (3–4): 27–31.

3

THE JEWISH EXPERIENCE OF ANTISEMITISM

Dave Rich

Research into antisemitism focuses overwhelmingly on the antisemites themselves: who they are, what they say, what motivates them and how they think. But antisemitism matters because it has a real impact on people – mostly, but not exclusively, Jewish people – in their daily lives. It matters because antisemitism is not only a way of thinking but also a pattern of behaving; and when antisemitism translates from an idea into an action, it can have dramatic and devastating consequences. This essay will concentrate on the people who experience these consequences, using data gathered by the Community Security Trust (CST) and the European Union Fundamental Rights Agency as well as other resources. It will assess what this data tells us about how Jewish people experience antisemitism in modern Britain: where, when and on whom it strikes, and how it makes British Jews feel about their own safety and belonging. And it will draw some lessons for others, by showing that when antisemitism reaches a particular level of virulence, it is not only Jews who are in danger.

Targets and Incidents

The Community Security Trust is a Jewish community organisation that, amongst other functions, provides support to victims of antisemitic hate incidents and hate crimes. (Full disclosure: CST is also my employer.) It publishes biannual reports analysing data compiled from the complaints of antisemitism received from victims, witnesses, security guards at Jewish buildings, its own volunteers and through a national information-sharing agreement with police forces. The foundation of all these reports is the experience of individual Jewish people who suffer antisemitism, and at times this can be

DOI: 10.4324/9781003322320-4

harrowing. In August 2021, Jacob Lipschitz, a 63-year-old Jewish man, was walking through the Stamford Hill area of North London when a random passer-by suddenly punched him on the side of the head, knocking him unconscious. Mr. Lipschitz fell into a wall and then to the floor, where he woke up with a broken ankle and injuries to his head. It took an operation to fix his ankle, but the psychological trauma was much longer lasting. Diagnosed with Post-Traumatic Stress Disorder as a result of the attack, over a year later Mr. Lipschitz was still suffering. 'I am not the same confident person I used to be', he told the court. 'I am scared' (CST 2022c).

The impact of antisemitic hate crime does not stop with the individual. The person who assaulted Mr. Lipschitz, Abdullah Qureshi, also attacked at least two other Jewish people in Stamford Hill that day, including one child. News of this series of violent anti-Jewish attacks spread quickly, aided by shocking CCTV footage of the assault on Mr. Lipschitz. News headlines led to collective fear across the Jewish community as the police hunted for the assailant. The video of Mr. Lipschitz being punched to the floor went viral. The episode revived feelings that repeat every time antisemitic attacks of this nature reach a level of seriousness that attracts media attention. 'Spate of anti-Semitic attacks makes the Sabbath a day of fear in Stamford Hill', read a headline in the *Independent* in 2005 (Akbar 2005). 'Four incidents in 10 days "instilled fear" in Charedi community', reported the *Jewish News* in 2022 (Mendel 2002). And on it goes.

The challenge is to translate these individual incidents into data that sheds light on who is being targeted by anti-Jewish hate crime offenders, and the circumstances and contexts in which these incidents occur. In 2021, for example, 57 per cent of victims of antisemitic incidents reported to CST were male, 35 per cent were female and in 8 per cent of incidents mixed groups of male and female victims were attacked – a family walking to synagogue perhaps, or groups of Jewish schoolchildren on their way home from school (Community Security Trust 2022:33).[1]

However, national data tells us that when it comes to the question of who suffers from crime, there is no significant difference between the genders. Although there are differences when it comes to specific categories of crime, taken as an aggregate the experience of crime is roughly the same in quantity, or close enough, whether you are male or female (Office of National Statistics 2021). This poses the question of why, when it comes to antisemitic hate crimes, Jewish men are significantly more likely to be targeted than Jewish women. One answer to this shines a light on an important aspect of how antisemitism affects Jewish people, and that is the question of visibility. Antisemitic hate crimes are more likely to affect people who can be identified as Jewish by their assailant. In London, antisemitic hate crimes occur primarily in Hackney and Barnet, the two boroughs where London's largest Jewish communities live. In contrast, Metropolitan Police data shows that the borough with the highest totals for other types of racist or religious hate crimes is Westminster, the heart of the city where everybody mixes. This contrast between the locations of antisemitic hate crimes compared to other racist and religious strands reflects the visible Jewish presence in Hackney and Barnet, rather than the presence of more antisemites.

This is logical, but it also means that antisemitism does not affect the varied and different parts of the Jewish community in equal ways, because Jewish visibility is a fluid concept. In the Strictly Orthodox or Haredi community, Jewish men wear distinctive dress, with long black coats, large black hats, beards and side curls. Other Jewish men who are religious, but not Haredi, may wear a *kippah* – a religious skullcap. There are children who go to Jewish schools and are visibly Jewish on schooldays, when they are wearing their uniform, but not at the weekend. Visibility may be indicated by a piece of jewellery with a Star of David or Hebrew writing, or simply by the fact that you are wearing smart clothes and walking near a synagogue on a Saturday morning. Or it may be that a Jewish person has no specific markers of visibility, but still appears to be Jewish to others due to some imperceptible Jewish 'look'. And what counts as visibly Jewish to one person may not register to someone else.

Jewish visibility, then, influences where antisemitism occurs and who it affects. The Haredi community is concentrated much more in Hackney than in Barnet, where Jewish expression and religiosity display a far wider variety, and this may explain why, in the year October 2022, there were more antisemitic hate crimes recorded in Hackney than in Barnet, even though the 2021 census shows that over three times as many Jews live in Barnet than in Hackney. This is also relevant to the discrepancy in how Jewish men and Jewish women experience hate crimes. Unlike Haredi men who wear a very specific and identifiable clothing, women in the Haredi community are only required to dress 'modestly'. Even in more mainstream Jewish traditions, there is no female equivalent to the male *kippah* head covering. The likelihood that the more prominent visibility of Jewish men compared to Jewish women plays a role in the imbalance in their experience of antisemitic hate crime is similar, although reversed, to the pattern of anti-Muslim hate crime which affects Muslim women more than men – because in Islam it is women who wear distinctive clothing such as the *hijab*. This religious clothing is not just a way for antisemites to identify Jewish targets: it is an affront to those who are repelled by difference, who consider any deviation from their own idea of British culture to be a threat.

Experiences and Responses

The impact of this pattern of offending on Jewish people was teased out in survey work done by the European Union Agency for Fundamental Rights in

2012 and 2018. These two surveys measured Jewish perceptions and experiences of antisemitism across several EU member states (which included the United Kingdom at that time), and one of its many findings was that most Jewish people will, at some time or another, attempt to hide the fact they are Jewish because they are fearful about being attacked. According to the 2018 survey, 17 per cent of Jewish people in the United Kingdom always or frequently 'avoid wearing, carrying or displaying things that might help people recognise you as a Jew', and a further 43 per cent occasionally do this. Twenty-seven per cent of British Jews even sometimes choose not to go to a Jewish event or site because they would not feel safe, either at the event or on the way to and from it. Across the 12 EU countries surveyed in 2018, 71 per cent of Jews always, frequently or occasionally take these steps. This reflects a genuinely held fear of antisemitism: in the UK, 29 per cent of Jews said they worry about being a victim of verbal abuse or harassment, and 20 per cent feared physical attack (European Union 2018:34–38).

These are staggering figures that immediately take us to the direct, personal impact of antisemitism on Jewish people's willingness to live an openly Jewish life. It is a fundamental democratic principle that the freedom to practice one's religion, and to take an equal share of the benefits of living in an open, liberal society, ought to be available to everybody irrespective of their faith or ethnicity. The data suggests that Jews are sometimes excluded from enjoying this right. Whether it is the Jewish school student removing their blazer before they get on the public bus home, or the Jewish football fan who replaces his *kippah* with a team baseball cap before he goes to the match, antisemitism has a restricting impact on the self-confidence of some Jews to be Jewish in public.

The evidence about where Jewish people most encounter antisemitic comments suggests a notable variety. According to the 2018 European Union Agency for Fundamental Rights survey, Jewish people in the EU were most likely to encounter negative statements about Jews online or in the media, at political events, in social situations or in other public places. Jewish people were almost twice as likely to hear antisemitic statements in academia as they were at sports events. Discrimination, although less frequent, was most likely to occur in a work context (European Union 2018). In other words, antisemitism can happen anywhere that Jews go in their daily lives. CST's antisemitic incident data suggests that the most common type of antisemitic incident involves a random passer-by shouting verbal abuse at a visibly Jewish person who they happen to encounter in the street. It is a daily risk that, once experienced, is not forgotten.

Antisemitism does not only affect the direct victims of hate crimes. The most high-profile attacks ripple out across the community, creating indirect trauma and anxiety amongst people far from the scene of the actual hate crime. Unsurprisingly, this phenomenon is at its most acute when antisemitism is rampant and when it attracts intense media, political and public attention. In May 2021, an escalation in violence in Israel and Gaza triggered a sharp spike in anti-Jewish hate incidents in the United Kingdom. The most notorious episode of antisemitism during this period involved a convoy of cars that drove from the north of England to London one Sunday afternoon, with Palestinian flags stuck to the car bonnets and waving out of the windows. As the convoy passed through North London towards the centre of the capital, it went through neighbourhoods with large Jewish communities, and this did not escape the notice of the people in the cars. Several Jewish people reported abuse shouted at them out of the car windows, but it was the behaviour of one carload of protestors – as ever in today's social media age, captured on film by a local resident – that went viral. As the convoy was stationary at a set of traffic lights on Finchley Road, a main arterial route into London, one of the convoy participants used a megaphone to broadcast unadulterated hate. 'Fuck the Jews', he shouted, 'fuck their mothers, fuck their daughters, and show your support for Palestine . . . we have to send a message' (Sussex Friends 2021).

The message went around the world. 'I've never felt the proximity of ancient hatred here so strongly as today', tweeted one British Jew, the daughter of a Holocaust survivor, who declared herself too frightened to go into the centre of London, her home city (Rich 2021). The *Washington Post* featured the convoy as the main element in a story about British antisemitism, as did the *Sydney Morning Herald* (Hassan 2021, James 2021). 'Europe's worrying surge of antisemitism', was how Human Rights Watch described what was happening (Ward 2021). When we think of the impact of antisemitism, our first thoughts naturally go to the direct victims. But when anti-Jewish attacks reach such intensity that they become the subject of international media focus, it affects the reputation of Britain as a whole.

This is a pattern that has been seen before whenever Israel is at war, and the wave that occurred in 2021 had a particular impact on younger people. In May 2021, CST recorded 95 antisemitic incidents affecting people and property in the school sector, compared to 54 such incidents during the whole of 2020. One group of Jewish schoolgirls heading home on a London bus were verbally abused by a girl from another school, who shouted 'Free Palestine and f**k Israel' and 'Stupid Jews' at them. At another London secondary school, students repeatedly shouted 'Free Palestine' at the school's Jewish teachers – and only at the teachers who were Jewish. One Jewish girl in South London had already endured a year of antisemitic bullying when the outbreak of conflict in Israel in May 2021 made things considerably worse. What started with shouts of 'Free Palestine' led to Nazi salutes from fellow students. She ended up having to leave her school and now journeys to North London every day to a Jewish school where she feels safe (Rose 2022).

In that individual case, antisemitism drove a young Jewish person to move schools, but at its most intense antisemitism can even motivate emigration. Stories of large-scale migrations of Jewish populations fleeing pogroms, massacres and state oppression are the stuff of Jewish history, but they do not reside only in the past. In the first two decades of this century, between 15 and 20 per cent of the French Jewish community left France for other countries, primarily Israel, the United Kingdom, Canada and the United States (Della Pergolo and Staetsky 2020:30). This migration occurred at a time of repeated antisemitic murders and terrorist attacks in France, and while this was not the only reason they all left, it was a major contributing factor. The terrorist attacks on the Ozar Hatorah school in Toulouse in 2012 and the Hyper Cacher supermarket in Paris in 2015 were merely the most horrific individual instances of antisemitic violence in France during that period. The murders of Ilan Halimi, Mireille Knoll and Sara Halimi (no relation), and a background drumbeat of daily abuse, led many French Jews to determine that their futures lay elsewhere. Some have since returned, and in May 2021, France did not experience a similar surge in anti-Jewish violence and harassment as that seen in the United Kingdom, United States and elsewhere. But blood changes the equation, and the sense of insecurity engendered by France's series of antisemitic murders will take a long time to dissipate.

Anti-Jewish terrorism is the most acute expression of antisemitic hatred, and it imposes a heavy burden on Jewish communities. In the past decade, Jewish communities in Paris, Brussels, Copenhagen, Halle, Pittsburgh and Poway have all suffered deadly terrorist attacks either by jihadists or by neo-Nazis. Other countries, including the United Kingdom, have seen plots foiled by police intervention. The emotional legacy that this leaves on those communities is plain; what often goes less recognised are the psychological and financial consequences for all Jewish communities that face a similar danger. In the UK, the government provides £14 million per year to pay for security guards at Jewish schools, synagogues and other community buildings. This funding has been in place in one form or another since 2010, when the amount was approximately £2 million and was limited to paying for guards at state-funded Jewish faith schools. It was vastly increased in both scale and scope in 2015, as a response to the wave of Islamic State terrorism that hit Europe, and its Jewish communities in that year (Home Office 2022). On top of this government funding, between 2007 and 2021, the Community Security Trust (CST) provided or pledged £15 million in grants to Jewish buildings to install and upgrade their physical security infrastructure (Community Security Trust 2022b). This encompasses gates, fences, alarms, cameras and the whole panoply of security equipment required to prevent terrorists from accessing Jewish people inside their synagogues, schools, community centres and care homes, all linked to a state-of-the-art control centre staffed around the clock. These grants come from donations raised from within the Jewish community, and they are usually provided by CST on a match-funded basis, meaning that the locations accessing the grants need to provide a similar amount themselves. If you add in the annual budget of running CST as an organisation – almost all of which also comes from donations – the overall combined cost to both the Jewish community and the public purse of securing Britain's Jewish community comes to somewhere in the region of £22 million per year.

For a community of just 300,000 people, this is a significant sum – and it only relates to one country. Across Europe, Jewish communities face a similar challenge of raising the funds, either from within their own community or from their governments, to ensure that communal life is protected from the randomness of terrorist outrages. In 2016, the then President of the European Jewish Congress, Dr. Moshe Kantor, told the European Commissioner for Financial and Economic Affairs Pierre Moscovici that 'This places a huge financial burden on our communities, and one that is virtually impossible for us to meet without state and EU involvement' (European Jewish Congress 2016). The following year the Organization for Security and Co-operation in Europe (OSCE) Office for Democratic Institutions and Human Rights recognised that 'The need to build or harden security perimeters is a financial burden often borne by Jewish institutions instead of governments, diverting funds from religious, cultural and educational activities.' This financial burden too often falls on small Jewish communities that can ill afford to divert much-needed funding from the core activities that lie at the heart of communal life. It is counterproductive to spend so much communal money on security that the community cannot afford to do the things that the security is supposed to protect. The OSCE recommended that governments could provide 'financial resources that can help address the security needs of Jewish communities, for example, funding a security guard or installing security equipment' (OSCE 2017:ix, 35). In 2021, the United States Commission on International Religious Freedom (USCIRF), a bipartisan U.S. federal agency, surveyed the state of play regarding antisemitism in 11 different European countries and heard a consistent plea from communal leaders. 'With the exception of France', their report noted, 'all Jewish community leaders responded that physical security measures at Jewish institutions were adequate to the threats assessed. The most common complaint was that Jewish communities bore excessive financial burdens for necessary security measures such as private security guards. Several governments covered all or a vast majority of security costs, including Hungary, Norway, and the UK' (United States Commission on International Religious Freedom 2021:3). In other words, Jewish communities have adapted to the dangers posed by antisemitism and, mostly, developed sufficient security measures to cope; but the cost of doing so has been onerous, and in some cases debilitating.

Ideology and Society

This anti-Jewish terrorism is not an isolated phenomenon. The antisemitism that drives it is part of a wider world view that rejects democracy, equality and the rule of law. It is a world view that generates terrorist violence against a range of people and institutions; as such, anti-Jewish terrorism should not be seen solely as a danger to Jews but as a manifestation of an ideology and set of beliefs that threatens the whole of society. The connection between anti-Jewish violence and the threat to wider society was illustrated in Paris in January 2015, in the successive terrorist attacks targeting the Charlie Hebdo office and then, a few days later, the Hyper Cacher kosher supermarket. A total of 17 people were murdered in the linked attacks across three days (including a policewoman who was killed on the day in between the two main incidents). The jihadist ideology that underpinned the taking of hostages at a kosher shop, seeing Jews as an eternal foe of Muslims whose lives can be forfeit, is connected to a broader rejection of democracy and liberalism that also sought to justify the murder of secular journalists for their work. Antisemitism creates a demonic figure of 'the Jew' and projects it from ancient times into a set of conspiracy theories that seek to explain the ills of the modern world. In so doing, it propels the extremist ideologies that cause murder and mayhem across society, even when no Jews are targeted. The lead hijacker in the 9/11 terrorist attacks in the United States, Mohammed Atta, 'considered New York to be the center of world Jewry, which was, in his opinion, Enemy Number One', noted Küntzel (2022). Al-Qaeda leader Osama bin Laden, responsible for the overall 9/11 plot that brought down the World Trade Center towers and brought the simmering conflict between radical Islamism and the West into the open, believed that 'The Jews' controlled the U.S. economy and media, 'and now control all aspects of your life, making you their servants and achieving their aims at your expense'. There were other factors and motivations involved in al-Qaeda's decision to attack the United States, but it would be a mistake to ignore the confluence of antisemitic conspiracy theories and their deep hatred and mistrust of the United States (Küntzel 2022).

Neo-Nazis also turn to antisemitism to explain and justify their attacks on other, non-Jewish, targets. In May 2022, Payton Gendron, a white supremacist in the United States, shot dead ten people, mostly African Americans, at a supermarket in Buffalo, New York. Gendron targeted that supermarket because its customers were mostly black, and that is who he had chosen to kill. But like so many extreme right-wing terrorists today, before doing so he wrote a lengthy political manifesto that he posted online, and in this manifesto and his other online postings he made it clear that despite the fact he set out to kill black people, the ultimate enemy are still the Jews. 'All practicers [sic] of modern Judaism must be killed', Gendron wrote on Discord. 'There are no innocent Jews on this Earth. . . . Jews can not be considered white, they are the enemy of all.' He even felt obliged to explain to his followers why he had chosen not to murder Jews when '(((they))) are the real problem. (((they))) have caused this white genocide we see today.'[2] 'The reason why I don't attack them and instead the negroes', he explained, 'is that their population boom will be more difficult to deal with in the future, and my killings will prevent some of that and hopefully separate negros and whites more'. On the other hand, he argued, killing Jews will not defeat them, 'but turn millions of people against the Jew and the Jew no longer can regain their power'. It is a frightening level of delusion that is used to justify appalling crimes.

Similar thinking lay behind the shooting of two men outside a bar in Bratislava used by the LGBT+ community. The perpetrator of this terrorist attack, a 19-year-old Slovakian white supremacist called Juraj Krajčík, was, like Gendron, deeply antisemitic. His pre-attack manifesto opened with this stark declaration (emphasis in the original):

It's the jews.
It's the jews.
It's the jews.

Yet Krajčík, like Gendron, did not choose to murder Jews: he targeted gay men. His explanation for this was that every manifestation of what he considers to be deviancy or degeneracy is an extension of ZOG, the Zionist Occupation Government, that dominates and controls the world. Therefore, murdering gay men, black people or anybody else who Krajčík deemed an enemy of his fantasy vision of a pure white race, strikes a blow against the Jewish-controlled system that he believed threatens a white genocide. Juraj Krajčík was viciously homophobic, just as Payton Gendron was irredeemably racist, but for both, Jews remained the ultimate enemy.

This antisemitic, conspiracist world view is not limited to violent neo-Nazis. British politics felt its backwash in the years when antisemitic invective became commonplace in arguments over, and within, the Labour Party under Jeremy Corbyn's leadership. The antisemitism that emanated from far-left circles during that period was very different from the terroristic ideology of Krajčík or Gendron: it did not involve a comparable level of violence, although there were plenty of antisemitic (and, notably, misogynistic) threats that promised to do just that. But that antisemitism was present to an alarming degree has been affirmed by a range of sources. CST's antisemitic incident data, for example, shows that in 2018 surges in antisemitic hate incidents recorded by CST correlated, in part, with periods when arguments over Labour Party-related antisemitism were especially intense and high-profile.

One-third of the 150 antisemitic incidents logged by CST in August 2018 'were related to antisemitism in the Labour Party, or to arguments about allegations of antisemitism in Labour' (Community Security Trust 2019). In 2019, the same occurred: 'the relative peaks of antisemitic incidents that CST recorded in 2019 correlate most closely to periods when discourse around Jews and antisemitism was prominent in news and politics due to the ongoing allegations of antisemitism in the Labour Party' (Community Security Trust 2020). Separate investigations into the phenomenon by the Equality and Human Rights Commission, by internal Labour Party staff and by Martin Forde QC in an independent report commissioned by the party, all found that the problem of antisemitism in the party was real, serious and not exaggerated.

The crucial point, though, is that this did not only affect Jewish members of the Labour Party. Non-Jewish Labour Members of Parliament such as John Mann, Ian Austin or Joan Ryan were all targets of antisemitism because they were, in the eyes of their harassers, too closely associated with the Jewish community or with Israel. All were subjected to allegations that they were in the pocket of Israeli paymasters who used their supposed financial muscle to suborn MPs and subvert British democracy. Often, it was the very act of speaking out against antisemitism that intensified the antisemitic abuse, and you didn't have to be Jewish to experience it.

This is the ultimate twist when we talk about the victims of antisemitism: it is not limited to Jews, because antisemitism is not (or not only) a simple prejudice towards people who are different. In its most developed form, it is an entire world view, a way of explaining social and political change that relies on conspiracy theories and ancient stereotypes to frame Jews as the hidden power pulling everyone else's strings. It's the reason why Ayatollah Khamenei has blamed the 2022 riots in Iran on meddling by the 'fake Zionist regime' (Khamenei 2022). When we talk about the victims of antisemitism, we start with the random Jewish people verbally abused in the street, schoolchildren bullied when Israel is at war or Jewish Members of Parliament and other high-profile community leaders harassed by abuse and threats from online trolls. But ultimately, the victims of antisemitism encompass entire societies that have, in different times and places, been captured by this putrid fantasy.

Notes

1 Figures given are for those incidents for which CST obtained a description of the victim, which accounted for 60 per cent of all incidents reported to CST during 2021.
2 The use of triple parentheses ((())) is an online code used by far-right extremists to identify Jewish people.

References

Akbar, Arifa (2005) 'Spate of anti-Semitic attacks makes the Sabbath a day of fear in Stamford Hill', *Independent*, 22 January.

Community Security Trust (2019) *Antisemitic Incidents Report 2018*, London: CST.

Community Security Trust (2020) *Antisemitic Incidents Report 2019*, London: CST.

Community Security Trust (2022a) *Antisemitic Incidents Report 2021*, London: CST.

Community Security Trust (2022b) *2021 Annual Review*, London: CST.

Community Security Trust (2022c) 'Abdullah Qureshi finally found guilty of antisemitic hate crimes'. Available: https://antisemitism.org/abdullah-qureshi-finally-found-guilty-of-antisemitic-hate-crimes-as-caa-and-others-vindicated-for-pressuring-cps-to-reinstate-racially-religiously-aggravated-charges/ (accessed 24 March 2023).

Della Pergolo, Sergio and Daniel Staetsky (2020) *Jews in Europe at the Turn of the Millennium: Population Trends and Estimates*, London: Institute for Jewish Policy Research.

European Jewish Congress (2016) 'EJC president Dr. Moshe Kantor raises security concerns for Jewish communities at meeting with European Commissioner Pierre Moscovici', 26 January. Available: https://eurojewcong.org/ejc-in-action/statements/ejc-president-dr-moshe-kantor-raises-security-concerns-for-jewish-communities-at-meeting-with-european-commissioner-pierre-moscovici/ (accessed 12 December 2022).

European Union (2018) *Experiences and Perceptions of Antisemitism: Second Survey on Discrimination and Hate Crime Against Jews in the EU*, Publications Office of the European Union. Available: https://fra.europa.eu/en/publication/2018/experiences-and-perceptions-antisemitism-second-survey-discrimination-and-hate (accessed 12 December 2022).

Hassan, Jennifer (2021) 'During Israel-Hamas conflict, British Jews come under physical and verbal attack', *Washington Post*, 21 May.

Home Office (2022) 'Protective security grant funding for Jewish institutions to continue', 12 April. Available: www.gov.uk/government/news/protective-security-grant-funding-for-jewish-institutions-to-continue (accessed 12 December 2022).

James, William (2021) 'Britain's Jews should not have to endure 'shameful racism', says Boris Johnson', *Sydney Morning Herald*, 17 May.

Khamenei, Ayatollah (2022) *Twitter*, 3 October. Available: https://twitter.com/khamenei_ir/status/1576886347151069184 (accessed 12 December 2022).

Küntzel, Matthias (2022) '9/11 and the globalisation of antisemitism', London Centre for the Study of Contemporary Antisemitism. Available: https://londonantisemitism.com/news/matthias-kuntzel-9-11-and-the-globalization-of-antisemitism/ (accessed 12 December 2022).

Mendel, Jack (2002) 'Four incidents in 10 days "instilled fear" in Charedi community', *Jewish News*, 4 February.

Office of National Statistics (2021) *Victims of Crime*, 21 June. Available: www.ethnicity-facts-figures.service.gov.uk/crime-justice-and-the-law/crime-and-reoffending/victims-of-crime/latest#by-ethnicity-and-gender (accessed 12 December 2022).

OSCE (2017) *Understanding Anti-Semitic Hate Crimes and Addressing the Security Needs of Jewish Communities: A Practical Guide*, Vienna: OSCE Office for Democratic Institutions and Human Rights.

Rich, Barbara (2021) *Twitter*, 16 May. Available: https://mobile.twitter.com/Barbara-Rich_law/status/1393974090655019016 (accessed 12 December 2022).

Rose, David (2022) 'My daughter was driven out of her school by antisemitic bully-ing', *Jewish Chronicle*, 14 July.

Sussex Friends (2021) *Twitter*, 16 May. Available: https://twitter.com/SussexFriends/status/1393925736851984385 (accessed 12 December 2022).

United States Commission on International Religious Freedom (2021) *Antisemitism in Europe: Implications for U.S.* Policy, Washington, DC: USCIRF.

Ward, Benjamin (2021) 'Europe's worrying surge of antisemitism', *Human Rights Watch*, 17 May.

4

THE LEFT AND THE JEWS

Time for a Rethink

Alan Johnson

When we talk about the Jews and the UK left, we are talking about a relationship in crisis.[1] Our questions tonight: What went wrong? Can it be rescued? Let me begin with some pre-emptive remarks.

First, I am better placed to talk about the left than the Jews. Although I probably spend more time with Jews and in Synagogues than many in the room, I am not Jewish. But I am a person of the left and have been since the late 70s when I was a teenage volunteer in *Days of Hope* radical bookshop in Newcastle (or *Haze of Dope* as some called it). Second, I do not think the left in the UK should be uncritical of Israeli policy. The left in Israel is not, so why should we be? Third, despite some recent polls, I don't think British Jews are about to start hiding in their cellars. Professionals who deal with antisemitism do not see a wave of popular antisemitism but rather three distinct political antisemitisms; on the dwindling far-right; in parts – I stress *parts* – of the British Muslim community; and in parts – again, I stress *parts* – of the left.

It's this strand of distinctively *left-wing* hostility to Jews that I want to make some remarks about tonight. It has never been the dominant strand of opinion on the left, and it is not so today; not by a long chalk. But it has always existed, it is growing today, and it must be part of any account of the breakdown in the relationship between Jews and the left.

It was called the 'socialism of fools' in the 19th century. It became an 'anti-imperialism of idiots' in the 20th century. And it takes the form of a wild, demented, unhinged form of 'anti-Zionism' – not mere 'criticism of Israeli policy' – that demonises Israel in the 21st century.

DOI: 10.4324/9781003322320-5

The socialism of fools and the anti-imperialism of idiots

Let's begin with a short 'Who said this?' quiz. Who said 'The whole Jewish world constitutes one exploiting sect, one people of leeches, one single devouring parasite closely and intimately bound together not only across national boundaries but also across all divergences of political opinion'? That was the 19th-century anarchist, Mikhail Bakunin.

Who wrote 'Whoever fights against Jewish capital . . . is already a classfighter, even if he does not know it . . . Strike down the Jewish capitalists, hang them from the lamp posts!'? That was Ruth Fischer, a leading figure in the German Communist Party in the early 1920s.

Who said 'Wherever there is trouble in Europe, wherever rumours of war circulate and men's minds are distraught with fear of change and calamity, you may be sure that a hooked-nosed Rothschild is at his games somewhere near the region of the disturbances'? Well, that was an editorial in *The Labour Leader*, organ of the Independent Labour Party (ILP) in 1891.

I could go on. Trust me, these quotes are not aberrations. Read Steve Cohen's seminal work *That's Funny, You Don't Look Antisemitic* (1984), for the entire sorry story about left-wing antisemitism. But that is ancient history, you might say. What about today? Well, left-wing antisemitism never went away. It became the 'anti-imperialism of idiots' in the last third of the 20th century, when vicious, well-funded and long-running anti-Zionist campaigns were conducted by the Stalinist States, in alliance with the authoritarian Arab states and parts of the Western left.

Those campaigns laid the ground for the form taken by left-wing antisemitism today – I call it antisemitic anti-Zionism, which bends the meaning of Israel and Zionism out of shape until both become fit receptacles for the tropes, images and ideas of classical antisemitism. In short, *that which the demonological Jew once was, demonological Israel now is*: uniquely malevolent, full of blood lust, all-controlling, the hidden hand, tricksy, always acting in bad faith, the obstacle to a better, purer, more spiritual world, uniquely deserving of punishment and so on.

Antisemitic anti-Zionism has three components: a programme, a discourse and a movement.

First, antisemitic anti-Zionism has a *political programme*: not two states for two peoples, but the abolition of the Jewish homeland; not Palestine alongside Israel, but Palestine instead of Israel.

Second, antisemitic anti-Zionism is a demonising intellectual discourse (Johnson 2015a). The left is imprisoning itself within a distorting system of concepts: 'Zionism is racism'; Israel is a 'settler-colonialist state' which 'ethnically cleansed' the 'indigenous' people, went on to build an 'apartheid state' and is now engaged in an 'incremental genocide' against the Palestinians. And there is the ugly phenomenon of Holocaust Inversion – the deliberate and systematic Nazification of Israel in street placards depicting Netanyahu as Hitler, in posters equating the IDF and the SS, in cartoons portraying Israelis as Nazis, and even in the language of intellectuals (Klaff 2014).

Third, antisemitic anti-Zionism is a presence within a global social movement (the Boycott Divestment and Sanctions, or BDS movement) to exclude one state – and only one state – from the economic, cultural and educational life of humanity: the little Jewish one.

And this is the real concern about Jeremy Corbyn. Not that he *indulges in* antisemitism himself, but that he has a record of indulging the antisemitism of others when it comes to wearing an 'Israel' badge. And these days, it almost always does. For example, Corbyn defended the vile antisemitic Palestinian Islamist Raed Saleh. Even though Saleh's murderous Jew-hatred was a matter of public record (hell, a matter of court records, come to that), Corbyn called Saleh 'an honoured citizen who represents his people extremely well' and invited him to take tea on the terrace of the House of Commons. Mind you, not many on the left could rouse themselves to object to Saleh. Mehdi Hassan, then the Political Editor of *The New Statesman*, argued that the criticism of Salah was an example of the media's 'lazy and simplistic demonisation of Muslims'.

Today is springtime for left-wing antisemitic anti-Zionism. We have a left-wing poet, Tom Paulin, who compares the Israeli Defence Forces to the Nazi SS. We have a left-wing Church of England vicar, Stephen Sizer, who links to an article saying the Jews did 9/11, and then says, anyway, prove that they didn't. We have a left-wing comedian, Alexei Sayle, who jokes that Israel is 'the Jimmy Saville of the nations'. Jenny Tonge, a left-leaning peer of the realm, demands an enquiry into whether the rescue mission sent by Israel to Haiti in 2010 had a secret agenda of harvesting organs for Jews in Israel. And we have trade unions breaking links with Israel and *only* Israel, left-wing protestors shouting down the Israeli theatre troupe at The Globe, and *only* the Israeli group.

Beinazir Lasharie, a Labour councillor in Kensington and Chelsea shared a video on Facebook claiming that ISIS is run by the Israeli secret service, and another one saying that she had heard 'compelling evidence' that Israel is behind ISIS. 'I've nothing against Jews . . . just sharing it!', she added. Antisemitic anti-Zionism, you see, *never* has anything 'against the Jews'. (The Labour Party has since suspended Lasharie, pending an investigation.)

There is relentless left-wing intellectual incitement, too. It has turned some of our universities into madhouses. Ilan Pappe says US policy in the region is 'confined to the narrow route effectively delineated . . . by AIPAC'. Yitzhak Laor claims that IDF 'death squads' are guilty of 'indiscriminately killing', and of acts of 'sadism', including 'mass starvation'. Omar Barghouti claims Israel has an 'insatiable appetite' for 'genocide and the intensification of ethnic cleansing'. Yehuda Shenhav in his book *Beyond the Two-State Solution* claims Israel is 'an aggressive war machine', seeking 'the annihilation of the Palestinian people'. The introduction to Noam Chomsky and Ilan Pappe's book *On Palestine* – currently prominently displayed in our high street bookstores – spreads the lie that in 2014 Israel was engaged in the 'systematic carpet bombing of an entire population'. (You have to read that again, slowly, to grasp just what a monstrous piece of demonisation and incitement it is.)

What can we say about each of these examples?

Each is self-consciously 'left-wing', broadly defined. Each is 'intellectual' in the Gramscian sense of being informed by a world view. And that world view is found in the murky borderlands where a modern anti-Zionism of a particularly excessive and obsessive kind co-mingles easily with classical antisemitic tropes, images and ideas.

How can we explain the breakdown of the relationship?

The occupation is a big part of the crisis in the relationship between the Jews and the left, of course. Whatever can be said about the self-defensive character of the Six-Day War in 1967, or about the serious security concerns that make Israel unwilling to simply walk out of the West Bank without an agreement, or about the actual reasons for the rejection of the Israeli peace proposals at the Camp David and Annapolis talks, one brute fact remains – and for most people it's the only fact that matters, I get that – the Palestinians do not have a state or a vote and pretty soon it will be 50 years since 1967.

But that isn't the whole story by any means.

The left also needs to think harder about our relationship to a couple of our own values – assimilation and universalism. We need to understand better how we have *misused* those values in our understanding of Israel and the Jews and, as a result, have *misshapen* our relationship with Zionism as a project and Israel as a state.

What do I mean? In the late 19th century, most of the left felt that assimilation was the only acceptable Jewish response to rising antisemitism. For example, Lenin – setting up the 'Good Jew/Bad Jew' dichotomy that has been dear to the left ever since – wrote that 'the best Jews have never clamored against assimilation.' Many on the left disapproved of the survival of Jewish*ness* – of the Jews as a *people* with the right to national self-determination as opposed to individuals with civil rights.

The left hoped to dissolve Jewish peoplehood in the solvent of progressive universalism. The proletariat, understood as the universalist class par excellence, was to make a world revolution that would solve 'the Jewish question' once and for all, 'in passing'.

But this left-wing universalism was always 'spurious' as Norman Geras put it, because it singled out the Jews as 'special amongst other groups in being obliged to settle for forms of political freedom in which their identity may not be asserted collectively'. 'Jews', Geras noted, 'must be satisfied, instead, merely with the rights available to them as individuals' (Geras 2013).

And yet, in the 19th century and the early 20th century, many European Jews were zealots for both universalism and assimilation; *it was the name of their desire too*. But here's the thing. *World history went another way* and Jewish history went with it. However, the left did not get the memo. *That's* the other explanation for the crisis in the relationship of the left and the Jews today.

This is the way that history went: the failure of the European socialist revolution, the rise of Fascism and Nazism, the unprecedented transformation of the assault upon the Jews in the form of the Shoah, an industrial-scale genocide in the heart of Europe, the expulsion of the Jews from the Arab lands, and the degeneration of the Russian Revolution into Stalinism and antisemitism. All this left the appeal of assimilationism and universalism in tatters.

In response, Jews insisted on defining their own mode of participation in modernity and in universal emancipation: support for Zionism and a homeland for the Jews; the creation of Israel, a nation state in a world of nation states. Whether they moved to Israel or not, that was the choice of all but a sliver of world Jewry. And that remains the case today.

Crucially, parts of the left – by no means all – failed to adapt to this great rupture in world history. This is all important, for it utterly transformed the political meaning of 'anti-Zionism'. Anti-Zionism meant one thing in the early 20th century: an argument among Jews, mostly, about how best to meet the threat of antisemitism. Anti-Zionism has come to mean something entirely different *after* the Holocaust and *after* the creation of the State of Israel in 1948: it has come to mean a programme of comprehensive hostility to all but a sliver of world Jewry, a programme for the eradication of actually existing Jewish self-determination.

Things got even worse. Left-wing anti-Zionism has been converging with some forms of Arab nationalism and even political Islamism – which are both now coded as singularly progressive. The left has its own version of Orientalism which infantilises the Palestinians and Arabs, puts them beyond criticism, and makes them the subject of endless Western left-wing delusions. For example, take Jeremy Corbyn's truly incredible claim that Hamas and Hezbollah are 'bringing about long-term peace and social justice and political justice in the whole region'.

This convergence between parts of the left and Arab nationalism, and later Islamism, was smoothed by two developments *on* the left. In the East, the Communist bloc's decades-long 'anti-Zionist' propaganda campaign injected an 'anti-imperialism of idiots' into the global left during the Cold War. We are talking about the mass publication and global distribution of antisemitic materials through the Communist Parties and their fellow travellers. Anthony Julius's book *Trials of the Diaspora* gives one telling example: 230 books were published in the USSR *alone* from 1969–1985 just on the subject of non-existent Zionist-masonic conspiracy against Russia. These books had a combined print run of 9.4 million (Julius 2010).

In the West, David Hirsh has observed that whereas anti-imperialism was previously 'one value amongst a whole set – democracy, equality, sexual and gender liberation, anti-totalitarianism' included – it was raised to a radically new status in the 1960s in the West as 'the central value, prior to and above all others'. And with this, a new Manicheanism descended on the left. Israel-Palestine was reframed. No longer were one people involved in a complex unresolved national question with another people. Now Israel became 'a key site of the imperialist system' and the Palestinians became 'the Resistance' to imperialism (Hirsh 2007).

Left-wing 'common sense' shifted accordingly. Now, to support Israel's enemies – *whatever* these enemies stood for, *however* they behaved – was a left-wing 'anti-imperialist' duty: in other words, antisemitism went 'progressive'. Writing in the *New Statesman*, I called this intellectual malady 'Campism' (Johnson 2015b). But whatever word is used, we need the concept. How else can we explain why Judith Butler – a leading lesbian, feminist and socialist academic – could claim idiotically that 'Understanding Hamas and Hezbollah as social movements that are progressive, that are on the left, that are part of a global left, is extremely important' (see Johnson 2013).

When the left can no longer distinguish the fascistic from the progressive, we really do have a problem.

How can the relationship be put back together?

In brief, not by taking an 'Israel right or wrong' approach. Wrong in principle, that approach will only make worse the problem at the heart of the relationship between the Jews and the left. And nor should we give up on our duty to support a Palestinian state as an expression of self-determination of the Palestinian people. But look, we do need to radically rethink our demented 'anti-Zionism'. We, left-wingers, must rethink our rejection of the right to national self-determination of just one people, the Jewish people. We must rethink our commitment to boycott just one state in the whole wide world, the little Jewish one. That singling-out is antisemitic *in consequence*, I am afraid, whatever the motivations of individual boycotters. Those left-wing refusals and those left-wing commitments are now, frankly, dangerous. We have to see that this left-wing anti-Zionism coexists, cheek by jowl, with *a family* of anti-Zionisms, that some of the family members are vile and murderous, and that the left has become hopeless at policing its own borders.

Our task is huge: to build an intellectual firewall separating sharp criticism of Israeli policy – which is legitimate, as it is for any nation state, and which, even when unfair, remains non-lethal – from the spreading demonology of Zionism and Israel which is not legitimate and which can be lethal. Beyond that, we need to hold our nerve, restate some basic truths and think more creatively about how we can act in the world to make a positive contribution to securing these truths: that peace will only come through engagement and deep mutual recognition between the two peoples, that there is no alternative to negotiations and mutual compromise, and that a final status agreement will secure two states for two peoples.

Note

1 This chapter was first published in *Fathom* in 2015.

References

Cohen, Steve (1984) *That's Funny, You Don't Look Anti-Semitic*, Leeds: Beyond the Pale Collective. A 2005 edition, foreword by Jane Ashworth, can be downloaded at the Alliance for Workers Liberty website. Available: www.workersliberty.org/files/2020-11/thatsfunny.pdf (accessed 9 November 2022).

Geras, Norman (2013) 'Alibi antisemitism', *Fathom*, Spring. Available: https://fathomjournal.org/alibi-antisemitism/ (accessed 9 November 2022).

Hirsh, David (2007) *Antisemitism and Anti-Zionism: Cosmopolitan Reflections*, New York: Institute for the Study of Global Antisemitism and Policy. Available: https://isgap.org/wp-content/uploads/2013/08/ISGAP-Working-Papers-David-Hirsh.pdf (accessed 9 November 2022).

Johnson, Alan (2013) 'Book Review. Parting Ways: Jewishness and the Critique of Zionism', *Fathom*, Spring. Available: https://fathomjournal.org/book-review-parting-ways-jewishness-and-the-critique-of-zionism/ (accessed 9 November 2022).

Johnson, Alan (2015a) 'Intellectual incitement: The anti-Zionist ideology and the anti-Zionist subject', in Cary Nelson and Gabriel Noah Brahm (eds.), *The Case Against Academic Boycotts of Israel*, New York: Wayne State University Press, 259–281.

Johnson, Alan (2015b) 'No, Jeremy Corbyn is not antisemitic – but the left should be wary of who he calls friends', *New Statesman*, 2 September. Available: www.newstatesman.com/politics/2015/09/no-jeremy-corbyn-not-antisemitic-left-should-be-wary-who-he-calls-friends (accessed 9 November 2022).

Julius, Anthony (2010) *Trials of the Diaspora: A History of Anti-Semitism in England*, Oxford: Oxford University Press.

Klaff, Lesley (2014) 'Holocaust inversion and contemporary antisemitism', *Fathom*, Winter. Available: https://fathomjournal.org/holocaust-inversion-and-contemporary-antisemitism/?highlight=Klaff%20 (accessed 9 November 2022).

PART 2

Contemporary Left Antisemitism

5

WHAT IS LEFT ANTISEMITISM?

Sean Matgamna

Left-Wing Antisemitism: Three Confusions

What is 'left-wing antisemitism'? Where is it manifested? What is to be done about it? There are three confusions or obfuscations that stand in the way of rational discussion of what we mean by 'left-wing antisemitism'.[1]

The first is that left-wing antisemitism knows itself by another and more self-righteous name, 'anti-Zionism'. Often, your left-wing antisemite sincerely believes that he or she is only an anti-Zionist, only a just if severe critic of Israel.

The second is that talk of left-wing antisemitism to a left-wing antisemite normally evokes indignant, sincere and just denial of something else! 'No, I'm not a racist! How dare you call me a racist?'

No, indeed, apart from an atypical crackpot here and there, left-wing antisemites are not racist. But there was antisemitism before there was late-19th- and 20th-century anti-Jewish racism. And there is still antisemitism of different sorts, long after disgust with Hitler-style racism, and overt racism of any sort, became part of the mental and emotional furniture of all halfway decent people, and perhaps especially of left-wing people.

Left-wingers are people who by instinct and conviction side with the oppressed, the outcasts, those deprived of human rights, with the working class and the labour movement. We naturally side against the police, the military and the powerful capitalist states, including our 'own'. We are socially tolerant; in contrast to 'hang 'em, flog 'em, build more jails' people; we look to changing social conditions rather than to punishment to deal with crime – we are people who want to be Marxists and socialists, and consistent

DOI: 10.4324/9781003322320-7

democrats. Confused some such people may be, racists they are not. We are not saying that left-wing antisemites are racists.

The third source of confusion and obfuscation is the objection: 'You say I'm an antisemite because I denounce Israel. I'm not anti-Jewish when I denounce Israel, but anti-Zionist.' And sometimes, at this point, you get the addition: 'By the way, I am myself Jewish.'

The objector continues: Israel deserves criticism. Even the harshest criticism of Israel's policies in the West Bank and Gaza, and of Israel's long-term treatment of the Palestinians, is pro-Palestinian and anti-Zionist, not antisemitic. To equate criticism of Israel with antisemitism is just crude and hysterical Zionist apologetics.

No, by 'left-wing antisemitism', we emphatically do not mean political, military or social criticism of Israel and of the policy of Israeli governments. Certainly, not all left-wing critics of Israel or Zionism are antisemites, even though these days all antisemites, including the right-wing, old-fashioned and racist antisemites, are paid-up 'anti-Zionists'.

Israel frequently deserves criticism. Israel's policy in the Occupied Territories and its general treatment of the Palestinians deserve outright condemnation. The oppressed Palestinians need to be politically defended against Israeli governments and the Israeli military. The only halfway equitable solution to the Israel–Palestine conflict, a viable, independent Palestinian state in contiguous territory, side by side with Israel, needs to be argued for and upheld against Israeli power.

The newspaper I support, *Solidarity*, condemns Israel's treatment of the Palestinians. We defend the Palestinians and champion an independent Palestinian state side by side with Israel.

The difference here between left-wing antisemites and honest critics of Israel – a category which includes a very large number of Israeli Jews as well as Israeli Arabs – is a straightforward one of politics, of policy.

The left-wing antisemites do not only criticise Israel. They condemn it outright and deny its right to exist. They use legitimate criticisms and utilise our natural sympathy with the Palestinians, not to seek redress and not as arguments against an Israeli government, an Israeli policy, or anything specifically wrong in Israel, but as arguments against the right of Israel to exist at all. Any Israel. Any Jewish state in the area. Any Israel, with any policy, even one in which all the specific causes for justly criticising present-day Israel and for supporting the Palestinians against it have been entirely eliminated.

The root problem, say the left-wing antisemites, is that Israel exists. The root 'crime of Zionism' is that it advocated and brought into existence 'the Zionist state of Israel'.

Bitterly, and often justly, criticising specific Israeli policies, actions and governments, seemingly championing the Palestinians, your left-wing antisemites seek no specific redress in Israel or from Israel, demanding only that Israel should cease to exist or be put out of existence.

They often oppose measures to alleviate the condition of the Palestinians short of the destruction of Israel. Thus the petitions and chants on demonstrations: 'Two states solution, no solution!' They use slogans like 'Free Palestine' precisely because they can be understood in different ways, depending on your definition of 'Palestine'. Therefore, they can accommodate those who, without having studied the complexities or the history of the Jewish–Arab conflict, instinctively side with the oppressed and outmatched Palestinians, and for whom 'Free Palestine' means simply that Israel should get out of the Occupied Territories. And it can also accommodate those, like the proponents of the slogan, the political Islamists of the Muslim Association of Britain/Muslim Brotherhood and others, who define 'Palestine' as pre-Israel, pre-1948 Palestine, and by 'Free Palestine' mean the destruction and abolition of Israel, and the elimination in one way or another of the Jewish population of Israel, or most of them.

The political differences spelled out here are easily understood. But why are the drive and the commitment to destroy Israel antisemitism, and not just anti-Zionism?

Because the attitude to the Jewish nation in Israel is unique, different from the left's attitude to all other nations; and because of the ramifications for attitudes to Jews outside Israel. Apart from a few religious Jews who think the establishment of Israel was a revolt against God, and some Jews who share the views of the leftists whom we are discussing here, those Jews outside Israel instinctively identify with and support Israel, however critically. For the left-wing antisemite, they are therefore 'Zionists', and proper and natural targets of the drive to 'smash Zionism'.

The attitude of the 'anti-Zionist' left to Israel brings with it a comprehensive hostility to most Jews everywhere – those who identify with Israel and who defend its right to exist. These are not just people with mistaken ideas. They are 'Zionists'.

In colleges, for example, where the anti-Zionist left exists side by side with Jewish students, this attitude often means a special antagonism to the 'Zionist' Jews. They are identified with Israel. They, especially, are pressured either to denounce Israel, to agree that it is 'racist' and 'imperialist' and that its existence is a crime against the Arabs – or else be held directly and personally responsible for everything Israel does, has done, or is said to have done.

In such places, where the left 'interfaces' with Jews, the logic of the unique attitude to Israel takes on a nasty persecuting quality. In the past, in the mid-1980s, for example, that has taken the form of attempting to ban Jewish student societies. Non-Jews who defend Israel's right to exist are not classified in the same category.

But is the attitude of the 'absolute anti-Zionists' to Israel really unique? There are seeming similarities with left attitudes to one or two other states – Protestant Northern Ireland, apartheid South Africa or pre-1980 white-ruled Rhodesia (Zimbabwe) – but the attitude to Israel is unique, because the reality of Israel cannot properly be identified with Northern Ireland, apartheid South Africa or white Rhodesia.

In apartheid South Africa and white Rhodesia, a minority lorded it over the big majority of the population, exploiting them. Israel is a predominantly Jewish state consisting of all classes. The Jewish nation does not subsist, and never has subsisted, on the exploitation of Arab labour, or depended in any essential way on such exploitation.

The general left hostility to the Northern Ireland Protestants – who are not exploiters of Catholic labour, and who are the compact majority, if not of the Six Counties, then of the north-east half of the Six Counties – is the closest to the attitude to Israel.

But it is not widely believed on the left that the Northern Ireland Protestant-Unionists simply have no right to be there. The right of the Jews to 'be there' *is* denied in those sections of the left that we are discussing. The organisation of Jewish migration to Palestine – that was the root 'crime' of Zionism, of which the 'crime' of establishing Israel was only a further development. The 'solution' is not only to undo and abolish Israel but to reverse Jewish 'migration' – which now includes people born there, to parents born there – and to roll the film of Middle Eastern history backwards.

The prerequisite for left-wing antisemitism is the catastrophic decline in the culture of the left over the last decades, a decline which allows people who want to be socialists to chant 'Sharon is Hitler, Israel is Nazi' and similar nonsense without checking on the words, without pausing to listen to what they are saying, or to think about it. The specific framework within which what we have been describing exists, and without which it probably couldn't exist in these 'left-wing' forms, is the poisonous and systematic misrepresentation and falsification of the history of the Jewish–Arab conflict and of the Jewish people in the 20th century. We can only touch on that here.

In real history, Jews fled to Palestine, where a small Zionist colony and a small pre-Zionist Jewish community already existed, from persecution in Europe in the 1920s, 1930s and 1940s. In the 1930s and 1940s, they fled for their lives from Nazism, which killed two out of every three Jews alive in Europe in 1939, in a world in which no non-persecuting state would let them, or enough of them, in. They fled to the existing Jewish national minority in Palestine (a long-established minority which, though small, was, for example, the majority in Jerusalem in 1900).

While Hitler was organising mass slaughter, Britain shut out Jews from Palestine, interning those who tried to enter. Overloaded, unseaworthy boats carrying illegal cargoes of Jews sank in the Mediterranean trying to get to Palestine (for example, the Struma, in which over 700 people died).

Israel was set up by those Jews on licence from the UN, which stipulated two states in Palestine, one Jewish and one Arab. When the State of Israel was declared in May 1948, the surrounding Arab states invaded. Jordan, Iraq and Egypt were then British-dominated, and some of the armies were staffed by British officers.

The Israelis defended themselves and won. In the war, three-quarters of a million Palestinian Arabs were driven out or fled; in the same period and afterwards, about 600,000 Jews were expelled from or fled Arab countries.

In the Arab invasion of 1948, the Arab-Palestinian state was eliminated. Most of its territory went to Jordan and fell under Israeli control in the war of 1967. That was a tremendous tragedy that will only be redressed when an independent Palestinian state takes its place alongside Israel.

This complex and tragic history is presented by the 'absolute anti-Zionist' left as a conspiracy of Zionism, conceived of as a demonic force outside general history and outside Jewish history. It is not rare to find 'left anti-Zionists' arguing that this Jewish-Zionist conspiracy was so all-powerful that it was able even to manipulate Adolf Hitler and the Holocaust in which six million Jews died (see the play by the veteran Trotskyist Jim Allen, *Perdition*, of which Ken Loach planned a performance at a London theatre in 1987). The core idea, the root of modern left-wing antisemitism, is that Israel, in one way or another, is an illegitimate state; and that therefore, in one way or another, it should be done away with. If its citizens will not be the first in history to voluntarily dismantle their nation state and make themselves a minority in a state run by those whom they have had to fight for national existence; if they will not agree to voluntarily dismantle Israel and create a 'secular democratic Arab state', in which Israeli Jews can have religious but not national rights – then they must be overwhelmed and compelled to submit or flee by the Arab states, now or when they are strong enough.

Beginning with the benign-seeming proposal to sink Israel into a broader Arab-majority entity in which 'everyone could live in peace', the chain of logic rooted in the idea that Israel should not have come into existence, that it is an illegitimate state, leads directly – since Israel will not agree to abolish itself – to support for compulsion, conquest and all that goes with it. Israel must be conquered.

Even the work of a writer like the American socialist Hal Draper can feed into this poisoned stream. While Draper made valid and just criticisms of Israel, he accepted that it had a right to exist and a right to defend itself. He denounced those who wanted to destroy it. But he made his criticisms in the tone and manner of a prophet denouncing sin and iniquity. He too thought that Israel was an illegitimate state, that it should never have come into existence and should go out of existence as soon as possible.

By agreement, and only by agreement, he believed; but the subtleties get lost. There is nothing to stop someone swayed by Draper's denunciations of Israel, and accepting his idea that Israel is an illegitimate state, then impatiently insisting: if not by agreement, then by conquest.

And so an increasingly disoriented SWP-UK could look to a Saddam Hussein to 'free Palestine', that is, conquer Israel.

The point here is that states and nations are the products of history. There is no such thing as an illegitimate nation or a 'bad people' which does not deserve the same rights as other peoples.

The antisemitic left today, which depicts Israel as the hyper-imperialist power – either controlling US policy or acting as its chief instrument, the story varies – is in the grip of an 'anti-imperialism of fools'. And that in practice leads to a comprehensive hostility to Jews not far from what Bebel called the socialism of fools. One of the great tragedies of contemporary politics is that many young people, whose initial instincts to oppose Bush and Blair in Iraq and to support the Palestinians are initially healthy, are being poisoned with 'left-wing' antisemitism.

'Left-wing antisemitism' is, in short, first a denial of Israel's right to exist and, what is rooted in that denial, a comprehensive hostility to pro-Israel Jews, that is to most Jews alive, branding them as 'Zionists' and seeing that description as akin to 'racist' or 'imperialist'. It exempts only those Jews who agree that Israel is racist imperialism in its most concentrated essence, and oppose its continued existence.

The general antidote to this anti-imperialism of fools is the propagation of rational democratic and socialist politics. Such politics focus on a political solution to the Arab–Israeli conflict. They measure and criticise Israel – and the Arab states – according to their stand in relation to that just solution – the establishment of an independent Palestinian state alongside Israel.

There is an immediate 'antidote' to left-wing antisemitism too, and it is a very important task for Marxist socialists like those who publish *Solidarity*: relentless exposure and criticism of their politics and antics – without fear of isolation, ridicule or the venomous hostility of the vocal and self-righteous left-wing antisemites.

Left-Wing Antisemitism: Eight Features

We need to specify what 'left antisemitism' consists of, in order to debate, educate and clarify. These, I think, are its main features.

1. The belief that Israel has no right to exist. That is the core of left antisemitism, though it comes in more than one version and from more than one root, ranging from the skewed anti-imperialism of the Orthodox Trotskyists through Arab nationalism to Islamic chauvinism. Advocacy of the

destruction of Israel, which is what separates left-wing and Islamist anti-semites from honest critics of Israeli policy, should not be tolerated in the labour movement and in the serious left.

2. The belief that Israeli Jewish nationalism, Zionism, is necessarily a form of racism. That this racism can only be expunged if Israel, Zionists and Jews abandon Israeli nationalism and support of any kind for Israel. That Jewish students, for example, can only redeem themselves if they agree that the very existence of Israel or of an Israeli Jewish nation is racist.

3. The view that Israel alone is responsible for the conflict with the Arab states (and, now, with Islamic states). The idea that Israel alone is respon-sible for creating Arab refugees, and is uniquely evil in doing so. In real history, the Arab states mostly refused the Palestinians citizenship or even the right to work.

4. The claim that the Palestinians have a 'right of return', that is, the right to the organised settlement in Israel of six million people (only a tiny and dying-off number of whom were born in what is now Israel) is one of the many codes for in fact demanding the self-abolition of the Jewish state and justifications for war to conquer and abolish it because it will not abolish itself. It is not the equivalent of free immigration to the UK, or even of mass migration to the UK of millions from Syria, Libya and Africa. Its equivalent for Britain would be the settlement in the country, organised by a hostile authority, of 60 million people. Socialists should of course be in favour of agreements between Israel and the Palestinians for compensation and for letting individual Palestinians into Israel. Sup-port for a collective right of return is only another form of the demand to conquer and destroy Israel, if it will not surrender.

5. The idea that the forced migration of 700,000 Arabs was a unique evil is also extravagantly wrong. In 1945, 12 million to 14 million Germans were driven out of Eastern Europe. They were driven into a Germany reduced to ruins by wartime bombing, where economic life had seized up and millions were starving. Only fringe German nationalists now propose to reverse that forced population movement and to drive out the Poles, Czechs, Russians, etc., who live where Germans once lived.

6. There is a peculiar dialect of Holocaust semi-denial current on the left. I have never heard of anyone on the left who denies that six million Jews were murdered by the Nazis. What the anti-Zionist left habitually deny is that this unique fact of history had repercussions that we should at least recognise and try to understand, with some sympathy for the surviving Jews and their descendants. On the left, the Holocaust is not denied, but it is relegated almost to the status of a 'virtual fact'. In truth, the Holo-caust discredited all Jewish-assimilationist programmes, including ours, the socialist one. It created and hardened the will for a Jewish solution to the Jewish question and for the creation of Israel. There is nothing

to be surprised at or scandalised by in that. The Holocaust should be appreciated as a real fact of history, with repercussions and reverberations, and not as something outside the history we are all part of, as a sort of sideshow, as a two-dimensional hologram rather than the enormously weighty, reverberating event it was and continues to be.

7. The idea that there are good peoples entitled to all rights and bad peoples entitled to none. That too is something I have never heard anyone voice plainly and explicitly. But it is there as an implicit subtext in the idea that we are concerned with national rights only for the presently oppressed, that is, in this case, the Palestinians.

8. The belief that there is a 'one-state solution'. But there is not. Not, as now, by Israeli domination of the whole territory and Palestinians living indefinitely in a purgatory of Israeli occupation, nor through a Palestinian state 'from the river to the sea' incorporating Israel after its Jewish population has been killed or overpowered by Arab or Islamic states. The only just solution that can serve both Jews and Arabs is two states: a sovereign Palestinian state in contiguous territory, side by side with Israel. If, as may be possible, a Palestinian Arab state is made impossible by the spread of Israeli settlements, then the future will be grim indeed for both Palestinian Arabs and Israeli Jews.

Note

1 This essay was first published in Sean Matgamna's book, *The Left in Disarray (Workers Liberty Press, 2017)* and we are grateful to him for granting permission to make it available to *Fathom* readers in 2018 and again here.

6

ANTI-ZIONISM AND ANTI-SEMITISM

Michael Walzer

Three Forms of Jewish Anti-Zionism

Anti-Zionism is a flourishing politics today on many university campuses and on parts of the left, and the standard response from many Jewish organisations and from most of the Jews I know is to call it the newest version of anti-Semitism.[1] But anti-Zionism is a subject in itself; it comes in many varieties, and which ones are anti-Semitic – that's the question I want to address here. I take 'Zionism' to mean a belief in the rightful existence of a Jewish state, nothing more. Anti-Zionism denies the rightfulness. My concern here is with left-wing anti-Zionism in the United States and Europe.

Most versions of anti-Zionism first appeared among the Jews. The first, and probably the oldest, takes Zionism to be a Jewish heresy. According to Orthodox doctrine, the return of the Jews to Zion and the establishment of a state will be the work of the Messiah in the days to come. Until then, Jews are required to accept their exile, defer to gentile rulers and wait for divine deliverance. Political action is a usurpation of God's prerogative. Zionist writers hated the passivity that this doctrine produced with such passion that they were called anti-Semites by orthodox Jews, who would never have given that name to their own rejection of the Zionist project.

'Waiting for the Messiah' has a left version, which might be called 'waiting for the revolution'. Jews (and other minorities) were often told that all their problems would be solved, and could only be solved, by the triumph of the proletariat. Many Jews took this to be an expression of hostility, a refusal to recognise the urgencies of their situation. But I don't see anti-Semitism here, only ideological rigidity and moral insensitivity.

The second Jewish version of anti-Zionism was first proclaimed by the founders of Reform Judaism in 19th-century Germany. There is no Jewish

DOI: 10.4324/9781003322320-8

people, they insisted, only a community of faith – men and women of the Mosaic persuasion. Jews could be good Germans (or good citizens of any state) since they were not a nation like the other nations and did not aspire to a state of their own. Zionism was perceived as a threat to these good Germans, since it suggested that they had an allegiance elsewhere.

Many leftists have adopted this denial of Jewish peoplehood, and then they go on to claim that a Jewish state must be a religious state, something like a Catholic or Lutheran or Muslim state – political formations that no leftist could support. But Reform Jews adopted this position knowing that most of their fellow Jews didn't share it. If the nation is a daily referendum, as Ernest Renan said, the Jews of Eastern Europe, the great majority, were voting every day for peoplehood. They weren't all looking for a homeland in the land of Israel, but even the Bundists, who hoped for autonomy in the Tsarist empire, were Jewish nationalists.

The early Reformers wanted to change the course and character of Jewish history; they weren't ignorant of that history. Leftists who argue against Jewish peoplehood are, mostly, ignorant. They aren't, however, the victims of what Catholic theologians call 'invincible ignorance', so we need to worry that what they don't know, they don't want to know.

If they were interested, they could learn about the radical entanglement of religion and nation in Jewish history – and about its reasons. You cannot separate religion from politics; you cannot set up a 'wall' between church or synagogue and state, if you don't have a state. Zionism was from its first days an effort to begin the process of disentanglement and to establish a state in which secularism could succeed. There are Jewish zealots in Israel today who oppose that effort – as there are Hindu nationalists and Muslim zealots who oppose similar efforts in their own states. One would expect leftists to defend secularism everywhere, which would require them to acknowledge the value of the original Zionist project.

I won't say that it is anti-Semitic to assume, lazily, that Jewishness is a purely religious identity. But the refusal to recognise that large numbers of identified Jews are not religious is a little odd. We don't call them 'lapsed Jews' (the way we call irreligious Catholics 'lapsed'); they are simply Jews. The assumption that there is no Jewish people that includes the faithful and the faithless, which is so easily corrected, must have a reason. It enables leftists who have supported so many national liberation movements to deny that Zionism is a movement of that sort: it can't be, because there is no Jewish nation. So it's a convenient argument, but that isn't a good reason for making it.

The third version of Jewish anti-Zionism takes both religious and political forms. The religious argument serves also as an explanation of the long diaspora years. The Jews, on this view, are too good for statehood. The politics of sovereignty requires a toughness and brutality that are better suited to the gentile nations. The Jews, shaped by the Sinai covenant and by a long history of dispossession and persecution, can't and shouldn't try to imitate the gentiles. You might call this a philo-Semitic doctrine; the only difficulty is that it has no empirical basis. Even before 1948, the Jews survived as a nation in mostly hostile environments by using all the necessary political means, often with considerable skill.

The political version of this argument isn't much better: it holds that the years of statelessness have turned the Jews into the first cosmopolitans. They are a people indeed, but a post-Westphalian people. Ahead of everyone else, they have transcended the nation state. Zionism is a regression from diaspora universalism.

But the Zionist achievement, the state of Israel, is a definitive refutation of this characterisation of the Jewish people. It reveals cosmopolitanism to be the programme of some Jews, not a description of all Jews. And why should this be a programme only, or first of all, for the Jews? Even if some Jews want to be cosmopolitans – a light unto the nations or, better, a light against the nations – why do so many non-Jewish leftists insist that all Jews take on this role, rather than claiming it for themselves? I can think of better candidates for a post-Westphalian politics. Let the French transcend the nation state; after all, they started the whole business with the *levée en masse* of 1793; the Marseilles, the first national anthem; the tricolour, the first national flag; and all the revolutionary oaths. Or the Germans, or the Danes, or the Poles, or the Chinese . . .

Leftist Versions of Anti-Zionism

So here's the rub. The most common leftist version of anti-Zionism derives, so its protagonists say, from a strong opposition to nationalism and the nation state. Early on in the history of the left, this was a plausible argument with wide extensions, and it was made by many Jews. Rosa Luxemburg, for example, wrote with equal loathing about Poles, Ukrainians, Lithuanians, Czechs, Jews and 'ten new nations of the Caucasus . . . rotting corpses [that] climb up out of hundred year old graves . . . and feel a passionate urge to form states'. The only thing I admire about Luxemburg's loathing is its universalism. But that's precisely the feature missing from much contemporary leftism, where the loathing is much more limited.

There have been many opportunities for the application of Luxemburg's argument. The second half of the 20th century saw the collapse of the British, French and Soviet empires and the creation of more nation states than had existed in all of world history until then. A few leftists dreamed of turning the old empires into democratic federations, but most supported pretty much all the post-imperial creations – with less enthusiasm, perhaps, in the Soviet case – except one. Think of the missed chances to oppose the nation state!

Why support Vietnamese nationalism, for example, when the obviously correct position with regard to Vietnam, Laos and Cambodia (the three parts of French Indochina) was one multinational state? Why didn't leftists call for the incorporation of Algeria as a province of France, with its citizens enjoying all the rights proclaimed by the French Revolution? The Algerian FLN, championed by the international left, created instead a nation state that has failed dismally to deliver those rights. I remember how enthusiastic people on the left were about U Nu's Burma, now Myanmar and a prime example of what's wrong with nationalism. Burma should have been a province of India, bringing Buddhists, Hindus and Muslims together in one state, but no one on the left argued for that. The British ruled Sudan as the 'Anglo-Egyptian Sudan' and surely the two African countries, freed from Anglo imperialism, should have been joined: one state. Why didn't leftists object to Sudanese liberation? Or to the Eritrean separation from Ethiopia? Why didn't they call for one Baltic state instead of the nationalist threesome, Latvia, Lithuania and Estonia?

I could pose many similar questions, but there is a single answer to all of them. The nation state was in all of these cases the people's choice, the democratic option even when it didn't lead to democracy. So leftists were right to support the Vietnamese, the Algerians and all the others. But then, why not the Jews? And why, now that a Jewish state exists and is very much like all the other states, is it on the receiving end of such a singular version of Luxemburgian loathing?

Why Is Luxemburgian Loathing Reserved for Israel?

The common answers to that last question are, first, that the creation of the state of Israel required the displacement of 700,000 Palestinians. Israel is a 'settler-colonial' state – like many other states if you go back far enough, but let's leave that aside. The more immediate history is telling. There was no displacement of Palestinian Arabs in the 1920s and 1930s; despite Zionist colonisation, the Arab population actually grew not only because of the birthrate but also because of immigration, mostly from Syria (the first British census in 1922 showed an Arab population of 660,267; the figure for 1940 was 1,068,433). There was no displacement during World War II when Jewish immigration slowed. And the state of Israel was proclaimed, first by the UN in 1947 and then in Tel Aviv in 1948, before the large-scale displacement began – so the idea that statehood 'required' displacement can't be right. It was the invasion of the new state by five Arab armies that led both to the flight of many Palestinian Arabs (Jews didn't flee, because they had no place to go) and the expulsion of many others (Jews weren't expelled, because the Arab armies lost the war). The numbers who fled and who were expelled are fiercely debated; they were large in both cases. Still, without the war, there would be nothing to debate – very few refugees would be in camps today. The Nakba was a tragedy that took two agents, two political movements and soldiers from both sides to produce.

And what about the flights and expulsions that have happened elsewhere, most obviously when the modern states of Turkey and Pakistan were created? Oddly, I haven't heard the legitimacy of those states questioned by leftist writers, even when the policies of their governments are criticised, as they should be. (The force of 'whataboutism' is often denied, but I think it is a powerful critique of one-eyed men and women who show great indignation at events *here*, wherever *here* is, and no interest at all in similar events elsewhere. Surely the phenomenon ought to be noticed.)

But – the second reason often given for anti-Zionism – Israel oppresses the Palestinians both in Israel proper and in the occupied West Bank. I won't address the more toxic forms of this critique: that Israel is a Nazi-like state, a uniquely evil state, a child-killer state – which do in fact reinvent or update the tropes of classic anti-Semitism. But there is much to criticise; my Zionist friends in Israel have fought for years for full equality at home and against the cruelties of the occupation and the zealotry of the settler movement. Fierce opposition to the policies of the current Israeli government (as of August 2019, with no improvement in sight) seems justified to me, the fiercer the better. I will provide a list of what needs to be said since I want to be recognised as a defender of Zionism but not an apologist for what people calling themselves Zionists are doing in Israel today – and were doing yesterday, too. (Defenders of Palestinian nationalism might consider providing a similar list of the pathologies of Palestinian politics.)

- Israel's Arab citizens face discrimination in many areas of common life, especially in housing and in the appropriation of state funds for education and infrastructure.
- With the recent Nation-State Law, the Knesset in effect gave the finger to its Arab citizens. Though the law has no legal consequences, it announces a second-class citizenship.
- The West Bank is a scene of invasive settlement, seizure of land and water, and lawless military rule.
- Settler thugs act violently against Palestinians on a daily basis, without effective restraint from the Israeli police or army.
- The current government uses anti-Arab incitement as a method of rule and is aiming at a single state dominated by what will soon be a Jewish minority (I will come back to 'one state' later).

There is more, but this will be enough to make the point: criticism of this sort has nothing to do with anti-Zionism or anti-Semitism. These are the policies of governments, but governments only rule states; they don't embody them.

Governments come and go – at least, we hope they do – while states endure for the sake of the men and women whose common life they protect. So criticising the governments of Israel shouldn't involve opposition to the existence of the state. The brutality of the French in Algeria required fierce criticism, but none of the critics that I remember opposed French statehood. The brutal treatment of Muslims in Western China today calls for fierce criticism, but no one is demanding the abolition of the Chinese state (although China is, in practice if not in theory, a Han nation state).

Some leftists claim that the long years of the occupation and the right-wing nationalism of the Netanyahu government reveal the 'essential character' of the Jewish state. This must be awkward for those men and women on the left who learned long ago, chiefly from feminist writers, to renounce essentialist arguments. Does the long history of intervention in Central America reveal the essential character of the United States? Maybe the opponents of intervention and occupation are more essential. Anyway, do states really have essences?

Many leftists these days simply endorse Palestinian nationalism without worrying about its essential character or even thinking about the programme of the nationalists, who are often explicit in demanding the whole thing: 'from the river to the sea'. There are Zionist Jews (in the government today) who make the same demand with equal fervour. Surely leftists should oppose both – with a similarly determined opposition. Those leftists who call for 'one state', with equal rights for Jews and Palestinians, would probably say that they are doing exactly that. Theirs is a programme that seems to reflect a consistent abhorrence of nationalism and the nation state – consistent, at least, in this one case.

But 'one state' means the elimination of one state, the existing Jewish state, and how exactly are the 'one-staters' going to achieve that? How do they plan to defeat the Jewish state and the national movement that produced it – or, alternatively, how do they plan to defeat Palestinian nationalism? What would the new state look like? And who would make decisions about immigration policy? (Immigration is the issue that scuttled bi-nationalism in the years before and immediately after World War II.) Finally, what if the new state – the most likely outcome – looked very much like Lebanon today? Given recent Middle Eastern history and given the history of Israel-Palestine, peaceful coexistence and equal rights under one government is a very sweet fantasy, but a fantasy still.

Surely, it would be better to add a state rather than subtract one – and allow both national movements to attain (or hold onto) the sovereignty they seek. The two-state solution may also be a fantasy; there are significant political forces, on both sides, aligned against it. But there is also realism here. We know how to create nation states; there is a lot of experience to build on. We don't know how to create the ideal political community that the one-staters claim to want. And we don't want, or we shouldn't want, the kind of state they are likely to create.

Creating nation states – that's pretty much the policy leftists have defended throughout the postcolonial period. Yugoslavia is the obvious exception, where many leftists opposed the creation of seven new nation states, preferring the tyrannical regime that once held the seven nations together. Another inconsistency: if tyranny is the alternative to national liberation, leftists should and most often do choose liberation. And the choice is a good one, for there is a lot of evidence that nations need states – often to protect them from foreign oppression. You can take the evidence for this from the history of the Jews – or the Armenians, or the Kurds, or the Kosovars or the Palestinians. The strongest political forces in all these countries aim at a state of their own. And if the other four, why not the Jews?

Why Not Zionism?

Why not Zionism? Because the Jews aren't a people; because they should be more cosmopolitan than anyone else; because the Zionist state has had some terrible governments; and because no one should have a state (even if almost everyone does). Each of these claims can be made and reasons given, but the way they are made in the world today is bound to arouse suspicion. It is at least possible, and sometimes it seems likely, that the people making them also believe that Jews ran the slave trade, that the Zionist lobby controls U.S. foreign policy (as Representative Ilhan Omar has said), that Jews are disloyal to every country in which they live except Israel, and that Jewish bankers control the international financial system. There are too many men and women who believe these things – on the left as well as on the right. They are anti-Semites or fellow travellers of anti-Semites, and their anti-Zionism is probably tightly connected to their anti-Semitism (though there are now pro-Israel anti-Semites among, for example, American evangelicals and Eastern European right-wing nationalists).

Men and women on the left need to be sharply critical, especially critical, of other leftists who hold these views. It is obviously easier to condemn right-wing anti-Semites and pretend that anti-Semitism doesn't exist on the left. But it does; indeed, it has been a regular topic here in *Dissent* (see, among other pieces, George Lichtheim, 'Socialism and the Jews', July–August 1968, and Mitchell Cohen, 'Anti-Semitism and the Left That Doesn't Learn', January 2008). It may well be true that right-wing anti-Semitism poses the greater danger to Jewish well-being, but the leftist version should not be underestimated.

Still, I am sure that a lot of anti-Zionists and many leftist anti-Zionists don't believe any of the anti-Semitic fables. Maybe they are willfully ignorant about the Jewish people, maybe they are peculiarly focused on the Jewish state, and maybe they just don't like Jews (as George Carey, the former Archbishop of Canterbury, said about Jeremy Corbyn). Maybe. But when it comes to leftist debates about Israel, Zionism is the issue, and it is Zionism that we should talk about. For all the reasons I've given, what's wrong with anti-Zionism is anti-Zionism itself. Whether you are an anti-Semite, a philo-Semite or Semiticly indifferent, this is a very bad politics.

Note

1 This essay was first published in the Fall 2019 issue of the US journal *Dissent* and we are grateful to Michael Walzer and the editors for permission to make it available to *Fathom* readers at that time and again here. Joshua Leifer's reply and Michael's rejoinder can be read at the *Dissent* website.

7

ALIBI ANTISEMITISM

Norman Geras

In Marx's essay 'On the Jewish Question', written in 1844, there are two contrasting sets of themes vis-à-vis the Jews.[1] In Part II of the essay, Marx deploys some well-known negative stereotypes, according to which: the mundane basis of Judaism is self-interest, egoism, or, as Marx also calls it, 'an anti-social element'; the worldly religion of the Jew is huckstering; and the Jew's jealous god – 'in face of which no other god may exist' – is money. The emancipation of the Jews is said by him to be equivalent to the emancipation of mankind *from* Judaism. Part I, on the other hand, presents a version of secular democracy in which the Jews, like any religious or other particularistic grouping, may retain their religion and their separate identity consistently with the state itself rising above such particularisms, and rendering these politically irrelevant.

Though Marx himself regards this – political emancipation – as an incomplete form of emancipation, he nonetheless articulates a genuine type of moral universalism: different faiths, ethnicities and peoples have a right to assert their specific identities and shared beliefs within the free secular order of the democratic state. The distinctions between such groups just cease to have a political bearing. Marx does not extend this argument beyond the single state to the global arena (that not being part of the discursive context), but the correlate at international level of what he argues in Part I of 'On the Jewish Question' is today embodied in the notion of a right of nations to self-determination, as affirmed in Article 1.2 of the United Nations Charter.

The contrasting themes of Marx's essay may be taken as emblematic of the state of affairs obtaining today between Jews and the left. It is not difficult

DOI: 10.4324/9781003322320-9

to understand the long affinity there has been between them. Common traditions of opposition to injustice, the commitment within liberal and socialist thought to ideals of equality (whether this is equality under the law or equality in substantive economic terms), opposition to racist and other similar types of prejudice – these things have long served to attract Jews to organisations and movements of the left, and they still do.

Israel as Alibi

At the same time, that affinity has now been compromised by the existence of a new climate of antisemitic opinion *within* the left. This climate of opinion affects a section of the left only, and not the whole of it. But it is a substantial section. Its convenient alibi is the state of Israel – by which I mean that Israel is standardly invoked to deflect the charge that there is anything of antisemitism at work. Israel, so the story goes, is a delinquent state and, for many of those who regard it so, a non-legitimate one – colonialist, imperialist, vehicle of oppression and what have you. Similarly, diaspora Jews who defend Israel within their home countries are not seen as the conduit of Jewish interests and/or opinion in the normal way of any other democratic articulation; they are treated, rather, as a dubious force – the notorious 'Jewish lobby' – as if their organised existence were somehow improper.

These themes pitch those who sponsor them out of a genuine, and into a spurious, type of universalism: one where the Jews are special amongst other groups in being obliged to settle for forms of political freedom in which their identity may not be asserted collectively; Jews must be satisfied, instead, merely with the rights available to them as individuals. I call this a spurious universalism because people's rights to live as they will (subject to the usual constraint of not harming others) is an incomplete right – a truncated and impaired right – if it does not include the freedom to associate with others of their own kind.

To repeat: Israel has been made an alibi for a new climate of antisemitism on the left.

But could it not be, perhaps, that there is no such climate? Could it not be that Israel's critics are just what they say they are, no more and no less: critics of the policies of successive Israeli governments, just in the same way as there are critics of the governments of every country? Well, it *could* be. There has been enough to criticise, goodness knows – from the long occupation of the West Bank and Gaza to the policy of permitting Jewish settlements on Palestinian land. It not only could be, it even in many cases is, since there are both critics and criticisms of Israel which are not antisemitic – such as the two criticisms I just made. Yet, if it both could be and is, it also in many cases is not. Much of the animus directed at Israel today is of a plainly antisemitic character. It relies (just as Marx did in Part II of 'On the

Jewish Question') on anti-Jewish stereotypes. This can be shown with near mathematical precision; I endeavour to show it in the rest of what I have to say.

Antisemitism as Epiphenomenal

A first form of the Israel alibi for contemporary antisemitism is the impulse to treat such of the antisemitism as there is acknowledged (by whomever) to be – in Europe, in the Arab world – as a pure epiphenomenon of the Israel–Palestine conflict. One instance of this was the statement by film director Ken Loach in March 2009 that if there was a rise of antisemitism in Europe this was not surprising: 'it is perfectly *understandable*' (my emphasis), he was reported as saying, 'because Israel feeds feelings of antisemitism'. The keyword here is 'understandable'. This might just mean 'capable of being understood'; but since more or less everything is capable of being understood, it would be pointless to use the word in that sense about the specific phenomenon of a rise in antisemitism in Europe. 'Understandable' also means something along the lines of 'excusable' or, at any rate, not an issue to get excited about. To see plainly the way in which Israel acts as an exonerating alibi in this case, one need only imagine Loach, or anyone else on the left, delivering themselves of the opinion that a growth of hostility towards, say, black people, or towards immigrants from South Asia, or from Mexico, was *understandable*.

Another instance of this first form of the Israel alibi is provided by a thesis of Gilbert Achcar's concerning Holocaust denial in the Arab world. Achcar is a professor at the School of Oriental and African Studies in London and a longtime leftist; he is the editor of a volume of essays on *The Legacy of Ernest Mandel*. Holocaust denial – as I shall merely assert and not argue here – is a prominent trope of contemporary antisemitism; it is indeed continuous with a practice of the Nazi period itself, when camp guards and the like would mock their Jewish victims by telling them that not only were they doomed to die, but also all knowledge of what had happened to them would be erased. They would be forgotten; the world would never know. Achcar accepts that Western Holocaust denial is an expression of antisemitism. Much Arab Holocaust denial, on the other hand, he puts down to such factors as impatience in the Arab world with Western favouritism towards Israel, a suspicion that the Holocaust has been 'amplified' for pro-Zionist purposes, and exasperation with the cruelty of Israel's treatment of the Palestinians.

Whether or not these explanations are valid, a racist belief does not cease to be one on account of its having context-specific causes. No one on the left would dream of suggesting that a belief that black people were lazy, feckless or simple-minded was less racist for being held by a certain group of white people on account of motives which eased their way towards that belief.

But the Israel alibi is currently exceptional in its legitimating power in this respect.

No Antisemitism Without Deliberate Intent

A second form of the Israel alibi for antisemitism is the plea that antisemitism should not be ascribed to anyone without evidence of active hatred of Jews on their part and without, that is to say, some clear sign of antisemitic *intent*. A well-known case of this second form arose with Caryl Churchill's play 'Seven Jewish Children' following upon Israel's invasion of Gaza in 2008–2009. This play puts into Jewish mouths the view that Palestinians are 'animals' and that 'they want their children killed to make people sorry for them'; but that there is no need to feel sorry for them; that we – the Jews – are the chosen people and that it is our safety and our children that matter; in sum, that 'I wouldn't care if we wiped them out.' I will not insist here on how this echoes the blood libel; it is enough that Churchill ascribes to the Jews, seeing themselves as chosen, murderous racist attitudes bordering on the genocidal. On the face of it, one would think, this is a clear candidate for antisemitic discourse.

Churchill, however, disavowed that charge when it came from critics. She did so on the grounds of what one might call an innocent mind. No antisemitism had been intended by her. On the one hand, the blood libel analogy had not been part of her thinking when she wrote the play; on the other hand, those speaking the offending lines in it were not meant to be Jews in general, merely individual Israelis. Churchill is evidently innocent here of any memory of the figure of Shylock in *The Merchant of Venice*, long thought of, despite his being only one character, as putting Jews in a bad light. She is innocent, too, of her own generalising tendencies in naming her play 'Seven *Jewish* Children' and then linking the broad themes of the Jews as victims of genocide and as putative perpetrators of it in their turn.

Contemplate, briefly, the idea of a sociology of racism in which racism was held to be a matter exclusively of mental *attitudes*, of what some given person or group of persons had in their minds and, most particularly, of hatreds explicitly formulated; but not also of a language that embodies negative stereotypes, or of unconscious prejudicial assumptions, or of discriminatory practices and so forth. For no other kind of racism would such a narrowly conceived sociology be taken seriously even for a moment.

A much more recent instance of the same thing is Günter Grass's poem 'What Must Be Said'. It imputed to Israel, on the basis of absolutely nothing in the way of evidence, a genocidal ambition against the Iranian people. Grass has been defended in his turn on the grounds that he is not personally an antisemite – as if this might settle the question of whether or not his poem contained antisemitic tropes.

Programmatic Rhetoric

Grass's poem may serve, also, to introduce a third form of what I am calling alibi antisemitism. For the poem contains a reference to the 'loudmouth' president of Iran – Mahmoud Ahmadinejad – at once Holocaust denier and lead spokesman for removing Israel from the page of history. Like others for whom this is a central goal, the loudmouth president sometimes has the benefit of the consideration that such talk is mere rhetoric, and so not to be treated as in earnest.

And you do not have to go far to find either journalists or activists of the left similarly playing down antisemitic elements within the programmatic objectives of Hamas and Hezbollah: not just their commitment to getting rid of Israel; also openly Jew-hating statements, as for example in the Hamas Charter. This latter document cites 'The Protocols of the Elders of Zion' as authoritative and as establishing a Zionist ambition to dominate the world. It has Jews hiding behind rocks and trees against the threat (which it celebrates) that Jews will in due course be killed.

Leftists and liberals of a would-be pragmatist turn of mind can appear remarkably untroubled by this sort of thing. Either the offending contents of the Hamas Charter are consigned by them to a receding past, or they are said not to represent the thinking of a moderate section of Hamas willing to contemplate a long-term (though not unlimited) truce with Israel. It is never explained by such pragmatists why, if the anti-Jewish components of the document are a thing of the past, no longer relevant, of merely rhetorical status, they have not been, or cannot now be, amended away.

I shall leave aside here the question of whether or not there are sound tactical reasons for Israel to consider negotiating with Hamas; it is not germane to my present concern. However, and as before, one should try to imagine a person of the left able to adopt so casual and indulgent an attitude to *other* openly racist discourses, able to treat them as merely rhetorical racism – while continuing to be held in respect within the left or liberal political milieu to which he or she belongs. It doesn't happen. Only Israel provides a pretext in that milieu for the mere-rhetoric plea. By some convenient metonymy, people saying 'Jews' may be taken really to mean 'Israel'. And Israel today is fair game for being hated.

A Climate of Complicity

The fourth and final alibi phenomenon I shall deal with is more oblique. It consists neither of the direct expression of antisemitic themes nor of attempts to explain these away, but rather of turning a blind eye. It is relevant to the case here, all the same, since prejudice makes its way more successfully when there is a certain tolerance of it by others, not actively hostile themselves but indulgent towards those who are.

I will take as my example of this the *Guardian* newspaper today. This once great paper of British liberalism now provides space on its opinion pages for the spokesmen of Hamas, the contents of its programmatic charter notwithstanding; provides space on its letters page for philosophers justifying the murder of Jews; and provides space on its website for people who deploy well-known antisemitic themes even while professing that they have nothing whatever against Jews. The *Guardian* is, as you would expect, on record as being vigorously opposed to racism: as, for example, when it referred in a leader of November 2011 to 'a message that is not heard often enough . . . that racism is never acceptable, wherever it takes place'.

Instructive, in the light of that, is to examine how the paper reacted editorially to the Toulouse killings. On 20 March of this year, before the identity of the killer was known and when it was assumed he was from the French far-right, the Guardian echoed the sentiment I have just quoted from its November leader, saying that 'the [French] republic will come together in the face of such an assault on its minorities.' While cautioning against speculation about the killer's motives, it nonetheless allowed itself to allude to Sarkozy's lurch to the right, his claims of 'there being too many immigrants in France', and other such expressions of xenophobia. This may be seen as an instance of treating racism as unacceptable 'wherever it takes place'. Two days later, once it was known that the killer was Mohammed Merah, an Islamist jihadi who had said he wanted to avenge the deaths of Palestinian children, a second *Guardian* editorial endorsed Sarkozy in 'condemn[ing] any attempt to denigrate the French Muslim community by associating it with the mad crimes of a terrorist'; and then added precisely nothing about the kind of ideas which might have been influential in Merah's willingness – not as a Muslim but as an Islamist and jihadi – to slaughter three Jewish children. 'Mad crimes of a terrorist' was all, and not so much as a breath about antisemitism. But the killing of Jewish children, even if to avenge the deaths of Palestinian children, is antisemitism of the most unadulterated kind. Those children were guilty of nothing and were killed by Merah *because* they were Jewish.

A liberal newspaper, committed to racism's never being acceptable anywhere, can find the words to name the poison that is right-wing anti-immigrant xenophobia, but not the word for hatred of Jews. Incomprehensible – but for that familiar alibi, Israel as a cause.

Conclusion

It is a moral scandal that some few decades after the unmeasurable catastrophe that overtook the Jewish people in Europe, these antisemitic themes and ruses are once again respectable; respectable not just down there with the thugs but pervasively also within polite society, and within the perimeters of a self-flattering liberal and left opinion. It is a bleak lesson to all but those unwilling to see. The message of 'never again' has already proved to have been too sanguine. Genocides still occur. We now know, as well, that should a new calamity ever befall the Jewish people, there will be, again, not only the direct architects and executants but also those who collaborate, who collude, who look away and find the words to go with doing so. Some of these, dismayingly, shamefully, will be of the left.

This is not a hopeful conclusion, but it is a necessary one. The best of hope in politics must always be allied to a truthful realism. We need to know what we are up against.

Note

1 Karl Marx, 'On the Jewish Question', in *Early Writings* (1975), Harmondsworth: Penguin Books, 211–242. This chapter is based on an earlier presentation by Norman Geras to the YIVO Conference on Jews and the Left held in May 2012 in New York City, and was first published in *Fathom* in 2013.

8

LIKE A CLOUD CONTAINS A STORM

Jean Améry's Critique of Anti-Zionism

Marlene Gallner

The Shoah-victim Jean Améry, author of the searing memoir *At The Minds Limits: Contemplations by a Survivor on Auschwitz and its Realities* (1980/1966), was also an extraordinarily sensitive critic of the German post-war society and of what we have learned to call the 'new antisemitism'.[1] When, in the 1960s, anti-Zionism grew rapidly in the German public discourse, especially within the left-wing student movement, Améry published several essays on the relationship between antisemitism and anti-Zionism. 'Anti-Zionism contains antisemitism like a cloud contains a storm', he wrote in the German newspaper *Die Zeit* (Améry 2005:133). He was the first to publicly address left-wing antisemitism in Germany. His essays give eloquent voice to contemporary concerns and – in their radicalism and their ability to penetrate the inner life of the relationship between antisemitism and anti-Zionism – are in advance of many contemporary contributions. This essay contributes to the work of making Améry's acute intelligence and moral urgency available as a resource today.

Biography

To fully comprehend Améry's work, it has to be situated within his personal history. He described himself as the 'political and Jewish Nazi-victim that I was and am' (Améry 2002:16). His reflections on the experience of being exposed to a murderous collective and on the persistence of suffering as a Shoah-victim course through all his work.

Améry was born in 1912 as Hans Maier in Vienna. His father was proud of his old Vorarlberg Jewish descent yet Améry himself grew up non-religious. After an unsteady but happy childhood and youth in the Austrian

DOI: 10.4324/9781003322320-10

Salzkammergut and Vienna, he took his first steps as a writer and publisher. However, Améry soon faced discrimination and persecution and so in 1938, together with his wife, he fled to Brussels. Two years later, Améry was imprisoned in an internment camp in Southern France. After his successful escape back to Belgium, he joined a communist resistance group, but in 1943 was recaptured and subsequently tortured by the Schutzstaffel (SS) in Breendonck for his political opposition. When it became apparent that Améry was not only a political opponent of the Nazis but also a Jew, he was deported to Auschwitz and later on to other concentration camps. In 1945, he was liberated by the British Army from Bergen Belsen camp and he returned to Belgium where he began his struggle to cope with being a Shoah-victim. One consequence of that struggle was that he changed his name to Jean Améry.

He never returned to live in Germany or Austria but nonetheless remained a perceptive observer and critic of the German post-war society. It was not until 1966, when Améry was already 54, that the publication of *Jenseits von Schuld und Sühne* brought his writings to a larger audience. *Jenseits von Schuld und Sühne*, available in English translation as *At the Mind's Limits: Contemplations by a Survivor on Auschwitz and Its Realities* is a sharp and unforgiving reflection on his experiences as a Nazi-victim. What makes Améry's thinking so unique is that he branched out from the solely historiographic terrain of grasping National Socialism and took one step further to describe the moral philosophical dimension of the Shoah and its aftermath.

After *Jenseits von Schuld und Sühne*, his newly gained recognition allowed Améry to publish his own explicitly political interventions about contemporary social trends, especially what he saw as the failure to properly confront the Nazi past and the appearance of a new face of antisemitism. With the exception of his writings on suicide, all his political works now centred on the new antisemitism and the importance of the Jewish State.

Israel and the Jews

Although Améry was not religious and had no connection to Israeli culture or language, the existence of the State of Israel was for him 'more important than any other' (Améry 2005:134). For him, Israel meant that Jews, wherever they lived, could find shelter from antisemitism, which was crucial after the experience of Auschwitz. He defines being a Jew not by religion or race but by the common threat of antisemitism. It is a distinctively negative definition.

In *Jenseits von Schuld und Sühne*, Améry described the unbearable tension between what he calls the compulsion and the impossibility of being a Jew. Not seeing oneself as a Jew, yet being made one 'from the outside', so to speak, constitutes the tension. It was not until the anti-Jewish racial laws enacted by the Nazis in 1935 that Améry fully understood that it was not *his* choice to define who is and who is not Jewish, but rather the choice of the antisemite. This reversal was not new, but the Nuremberg Laws gave an alarming new dimension to it. After the experience of the Shoah, Améry never again trusted promises to protect the Jews. He remained wide awake and could not cast off his seismographic sensitivity to the continued, if disguised, existence of antisemitism.

Améry offered two reasons for the 'existential bond' every Jew has to the State of Israel, whether he believes in Zionism or not (Améry 2022d:53). First, Israel allows Jews not to depend on the external image imprinted on them. 'It is the country where the Jew is not a usurer but a farmer, not a pale stay-at-home but a soldier, not a wholesale merchant but a craftsman' (Améry 2022d:53). This also has implications for all Jews in the diaspora. Israel is the reason that enables them to be equally humans like their fellow citizens. Second, antisemitism, and the threat of death it carried, did not disappear when the Allies defeated the German death machinery in 1945. Améry did not suggest that every Jew should leave their native country and emigrate to Israel. His concern was the '*option*' to find shelter (Améry 2022d:54). If the Jewish State perished, it would 'bequeath to its inhabitants nothing but the slaughtering knife of their opponents' (Améry 2022d:54).

Antisemitism and Anti-Zionism

I have already noted that Améry wrote in 1969 that 'Anti-Zionism contains antisemitism like a cloud contains a storm' (Améry 2005:133). Anti-Zionism was the new 'honourable antisemitism' that was now turned against Israel as the object of the same old and dangerous resentments (Améry 2005:133). The 'emotional infrastructure' and the psychological mechanisms of the antisemites remained the same (Améry 2022a:36). Antisemitism, to Améry, had nothing to do with the Jews and everything to do with the antisemites who were engaged in psychological projection.

Améry observes that the victim of antisemitism suffers, while the antisemite, the one with the actual psychological 'disorder', does not feel psychological strain: 'I know that what oppresses me is no neurosis, but rather, precisely, reflected reality' (Améry 1980:96). In psychoanalytic terms, antisemitism may be understood as an illness. And yet, it is no actual disorder because the antisemite is never impaired by it. It is modern society itself, which dialectically brings the antisemitic mindset forward. For the potential victim of antisemitism, the choice is either an accommodation with or a revolt against this reality. However, he or she always has to expect antisemitic outbursts. Hence, Améry writes his warning: 'But since the sentence passed on me by the madmen can, after all, be carried out at any moment, it is totally binding, and my own mental lucidity is entirely irrelevant' (Améry 1980:96).

After the Shoah, Jew-hatred changed its constitution. While physical attacks on Jews still existed, and are even increasing in recent years, its most virulent form today is *anti-Zionism*. It is not as easy to recognise, although the motives and even the stereotypes remain the same. Adapted to present-day circumstances and articulated in ways that are socially acceptable, at least in certain circles, antisemitism today is often the storm contained within the cloud of anti-Zionism. While open hostility to Jews remains on the far-right and Islamic parts of the political spectrum, anti-Zionist resentment in Western countries is widespread. The new antisemite refuses to see himself as an antisemite. He proudly identifies as an anti-Zionist and thinks that thereby he has preserved his honour. But Améry points out that 'classical antisemitism is taking on a contemporaneous guise. Yet its previous guise too lives on: a rare case of genuine coexistence' (Améry 2022a:34). Furthermore, he sees the new antisemitism today as more dangerous than the old, right-wing antisemitism that was and still is easy to identify. In the 1960s, Améry was reminded of National Socialist Europe: the call for the death of Jews, this time Zionists, was getting louder. He doubted that historical education could help abolish antisemitic prejudice because 'anti-Zionism is nothing other than an updated version of the age-old and evidently ineradicable, utterly irrational hatred that has been directed against the Jews since time immemorial' (Améry 2022d:52).

Antisemitism of the Left

Améry was utterly shocked to see that it was first and foremost the left that supported this new antisemitism. He had always seen himself as part of the radical left, at a time when leftist groups were the only ones to actively oppose antisemitism. And now his closest allies were betraying their own principles. So it was that his loss of trust in the world as a Shoah-victim was reinforced 20 years later as a politically homeless leftist. His involuntary yet necessary estrangement from the left makes his critique all the more poignant.

By the 1960s, left-wing antisemitism was no longer only a phenomenon of Soviet loyalists. Now, it was embraced by the independent, so-called New Left. In the years immediately after the Shoah, the German public was relatively well-disposed towards the young Jewish State, though Améry believed that this was a cheap way to assuage guilt feelings. But in the 1960s, he describes how a gasp of relief could be felt in Germany in response to the rise of anti-Zionism. Finally, Germans could blame the Jews as oppressors, and they could feel morally superior (see Améry 2022a:35).

The left-wing student movement in West Germany was a reaction against the conservatism of the previous two decades. The Auschwitz trials in Frankfurt saw many young Germans begin to openly question the Nazi past of the older generation, but they did not, as they should have done, *break* with their fathers. Pacifist views spread throughout German society while at the same time popularity of the Palestinian 'liberation' struggle grew. The

Six-Day War, in which Israel took over the West Bank from Jordan and Gaza from Egypt, was abused as a justification to now blame Israelis as the cruel persecutors. It was a rationalisation; a welcome opportunity to utter long-suppressed reflexes.

In modern antisemitic ideology, the moral mantra of the left – to always be on the side of the weak against the mighty – gets upended. The antisemitic delusion attributes enormous power to the Jews, and the new antisemitism repeats the delusion for Israel. While Israel is faced with annihilation at the hands of hostile neighbours that outnumber her, Israel is imagined by the left to be an almighty oppressor and is therefore seen as its natural enemy (see Améry 2022a:38). Améry does not euphemise the suffering of the Palestinians but stresses Israel's fight is for survival and 'the preservation of a shelter for the Jews of the diaspora' (Améry 2022b:44). The Jews from the Arab countries 'would long since have perished under dramatic circumstances' if it was not for the Jewish State they escaped to in the late 1940s and early 1950s (Améry 2022b:44). And yet, the left today does not mobilise when it comes to actual crimes against humanity in Syria, Iraq or Iran, but when the Israeli army strikes back against rockets from Gaza, the left-led demonstrations are huge.

Left-wing antisemitism pained Améry: 'How did Marxist dialectical thought come to lend itself to the preparation of the coming genocide?' (Améry 2022b:41). He tried to find answers. He thought there was a 'generational problem' (Améry 2022b:41). The New Left was young not only on a theoretical field but also as people. Most had not witnessed the Nazi past. Therefore, argued Améry, they failed to see what was specific to National Socialism: eliminationist antisemitism (see Améry 2022b:42). Instead, the New Left falsely subsumed National Socialism under the heading of Fascism and ignored the eliminatory antisemitism. In short, *the vast majority of the left does not make the Shoah, the irrational extermination of Jews, a point of reference for their social theory.* They do not see the inherent threat of death carried by antisemitism and its differences to racism and other forms of group-related enmity. They view Israel as an aggressor against the Palestinian Arabs and they declare solidarity with the allegedly weak against the strong. Antisemitism in the shape of anti-Zionism becomes acceptable, or in Améry's words 'honourable'.

In a talk given in 1976 at the Brotherhood Week, an interfaith event of the Society for Christian-Jewish Cooperation, Améry called for the left to rethink its stance towards Israel (see Améry 2022e:69). Since then, the problem of antisemitism on parts of the left, internationally, has only worsened, especially since alliances have been formed with traditional right-wing and Islamic antisemitism. Améry's demand is more pressing today than ever.

The Categorical Imperative After Auschwitz

Améry brings to mind what it means to translate Theodor W. Adorno's categorical imperative – 'Mankind has to arrange their thoughts and actions so that Auschwitz will not repeat itself, so that nothing similar will happen' – into concrete terms (Adorno 2003:358). The Shoah is the brutal manifestation of a society in which we can trust neither reason nor the self-preservation drive of perpetrators. Eliminationist antisemitism constituted the core of Nazi ideology, which is why even when the tide of World War II turned against Germany, it remained the regime's priority. The mania went so far that even when the war was foreseeably lost, the killing of Jews did not stop until the total defeat of the Germans. The Nazis were willing to sacrifice themselves in order to eliminate what they saw as 'world Judaism'. In contrast to other horrible and cruel genocides, the Shoah is unprecedented because of this absence of instrumental reason. That is why a new categorical imperative after Auschwitz is required. Kant's categorical imperative – act only in accordance with that maxim through which you can at the same time will that it become a universal law – and at a later date Marx's – overthrow all conditions in which man is a degraded, enslaved, neglected, contemptible being – are no longer sufficient. Today, we also need Adorno's.

History has shown that Jews cannot rely on others to come to their rescue and that the existence of a Jewish State is essential to prevent a new Shoah. Because of this, Israel differs from every other state in the world. Today, believed Jean Améry, 'Anyone who questions Israel's right to exist is either too stupid to understand that he is contributing to, or is intentionally promoting an über-Auschwitz' (Améry 2022c:49).

Note

1 This chapter was first published in *Fathom* in 2016.

References

Adorno, Theodor W. (2003/1966) 'Negative Dialektik', in Rolf Tiedemann (ed.), *Gesammelte Schriften Bd. 6: Negative Dialektik. Jargon der Eigentlichkeit*, Frankfurt am Main: Suhrkamp, 7–412. Translation M. G.

Améry, Jean (1980/1966) *At the Mind's Limits. Contemplations by a Survivor on Auschwitz and Its Realities*, Bloomington: Indiana University Press.

Améry, Jean (2002/1976) 'Jenseits von Schuld und Sühne', in Irene Heidelberger-Leonard and Gerhard Scheit (eds.), *Werke Bd. 2: Jenseits von Schuld und Sühne. Unmeisterliche Wanderjahre. Örtlichkeiten*, Stuttgart: Klett-Cotta, 7–177. Translation M. G.

Améry, Jean (2005/1969) 'Der ehrbare Antisemitismus', in Irene Heidelberger-Leonard and Stephan Steiner (eds.), *Werke, Bd.7: Aufsätze zur Politik und Zeitgeschichte*, Stuttgart: Klett-Cotta, 131–140. Translation M. G.

Améry, Jean (2022a/1969) 'Virtuous antisemitism', in Marlene Gallner (ed.), *Essays on Antisemitism, Anti-Zionism, and the Left*, Bloomington: Indiana University Press, 34–40.

Améry, Jean (2022b/1969) 'The new left's approach to "Zionism"', in Marlene Gallner (ed.), *Essays on Antisemitism, Anti-Zionism, and the Left*, Bloomington: Indiana University Press, 41–45.

Améry, Jean (2022c/1973) 'Jews, leftists, leftist Jews: The changing contours of a political problem', in Marlene Gallner (ed.), *Essays on Antisemitism, Anti-Zionism, and the Left*, Bloomington: Indiana University Press, 46–49.

Améry, Jean (2022d/1976) 'The new antisemitism', in Marlene Gallner (ed.), *Essays on Antisemitism, Anti-Zionism, and the Left*, Bloomington: Indiana University Press, 50–54.

Améry, Jean (2022e/1976) 'Virtuous antisemitism: Address on the occasion of Jewish-Christian brotherhood week', in Marlene Gallner (ed.), *Essays on Antisemitism, Anti-Zionism, and the Left*, Bloomington: Indiana University Press, 58–73.

9

WHAT CORBYN'S FAVOURITE SOCIOLOGISTS GREG PHILO AND MIKE BERRY GET WRONG ABOUT CONTEMPORARY ANTISEMITISM

Matthew Bolton

Controversially reinstated in the Labour Party but denied a return to the Parliamentary Labour Party by the leader Keir Starmer, Jeremy Corbyn's defiant response to the 2020 Equality and Human Rights Commission (EHRC) report, which found the party had breached the Equality Act in its treatment of Jewish people under his leadership, continues to roil the UK left.[1]

In his initial statement, Corbyn said he did not 'accept all of [the report's] findings', because in his view the 'scale' of antisemitism had been 'dramatically overstated for political reasons by our opponents inside and outside the party, as well as by much of the media'. In a later interview, Corbyn clarified that this claim was based on supposed disparity between the general public's perception of the number of Labour members 'under suspicion of antisemitism' and the actual number of formal complaints. While his most recent intervention, released shortly before the hearing which readmitted him to the party, made 'clear' that 'concerns over antisemitism' were not 'overstated', he did not withdraw his contention that the 'scale' of the problem had been exaggerated.

On the face of it, Corbyn's argument is flatly empirical, resting on raw numbers and unrelated to the wider question of antisemitism on the left. But this ostensibly value-free statement is premised on a series of ideological presuppositions that, once unpicked, demonstrate that the anti-Jewish discrimination the EHRC confirmed is not an inexplicable anomaly or random occurrence. Rather, it derives from a specific world view, bordering on conspiracy theory, that has come to dominate large swathes of the left, and which is all too often receptive to antisemitism.

DOI: 10.4324/9781003322320-11

The 'Bad News' Model

Corbyn dutifully prefaced his comments with the disclaimer that 'anyone claiming there is no antisemitism in the Labour party is wrong. Of course there is, as there is throughout society, and sometimes it is voiced by people who think of themselves as on the left.' This idea, that any antisemitism in Labour is merely a reflection of that within wider society, is drawn from a 2017 survey by the Institute of Jewish Policy Research (see Staetsky 2017). The JPR found that 30 per cent of the British public agreed with at least one derogatory statement about 'Jews as Jews', such as 'Jews get rich at the expense of others', or 'exploit Holocaust victimhood for their own purposes'. This percentage – 30 per cent – was the same for those who self-identified as being on the left. By contrast, the percentage of self-identified right-wingers in agreement with such statements was 20 per cent higher than average. The conclusion typically drawn by Corbyn supporters is that the home of true antisemites is on the right – but that, given the size of Labour's membership, it is sadly inevitability that a small number will end up within the party. This latter group might 'think of themselves' as being on the left, but are in fact interlopers. Corbyn's sole 'regret' when it comes to antisemitism relates to the failure to unmask and remove these intruders from the party speedily enough. But the notion that the left or Labour might have a *particular* problem with antisemitism, beyond that of society in general – or that there might be a particular form of antisemitism within leftist circles that cannot be immediately reduced to that of the right – is seen as a distortion of the evidence.

This raises the question of who might be distorting that evidence, and to what end. Corbyn's answer here draws on *Bad News for Labour*, a 2019 book on the antisemitism crisis (Philo et al. 2019). Its central thesis is constructed around a single opinion poll, in which respondents were asked to estimate the percentage of Labour members subject to antisemitism complaints. Two-thirds had not heard of the Labour antisemitism crisis or were not sure. Among those who had, the mean estimate – found by adding all responses together and dividing the total by the number of respondents – was 34 per cent, although the single most popular answer was between 0 and 9 per cent. Philo and Berry – and now Corbyn – argue that the disparity between the average of respondents' estimates and the true number of complaints was the result of an antagonistic media deliberating blowing a miniscule problem out of all proportion in order to attack the left.

Philo and Berry's findings and methodology have been comprehensively dismantled elsewhere (Allington 2020, Brown 2019). It is only worth adding here that, regardless of the total number of formal complaints, the fact that a substantial amount of them involved the leader of the party and his close associates seems far more relevant to understanding public perception than a random cohort's ability to pluck abstract percentages out of the air.

It is true that some reporting bordered on the hysterical, such as claiming Corbyn 'danced a jig' towards the Cenotaph. But for much of his leadership, the media actually *underplayed* the seriousness of the antisemitism charges against him. There was an incessant focus on his description of Hamas and Hezbollah as 'friends', for instance, allowing him to portray himself as a diplomatic broker using 'inclusive language' to talk to 'both sides'. But journalists repeatedly failed to press him on his very next sentence in the same speech, where he extolled Hamas as 'dedicated to . . . peace and social justice and political justice' – a far more damning charge, and far more difficult to deflect with empty platitudes.

But rather than picking more holes in Philo and Berry's argument, it is more instructive to focus instead on the general world view underpinning their analysis. *Bad News for Labour* is the latest instalment in a long series of *Bad News* books. Initially focused on media reporting of industrial disputes, in recent years they have centred on the Israel–Palestine conflict. What connects the series is the idea that mass media systematically distorts its coverage to manipulate public opinion at the behest of powerful interests. While more sophisticated cultural analyses emphasise both the contested nature of media production and the ability of individuals to actively 'decode' the media they consume, for Philo and Berry, the media is a homogenous propagator of mystification and the public merely a passive victim of ideological trickery.

In *Bad News from Israel* (2004) and *More Bad News from Israel* (2011), Philo and Berry argue that the media consciously misrepresents the conflict to cover up Israeli crimes. Their assumption is that if the British public were told 'the truth', then their manufactured support for Israel would disintegrate. Given the supposed power and one-sidedness of the media narrative, it is somewhat surprising to read the JPR's finding that a third of British people hold an unfavourable view of Israel, while only one-fifth are favourable. A mere 6 per cent sympathise with Israel when it comes to the conflict, with 18 per cent favouring the Palestinians. But even if we accept the claims of a pro-Israeli bias within the media, Philo and Berry's version of the 'truth' is little better. Rather than the story of two national movements, each with legitimate territorial claims, coming to conflict in tragic circumstances, we get instead an uncritical regurgitation of the work of such 'impartial' sources as Norman Finkelstein and Noam Chomsky. Here Jewish national aspirations, even in the wake of the near annihilation of the European Jewry, are portrayed as illegitimate, reactionary and imperialistic, while Palestinian claims to nation statehood are presented as authentic, indigenous and emancipatory. What I have described elsewhere as the *intrinsic* relation between Israel, Zionism and antisemitism is severed, with antisemitism now presented as an unfortunate but ultimately rational *extrinsic* response to Israeli actions (Bolton 2020). Philo and Berry thus reduce the messy complexity of the Israel–Palestine conflict to a Manichean struggle between two monolithic discourses – the 'bad news' of lies, manipulation and distortion, and the 'good news' of their own unquestionable truth and righteousness. Any argument which refuses this binary premise is immediately suspect, and more likely than not itself the result of ideological manipulation.

False Flags

Once this seductively simple formula – which has the self-confirming logic of all conspiracy theories – has been established, it can be applied to almost any event. Thus when David Miller, Philo's protege and a contributor to *Bad News for Labour*, is not bemoaning the 'influence' that 'Zionists . . . have over the British Left and British politics more widely', he has argued that Bashar al-Assad's chemical attacks on rebel-held areas in Syria were 'managed massacres' staged by the rebels themselves in collaboration with the media (Kennedy 2020). (A BBC radio documentary recently revealed that Corbyn himself believes the White Helmets, a Syrian humanitarian organisation that has been the subject of multiple conspiracy theories, to be 'highly suspicious' because they have received funding from the British government. See BBC 2019). Similarly, over recent months, there has been a sharp rise in leftists arguing that the ongoing genocide of Uyghur Muslims in Xinjiang is a media fiction concocted by Western 'neo-cons' seeking a 'new Cold War' against China. This new mode of 'radical' genocide denial replicates that prevalent during the Yugoslav wars of the 1990s, when Corbyn's mentor Tony Benn claimed Bosnian Muslims were bombing themselves to incriminate Slobodan Milosevic's Serbian regime and his Bosnian-Serb allies (Benn 2009). Corbyn himself would later sign a Parliamentary motion denying the genocide in Kosovo (UK Parliament 2004). It is not surprising, then, to find Edward Herman – whose co-authored book *The Politics of Genocide*, according to George Monbiot, 'downplay[s] or dismiss[es] both the massacre of Bosniaks at Srebrenica in 1995 and the genocide of Tutsis committed by Hutu militias in Rwanda in 1994' – providing a glowing endorsement for *Bad News From Israel* (Monbiot 2012).

For all the supposed empirical rigour deployed by Philo, Miller and Finkelstein, theirs is at root a wholly irrational world view, in which reality is entirely dissolved into representation. Society is deprived of any objective basis and collapses into the pure contingency of competing propaganda claims. In a world entirely driven by secretive machinations, everyone is a dupe – aside from the good authors themselves. But it is notable that, for all the supposed radicalism of their totalising critique of the 'mainstream media', the end result is invariably the unquestioning acceptance of 'alternative' narratives pushed by authoritarian states and their compliant media channels, especially if they purport to be 'anti-imperialist' – namely, anti-American and anti-Israeli. It is also striking how often Muslim people are accused of collaboration with the imperialists and the media. That Palestinians are an outlier here suggests that the contemporary left's propensity to inflate 'the idea of Palestine' into a signifier for emancipation-in-itself has less to do with supporting actual Palestinians than it has opposing the 'Zionists' who stand in the way of universal freedom.

Nor is it coincidental that this same 'false flag' logic is at work in Norman Finkelstein's theory of a so-called 'Holocaust Industry', a Jewish-led media conspiracy to exaggerate the unique elements of the Nazi genocide in order to shield Israel from criticism and 'shakedown' credulous Gentiles. Johnson has critically examined Finkelstein's tendency to '[normalise] antisemitism by telling his audiences that most Jews believe in their group's superiority, talk too much about the Holocaust, are over-represented in the media and use that over-representation for Jewish ends' (2018:122). And here the findings of the second, strangely neglected, half of the JPR report become of interest. Not only did the JPR find that the 'very left-wing' – those most likely to be Corbyn supporters – are 20 per cent more likely to hold anti-Israel views than the general population, they are also far more likely to agree with anti-semitic statements such as 'Israel has too much control over global affairs' and 'Israel has interests at odds with the interests of the rest of the world'. Moreover, the JPR found that the stronger a person's anti-Israel views, the more likely they are to hold antisemitic attitudes about 'Jews as Jews'. The most commonly held views within this cohort were that Jews have inter-ests that 'are very different from the interests of the rest of the population'; 'have too much power in Britain' – including over the media and, as Finkel-stein maintains, 'exploit Holocaust victimhood for their own purposes'. It is thus here – at the intersection of antisemitic anti-Zionism and traditional Judeophobia, where leftists are overrepresented – that the true source of the Labour antisemitism crisis is to be found. It is not an import from the right, or a random statistical quirk, but rather a homegrown problem with roots that are specific to the left.

Corbyn and his supporters would no doubt seek to refute these particu-lar JPR findings by relying on a categorical distinction between 'Jews' and 'Zionists'. But that distinction simply does not hold when half of all Jews live in Israel and the rest overwhelmingly have some kind of affinity with Israel, however mild (Miller et al. 2015). For Corbyn, those facts are allowed no relation to the history of antisemitism or to the question of whether his brand of absolutist anti-Zionism is (in practice) antisemitic. Instead, both groups, the Jews in Israel and the Jews in the diaspora, are seen as having been duped by 'bad news', that is, propaganda about Israel and propaganda about Corbyn's Labour. The alternative to condemning British Jews to the status of fools at best, or liars and propagandists at worst, is for the left to acknowledge that the way it has long understood antisemitism, Israel and the idea of Jewish nationhood is not only historically and conceptually flawed but *itself* tainted with antisemitism. But this would mean challenging not just axiomatic beliefs about Israel but an entire world view, one built on conspiracy, irrationality and projection. Corbyn's statement, and ongoing refusal to withdraw it, is thus as much a defence of this ideological edifice as it is an evasion of his responsibility for the crisis.

Note

1 This chapter was first published in *Fathom* in 2020.

References

Allington, Daniel (2020) 'Review: Bad news for labour: Antisemitism, the party, and public belief', *Journal of Contemporary Antisemitism*, 3 (1): 127–133.

BBC Radio 4 (2019) *Intrigue: Mayday*, Episode 8: False Flags, November. Available: www.bbc.co.uk/programmes/m000pchw (accessed 31 October 2022).

Benn, Tony (2009) 'Tony Benn on Bosnia: "The main enemy is NATO"', Workers Liberty website. Available: www.workersliberty.org/story/2009-04-02/tony-benn-bosnia-main-enemy-nato (accessed 31 October 2022).

Bolton, Matthew (2020) 'Conceptual vandalism, historical distortion: The labour antisemitism crisis and the limits of class instrumentalism', *Journal of Contemporary Antisemitism* 3 (2): 11–30.

Brown, Sarah (2019) 'Book review – Bad news for labour: Antisemitism, the party and public belief', *Fathom*. Available: https://fathomjournal.org/book-review-bad-news-for-labour-antisemitism-the-party-public-belief/ (accessed 31 October 2022).

Johnson, Alan (2018) 'Denial: Norman Finkelstein and the new antisemitism', in Jonathan Campbell and Lesley Klaff (eds.), *Unity and Disunity in Contemporary Antisemitism*, Boston: Academic Studies Press, 115–135.

Kennedy, Dominic (2020) 'Lecturer David Miller quits "Zionist" labour party', *The Times*, 16 June. Available: www.thetimes.co.uk/article/zionists-have-taken-over-labour-xczt85sck (accessed 31 October 2022).

Miller, Stephen, Margaret Harris and Colin Shindler (2015) *The Attitudes of British Jews Towards Israel*, London: Department of Sociology, School of Arts and Social Sciences, City University.

Monbiot, George (2012) 'My fight may be hopeless, but it is as necessary as ever', *The Guardian*, 21 May. Available: www.theguardian.com/commentisfree/2012/may/21/ratko-mladic-genocide-denial (accessed 31 October 2022).

Philo, Greg and Mike Berry (2004) *Bad News From Israel*, London: Pluto Press.

Philo, Greg and Mike Berry (2011) *More Bad News From Israel*, London: Pluto Press.

Philo, Greg, Mike Berry, Justin Schlosberg, Anthony Lerman and David Miller (2019) *Bad News for Labour: Antisemitism, the Party and Public Belief*, London: Pluto Press.

Staetsky, Daniel L. (2017) *Antisemitism in Contemporary Great Britain: A Study of Attitudes Towards Jews and Israel*, London: Institute for Jewish Policy Research.

UK Parliament (2004) 'Early day motion: John Pilger and Kosovo'. Available: https://edm.parliament.uk/early-day-motion/26919 (accessed 31 October 2022).

10

ANTISEMITISM AND THE LEFT

A Memoir

Kathleen Hayes

The beliefs that give our lives meaning are passed down to us by people we cherish.[1] For those on the left, these men and women are often dearer than family: comrades with whom we have worked and fought; shared jokes, drinks and beds; and endured a third round of brain-numbing discussion on a glorious summer day while other people thoughtlessly picnicked in the park. Our evolving sense of what is true is inextricably entwined with our respect and, most of all, our love for the person who teaches it to us. We think that the things they say and write and the ideas in the books they recommend must be true – because we know them to be honourable, intelligent people and we love them.

I was a devoted Trotskyist for 25 years. My initiation took place at a protest against Natan Sharansky. It was 1987. I was a callow 19-year-old Berkeley student and anti-apartheid activist; my soon-to-be comrades were the smartest, funniest, most good-hearted yet irreverent people I had ever known. There was, predictably, a guy in the picture – my genial bespectacled boyfriend who had introduced me to the party – and the uneasy suggestion that my sudden conversion to Marxism wasn't a purely intellectual epiphany. I had almost certainly never heard of Sharansky, but when an older comrade I particularly admired asked me, a glint of mischief in her eyes, whether I'd like to come to a 'bright red demo' against an anti-communist traitor who had spied on the Soviet workers state, I'd heard almost everything I needed. I joined their small picket line in front of the San Francisco hotel where Sharansky was speaking, and when it was over, I soaked up my new comrades' attention and praise like a parched little flower after a long drought.

'I never saw any antisemitism', we so often hear today. And so I didn't, or seldom did, in the decades of leftist political activity that followed. It was

DOI: 10.4324/9781003322320-12

embedded in the fabric, a thread that ran unseen throughout an avowedly emancipating world view and was inextricable from it. It stitched together a legacy that included Marx's sometimes-troubling writings about Jews; subterranean beliefs about an association between Jews, trade and capitalism; longstanding hostility to Jewish 'particularism'; and a Marxist heritage that could claim some principled opponents of antisemitism in its ranks but also many who were ambivalent or complacent about it, sometimes with deadly consequences, some outright antisemites and every shade between. I suspected none of this the day I joined that picket line: quite the contrary, despite all the fulminating against Zionism and the Anti-Defamation League. A prominent sign carried that day – '20 million Soviet citizens died smashing Third Reich!' – established beyond all doubt that the party was firmly on the side of good against evil. And, of course, staunchly against antisemitism.

So it takes hold. A certain way of thinking and feeling begins to flourish, in which you are on the side of progress and good, with people and a cause you grow to love more than life itself; while on the other side of that divide are The Jews – or, at least, the vast majority of Jews who do not unambiguously renounce Israel to the left's satisfaction. In this essay, I will not be tracing the history of antisemitism in the Marxist movement, or its extension to the left more broadly. Many historians and sociologists have done that already (e.g. Robert Wistrich, David Hirsh, Dave Rich, Robert Fine and Philip Spencer), and all I will do here is express appreciation for their work.[2] What I will try to do instead is describe how unrecognised antisemitism gained a hold over me; the purpose I think it served; and how I came to, at least consciously, recognise and reject it.

I'm not placing myself at the centre of this account because I'm fond of self-exposure. In fact, this is the most difficult thing I've ever written. Although I've told a few supportive new friends about my ignominious past and mentioned it in a recent master's dissertation for Birkbeck about antisemitism and the left, this is by far my most personal and public account. It's not only hard because I'm admitting I held some horrible views and was maybe simply an idiot; but because despite everything, part of me cringes at the thought I'm betraying people and a cause that provided meaning to my every breath for many years. It's probably not coincidence that as I have been writing this, I keep dreaming of my former comrades. I often have nightmares involving them (oh God, I have to sell that newspaper again), but these past nights my comrades are laughing or embracing me. Despite the affection they show, I know they have appeared to tell me they do not want me to write, that they hate what I am writing and the person I have become, and this knowledge makes every word an act of will. I'm writing anyway, in the hope that some good may yet come from my experience – first, that it might provide a different, or at least fuller, perspective to those committed to studying and fighting antisemitism; and second, that it might help others who thought as I once did to at least question their views.

A Seduction

I joined the party, beginning with its youth organisation, because I wanted to fight for a better world and had become convinced Marxism was key to that. This is what I told myself and others countless times over the years that followed – and indeed, I remember my moment of decision as a conscious, reasoned act, one marking me as someone willing to swim against the stream. But it wasn't that simple; truly life-altering decisions never are. I can recount the arguments that convinced me, but what really made my conversion all but inevitable was my respect and, most of all, my love for the people who argued with them. Some might call my decision a leap of faith, but although there is much truth to that, I prefer to compare it to a seduction. My sun-dappled Southern California childhood had given me everything except a sense of belonging and purpose, and I was ripe to give myself. I discovered the dubious euphoria of surrender to the party.

It came at a price. Wine-fuelled parties, jokes and selfless dedication to rid the world of all oppression: that was one side of party life. The other was brutal. It takes hold inexorably like an abusive relationship; by the time you start to think of leaving, as you inevitably must, your soul is so fully theirs that life outside is viewed as no better than death. So you immerse yourself ever more deeply into the party. You lie to your parents and any non-party friends you might have, both because your membership is a secret and because they wouldn't understand. Your world shrinks to a succession of meeting rooms in which your dear, witty, intelligent comrades periodically accuse each other – and sometimes, devastatingly, you – of capitulating to the bourgeoisie. You survive your victimisation, barely, and await vengeance by becoming one of the accusers. It is quite sick. Yet the beating heart of this toxic cycle is the most fervent and loving dedication to humanity found on this side of sainthood.

This is the authoritarian organisation, in which a hunger for meaning, community and fulfilment is alternately fed and starved. My party proclaimed itself committed to total equality, while an invisible nexus of sex, power and what I experienced as love served to entrench and sanction hierarchy and oppression. At the pinnacle stood the Great Leader, whose every pronounce-ment was regarded with reverence. No one acknowledged or even saw how power ineluctably determined decisions 'freely' made, or how it enabled the toleration of certain behaviours which can only be deemed abuse. We all, myself included, performed mental acrobatics when necessary to defend the Great Leader's integrity and that of the party. We learned not only to lie but – since we simultaneously believed in our absolute scrupulousness – to believe the lies. We forgot the mental somersaults that had careened through our heads until we reached the accepted version of truth. The reward was a renewed sense of unity against our enemies, whose rendition of truth was wrong because it was against the party.

Comrades and Enemies

This is the context in which antisemitism took root. The party needed enemies as a way of cohering itself and had them in abundance. The capitalist ruling class was one obvious, if distant target, but far more venom was spewed against other leftists, some of whom I learned to hate with the fervour of a Maoist Red Guard. Then there were the 'bourgeois feministssssss' (uttered with a hiss), against whom the party's fulminations sometimes reached such borderline-obscene fury it was close to misogyny. But most of all there were the reactionary, preternaturally sinister 'Zionistsssssss'. And I was no more capable of questioning my beloved party's attitude towards Zionism and Israel than I was of challenging the belief that the earth is round.

The pattern was repeated with regard to the Soviet Union: authoritarianism writ large. Lenin was the paradigmatic Great Leader, and the October Revolution was the battle line between the righteous and their many enemies. The dispiriting realities of America in the late 20th century could be forgotten by immersing ourselves in a history populated by Bolshevik heroes and counter-revolutionary villains – much as those in a less secular age drew solace from *The Lives of the Saints*. The injunction to hail the October Revolution made it completely impossible to consider, even in the hidden depths of one's mind, whether the 'bureaucratic abuses' attributed to Stalinism might have begun earlier, with the Great Leader himself; and it meant that no matter how harshly we denounced Stalinism as Trotskyists, we had to suppress a sometimes-troubling legacy of our own. The binary view of October as something one is either for or against inevitably cast Jews – beginning with but not limited to Zionists – as enemies.

Historians have documented how a deluge of antisemitic Stalinist propaganda took root in the left during and after the Six-Day War, resulting in an increasingly foam-flecked anti-Zionism.[3] My party was undoubtedly one to respond in this way: although their newspaper articles continued to assert Israel's right to exist, those diligent formulations were effectively negated through vitriolic anti-Zionism. But there is another consequence of the 1967 war that has received less attention: how afterwards increasing numbers of Soviet Jews attempted to emigrate to Israel or the West, were refused by Soviet authorities, and were declared enemies of the Soviet workers state in echoes of the notorious antisemitic Stalinist show trials. The Cold War in the 1970s and 1980s was to some extent fought over the bodies of Soviet Jews, 'refusenik' dissidents like Sharansky. Pro-Sovietism and antisemitism went hand in hand.

The Palestinian struggle filled the vacuum left by the Soviet Union's collapse. Communism is dead, but the Intifada lives. Burgeoning anti-Israel protests and pro-Palestinian campus activism provided a sense of solidarity that warmed a cold and lonely world. Very rarely, my party objected to some display of antisemitism by our fellow defenders of the Palestinians, but it had to be extreme and crude: blood libels or plainly antisemitic references to the Rothschild family. Swastikas were obviously antisemitic outrages – unless they were twinned with the Star of David, in which case they denoted justified outrage at the Zionist jackboot. It didn't occur to me there was anything wrong with this, or with the party's frequent use of terms associated with Nazism – 'untermenschen', 'master race' and of course 'Holocaust' – to describe Zionism's ideology and goals. I swam in a sea of antisemitism for years and didn't notice the water was filthy.

There's one related issue that deserves note: the role of the Jewish anti-Zionist leftist. My party, like so many others, contained many Jewish members, some of whom were central to developing the party's line on Israel. They gave it a legitimacy that would have been impossible otherwise. The party's 'Near East expert' – a scholarly, mild-mannered Jewish guy prone to exclaiming 'Oy gevalt!' – could not be an antisemite. Or so I thought. I also assumed I couldn't be an antisemite because of my own family background: although my name is Irish, on my mother's side I am Dutch-Jewish. Of all I'm ashamed of, near top of the list is how I invoked my great-grandfather, murdered in Auschwitz, to prove (to myself, if no one else) my innocence of antisemitism. Yet for all my shame, I don't think anything is gained by declaring myself an antisemite. There needs to be a better way of looking at this, one that rejects the dichotomy between antisemites and non-antisemites. What exist, rather, are myriad shades of grey, which shift over time according to unrecognised need. And which, sometimes, put us at war with our own identities.

After the Party: Hangover and Sobriety

Fast-forward to 2016. I'd been living and doing political work with the party in London for several years. I quit the party that year for a combination of political and personal reasons I won't go into, except to say it shook my faith in my comrades as compassionate beings. A more devastating personal experience soon after I quit left me reeling. I felt incredibly alone and betrayed. I'd thought my comrades were more than family and more than friends. It transpired they were neither; that transcendent love had been all in my head.

Only these painful personal shocks made it possible for me first to question, then to see what had been hiding in plain sight all along: first the party's streak of misogyny and the Great Leader's direct role in it; then the disturbing brutal side of the October Revolution and the Bolsheviks I'd revered. My former beliefs shattered, one after another, in the loneliest, most disorienting time of my life.

I'd joined Labour, like so many far-left enthusiasts of Jeremy Corbyn, the moment I quit; and like so many others I'd insisted the antisemitism charges simply reflected right-wing attempts to smear him and socialism. But after watching the Panorama documentary 'Is Labour Anti-Semitic?' twice, I decided to do some fact-checking. My first assignment was clear cut: investigating the truth behind Ken Livingstone's claims that the Zionists had collaborated with the Nazis which, I'm ashamed to say, I believed completely. My former party swore by the same book by Lenni Brenner, *Zionism in the Age of Dictators*, that Livingstone cited. My search soon brought me to a *Fathom* article by Paul Bogdanor, debunking Brenner, which I found devastating. (Editor's note. See Chapter 18 in this collection.) I kept reading. And finally, sickened, realised that the people and beliefs I'd loved with all my heart – and I – had been horribly, shockingly wrong.

So I kept reading *Fathom*. Shoutouts to a few of you: Alan Johnson, Philip Spencer, the late Norman Geras and Susie Linfield. Yet even well after I'd accepted much of what *Fathom* had to say about antisemitism, I was confounded when I considered that I was reading and agreeing with – my God – *Zionists*. I thought perhaps I'd lost my mind. It took a long time, and many books and articles, before I could ask the question that never occurred to me all those years I was an anti-Zionist – 'What is Zionism, actually?' – and wonder how and why self-determination for the Jewish people came to be seen as the epitome of evil. I had to be painfully stripped of my most precious possession – the love of my comrades – before I could even pose that question and start looking for answers.

Songs of Love and Hate

Eve Garrard's brilliant essay 'The Pleasures of Antisemitism' notes that antisemitism is less about thoughts than feelings: the transgressive pleasure of hate. (Editor's note. See Chapter 29 in this collection.) To this, I would only add that the hate has a corollary, love. For the left, love for one's comrades, party, the Soviet Union (once), or even socialism demands someone to hate – someone against whom hate (or a vaguer hostility) is sanctioned by those who have authority over us. Jews, often in the form of Zionists, are the hate object that makes possible the leftist's most transcendent love. This is what makes it so intractable: its inextricable association with all the leftists finds righteous and dear. Others (e.g. those 'feministsssss') may occasionally fill the role of hate object. However, from Marx's day onwards, the left has most readily found it in Jews.

Ours is an increasingly fragmented world, and each of us seeks meaning and comradeship where we can. We choose our tribe, with cherished people and beliefs, and cling to them as if our lives depend on it, which in a sense it does. I get the fervour of Corbyn's supporters. It's the Great Leader thing all over again. They love him and need to believe in the hope he seems to offer; as a result, they perceive criticism of him as almost an existential assault. They believe they are doing the courageous and principled thing in defending him against his opponents, whom they cannot but view as completely malevolent. In this febrile climate, it may seem futile to convince anyone she might be wrong about something as ugly as antisemitism.

Yet successes are possible, minds changed here and there: count me as one. So thank you, *Fathom*. As Karl Kautsky wrote Jean Jaurès in 1899, saluting him for taking up the fight for Dreyfus and against antisemitism: 'I wish your noble work full success and shake your hand with friendship.'

Notes

1 This chapter was first published in *Fathom* in 2021.
2 The most comprehensive survey of left antisemitism is the late Robert S. Wistrich's 648-page book, *From Ambivalence to Betrayal: The Left, the Jews and Israel*, 2012, Lincoln NE: University of Nebraska Press.
3 See the chapters by Tabarovsky and Gansinger as well as Herf's interview in this collection.

11

DENIAL

Norman Finkelstein and the New Antisemitism

Alan Johnson

The concept of a 'new antisemitism' directs our attention to some of the ways in which some people talk about Israel, Israelis and 'Zionism', suggesting that these ways have left the terrain of 'criticism of Israeli policy' and become something much darker.[1] The concept is concerned to distinguish between legitimate criticism of that policy (most obviously, of the occupation of the territories, the settlement project, the treatment of minorities in Israel, and the degree of force Israel uses to restore deterrence against Hamas) and an essentialising, demonising and dehumanising discourse which bends the meaning of Israel and Zionism (and most Jews) out of shape until they are fit receptacles for the tropes, images and ideas of classical antisemitism.

The concept alerts us to antisemitism's tendency to shape-shift through history. And to the possibility that since the creation of a Jewish state, in some quarters at least, what 'the Jew', demonised and essentialised, once was, Israel, also demonised and essentialised, now is: malevolent in its very nature, all-controlling, full of blood lust, and the obstacle to a better, purer and more spiritual world.

The new antisemitism, which might also be called antisemitic anti-Zionism, has three components: a political programme to abolish the Jewish homeland, a discourse to demonise it, and a movement to make it a global pariah state. The old antisemitism – which has not gone away, but co-mingles with the new form – believed 'the Jew is our Misfortune.' The new antisemitism proclaims, 'the Zionist is our misfortune.' The old antisemitism wanted to make the world 'Judenrein', free of Jews. The new antisemitism wants to make the world 'Judenstaatrein', free of the Jewish state which all but a sliver of world Jewry either lives in or treats as a vitally important part of their identity.

DOI: 10.4324/9781003322320-13

We have no right to be disbelieving of this development. After all, antisemitism has never really been about the Jews, but about the need of some non-Jews to scapegoat Jews. As those needs have changed throughout history, the physiognomy of antisemitism has also changed.

Norman Finkelstein, the New Antisemitism and the 'Holocaust Card'

For Norman Finkelstein, however, the concept of a new antisemitism is nothing but a 'variant' of the 'Holocaust card'. Playing the card has been simple enough for the Zionists: 'A central thesis of my book *Beyond Chutzpah*', writes Finkelstein, 'is that whenever Israel faces a public relations debacle its apologists sound the alarm that a "new anti-Semitism" is upon us' (Finkelstein 2006). His argument has proceeded as a would-be triple unmasking: of *the agencies* that promote the fraud of the new antisemitism, of *the motivations* of the fraudsters and of *the components* that make up the fraud.

Agencies

Finkelstein asks who has 'foisted the new antisemitism on the international agenda'? His answer: not 'honest and decent people' with 'ordinary moral values' but Israel's apologists (2005:5–6). (These two categories pretty much exhaust the cast of characters in Finkelstein's books.) He indicts Jewish 'impresarios' such as former ADL director Abraham Foxman and Jewish 'ancient divas' like the novelist Cynthia Ozick for creating 'the new antisemitism scam' with the backing of 'well-heeled "pro" Israel organisations and foundations' – the 'de facto agents of a foreign government' – supported by 'the Bush administration and Israel' (2005:61, 69, 62).

And everybody is in on the scam. From the UN Secretary General Kofi Annan to the left-wing veteran Todd Gitlin; from the Holocaust survivor Elie Wiesel to the National Executive Committee of the UK Labour Party; from successive US Administrations to those US University Presidents that are strapped for cash; from 'entrepreneurial black professors' like Henry Louis Gates Jr (2005:70) to the *Guardian's* widely respected Jonathan Freedland, assailed by Finkelstein as 'a hack who regularly plays the antisemitism card' (Stern-Weiner and Finkelstein 2016); and from all the 'organisations directly or indirectly linked to Israel or having a material stake in inflating the findings of antisemitism' (2005:8) to 'stupid Goys' such as the present author (2015a).[2]

Motivations

And why have Israel's apologists invented the new antisemitism? To 'taint any criticism of Israel as motivated by antisemitism' and to 'turn Israel (and

Jews) not Palestinians, into the victim' (2005:33). Decent moral people wishing to oppose the occupation are faced with a conspiracy by tricksy Zionists to 'cry wolf' in order to shut them up (2005:66) A 'smear campaign' (Stern-Weiner and Finkelstein 2016) has been designed 'not to fight antisemitism but rather to exploit the historical suffering of Jews in order to immunise Israel against criticism' (2005:22). It is all a 'sham', designed to 'whip up hysteria', and to function as a 'club . . . to assail Israel's critics' by portraying those critics as 'classical Jew-haters' (2005:76, 23, 28, 32). In short, the game is 'political blackmail' (Stern-Weiner and Finkelstein 2016). That assertion, endlessly repeated, is as far as Finkelstein's analysis of the motivations of the fraudsters goes.

Components

And how does the new antisemitism fraud work? How does it manage to 'silence . . . media', 'muzzle academic freedom' and 'undermine the most basic principles of human rights'? (2005:34, 70, 46). According to Finkelstein, there are three components: 'exaggeration and fabrication; mislabelling legitimate criticism of Israeli policy; and the unjustified yet predictable "spillover" from criticism of Israel to Jews generally' (2005:16).

Finkelstein argues that 'most' claims of antisemitism 'prove on investigation to be wildly overblown' (2005:67). He thinks they are 'trivial, nebulous, exaggerated and a lot just fabricated' (2015b).

David Hirsh, a leading UK scholar of contemporary antisemitism, accepts that 'the issue of antisemitism is certainly sometimes raised in an unjustified way, and may even be raised in bad faith', finding some examples on the Israeli right of the characterisation of advocacy of Israeli withdrawal from the West Bank as antisemitic (2010:47, 76). Our responsibility (at once analytical, political and moral) is to make a good-faith effort to *distinguish* between times when exaggeration or falsification *is* happening and times when it is *not*. My own attempt to do so can be found in my submission to the 2016 Labour Party enquiry into antisemitism and other forms of racism (Johnson 2016). But Finkelstein spurns this labour of distinction: 'the hysteria over a new antisemitism hasn't *anything* to do with fighting bigotry – and *everything* to do with stifling criticism of Israel' (2005:76).

Hirsh has observed that the *typical* form of the denial of the new antisemitism is 'the *ad hominem* attack which leaves the substance of the question at issue unaddressed' (2010:51). To be sure, Finkelstein's work is replete with that kind of thing. He smears the global campaign in the 1980s to free Soviet Jewry as a plot designed to 'vilify the Soviet Union' (2005:25); he questions the mental health, as well as the good faith, of those who claim to see a new antisemitism (2005:39, 40, 71); he dismissed the 2006 UK All-Party Parliamentary Report into Antisemitism because its author, Dennis Macshane

MP is a 'notorious Israeli Firster' (2006); he attacked Jonathan Freedland, (again), a sharp critic of Israeli policy, as a 'dull-witted creep' (Stern-Weiner and Finkelstein 2016); he avers that all the 'antisemitism mongers should crawl back into their sewers'; and so on.

Closely related to his love of the ad hominem is his addiction to what Freud called 'the tendentious joke'. As opposed to the 'innocent joke' which depends on verbal dexterity, the tendentious joke depends on the indirect expression of hostility or obscenity and is a very serious thing because it makes possible, thought Freud, 'the satisfaction of an instinct (whether lustful or hostile) in the face of an obstacle that stands in its way' (quoted in Storr 1989:86).

After posting a map on his website that suggested that Israel and Israelis should be transferred *en masse* to the USA, Finkelstein said that it was 'funny'. A favourite joke of his is that his sister got him onto Netflix only for him to discover that 'every third movie is about the Holocaust'. Although Netflix offers around 2,500 movies, all he found was 'Holocaust, Holocaust, Holocaust! Crazy!' (Finkelstein 2016 at 1:25:10–28). Another favourite joke of his is this one: 'To quote Gloria Gaynor's inspirational refrain, Jews "will survive" this onslaught of non-existent, pseudo and contrived anti-Semitism' (Finkelstein 2015c).

Enzo Traverso's Critique of Norman Finkelstein

In 2003, it was as a member of the editorial board of the critical Marxist journal *Historical Materialism* that I invited the Italian intellectual historian Enzo Traverso to review Norman Finkelstein's book *The Holocaust Industry* (Finkelstein 2000). Traverso took his critical distance, to put it mildly (Traverso 2003. All quotations are taken from this review). About Finkelstein's claims regarding Holocaust compensation payments, Traverso judged the book guilty of lumping together the Jewish Claims Conference, about which he thought 'most' of Finkelstein's points are 'probably correct', and the national commissions that were established in Europe which were based on 'completely different ethical and political rules' and which 'aimed to establish the truth and make amends for justice, not to seek profit'. Traverso noted that Finkelstein 'takes the side of Swiss banks, portraying them as victims of a Jewish "racket"'. In effect, Finkelstein had issued 'an absolution and whitewash' by portraying the banks as 'victims, even though they were the first to practice extortions and . . . not against powerful economic institutions . . . but a persecuted community, just before and during its extermination!'

Traverso didn't stop there. Finkelstein's denunciatory zeal, he observed, was not 'circumscribed and contextualised' but was a 'simplistic, sectarian, polemical and provocative' form of argumentation. His writing 'often seems to parody, in a very unpleasant way, the stereotype of a once-flourishing anti-Semitic literature'. The very title of Finkelstein's book, he pointed out, 'recall[ed] the old anti-Semitic myth of a "Jewish Conspiracy"' noting that the book was welcomed in Berlin by 'an enthusiastic public of nationalists'.

Traverso noted 'the simplistic and unilateral character' of Finkelstein's claim that the 'Holocaust Industry' was a plot to fend off criticism of Israel. Finkelstein had failed to reconstitute the complex 'itinerary of the Judeocide's collective remembrance within American society'. Instead, he had just trashed the very idea of collective memory and substituted 'a conspiratorial vision of history' in order to explain the rising salience of Holocaust remembrance in the culture. In doing so, he had ignored several research paths, each with an impressive literature, that had explained the rising importance of the Holocaust in Western culture in various ways: 'the return of repressed memory', the 'age of the witness', 'the birth of a particularist ethos among American Jews' and a 'generational shift in Germany and Europe'. All were 'unworthy in Finkelstein's eyes', so in lieu of a genuine historical analysis, we find only a gross simplicity verging on a conspiracy theory to account for the increased attention given to the Shoah: 'an alliance between US imperialism and the State of Israel, with the support of American Jewish elites'.

Traverso found repulsive Finkelstein's claim that Holocaust representations in books, poems, plays, paintings and films were nought but 'products of a propaganda machine'. What about the works of 'Andre Schwartz-Barth, Primo Levi, Jean Améry, Ruth Kluger, Imre Ketez and Victor Klemperer'? Traverso demanded to know. He was shocked that Finkelstein 'seems indifferent' to the fact that many expressions of Holocaust memory have been 'a powerful motor for the antifascist, anti-colonialist and antiracist struggles of several generations'. Traverso's summary judgement of Finkelstein's book was damning: a 'caricatural simplification of the historical process'.[3]

Debating Finkelstein

Finkelstein put on a political stand-up routine when I debated him at King's College London about the new antisemitism in March 2015. To a few hundred students, he told a rolling 'gag' about a 2014–2015 YouGov poll of antisemitic attitudes in the United Kingdom. His 'punch line' was that agreement to statements about Jews can't be an indicator of antisemitism if those statements are . . . *true* (laughs invited). For example, Finkelstein told the students that the 17 per cent of people who agreed with the statement 'Jews think they are better than other people' are not antisemitic because Jews *do* think that. Between 'the spectacular secular success of Jews in the Western world, and their theological chosen-ness, most Jews believe in their group's superiority' (Finkelstein and Johnson 2015).

He has told audiences that the 17 per cent who agreed that 'Jews have too much power in the media' are not antisemitic because Jews *are* over-represented in the media and they do use that over-representation for Jewish ends. For example, he claimed it was the over-representation of Jews in Hollywood that leads to the 'media's obsessive focus on the Holocaust' (Finkelstein 2015b). 'My impression is that every third film available for download, even in romantic comedies, seems to be about the Holocaust', he said, to more laughter. He has posed this rhetorical question: 'Who can seriously believe that the pro-Jewish bias of the corporate media has nothing whatever to do with the influential Jewish presence at all levels of it?' (2005:83).

Of the 13 per cent who agreed that 'Jews talk about the Holocaust too much in order to get sympathy', Finkelstein said there must be something wrong with the mental faculties of the 87 per cent who *didn't* agree. To more laughter, he asked the students, 'Doesn't every sane person think that Jews talk too much about the Holocaust?'

Taboos fell like nine pins that night. 'Jews are tapped into the networks of power and privilege', he said, and are 'the richest ethnic group in the United States' and so 'if you marry a Jew, it opens doors.' If some Jews faced a little stigma, *so what*? Such stigma is 'socially inconsequential', he reassured the hall. It is more socially consequential to be 'short, fat, bald or ugly than to be Jewish', he said, to more laughs. 'Look', he added, 'most people carry on in life, bearing these stigmas. It's called life. Get used to it.' Sitting next to Finkelstein that evening, it struck me that he had not mentioned to the students that Jews – not the 'short, fat and ugly' – had been singled out for murder by Islamists only two months earlier in Paris, and in Copenhagen only a month before. When I pointed this out to the students, I thought he looked uncomfortable (Finkelstein and Johnson 2015).

So blasé was Finkelstein that night that a press officer from the Stop the War coalition, not a group known to be friendly to Israel, stood up and objected: 'Hold on, we do need to take antisemitism seriously!'

To sum up, Finkelstein is a simplistic lumper who refuses to make the most elementary analytical distinctions, believing that the concept of new antisemitism hasn't *anything* to do with fighting bigotry – and *everything* to do with stifling criticism of Israel; a polemicist with an ugly and sectarian mode of argument and a prose style that is a parody of a once-flourishing antisemitic literature; a lover of the ad hominem attack which leaves the substance of the question unaddressed, preferring to parade before the readers his collection of 'stupid goys', 'ancient divas', 'dull-witted creeps', 'impressarios', 'hacks', 'Israel-Firsters' and 'antisemitism mongers' who should 'crawl back into their sewers'; a tendentious joker trading in the indirect expressions of hostility or obscenity; a conspiracy theorist who reduces the history of Holocaust memory to the machinations of the Zionist propaganda machine, and contemporary forms of antisemitism to a public relations exercise; a crude reductionist who prefers a caricatural simplification of the historical process to a careful reconstruction of the dynamics of either collective memory or protean hatreds; a man who normalises antisemitism by telling his audiences that most Jews believe in their group's superiority, talk too much about the Holocaust, are over-represented in the media and use that over-representation for Jewish ends, are tapped into the networks of power and privilege, and should stop complaining about antisemitism, as they have not arrived at 'Kristallnacht, let alone Auschwitz'; a man who believes it is too simple to say that accusations of Jewish responsibility for Israeli policy are antisemitic, too simple to say accusations of Jewish power antisemitic, and who thinks that if you want to really touch a Jewish nerve, you should make the analogy with the Nazis, because that's the only thing that resonates with them.

Notes

1 This chapter makes available an extract from 'Denial: Norman Finkelstein and the New Antisemitism', a chapter by Alan Johnson in *Unity and Disunity in Contemporary Antisemitism*, edited by Jonathan Campbell and Lesley Klaff (Academic Studies Press, Boston, 2018). The editors thank Academic Studies Press for permission to publish the extract in *Fathom* in 2018 and again in this collection.
2 I wrote, alarmed, about my 2015 debate with Finkelstein at *The Jewish Chronicle* (Johnson 2015). Finkelstein's mocking response was posted on his blog: ' "These are bad bad times" = "this is good business for stupid goys like me – who, if we weren't getting paid to defend Israel, would have to find a real job" ' (Norman G. Finkelstein Blog, 13 March 2015). In *Mein Kampf*, Hitler used the term 'dumb goyim' to refer to gullible gentiles who, thinking well of the Jews, were manipulated by them. He wrote that 'the Jews again slyly dupe the dumb Goyim.' This antisemitic trope is also found in Tom Paulin's poem *Killed in Crossfire*. As well as using the Nazi analogy ('the Zionist SS'), Paulin's poem depicted those gentiles who were, in his view, taken in by Israeli propaganda as 'dumb goys'. When his poem elicited a critical response, Paulin wrote a second poem disparaging 'the usual cynical Goebbels stuff'. See the brilliant discussion of Paulin's poem in Anthony Julius' *Trials of the Diaspora: A History of Antisemitism in England*, Oxford, Oxford University Press, 2010:236–240.
3 Hailed by the Marxist intellectual historian, Michael Lowy as 'the most gifted historian of his generation', it should be noted that Traverso is a sharp critic of Zionism and the policies of the State of Israel, most recently in his *The End of Jewish Modernity* (2013). His earlier works include *Understanding the Nazi Genocide. Marxism After Auschwitz* (London: Pluto Press, 1991) and *The Marxists and the Jewish Question. The History of a Debate, 1843–1943* (New Jersey: Prometheus Books 1994).

References

Finkelstein, Norman (2000) *The Holocaust Industry: Reflections on the Exploitation of Jewish Suffering*, London: Verso.
Finkelstein, Norman (2005) *Beyond Chutzpah. On the Misuse of Anti-Semitism and the Abuse of History*, Berkeley: University of California Press.
Finkelstein, Norman (2006) 'Kill Arabs, cry antisemitism', *Norman Finkelstein Blog*, 12 September. Available: www.normanfinkelstein.com/kill-arabs-cry-anti-semitism/ (accessed 12 November).

Finkelstein, Norman (2015a) 'Stupid goy', *Norman Finkelstein's Blog*, 13 March. Available: www.normanfinkelstein.com/these-are-bad-bad-times-this-is-good-business-for-stupid-goys-like-me-who-if-we-werent-getting-paid-to-defend-israel-would-have-to-find-a-real-job/ (accessed 21 November 2022).

Finkelstein, Norman (2015b) 'Dr. Norman Finkelstein on "the new antisemitism"', YouTube. Available: www.youtube.com/watch?v=fNLM-5rTFdU (accessed 12 November 2022).

Finkelstein, Norman (2015c) 'Are Penelope Cruz and Javiar Bardem anti-Semites? Is there a new "new anti-Semitism"? Part 4', *The Unz Review: An Alternative Media Selection*, 11 December. Available: www.unz.com/nfinkelstein/are-penelope-cruz-and-javier-bardem-anti-semites/ (accessed 12 November 2022).

Finkelstein, Norman (2016) 'Norman Finkelstein – the new anti-Semitism and the holocaust industry', You Tube. Available: www.youtube.com/watch?v=oPr8GYUK2EE (accessed 12 November 2022).

Finkelstein, Norman and Alan Johnson (2015) *Debate on the New Antisemitism*, London: Kings College (audio and transcript in author's possession).

Hirsh, David (2010) 'Accusations of malicious intent in debates about the Palestine-Israel conflict and about anti-Semitism: The Livingstone formulation, "playing the anti-Semitism card" and contesting the boundaries of antiracist discourse', *transversal* 1. Available: https://research.gold.ac.uk/id/eprint/7144/1/hirsh_transversal_2010.pdf (accessed 12 November 2022).

Johnson, Alan (2015) 'I debated with Norman Finkelstein at king's college. It was dire, and scary', *The Jewish Chronicle*, 12 March. Available: www.thejc.com/comment/opinion/i-debated-with-norman-finkelstein-at-king-s-college-it-was-dire-and-scary-1.65580?reloadTime=1649808000020 (accessed 12 November 2022).

Johnson, Alan (2016) *Antisemitic Anti-Zionism: The Root of Labour's Crisis. A Submission to the Labour Party Inquiry Into Antisemitism and Other Forms of Racism.* Available: www.bicom.org.uk/wp-content/uploads/2016/06/Prof-Alan-Johnson-Chakrabarti-Inquiry-submission-June-2016.pdf (accessed 12 November 2022).

Stern-Weiner, Jamie and Norman Finkelstein (2016) 'American Jewish Scholar behind Labour's "antisemitism" scandal breaks his silence', *openDemocracy*, 3 May.

Storr, Anthony (1989) *Freud: A Very Short Introduction*, Oxford: Oxford University Press.

Traverso, Enzo (2003) 'Uses and misuses of memory: Notes on Peter Novick and Norman Finkelstein', *Historical Materialism*, 11 (2): 215–225.

12

'TOXIC GIFTS'

Israel and the Anti-Zionist Left. An Interview With Susie Linfield

Susie Linfield

Delusions

Alan Johnson: *I have personally witnessed, again and again, nonsense about Zionism, Israel and the conflict being passed off as wisdom by intellectuals of the left.[1] I have seen Jacqueline Rose, repeating Arendt, tell an audience that the Zionist movement could have had a harmonious bi-national state in Palestine in the 1940s but refused to pick up the prize that was lying at its feet. I have debated Norman Finkelstein and heard him tell 300 students that 'Hamas does not have rockets' and watched them applaud. When I tell them a truth, that Hamas rockets reached the outskirts of Tel Aviv in the last conflict, they laugh. Your book reveals one of the roots of this phenomenon to be the left's 'calamitous obliviousness' to reality and its 'treacherous readiness to substitute ideology, wishful thinking, or sheer fantasy' in its place. You argue all this 'cannot lead us to an understanding of the past and therefore to what is either achievable or just in the future'. How do you explain this abandonment of the reality principle by the left?*

Susie Linfield: I am somewhat bewildered by it, in all honesty. I'm not sure I have a full explanation – though it's not entirely new. For a long time the left denied what was going on in the Soviet Union – although at least there were better reasons for that, especially during the war years when the Soviet Union was fighting Hitler and was the bulwark against fascism. But there was a denial of

DOI: 10.4324/9781003322320-14

the show-trials, the politically-caused famines, and the Gulag. I think it was the desperate wish for the revolution to succeed and a desperate wish for utopia on earth.

In terms of Israel: in the 1947–1948 period you have Azzam Bey, the head of the Arab League, promising 'a war of extermination' against the Yishuv – yet Hannah Arendt is busy saying the Jews should try for a something akin to a bi-national state (she was not precisely a bi-nationalist, but close enough). She even said this entity should be part of the British Commonwealth, although that empire was starting to collapse: the Indians had begun the 'Quit India' campaign. She was not only oblivious to what was going on in Palestine, but also to what was going on in the colonial world. Not wanting to be part of the British commonwealth was probably the only thing that Arabs and Jews in Palestine agreed on! It is unclear to me where she was getting her information from. As far as I can tell, she only spoke to the German Jewish intellectuals, but even they had rejected the bi-national idea by then because, as one early proponent, her friend Gershom Scholem, reluctantly observed, the Arabs had *rejected every single initiative* put forward by the Jews for bilateralism.

Wishful thinking on the left is combined with a Manichaean world view: extreme animus against Israelis, identified as the evil white colonists, combined with an idealisation of the Palestinians, cast as the oppressed non-white revolutionaries. But what follows from any kind of Manichaean world is falsity, bad politics, and bad political analysis, because the world itself isn't actually Manichaean. You can only preserve that structure by regularly buttressing it with great dollops of delusion. I think that's the 'theoretical' root of the left's denial of reality.

Even brilliant thinkers abandoned the reality principle. Arendt abandoned it in 1947–1948. Isaac Deutscher, Maxime Rodinson, and even I.F. Stone to some degree, professed to believe that the Arab world was about to revive itself in some kind of democratic progressive direction, when in fact the exact opposite was happening before their eyes. The rise and consolidation of the Saddams, the Assads and the Gaddafis was actually happening, the Arab world was going backwards to brutal dictatorship, its liberalising tendencies were being extinguished. Yet these people were too often unwilling to look and to see – though I would add that Rodinson, a scholar of the Arab world, did sometimes speak truth to power.

Part of that, frankly, was that it was very hard to get into some of these Arab countries, and someone like Deutscher – and I don't criticise him for this – was much more interested in western political movements than in the Arab world. It was the same with I.F. Stone. But that lack of knowledge, combined with a Manichaean world view and a desperate hope that the conflict could be resolved, has resulted in layer upon layer of fallacious, and therefore useless political analysis.

I also think a kind of narcissism is involved in all this political fantasising. When I read Jacqueline Rose writing about how this great bi-national opportunity was missed by the Zionists, I think she is projecting her own wishes and ideas onto people for whom they had absolutely no bearing and about whom she seems to know nothing. Western intellectuals tend to do this a lot and it is a kind of narcissism: 'I think something, therefore everyone else must'. Weirdly, although the people who do this think of themselves as anti-imperialist, this is itself a form of intellectual imperialism. I think that is true of Arendt too. She assumes that Hannah Arendt and Palestinian peasants must have the same ideas. Well, they didn't. Palestinian peasants did not want the same things that Hannah Arendt wanted. And there are many Palestinians in the West Bank and Gaza who do not, I'm pretty sure, share Jacqueline Rose's worldview: about Israel, or anything else. It's a kind of arrogance.

Non-Solutions

Alan Johnson: And what of the far-left proposal for a 'one-state solution'?

Susie Linfield: I went to a conference years ago and heard an anti-Zionist, Jewish Israeli put forward the 'one-state solution' idea. I approached him afterwards – this was before I wrote the book – and I asked him how he envisioned this one state coming about. Would Hamas suicide bombers be integrated in the IDF, I asked? What kind of education system would this new state have, because Israel and Palestine have very different education systems? What kind of foreign policy would it have? Would it become part of the Arab League? What would be the status of women, and their rights? What about gay rights? I posed a whole series of questions to him. He just shrugged and said 'yeah, ok, but it's a good *idea*'.

Although I'm rather despairing regarding the prospects of the two-state solution, I find the one-state prospect even more unrealistic. And if there ever is a one-state, it will not be the democratic state that leftists envisage. Again, the proposal is based on a refusal of the reality principle. One state will either be the one that the far right in Israel envisions – with no, or at least no equal, rights for Palestinians; or it will be the state that some Palestinian irredentists envision: an authoritarian state with Jews as a beleaguered minority, if many remain at all. Neither version would be secular, or bi-national, or democratic. Why would any leftist support this?

One state is sometimes put forth by leftists as the only 'just' solution for the violence and dispossession of the past. But justice is something that human beings make, and everything that human beings make is imperfect. Justice cannot vindicate all these years of suffering, on either side – because there is no vindication of suffering. I hate it when people say Israel vindicates the Holocaust. Nothing vindicates anything. The only thing that you can do is look to the future for something that is humanly possible and has enough justice upon which to build something real, something sturdy. That's what I am really arguing for in the book.[2]

People are not interchangeable. You cannot just smush people together, irrespective of history and culture, and assume they're going to meld into a peaceful, democratic and unified whole. Look at the breakup of Yugoslavia. Look at Lebanon. With Israel and Palestine, I do not believe that you can take two people who have murdered each other's children for a hundred years and expect them to combine into a peaceful democratic nation. I also believe very strongly that there should be one small place in the world with full, inalienable rights for all citizens but where the Jewish people have sovereignty, where Hebrew is the language, where Jewish history is taught, where a Hebrew culture can be cultivated, and where Jews can defend themselves when threatened. Several thousand years of Jewish history taught us the necessity of that. And given the rising antisemitism in the world, that is not an outmoded need.

Toxic Solidarities

Alan Johnson: *You claim that the left has engaged in a kind of political malpractice as a consequence of refusing to face the 'harsh, complicated realities' of the conflict. I think one form of this political malpractice is that much left-wing solidarity, being 'glib and uncritical', can sometimes be what you have called a 'toxic gift'. Albert Memmi believed the solidarity of the left could be bad for the colonised. Fred Halliday reflected on the terrible 'fate of solidarity' in our times. Can you talk a little about what you think has gone wrong with the idea of solidarity with the Palestinians?*

Susie Linfield: Well, it's *uncritical* solidarity – the writing of a blank check – that has been the problem. When you read the histories of the Palestinian movement, you quickly discover that there are some Arab historians who are very critical of the leadership of the Palestinian movement. (I refer to *real* historians, not to anti-Zionist propagandists.) One of the things that frankly surprised me in my research was to realise just how catastrophic that leadership has been. A small cadre of PLO militia believed for decades that they were going to destroy Israel by physical force, which was preposterous. They also believed, at various times, that they could overthrow the Jordanian state, radically change the politics of Lebanon to their liking, and foment a worldwide or at least a pan-Arab revolution. And in all this unbelievable grandiosity they were encouraged by the international left.

I think that was a terrible thing to do to the Palestinians. It was a complete misunderstanding, morally and politically, of the reality. The left's support for the delusions of the Palestinian movement has greatly contributed to the catastrophic situation of the Palestinians today. Hamas is still promising the Palestinians, against all evidence, that the armed struggle will defeat the evil Zionist entity. And again, we see the abandonment of the reality principle in favour of theoretical schemas. The idea that Israel was a fragile colonial implant, which could be easily toppled by the 'anti-imperialist armed struggle', had a tenacious hold, and in some places still does. That's what I meant by a toxic gift: being in uncritical solidarity with programmes that are morally revolting and politically unviable. Though there were some leftists, including Rodinson, the French journalist Alain Gresh, and the Pakistani activist Eqbal Ahmad – all strong supporters of the Palestinians – who begged the PLO leadership to adopt a non-exterminationist program that would appeal to ordinary Israelis.

Inverted Values

Alan Johnson: *By 2015, Fred Halliday was pointing out that parts of the left were revelling in the slaughter of civilian UN officials in Iraq, condoning the killing of children in Israel, and were willing to sacrifice the population of Lebanon to the 'national resistance' movement Hezbollah. Jeremy Corbyn even claimed that Hamas and Hezbollah were 'leading forces for peace and social justice in the region'. The fascistic is being misread as progressive by parts of the left.*

Susie Linfield: Yes, parts of the left, either through ignorance or maybe by just not caring, either refuses to criticise, or even 'critically' supports, some of the most grotesque regimes in the world under the aegis of 'solidarity' with 'the oppressed'. Of course, the oppressed in Zimbabwe or Syria were and are being oppressed by their own regimes, not by western colonialists, but that does not compute. Only the West can be opposed; to do otherwise is to give succour to 'imperialism'. Of course, there *are* imperialist interventionists in Syria: that is, Russia and Iran. Unsurprisingly, Iran is now aiding Russia in its attempt to crush Ukraine: another country, like Israel, that presumably has no 'right' to exist.

Fred Halliday began to elaborate a different approach. He said that we must look at the real lives of the people on the ground, not at the grandiose 'anti-imperialist' rhetoric of these dictatorships. Forget what the regime claims to be, and look hard at what it does, and at the human rights of the people living under it.

Take the Syrian war. You can easily find articles by Syrian leftists who are enraged at those parts of the western left that are, in effect, pro-Assad, and who view Assad as part of the axis of resistance to 'imperialism' (including, or maybe especially, to Israel) or as a secular bulwark against terrorism. These writers and activists – I think especially of Yassin al-Haj Saleh, a communist – have suffered enormously at the hands of this 'anti-imperialist' dictatorship and are absolutely furious: they say the left is guilty of rationalising the actions of a fascist butcher.

Traditionally, the left was opposed to terrorism. (Andre Malraux's *The Conquerors*, set in China in the 1920s, is a good illustration of this.) Yes, you had the Russian movements who assassinated the Tsar and some government officials, but planting a bomb in the middle of Saint Petersburg to kill civilians would have been incomprehensible to them – much less to the Bolsheviks. The classical Marxist left was opposed to terrorism, correctly arguing that it pushes the masses of people to the right and contradicts the principle of mass self-emancipation.

The real change on the left comes with the Algerian revolution. What was hitherto inconceivable – that the left would support, or excuse, or fail to condemn the killing of unarmed civilians – now becomes extremely conceivable, because the terrorism is justified as 'anti-colonialist' and the right of Western socialists to condemn the actions of such movements is now denied. In other words: if the movement's aims are just, everything it does must also be. And with the emergence of the Palestinian movement, which used terrorism as its *main* form of political activity for several decades, the left collapses and justifies terrorism, even romanticises it. To the point where some parts of the left substituted terrorism for actual political organising.

The great irony, and tragedy, in all this is that suicide bombings, which were deemed by some to be 'legitimate' if the targets were Israelis, have now spread throughout the Arab and Muslim world, and beyond: Think of Iraq, Syria, Somalia, Afghanistan. Pakistan. The list goes on, as does the suffering.

Notes

1 This chapter was first published in expanded form in *Fathom* in 2019. The excerpt published here was updated by Linfield in 2022. The full interview, 'Zionism and the Left: An interview with Susie Linfield', can be read at the *Fathom* website.
2 Susie Linfield (2019) *The Lion's Den: Zionism and the Left from Hannah Arendt to Noam Chomsky*, New Haven: Yale University Press.

PART 3

The Soviet Roots of Contemporary Left Antisemitism

13

SOVIET ANTI-ZIONISM AND CONTEMPORARY LEFT ANTISEMITISM

Izabella Tabarovsky

Introduction

In 1985, the KGB-supervised Anti-Zionist Committee of the Soviet Public, known by its Russian acronym as AKSO, issued a brochure, *Criminal Alliance of Zionism and Nazism*.[1] The brochure reported on a press conference that the Committee had held some months earlier. The site for the press conference, the press centre of the Soviet Ministry of Foreign Affairs, indicated the official blessing of the messages AKSO had to deliver. The brochure was translated into English and distributed abroad by Novosti Press Agency, a news service and an important arm of Soviet foreign propaganda.

A propagandistic document reporting on a propagandistic event, the brochure painted a harrowing picture of Zionism. Senior members of the AKSO, most of whom were prominent Soviet Jews (an intentional choice on the part of the KGB, meant to deflect accusations of antisemitism) claimed that they had irrefutable proof of Zionist co-operation with the Nazis. They described Zionists as facilitators of Nazi expansionism, accused them of falsely inflating the significance of antisemitism and Jewish victimhood in World War II, and claimed that the 1930s agreement that permitted the transfer of 60,000 German Jews to Palestine had made it 'easier for the Nazis to unleash World War Two'. They claimed that Zionists had colluded 'in the genocide against the "Slavs, Jews and some other peoples of Europe"'. Speakers concluded by rejecting, in advance, any attempts by the 'pro-Zionist press' to represent the committee's assertions as antisemitic, disassociated Zionists from Jews and promised that Zionism would never succeed in repudiating the 'historical reality' of cooperation between the Zionists and the Nazis.

DOI: 10.4324/9781003322320-16

The brochure might have read as a shocking smear that distorted history had it not been an integral part of a massive Soviet anti-Zionist campaign that entered a particularly active stage in 1967 (see Gansinger 2016 for an analysis of the anti-Zionist campaign in Communist Poland). Its language reflects its epoch – one marked by Cold War tensions, propagandistic jargon that permeated all aspects of Soviet public life, and virulent demonisation of Israel and Zionism. Alleged Zionist–Nazi collaboration and false equivalence between the two were among the campaign's centrepieces.

Designed by the KGB and overseen by chief Communist Party ideologues, the campaign had achieved numerous successes. For a significant portion of domestic and some foreign audiences, it succeeded at emptying Zionism of its meaning as a national liberation movement of the Jewish people and associating it instead with racism, Fascism, Nazism, genocide, imperialism, colonialism, militarism and apartheid. It contributed to the adoption of the notorious 1975 UN General Assembly Resolution 3379, which held Zionism to be a form of racism and paved the way for the demonisation of Israel within that organisation.

In the course of the campaign, hundreds of anti-Zionist and anti-Israel books and thousands of articles were published in the USSR, with millions of copies entering circulation in the country. Many were translated into foreign languages – English, French, German, Spanish, Arabic and numerous others. In 1970 alone, the comparison between alleged Zionist and Nazi racism – just one of the campaign's numerous memes – merited 96 mentions (Pinkus 1989:256). Demonisation of Zionism continued in films, lectures and radio broadcasts. Anti-Zionist cartoons, many of an obvious antisemitic nature, were a regular feature of Soviet publications.

The campaign used the significant Soviet broadcasting and publishing capacity abroad, as well as front organisations and friendly communist and other radical left organisations in the West and third-world countries to transmit its messages to foreign audiences. The US State Department viewed the AKSO committee as a tool in the Soviet arsenal of 'active measures' – 'covert or deceptive operations conducted in support of Soviet foreign policy'.

The antisemitic nature of this campaign was appalling. The main authors contributing content – many of whom had direct links with the KGB and top party leadership – relied heavily on antisemitic tropes borrowed directly from the *Protocols of the Elders of Zion*. Some in the group were closet admirers of Hitler and Nazism and used *Mein Kampf* as both a source of 'information' about Zionism and inspiration for their own interpretations.

The Soviets vehemently rejected accusations of antisemitism, arguing that they were 'Zionist tricks' and 'nefarious imperialist scheming'. But some 2.6 million Soviet Jews knew better. In 1976, during one of the peaks of the campaign, the Soviet Jewish activist Natan Sharansky said that he sensed 'the smell of pogrom' in the air.

The virulently antisemitic anti-Zionism that was so central to the late Soviet Union's propaganda seems to have faded from the West's collective memory. Yet, in a strange case of déjà vu for those who, like myself, have lived through the late Soviet anti-Zionist campaign or have studied it in detail, the same memes and ideas that were in use then continue to circulate in contemporary far-left anti-Zionist circles.

Political cartoons equating Israel with Nazi Germany that might as well have been lifted from Soviet newspapers have appeared on mainstream progressive blogs (Levick 2010). One-time London Labour mayor Ken Livingstone has claimed that 'Hitler was supporting Zionism before he went mad and ended up killing six million Jews.' Lenni Brenner's 1983 anti-Zionist book *Zionism in the Age of the Dictators* is built around a supposed Nazi-Zionist equivalency. References to Zionism and Israel as racist, imperialist, colonial, genocidal and apartheid abound in contemporary far-left discourse. The anti-Zionist discourse of the UK Labour Party, which in the Corbyn era led to a crisis over antisemitism, is replete with the same memes.

The similarity begs the question of the ideological origins of this discourse. Just as it is important to understand the ideological heritage of the far-right's antisemitic rhetoric, it is important to wrap our heads around the origins of the far-left's anti-Zionist discourse, particularly where it intersects with antisemitism. We can begin by re-examining what historian Jeffrey Herf calls 'the toxic ideological brew' that the communist anti-Zionist and anti-Israel campaigns left behind (Herf 2016:461).

'International Zionism' as a worldwide conspiracy to destroy socialism and spread imperialism

The idea of Zionism as a hostile ideology began to solidify in the post-World War II USSR in the late 1940s, once it became clear that Israel was aligning itself with the 'imperialist camp' rather than the Soviet Union. Allegations of Zionist conspiracy became a prominent feature of Stalinist purge trials. The Slánský Trial in Czechoslovakia featured the idea of 'international Zionism' as a worldwide conspiracy aiming to destroy socialism. Manufactured by the Soviet secret services, the trial tied together Zionism, Israel, Jewish leaders and American imperialism, turning 'Zionism' and 'Zionist' into dangerous labels that could be used against one's political enemies. The trial opened the door to vicious antisemitism (Jewish Telegraphic Agency 1952).

Over the following decade, the Soviet press continued a broad anti-Israel campaign. It received a boost with the trial of Adolf Eichmann in Jerusalem. The Soviets were determined to undermine the legitimacy of the trial, whose emphasis on the Holocaust challenged their concept of Slavic victimhood in World War II. One way to do so was to attack Israel's diplomatic relationship with West Germany, which the Soviets painted as a 'fascist' heir of Nazi Germany.

The 'obvious' conclusion was that Zionism was a natural bedfellow of fascists and Nazis. Drawing this parallel allowed the Soviets to tap into a visceral sentiment. For the Soviet people, whose sacrifice in World War II was enormous, Fascism and Nazism represented the greatest evil imaginable. By equating Zionism with these two, Soviet propaganda architects sought to create a visceral reaction – of a kind that didn't depend on fact but on a deep feeling.

By the 1960s, the Soviets' anti-Zionist propaganda arsenal widened courtesy of a book, *Judaism without Embellishments* by Trofim Kichko. A deeply antisemitic tract featuring Der Sturmer-like cartoons, it proposed that Judaism, with its concept of Jews as a chosen people, was an inherently racist religion and linked to American imperialism and Israeli colonialism. One of the cartoons showed a stereotypical Jewish capitalist licking a boot with a swastika painted on it (Jews in Eastern Europe Special Issue 1964).

The book initially generated a storm of indignation, including from foreign leftist groups, and the Soviets disavowed it – but only temporarily (Decter 1964). In the following years, Kichko became one of the key authors contributing to a huge volume of Soviet anti-Zionist propaganda.

Besides the ongoing advancement of the alleged Nazi-Zionist connection, his book introduced an idea that Soviet propagandists would use repeatedly in the coming decades: that Zionism was an outgrowth of Judaism and, as such, asserted Jewish racial superiority. The Soviets would use this line repeatedly over the years, including at the UN, as they worked towards the adoption of the 'Zionism Is Racism' resolution.

The turning point: the Six-Day War of 1967

It was the Arab–Israeli war of 1967, however, that really intensified Soviet anti-Zionist campaigning. For Moscow, which had supported the Arab forces, the war was a crushing defeat, handing a clear ideological victory to the 'imperialist' camp. At home, Israel's victory served as the catalyst for a national awakening among Soviet Jews. All of a sudden, the old enemy – international Zionism and its Jewish fifth column at home – seemed to be rearing its head. A new propaganda tool was needed to help shape public opinion at home and abroad.

On 7 August 1967, an article titled 'What Is Zionism?' appeared simultaneously in several Soviet publications. Its author, Yuri Ivanov, an employee of the KGB and the Central Committee apparatus, would go on to become one of the leading Soviet anti-Zionist writers. He took his cue from age-old tropes of Jewish conspiracy and influence: he presented Zionism as a centrally controlled international system that gripped the entirety of global politics, finance and the media, had unlimited resources, and sought to establish monopolistic control over the entire world (Gjerde 2018).

Similar articles followed, including one by Kichko, now back in favour. In 1968, he produced a new book, *Judaism and Zionism* which, building on his original ideas, blamed Judaism for the 'crimes' of Israeli 'aggressors'. 'There is a direct connection between the morality of Judaism and the actions of the Israeli Zionists', wrote Kichko. 'Weren't the actions of the Israeli extremists during their latest aggression against the Arab countries in keeping with the Torah?'

Kichko's book was one of many Soviet publications that attempted to show that the evils of Zionism could be traced back to Judaism, which had always been the bête noir of the Soviet struggle against religion and was persecuted with particular harshness. Even as a few synagogues continued to function into the 1970s and 1980s, the study of Hebrew was prohibited, and so was the training of the next generation of clergy, indicating that the Soviet leadership had clearly marked Judaism for extinction. The problem was that by painting every aspect of Jewish religion and tradition in black, Soviet claims that they were not antisemitic but simply anti-Zionist were rendered meaningless.

Next in the line of prominent Soviet anti-Zionist texts came Ivanov's *Caution: Zionism!* The state-owned press greeted this 1969 book with rave reviews. The initial 70,000 print run was followed by three additional reprintings. In the early 1970s, hundreds of thousands of copies were put into circulation. The book was translated into 16 languages and became one of Soviet anti-Zionism's foundational texts. It described Zionists as representative of colonialist-imperialist powers, hostile towards the working people of Palestine and cultivating an insatiable thirst for power. It portrayed Judaism as the world's most inhuman religion, one that had spawned the world's most vicious nationalism. The supposed connection between Zionism and Fascism received detailed treatment, as did the idea that 'Israeli militarism and West German neo-Nazism are fed from the same source.'

Like Kichko before him, Ivanov devoted ample space to detailing Judaism's idea of Jews as a 'chosen people', which, he aimed to show, demonstrated the supposedly racist underpinnings of Zionism. He also took time to discredit the idea of a single Jewish nation, calling the idea a Zionist invention that was 'false and reactionary in content'. This notion, he claimed, had prevented Jews from comfortably assimilating into their host nations, promoted a ghetto mentality, kept the Jews separate and consequently provoked antisemitism.

Some of these ideas could be traced back to the early Bolshevik discourse on the Jewish question, but in the new environment, they had a new purpose. With Ivanov's book, the Soviet ideologists were sending their Jewish citizens a clear message: assimilate or be viewed as adherents of the most racist, reactionary, and genocidal religion and ideology on the planet – and suffer the consequences.

The book came out at a crucial time. The Six-Day War led to a national awakening among Soviet Jews. Growing awareness of the tragedy of the Holocaust (the Soviets had sought to internally suppress information about the Jewish aspects of Hitler's war) was strengthening Soviet Jewry's Jewish identity. As the Soviet regime's antisemitic rhetoric intensified, more Soviet Jews began to reach out to the United States and Israel for help. Arrests and trials on charges of Zionist activity began (New York Times 1971). In 1970, a group of 16 refuseniks attempted to hijack an empty plane to fly it to freedom. They were arrested before they even got to the plane. The harsh sentences that the group received – including two death sentences, later commuted as a result of an international outcry – drew attention abroad to their plight. The campaign for Soviet Jewry began to gather steam in the West.

Inside the country, the increasingly antisemitic anti-Zionist campaign continued unabated. Ivanov and Kichko were among a dozen or so primary anti-Zionist ideologues who throughout the campaign's 20-year span produced some 50 books, with nine million copies in circulation. Historian Andreas Umland has shown how these texts propagated 'paranoid, conspiratorial anti-Zionism mixed with antisemitic, xenophobic, and ultra-nationalist messages, combined with anti-capitalist and anti-Western rhetoric'. Titles included *Fascism under a Blue Star*, which compared Zionism to Fascism; *De-Zionization* (translated into Arabic and published in Syria in 1979 on Hafez al-Assad's direction); and *Zionism and Apartheid*, a deeply antisemitic tractate whose author was a fan of Nazi ideology and borrowed directly from *Mein Kampf* for his writings (Umland 1999).

Soviet Jewry and the Nazi analogy

In 1983, two new books from the same genre received international attention thanks to the US Jewish organisations engaged in the campaign for Soviet Jewry. One was called *On the Course of Aggression and Fascism*. It detailed Zionism's alleged 'criminal alliance with the Fascists' and blamed the Zionists for the extermination of non-Zionist Jews during the Holocaust. The second, titled *The Class Essence of Zionism*, declared Jews a 'fifth column in any country' (Doder 1983). The two books were written by Lev Korneev, a notorious antisemite, and were so egregious they prompted an unexpected act of personal protest by a non-Jewish Soviet scholar. In the oppressive climate of the early 1980s USSR, it's doubtful if anyone followed in his footsteps (Jewish Telegraphic Agency 1983).

Each publication spawned endless reviews and 'analytical pieces' aimed at different audiences, including the military, party functionaries, trade unions and youth. The Academy played an important role in lending legitimacy to the effort through its 'scholarly' articles. Reporting on this output, the *Washington Post* observed in 1979: 'Soviet bureaucrats vehemently reject suggestions that "anti-Zionism" means "anti-Semitism." But to many Soviet Jews, it is a distinction without a difference.'

The campaign did not rely on printed word alone. The Soviets produced several documentaries to support the campaign. One was called *The*

Concealed and the Apparent: Goals and Actions of the Zionists. With its manipulation of historical footage, deeply antisemitic imagery and parallels between Zionism and Nazism, it was deemed to be so inflammatory that viewings were limited to selected audiences. Although it was never released to the broader public, the film serves as a stark visual testimony to the deep connections between Soviet-style anti-Zionism and antisemitism.

What drove this campaign was the Soviets' apparent belief that a vast Zionist conspiracy did in fact exist, and that this campaign aimed at undermining the Soviet Union and socialism itself. The more the West criticised the Soviets' human rights record and treatment of its Jewish minority, and the more Soviet Jewry expressed a demand to emigrate, the more the authorities felt confirmed in their belief, and the more the campaign intensified.

The authorities engaged numerous resources to discredit the very idea of emigration. They claimed that those who had done so experienced nothing but misery abroad and were begging to come back. For foreign audiences, the message was that Soviet discrimination against their Jewish citizens was fiction, and that Soviet Jews had no desire to leave their motherland. Geared at English-speaking foreign audiences in particular were English-language booklets, published by the same Novosti Publishing House that distributed other Soviet anti-Zionist propaganda abroad. The titles spoke for themselves: *Soviet Jews: Fact and Fiction*; *The Deceived Testify: Concerning the Plight of Immigrants in Israel*; and *Deceived by Zionism*.

By the mid-1970s, the KGB felt the Zionist threat was so acute that it warranted establishing a special department to focus specifically on Zionism. American Jewish organisations were viewed as a particularly important link in the presumed anti-Soviet Zionist conspiracy. The Soviets believed the international movement for Soviet Jewry to be a cynical manipulation manufactured from the top in order to give a black eye to the Soviet image abroad and meddle in the country's domestic affairs. Countless articles were devoted to discrediting it. According to Israeli investigative journalist Ronen Bergman, the Soviet secret services targeted some of the organisations involved in the movement by discrediting them and attempting to sow discord and confusion (Bergman 2016).

By the early 1980s, as US–Soviet relations were hitting a new low, and emigration demands were surging, the newly created Anti-Zionist Committee of the Soviet Public produced brochures and delivered press conferences on the evils of Israel and Zionism, including for foreign audiences. In a 1983 *Pravda* article announcing the launch of the Committee, its members declared Zionism to be a concentration of 'extreme nationalism, chauvinism, and racial intolerance, justification of territorial seizure and annexation, armed adventurism, a cult of political arbitrariness and impunity, demagogy and ideological sabotage, sordid maneuvers and perfidy' (Korey 2013:89). A 1985 TASS broadcast commenting on one of the committee's

English-language brochures announced: 'Zionist leaders are responsible for the deaths of thousands of Jews annihilated by the Nazis. It is precisely the Zionists who assisted the Nazi butchers by helping them to make up the lists of the doomed inmates of ghettoes, escorting the latter to the places of extermination and convinced them to resign to the butchers' (Korey 2013:111).

Global political warfare

The Soviets didn't limit themselves to fighting Zionism within their borders. An enemy such as this one had to be fought on multiple fronts, including through information warfare abroad. At their disposal was a powerful state-owned media apparatus whose goal was to 'spread the truth about the USSR in all the continents' (Hazan 2017:49). It published numerous newspapers and magazines with a combined circulation of tens of millions of copies per year in English, German, Spanish, Hindi, French, Arabic and other languages. Radio Moscow broadcast more than 1,000 hours per week, in 80 languages, to Europe, the Middle East, North and sub-Saharan Africa, and the Americas. The Soviet Union's main foreign broadcasting arm and primary carrier of foreign propaganda, the Novosti Press Agency, worked in over 110 countries. One of its tasks was to build relations with the local press (Hazan 2017:31, 34–61). Numerous friendship societies were established by the Soviets abroad as well as front organisations designed to promote Soviet international interests, mobilise sympathisers and offer propaganda support (Hazan 2017:103–114).

The Soviet relationships with the local media meant that they could rely on these outlets, whenever necessary, to inject prefabricated items of a propagandistic or disinformation nature into the global news stream. Novosti could then pick these up and disseminate them throughout their network (Hazan 2017:49). It was in this way that the Soviets scored one of their biggest Cold War disinformation successes: getting the CBS television anchor Dan Rather to broadcast to millions of viewers a version of a KGB-fabricated story of American scientists inventing the AIDS virus to kill African Americans and gay people.

The Soviets structured their foreign anti-Zionist messaging in accordance with their specific foreign policy priorities for that country or audience. 'Zionism played a role of a bugaboo', Israeli historian Nati Cantorovich told me, 'In Africa it was about South African apartheid and Zionism. In Latin America it was about American imperialism and Zionism. In Asia, it was Japanese revanchism and Zionism.'

In 1970, for example, *Soviet Weekly*, a Soviet English-language outlet that targeted the United Kingdom, reprinted, in four consecutive issues, an article that defined Zionism as 'not so much the Jewish nationalist movement it used to be but an organic part of the international – primarily American –

imperialist machinery for the carrying out of neocolonialist policies and ideological subversion' (Hazan 2017:150). In 1977, the same publication printed a piece titled 'Why We Condemn Zionism', which proclaimed Zionism to be a racist doctrine and characterised Israelis as 'worthy heirs to Hitler's National-Socialism' (Wistrich 2012:437). Several African programmes, broadcast on the same day in 1973 in English, French and Portuguese, claimed that Zionism had 'an ideological affinity with South African racism' and was 'part of the global strategy of imperialism aimed against the liberation movements' (Hazan 2017:152).

Numerous Soviet anti-Zionist books were translated and distributed abroad. According to Bergman, the 1979 Soviet anti-Zionist tractate titled *The White Book* was distributed to a variety of audiences in 32 countries, including not only US and Canadian Communist Party leaders but also 'parliament members, ministers and social activists from different countries, libraries, as well as representatives of international organisations, libraries, and higher education institutions' (Bergman 2016). Among the English-language propaganda brochures published by Novosti were *Zionism: Instrument of Imperialist Reaction, Soviet Opinion on Events in the Middle East and the Adventures of International Zionism*, and *Anti-Sovietism – Profession of Zionists, Zionism Counts on Terror* and others.

Senior members of the Anti-Zionist Committee of the Soviet Public regularly published articles in the foreign press and addressed foreign audiences. The head of the committee, General David Dragunsky, took part in Soviet Hebrew-language broadcasts directed at Israel. In October 1983, he appeared on Radio Damascus to boast of the Committee's successes and to claim that its anti-Zionist work was receiving broad support from outside the USSR, including from Israel. He assured audiences of the Committee's close relationship with the Arab world and especially Syria. Syria was one of the most militantly anti-Zionist states in the Middle East, and the Soviet-Syrian friendship treaty of 1980 specifically named Zionism a common enemy. In conveying his anti-Zionist message to Syrian audiences, Dragunsky was lending a helping hand to Soviet foreign policy objectives vis-à-vis the country (Korey 1989:35).

Arab-language anti-Zionist literature was an important part of Soviet propaganda directed at the Middle East. According to Bergman (2014), it served as source material for Mahmoud Abbas's 1982 Ph.D. dissertation. In the early 1980s, Abbas was enrolled at Moscow's Patrice Lumumba University, a school established to train future Third World elites in Marxism-Leninism and prepare them to become pro-Soviet influencers (Hazan 2017:87–88). He defended his dissertation at Moscow's Institute of Oriental Studies – an important institution within the Academy of Sciences, which regularly churned out 'scholarly' works demonising Zionism and Israel. During Abbas's tenure, the Institute was headed by Yevgeny Primakov, an Arabist with lifelong connections to Soviet intelligence in the Middle East, who would eventually head the Soviet foreign intelligence agency SVR. That Primakov personally appointed Abbas's dissertation advisor shows the importance that the Soviet foreign policy and intelligence establishments attached to the educational output of this already prominent Palestinian leader.

Abbas's dissertation was published as a book in 2011 in Arabic under the title *The Other Side: The Secret Relationship between Nazism and Zionism*. Several passages from the book reproduced in Bergman's 2014 article replicate some of the mainstays of the Soviet anti-Zionist campaign, including those concerning the alleged Zionist collaboration with the Nazis during the Holocaust and casting doubt on the number of Holocaust victims.

A particularly curious piece of historical falsification that made it into Abbas's book concerned Adolf Eichmann's capture by the Mossad. According to Bergman, Abbas wrote that the Mossad abducted Eichmann in order to prevent the high-ranking Nazi from revealing the secret of Zionists' role in the Final Solution. Strikingly, the very same piece of fabrication was employed by a member of the Anti-Zionist Committee of the Soviet Public at a press conference in Moscow in June 1983. At the event, Yuri Kolesnikov, author of numerous works demonising Zionism and Israel, claimed that during the war the Zionists were 'in league with the Gestapo and SS' and that the Israelis executed Eichmann years later 'to prevent the "sacred secrets" of this collaboration from becoming public'. The repetition of the same provocation by these two individuals, who shared a connection to Soviet propaganda and intelligence structures, shows that they were drawing on the same source for their anti-Zionist claims.

The toxic legacies of Soviet antisemitic anti-Zionism

We have yet to fully understand how much Soviet anti-Zionist propaganda has influenced the world. In those individual instances where this influence is evident, it is apparent just how negatively it impacted the lives of Jews around the globe. One instance of such influence is documented in Dave Rich's *The Left's Jewish Problem: Jeremy Corbyn, Israel and Anti-Semitism*. He details how the adoption of the 'Zionism Is Racism' resolution by the UN – an effort the Soviets spent a decade promoting – opened the door for British Students' Unions to campaign to restrict the activities and funding of Jewish societies on campuses or even ban them. The logic was simple: the UN has ascertained that Zionism is racism; Jewish societies declare their support for Israel; ergo Jewish societies are racist and cannot be tolerated on campus. British Student Unions 'mostly did this for honorable anti-racist reasons, but in doing so they discovered something disturbing', writes Rich. 'When you use the "Zionism is racism" idea as the basis for practical politics, you can end up with an antisemitic campaign' (Rich 2016).

In July 1990, less than a year before the USSR fell apart, *Pravda* published an editorial admitting to the wrongs of the anti-Zionist campaign of the previous quarter century. 'Considerable damage was done by a group of authors who, while pretending to fight Zionism, began to resurrect many notions of the antisemitic propaganda of the Black Hundreds and of fascist origin', it read. 'Hiding under Marxist phraseology, they came out with coarse attacks on Jewish culture, on Judaism and on Jews in general.' But the damage inflicted by the two decades of the campaign could not be undone with a single editorial. A 1990 Soviet poll showed that a significant percentage of Soviet citizens thought that Zionism was 'the policy of establishing the world supremacy of Jews' and an 'ideology used to justify Israeli aggression in the Middle East'.

Among the organisations that had risen to prominence as perestroika lifted controls over civil society were the virulently anti-Semitic Pamyat (Memory) and Otechestvo (Homeland), which blended fascist and neo-Nazi ideas with a form of Russian ethnic ultranationalism. Some of their leaders were the same ideologues who had manufactured the Soviet anti-Zionist campaign. In the summer of 1988, as the Russian Orthodox Church prepared to celebrate the millennium of the introduction of Christianity to Rus', rumours of impending pogroms sent the country's Jews into panic. Two million Jews left the country in the following decade.

Conclusion

One of the lessons that the Soviet anti-Zionist campaign teaches is that anti-Zionism and antisemitism have historically been deeply and possibly inextricably intertwined. True to their ideological tenets, the Soviets never attacked the Jews in purely racist terms. Accused of antisemitism, they indignantly claimed that they were simply anti-Zionist. But wherever and whenever they employed anti-Zionism for their political purposes, antisemitism blossomed.

Examples of other countries further prove this point. Poland's 1968 anti-Zionist campaign quickly degenerated into an antisemitic witch-hunt, resulting in expulsions and forced emigration of some 15,000 Jews (see Gansinger in this collection). Today, as some of the leading opinion-makers on the left are seeking to build consensus around the idea that anti-Zionism and antisemitism are not the same, understanding this history is vitally important. Claiming that anti-Zionism and antisemitism are not the same may make for an interesting intellectual exercise. What happens in practice is another matter.

At its core, the Soviet anti-Zionist campaign of 1967–1988 was a campaign of propaganda and disinformation. It built and weaponised narratives based on made-up or twisted facts. It distorted history. It employed classic propaganda tools such as deception, guilt by association, and repetition to inculcate the key messages. It shamelessly played on people's sentiments, and it used both Soviet Jews and Muslims as instruments of propaganda (Hazan 2017:230–293).

Despite its claims, the Soviet anti-Zionist campaign was hardly motivated by a search for justice, peace or liberation for the Palestinian people. Conceived by master propagandists, it was an instrument whose purpose was to divert attention, manipulate, solidify control, purge enemies, and broaden influence for one of the most oppressive regimes in humanity's history.

A particular trick of Soviet anti-Zionism, according to the Israeli historian Kiril Feferman, was that it 'proposed a version of antisemitism to Western audiences that did not have obvious antisemitic overtones' (interview with author). It did so by substituting anti-Zionism for antisemitism in its propaganda, which made it passable for the many well-intentioned, idealistic individuals who otherwise would have recoiled in disgust from this rhetoric. Yet, underneath the relatively benign covers, the messages of the campaign packed a powerful antisemitic charge.

The messaging emanating from today's far-left anti-Zionist camp is strikingly similar to the messaging of the Soviet anti-Zionist campaigns. From the claims of Zionist collaboration with the Nazis in the Holocaust, to the idea of Zionism as an inherently racist and oppressive ideology, to the concept of Israel as a settler-colonialist state that engages in genocidal behaviour and apartheid – all of these ideas were part and parcel of the Soviet anti-Zionist narrative.

More research is needed to shed light on the trajectory and impact of the ideas that the late Soviet anti-Zionist campaign brought forth. Soviet anti-Zionism borrowed from the Tsarist *Protocols* and Hitler's Nazi propaganda; it adapted those ideas to its Marxist-Leninist framework; and ended up fertilising the ideologies of post-Soviet Russian ultranationalism. Did its ideological precepts also influence the global left and its view of Zionism and Israel? If so, to what extent? Is it possible that some of those ideas have outlived the system that produced them? To answer these questions is to find a crucial missing link in our understanding of contemporary left antisemitism.

Note

1 This chapter was first published in *Fathom* in 2019.

References

Bergman, Ronen (2014) 'Abbas' book reveals: The "Nazi-Zionist plot" of the Holocaust', *Ynet Magazine*, 26 November.

Bergman, Ronen (2016) 'The KGB's middle east files: The fight against Zionism and world Jewry', *Ynet Magazine*, 12 January. Available: www.ynetnews.com/articles/0,7340,L-4886594,00.html (accessed 28 October 2022).

Decter, Moshe (1964) 'The Soviet book that shook the communist world', *Midstream: A Quarterly Jewish Review*, July: 3–6. Available: www.marxists.org/subject/jewish/kichko-2.pdf (accessed 28 October 2022).

Doder, Dusko (1983) 'Soviet book assails Jews', *The Washington Post*, 20 June. Available: www.washingtonpost.com/archive/politics/1983/06/30/soviet-book-assails-jews/3572b557-5028-4dda-8bc8-5e44c6b2c781/?utm_term=.3aff1a6fe4a8 (accessed 28 October 2022).

Gansinger, Simon (2016) 'Communists against Jews: The anti-Zionist Campaign in Poland in 1968', *Fathom*, Autumn. Available: https://fathomjournal.org/communists-against-jews-the-anti-zionist-campaign-in-poland-in-1968/ (accessed 28 October 2022).

Gjerde, Asmund Borgen (2018) 'The logic of anti-Zionism: Soviet elites in the aftermath of the Six-Day War', *Patterns of Prejudice*, 52: 271–292.

Hazan, Baruch A. (2017) *Soviet Propaganda: A Case Study of the Middle East Conflict*, New York: Routledge. [First published 1976, Keter Publishing House Jerusalem Ltd.]

Herf, Jeffrey (2016) *Undeclared Wars With Israel: East Germany and the West German Far Left, 1967–1989*, New York: Cambridge University Press.

Jewish Telegraphic Agency (1952) 'Prague trial throws Jews in communist countries into mortal fear', *Jewish Telegraphic Agency Archive*. Available: www.jta.org/archive/prague-trial-throws-jews-in-communist-countries-into-mortal-fear (accessed 28 October 2022).

Jewish Telegraphic Agency (1983) 'Non-Jewish Russian academic blasts notorious soviet anti-Semite', *JTA Daily News Bulletin*, 1 December. Available: http://pdfs.jta.org/1983/1983-12-01_226.pdf?_ga=2.200214958.1022698916.1666959724-1124417636.1666959724 (accessed 28 October 2022).

Jews in Eastern Europe Special Issue (1964) 'Antisemitism in the USSR', *Jews in Eastern Europe*, II (5), July. Available: www.marxists.org/subject/jewish/kichko.pdf (accessed 28 October 2022).

Korey, William (1989) 'The Soviet public anti-Zionist committee: An analysis', in Robert O. Freedman (ed.), *Soviet Jewry in the 1980s: The Politics of Anti-Semitism and Emigration and the Dynamics of Resettlement*, London: Duke University Press, 26–50.

Korey, William (2013) *Russian Antisemitism, Pamyat, and the Demonology of Zionism*, New York: Routledge. [First published 1995, Harwood Academic Press.]

Levick, Adam (2010) 'Anti-Semitic cartoons on progressive blogs', *Jerusalem Center for Public Affairs*. Available: https://jcpa.org/article/anti-semitic-cartoons-on-progressive-blogs/ (accessed 28 October 2022).

New York Times (1971) 'Leningrad court sentences 9 Jews', 21 May. Available: www.nytimes.com/1971/05/21/archives/leningrad-court-sentences-9-jews-prisoncamp-terms-range-from-one-to.html (accessed 28 October 2022).

Pinkus, Benjamin (1989) *The Jews of the Soviet Union: The History of a National Minority*, Cambridge: Cambridge University Press.

Rich, Dave (2016) *The Left's Jewish Problem: Jeremy Corbyn, Israel and Anti-Semitism*, London: Biteback Publishing.

Umland, Andreas (1999) 'Soviet antisemitism after Stalin', *East European Jewish Affairs*, 29: 1–2, 159–168.

Wistrich, Robert (2012) *From Ambivalence to Betrayal: The Left, the Jews, and Israel*, Lincoln and London: University of Nebraska Press.

14

COMMUNISTS AGAINST JEWS

The Anti-Zionist Campaign in Poland in 1968

Simon Gansinger

Introduction

Travellers at Dworzec Gdański, a train station in the north of Warsaw, may notice a plaque that says: 'Here they left behind more than they possessed.'[1] Put up in 1998, it commemorates the departure of thousands of Polish Jews who, 30 years earlier, were forced to leave the country for no other reason than their being Jewish. 'Everything started collapsing then', Halina Zawadzka, who had survived the Holocaust in Poland, wrote about her experience of 1968. 'The past was being repeated' (quoted in Głuchowski and Polonsky 2009:3). Organised by the Polish United Workers' Party (PZPR), the anti-Zionist campaign of 1968–1971 destroyed a Jewish community which had only just re-established itself. It was a gruesome example of left-wing anti-semitism inflected as 'anti-Zionism'.

The assault on the country's Jews teemed with declarations *against* anti-semitism. On countless rallies, people carried signs that read 'Antisemitism – No! Anti-Zionism – Yes!' Yet of the 8,300 members expelled from the Communist party, nearly all were Jewish (Blatman 2000:308). Almost 9,000 Jews lost their jobs, and hundreds were thrown out of their apartments (Wolak 2004:73). The regime allowed Jewish citizens to leave the country under two conditions: they must revoke their citizenship and they must declare Israel as the country of their destination. In this way, the regime legitimised the purge in the most cynical fashion: Why would these people go to Israel if they hadn't been Zionists all along?

Many Jews seized the opportunity. Whereas in April 1967, only 29 applied for exit visas to Israel, the number rose to 168 one year later and reached 631 in October 1968 (Szaynok 2009:156). Estimates of how many Jews left Poland between 1968 and 1971 vary. The most conservative holds

DOI: 10.4324/9781003322320-17

the number to be 12,000; earlier estimates believed that more than 20,000 were forced out of the country. The correct figure might lie somewhere in the middle, at about 15,000 (Eisler 2009:42). Fewer than 30 per cent ended up in Israel, with the rest going to other countries, primarily Sweden, France and the United States (Wolak 2004:116).

The Zionist 'fifth column'

After Israel's victory in the Six-Day War, the member states of the Warsaw Pact, with the exception of Romania, cut diplomatic ties with Israel. The developments in Poland, however, soon took a peculiar course. On 19 June 1967, one week after the suspension of diplomatic relations with Israel, Władysław Gomułka, the first secretary of the PZPR, made a remarkable comment on the domestic dimensions of the events in the Middle East. Some Polish Jews, he was sorry to hear, sympathised with the enemies of socialism, the 'Israeli aggressors', thereby forfeiting their claim to be loyal Polish citizens. These people were not just morally corrupt, they constituted a potential 'fifth column' in the country, which had to be eradicated before it could gain strength (Michlic 2006:247, Rozenbaum 2009:70).

The significance of Gomułka's 'fifth column' remark cannot be overstated. The term invoked a well-organised Zionist conspiracy whose centre was to be found in the Jewish community, which in 1967 counted no more than 30,000 members out of a Polish population of 32 million. When Gomułka gave his speech, he had already been exposed to the anti-Jewish fabrications of the Ministry of Internal Affairs (MSW) for some months. The ministry was led by Mieczysław Moczar, whose fervently antisemitic views were no secret to his comrades. Even before June 1967, high-ranking MSW officials took a special interest in the activities of Jewish institutions in Warsaw and popularised the notion of a Zionist infiltration among party circles. Under Moczar's lead, the MSW worked tirelessly to gather information on individual Jews and expose their alleged links to Israel – which meant, in most cases, to distort or invent these ties (Eisler 2009:43–46).

Also thanks to the opposition of politburo members against Moczar's machinations, Gomułka's imaginary Zionist enemy within Poland did not attract much attention in the broader public. With the exception of the military, where the majority of Jewish officers were dismissed, the anti-Zionist campaign did not gain traction until March 1968, when a full-blown assault on the 'fifth column' shook the country.

Antisemitism against protesting students

It is tempting to look at history as an orderly chain of events. But those entangled in this chain lack the comfort of hindsight. The order of things is lost on them, and so is the irony that posterity likes to attribute to history when it has collapsed into utter irrationality.

On 30 January 1968, 300 students protested the ban of the allegedly anti-Russian play *Dziady* by the 19th-century Polish romantic author Adam Mickiewicz, not suspecting that their courageous acts would usher in the anti-Zionist frenzy of March 1968. Needless to say, the student protests that preceded the purge of Zionists from the country had as little relation to the Middle East as had the anti-Zionist who, some weeks later, called on 'Zionists [to go] to Siam!' ('Syjoniści do Syjamu!'). This demand was emblazoned on banners at a rally. The writer, apparently, thought Zionists had come from Siam because of the phonetic proximity of the two terms in Polish (Eisler 2019:122). The history of antisemitism lacks order as much as the antisemites lack understanding. Until immediately before the campaign, the public was captivated by the academic protests and perfectly unperturbed by Zionism. The sudden appearance of the Zionist spectre in the chronology of student unrest reminds us not only of the deceitful continuity of historic events but also of the violent rupture of thinking, which is so typical of antisemitism.

As a punishment for their involvement in the *Dziady* protests, two students, Henryk Szlajfer and Adam Michnik, who happened to be Jewish, were expelled from the University of Warsaw. On 8 March, a Friday, their colleagues responded with a large demonstration at the university, which was brutally dissolved by security forces. The demand for freedom of speech and civil rights, however, was soon heard at campuses all over the country, and before the weekend was over, tens of thousands of students and sympathisers rallied for this cause.

The regime got nervous. The protests had grown too large in too short a time to be quietly suppressed. If the voice of the workers entered into the chorus of calls for free speech and free education, the student unrest could quickly evolve into a fully fledged rebellion. In the MSW headquarters, everything was prepared to defang the movement in its infancy. Moczar's men compiled lists of the alleged leading instigators, most of them Jewish. After Gomułka and other high-ranking party members had approved the document, it was handed to the press with the intention of neutralising the protests by kindling a campaign against alien provocateurs. The working masses, the reasoning seemed to be, would hardly join ranks with a Jewish elite.

'Complete removal of Zionist elements'

The publication of the list alone would have sufficed to brand the official propaganda against the student unrest as an antisemitic stunt. And while the official party organs were content with calling out Jewish-sounding names, it took the newspaper of the Catholic splinter group PAX, *Słowo Powszechne,* to link the events to Gomułka's fifth column and conjure up a Zionist cabal. According to the article 'To the students of the University of Warsaw', published on 11 March, the protests were part of a plot 'to undermine the authority of the political leadership of People's Poland'. Fortunately, the readers were assured, 'antisemitic sentiments are alien to [the Polish youth].' And so they certainly would not take it the wrong way when they are informed that the main organisers of the demonstration at the University of Warsaw were natural-born Zionists who 'held meetings at the "Babel" club at the Social and Cultural Association of Jews'.

The public readily took the hint. From now on, the media abounded with condemnations, denunciations and exposures of Zionist traitors. Within the next ten days, some 250 articles addressed the protests, a good portion of which endorsed the idea of a Zionist conspiracy. But the campaign was not restricted to hateful columns in magazines or outraged talking heads on television. In more than 100,000 public meetings in factories, in party offices, and even in sports clubs all over Poland, anti-Zionist resolutions were passed (Stola 2005:296). One representative resolution from the beginning of April (quoted in Lendvai 1971:115) demanded the 'complete removal of Zionist elements and other enemies of our socialist reality from the political, state administrative, educational, and cultural apparatus and also from social organizations. . . . Those who in their nihilism and cosmopolitanism poison the spirit and heart of the youth should lose their influence on it.' While the Jewish community was spared a nationwide pogrom, physical violence accompanied the aggressive rhetoric. Jewish journalists were beaten up, Jewish co-workers bullied and Jewish students subjected to particularly harsh treatment at the hands of Moczar's militia. In this atmosphere, which according to historian Dariusz Stola (2000:149) amounted to a 'symbolic pogrom', dozens committed suicide after they had found themselves publicly vilified and socially isolated.

Gomułka: 'Zionists will leave'

While the campaign certainly could not have been initiated without the knowledge and consent of Władysław Gomułka, the first secretary did not comment on its anti-Zionist spin for an oddly long time. More than one week after the publication of the incendiary article in *Słowo Powszechne*, on 19 March, he finally set out his views about the role of Zionism in the current events before a large assembly of party activists. The main culprits of the student unrest, he said, were revisionary and reactionary elements, some of whom, Gomułka noted, were Jewish. The Jewish population of Poland, he went on, could be divided into three groups: Polish, cosmopolitan and Zionist. While the first and largest group proudly served its fatherland and the second could at least be tolerated, the third group, 'Polish citizens who are emotionally and in their thoughts connected to the State of Israel', would leave the country. By making this division, Gomułka played down the importance of a Zionist conspiracy while at the same time acknowledging its existence. A significant portion of the audience expressed their discontent with the first secretary's perceived leniency and demanded that he give names. This open display of defiance, and Gomułka's futile attempts to calm the crowd, attested to the dynamic of the antisemitic witch-hunt, which had ceased to be a contained campaign controlled by the party.

Over the next few weeks, while Poland was gripped by the anti-Zionist fever, the Jewish community could not do more than hold their breath and wait for the frenzy to ebb away. In June 1968, the Central Committee decided to discontinue the campaign. At the Fifth Party Congress in November, Zionism was no longer on the agenda. When asked by a comrade whether the protests in March were linked to a Zionist conspiracy, the Attorney General (quoted in Lendvai 1971:182) replied, 'No, we have no proof whatsoever for this supposition.'

For the victims of the campaign, the supposition impacted brutally on their lives. In Łódź, where the antisemitic campaign raged without restraint, the city's newspapers dismissed Jewish journalists, the administration of the local eye clinic demanded baptism certificates from physicians, and the local PZPR propaganda bureau published educational material that approvingly quoted the *Protocols of the Elders of Zion* (Eisler 2009:51–52, Lendvai 1971:160). Within less than two months, the Jewish population of Łódź, once a thriving centre of Jewish culture and business, was driven out of the city.

Anti-Zionism and antisemitism

The plausibility of a Zionist conspiracy was hardly self-evident in 1968 in Poland. The absurdity of this idea was captured in a comment by a local farmer in Włoszczowa (quoted in Eisler 2009:54), who said, 'Up to now, we've heard that the peasants and workers ruled Poland, while in reality the Jews do.' One can easily sympathise with the bemused farmer of Włoszczowa: one bizarre idea had been superseded by another.

Most of the writers who have studied the campaign have argued that its anti-Zionism was simply antisemitism in disguise. This 'identity thesis' holds that anti-Zionism is a surface phenomenon that can be reduced to classical antisemitism. The meaning of anti-Zionism, then, consists in its being a direct translation of antisemitism into a socially permissible code: 'Zionists' equals 'Jews'. We know this mechanism from euphemisms that refer to a tabooed term – you say the first, but you mean the latter.

There is a lot to say in favour of the identity thesis. Apart from the fact that the campaign chiefly targeted Jews (and people who were believed to be Jewish), many of the classical elements of antisemitism were present during the events of 1968. Conspiracy theories, paranoia, anti-intellectualism and anti-cosmopolitanism, all of which featured in the campaign, had been part and parcel of the ideological repertoire of Jew-hatred since the 19th century.

Still, I believe there is more to it. When antisemitism appears as anti-Zionism, it is not merely replicated in a different language. Rather, it undergoes a profound transformation. The displacement of 'Jews' by 'Zionists' modifies the ideological structure of antisemitism. The object that is hated – that is, in Poland 1968, the Zionist – resonates with the 'obscure impulse', the unconscious motive that drives the antisemite and 'takes them over completely' (Horkheimer and Adorno 2002:140). Instead of being a disingenuous version of antisemitism, the anti-Zionism of March 1968 was one of its *inflections*.

I borrow the term 'inflection' from linguistics. In many languages, we have to change the structure of words in order to convey a certain meaning in accordance with the grammatical context. By inflecting the verb 'to be', for example, we get the word forms 'is' or 'was', and we use one or the other depending on whether we talk about the present or the past. Antisemitism can also be inflected. However, its grammatical context is society itself. In the example I mentioned, the word (or, to be more precise, the lexeme) 'to be' looks nothing like the inflected forms it corresponds to. It is, as it were, obscure, like the impulse of the antisemites, which, in the words of Max Horkheimer and Theodor W. Adorno, gives rise to a 'system of delusions' (2002:154). The forms these delusions take are irrational but not haphazard. The specific ideological expression of antisemitism at any one time is governed by its historical circumstances.

But what was the context that made the anti-Zionist inflection more adequate, more potent and more cohesive than its uninflected base form? The public disapproval of historical manifestations of antisemitism certainly played a part. But that was not all. The campaign of 1968 exemplifies the ideological innovation that anti-Zionism brings to antisemitism: the apprehension of the political conspiracy. When the crackdown on students turned anti-Zionist, it became an eminently political witch-hunt.

The role of the political is key to understanding the relation of anti-Zionism to traditional antisemitism. The old anti-Judaic and antisemitic images, such as the identification of Jews with the murderers of Christ or the identification of Jews with capital, had limited applicability under the social conditions of People's Poland, where the salience of the political was apparent to everyone. Instead, another aspect of antisemitism rose to prominence: the identification of Jews with the abstract state apparatus.

The address of the political conspiracy

The political conspiracy has always been a quintessential element of modern antisemitism, just as the Jewish dominance of the economy is antisemitic stock in trade. Both in the economic and the political sphere, the idea of a Jewish conspiracy stems from the desire to make social relations less complex and more tangible. The concretisation of the abstract is not a purely cognitive phenomenon: antisemites experience the world through their delusional representations.

The historian and political theorist Moishe Postone (1980:112) writes that in National Socialism Jews became the 'personifications of the intangible'. The campaign in Poland illustrates that the anti-Zionist image of Israel facilitates this process of delusional concretisation in the political sphere. The political conspiracy is made tangible in Zionism. And consequently, the political conspiracy can be attacked in Israel's lackeys, the 'Zionists'.

Spring 1968 in Poland offers us ample material to support this thesis. An article in the Army daily *Żołnierz Wolności* informed its readers about 'Israel's fantastic network throughout the world' that is the 'source of the might of the espionage services directed from Tel Aviv' (quoted in Lendvai 1971:142). Edward Gierek, who succeeded Gomułka as first secretary in 1970, pointed to the crooked political ambitions of the Zionists before an audience of 100,000 in Katowice: 'This is done in the interests of old political speculators who act without any scruples.' Gierek then delivered a sequence of well-known Jewish names, 'these Zambrowskis, Staszewskis, Słonimskis', all in the plural to erase any doubt that they are not individual human beings but representatives of a clandestine organisation (quoted in Institute of Jewish Affairs 1968:15). 'Zionism' is to overwhelming political power what 'the Rothschilds' are to the global financial cartel: the proper name for a paranoid idea.

One of the most prominent slogans during the campaign was the fight against 'international Zionism'. This oxymoron expresses the ideological function of the Zionist conspiracy in its most condensed form. The antisemite imagines the Jewish conspiracy as unbound and pervasive, that is, as 'international'. But they also seek to identify, grasp and eliminate it. In the distorted representation of Zionism, they give the conspiracy an address and a name, thereby melding together two complementary elements of antisemitism: the ubiquity of the hated object and the desire for concretisation.

The concretisation of the economic sphere is not at odds with the concretisation of political power. Antisemitism embraces the Rothschilds and the 'Zambrowskis, Staszewskis, Słonimskis' alike. The reckless profiteer of traditional antisemitism and Gierek's 'political speculators' are two forms, two inflections of the same antisemitic obsession to make the world accord with one's delusions. The article in *Żołnierz Wolności* is a case in point. Its author closes his tirade against Zionist traitors with the synthesis of old and new antisemitism: 'Their aim was to serve foreign interests, to serve imperialism and anti-Polish and anti-socialist subversion. Their homeland is the American dollar regardless of whether they receive it from Tel Aviv, Bonn, or

Washington.' For antisemites, Jews have always had control over economic power, and they have hated and envied them for this hallucinatory alliance with money. In anti-Zionism, the antisemitic hatred of Jews has further consolidated itself within the *political* realm.

In Poland, the purge of alleged Zionists from the military, the party, the administration and public institutions was the purge of the Jews from the political sphere. 'The word "political" and its derivatives', Stola writes, 'were those most frequently used [in March 1968] to depict the enemy' (2005:290). This is then the meaning of 'Zionism' in anti-Zionism: the Jew as a political being. As the antisemitic campaign of 1968 located its objects within the political sphere, it was, almost necessarily, bound to appear as anti-Zionist antisemitism.

On 15 March, a journalist of the party paper *Trybuna Ludu* intimated how international Zionism maintained its paradoxical character: '[The Zionist leaders] oblige the rest of the Jewish community, scattered all over the world – instigating among it feelings of nationalism and religious fanaticism – to lend an all-round support to Israel. . . . The assistance for which the Zionist leaders call is therefore an assistance for Israeli expansionism, behind which stand the forces of imperialism, particularly West German and American imperialism' (quoted in Institute of Jewish Affairs 1968:16). Throughout the campaign, the connection of Zionism to West Germany and the United States was a popular theme, although the pamphleteers could not quite agree on who manipulated whom. The fusion of the economic conspiracy and the political conspiracy can be seen in an article in *Głos Pracy* from 18 March: '[Zionism] hobnobbed with French and British capital and even was born under the influence of that capital. Recently it [put its] stakes on American and West German imperialism' (quoted in Institute of Jewish Affairs 1968:17).

Beyond Poland 1968

Antisemites want their objects to be easily identifiable and ready at hand. The Zionist bogey that was conjured up in March 1968 served this purpose. In the Zionist fifth column, the delusion of Jewish world dominance manifested itself in the political sphere. The Polish case helps us understand the ideological function of anti-Zionism within antisemitism: anti-Zionism localises a hitherto politically indeterminate conspiracy. And the grim fate of the 15,000 Polish Jews who were forced into emigration poignantly reminds us that the target of anti-Zionist antisemitism is not just the Jewish state but the people for whose protection it was founded.

Note

1 This chapter was published in *Fathom* in 2016 and was revised by Simon Gansinger in 2023. It is based on a conference presentation at the Institute for the Study of Contemporary Antisemitism at Indiana University, Bloomington. A longer version

of that presentation was included in Alvin Rosenfeld (ed.) *Anti-Zionism and Anti-semitism: The Dynamics of Delegitimization*, Bloomington: Indiana University Press, 2019, 341–368.

References

Blatman, Daniel (2000) 'Polish Jewry, the six day war, and the crisis of 1968', in Eli Lederhendler (ed.), *The Six-Day War and World Jewry*, Bethesda, MD: University Press of Maryland, 291–310.

Eisler, Jerzy (2009) '1968: Jews, antisemitism, emigration', in Leszek W. Głuchowski and Antony Polonsky (eds.), *Polin: Studies in Polish Jewry Volume 21: 1968 Forty Years After*, Liverpool: Liverpool University Press, 37–61.

Eisler, Jerzy (2019) *The 'Polish Months': Communist-Ruled Poland in Crisis*, translated by Jerzy Giebułtowski, Warsaw: The Institute of National Remembrance.

Głuchowski, Leszek W. and Antony Polonsky (2009) 'Introduction', in Leszek W. Głuchowski and Antony Polonsky (eds.), *Polin: Studies in Polish Jewry Volume 21: 1968 Forty Years After*, Liverpool: Liverpool University Press, 3–15.

Horkheimer, Max and Theodor W. Adorno (2002) *Dialectic of Enlightenment: Philosophical Fragments*, Stanford, CA: Stanford University Press.

Institute of Jewish Affairs (1968) *The Student Unrest in Poland and the Anti-Jewish and Anti-Zionist Campaign* [*sic*], Background Paper No. 9, [s.l.]: Institute of Jewish Affairs in association with the World Jewish Congress.

Lendvai, Paul (1971) *Anti-Semitism Without Jews*, New York: Doubleday.

Michlic, Joanna B. (2006) *Poland's Threatening Other: The Image of the Jew From 1880 to the Present*, Lincoln: University of Nebraska Press.

Postone, Moishe (1980) 'Anti-Semitism and national socialism: Notes on the German reaction to "holocaust"', *New German Critique* 19: 97–115.

Rozenbaum, Włodzimierz (2009) 'The march events: Targeting the Jews', in Leszek W. Głuchowski and Antony Polonsky (eds.), *Polin: Studies in Polish Jewry Volume 21: 1968 Forty Years After*, Liverpool: Liverpool University Press, 62–92.

Stola, Dariusz (2000) *Kampania antysyjonistyczna w Polsce 1967–1968*, Warsaw: Instytut Studiów Politycznych PAN.

Stola, Dariusz (2005) 'Fighting against the shadows: The anti-Zionist campaign of 1968', in Robert Blobaum (ed.), *Antisemitism and Its Opponents in Modern Poland*, Ithaca, NY: Cornell University Press, 284–300.

Szaynok, Bożena (2009) '"Israel" in the events of march 1968', in Leszek W. Głuchowski and Antony Polonsky (eds.), *Polin: Studies in Polish Jewry Volume 21: 1968 Forty Years After*, Liverpool: Liverpool University Press, 150–158.

Wolak, Arthur J. (2004) *Forced Out: The Fate of Polish Jewry in Communist Poland*, Tucson, AZ: Fenestra Books.

15

THE GERMAN LEFT'S UNDECLARED WARS ON ISRAEL

An Interview With Jeffrey Herf

Jeffrey Herf

Alan Johnson: *Tell us about the genesis of your book* Undeclared Wars on Israel: East Germany and the West German Far Left 1967–1981.[1]

Jeffrey Herf: I've been thinking about the topic of this particular book since 1978 when I was a graduate student in Frankfurt working on my dissertation at Brandeis University. I met – in my young leftist days – people on the left who were profoundly hostile towards Israel, and I found that very peculiar. I also met and learned from people in Frankfurt/Main who dissented from the anti-Zionist left. So, I began reading and writing about the peculiar anti-Israeli passion that emerged in both the international and West German left. That passion was global but it had added complexities and complexes in Germany after Nazism. I wanted to understand them. In 1990, after the unification of Germany, I worked in the archives of the former German Democratic Republic, (GDR) and learned a great deal about the turn of that East German government against Israel in the 1950s. I have thought about this issue ever since and became aware that although there were many German historians who were working on East Germany, there were few writing about East Germany's hostility toward Israel. Hence, I felt a responsibility to write this book.

Alan Johnson: *Why do you begin the book with the Stalinist anti-cosmopolitan purges of the 1940s and 1950s?*

DOI: 10.4324/9781003322320-18

Jeffrey Herf: For the Soviet Union in the early years of the Cold War its war-time alliance with capitalist Britain and the United States had become an embarrassment. So Stalin and the Soviet ideologue Andrei Zhdanov, in an essay entitled the 'Two Camp Policy' did everything they could to diminish the role of the West in the victory over Nazi Germany, diminish the significance of anti-Semitism, and pretend that the Soviet Union won the war largely on its own.

In the immediate post war years, the years of what I have called 'Israel's moment', the Soviet support for the Zionist project and then for the new state of Israel was firm and consequential. However, by fall 1949 when it became evident that the Jewish state was not going to be supportive of Soviet expansion in the Middle East, Stalin reversed course and began a policy of denunciation of Zionism as a tool of Western imperialism. So now there was a geopolitical reason – winning the Cold War in the Middle East – for the Soviets to turn against Israel. Geopolitics drew as well on a long-standing left-wing tradition of associating the Jews with capitalism and imperialism and that resurfaced in Stalin's mind and became very important in the anti-cosmopolitan purges in the Soviet Union and Eastern Europe from 1949 to 1953. From that point on, it became impossible to be a leading member of a communist party, or high ranking official in the Soviet bloc and at the same time remain a supporter of the state of Israel.

One manifestation of this anti-Semitism was the Slánský trial in Prague that involved 14 members of the Communist Party – 11 of whom were Jewish, including Rudolf Slánský, the former general secretary of the Communist Party. All were found guilty of being part of an American-Israeli conspiracy to destroy the communist regimes in Eastern Europe. Eleven, including Slánský, were executed by hanging. The trial should be understood in the context of Czechoslovakia's decision to send large amounts of arms to the Israelis in 1947–48 during the first Arab Israeli War. Those Czech officials sympathetic to Jews and to the Zionist project fell under retrospective suspicion of being part of a plot to overthrow the communist regimes. In East Germany, the anti-cosmopolitan purges led to the arrest and imprisonment of prominent communists such as Paul Merker, and the flight of leaders of the Jewish community to the West. Their 'crimes' also included sympathy for Israel.

Alan Johnson: *What form did East Germany's 'undeclared war on Israel' take?*

Jeffrey Herf: Well, it was not a matter of 'criticism of Israel' – a legitimate right of every government in the world. Rather, beginning in the 1960s, it encompassed a spectrum of antagonism that included: provision to Arab states and Palestinian terrorist organisations with guns, bullets, rocket-propelled grenades, landmines, anti-tank weapons, and rockets; political warfare and intelligence cooperation; formal political and military alliances between the upper echelons of the East German, Iraqi and Egyptian governments; state to state relations that involved the transfer of jet planes, tanks and heavy artillery; and agreements to provide the Palestinian Liberation Organisation and smaller Palestinian guerrilla fractions with arms to be fired at Israel and/or Israeli citizens.

Alan Johnson: *And UN leaders, such as General Secretary Kurt Waldheim, ignored detailed reports from Israeli representatives about this political warfare campaign and about the Arab states' armed attacks against Israel?*

Jeffrey Herf: Yes. The files of the United Nations, available through its online Official Documents System (ODS), offered abundant evidence of not only of the well-known antagonism to Israel by the Soviet bloc, Communist states, Arab, and Islamic states, and the PLO. Less well known is that those files show Israel presented its case to all members of the UN. That was possible because the UN permits its members to send reports to the Secretary General and the President of the Security Council. These reports were then circulated to all members of the UN. In the 1960s to 1980s, Israel's Ambassadors to the UN, Gideon Rafael, Chaim Herzog, Yosef Tekoah and Yehuda Blum, made excellent use of this system to send detailed reports of the ongoing terrorist campaigns leading to attacks on Israeli civilians. Outside the archives of the Israeli government, they are the most detailed record that we have about the ongoing terrorist campaign that was being waged by the PLO and its various branches (PFLP, PDFLP) against Israel in those years. The anti-Israel majority in the UN in those decades either ignored the information in those reports or worse, redefined terrorism as a legitimate form of 'resistance'.

Alan Johnson: *What motivated the East German communist leadership to wage this war?*

Jeffrey Herf: Anti-Zionism was the norm in Marxist-Leninist ideology. Brief post-war support for Zionism had been a result of the anti-Nazi passions of World War II, fresh memories of the Holocaust, and an expectation that a Jewish state would benefit Soviet foreign policy aims. The following four decades of Soviet bloc anti-Zionism was a return to Communist ideological normalcy that regarded Zionism as an anachronism, a deviation from class struggle, and a form of reactionary nationalism. Anti-imperialist nationalism was fine, but not Zionist nationalism. East Germany's war against Israel was a matter of ideological conviction that mirrored this broader Soviet bloc consensus.

East Germany took a prominent role in the Soviet bloc antagonism to Israel for another reason: it sought to gain diplomatic recognition from the Arab states when West Germany was trying to isolate it diplomatically and economically. The West German government in Bonn (the Federal Republic of Germany) defined East Germany as illegitimate and threatened to cut off diplomatic and economic ties with states that had such links to the GDR. The policy was called the Hallstein Doctrine, named after an official in the West German Foreign Office. East German diplomats sought to counteract the Hallstein doctrine by establishing diplomatic and political relations with countries outside the Soviet bloc. Otto Winzer, East Germany's foreign minister in the 1960s, made the argument that the key to breaking out of the isolation fostered by the Hallstein Doctrine was to play the anti-Zionist card by siding with the anti-Zionist Arab states – and the Palestinians. The fruits of Winzer's plan were seen in 1969 when Iraq, Syria, Egypt, Yemen and Libya all signed agreements to start diplomatic relations with East Germany, and each denounced Zionism. During the Six-Day War of 1967, Walter Ulbricht, the First Secretary of the ruling Socialist Unity Party and leader of the East German regime, in a major speech in Leipzig, denounced Israel and supported the Arab states. The East German support contributed to the Arab decisions two years later to initiate diplomatic relations with the GDR.

Alan Johnson: *You claim that East Germany pioneered a 'Eurocentric definition of counterterrorism'. What did that definition entail
and how did it shape the UN's attitude towards terrorism
aimed at Israel?*

Jeffrey Herf: I found this to be one of the most interesting aspects of the
research and writing. After East Germany signed agreements
in 1974 to support the PLO militarily and economically, the
Stasi, East Germany's state security and intelligence service,
had a serious problem. East Germany soon became a tran-
sit point for young PLO members to enter West Germany
traveling on foreign passports from East to West Berlin
where some engaged in terrorist attacks on Jewish institutions in West Germany or Western Europe. East Germany
had a reputation in the Middle East for being a supporter of
the PLO and the Arab states in their wars with Israel. Young
men, mostly, came from Beirut and Damascus and Cairo to
the Soviet Bloc and to East Germany where they received
military training and/or university fellowships. Some then
decided to travel to West Germany, West Berlin, or Western
Europe and attack the 'imperialists' who were supporting
Israel. Or they wanted to attack the Jewish institutions in
West Germany.

Leading Stasi officials understood that if Arabs, or Palestinian Arabs travelling from East Berlin committed terrorist
acts in the West, the West European and American intelligence services would very likely learn the itinerary of their
travels and hold the GDR accountable for not preventing
or even for facilitating the attacks. The East German leaders understood that if such attacks were traced back to the
GDR and the Soviet bloc it would put détente at risk and
with it the millions of deutschmarks that West Germany
was sending to East Germany.

So, leaders of the East German intelligence services pon-
dered how to continue to support terrorism aimed at Western
interests, and at Israel, but prevent terrorist attacks in West
Germany and Western Europe that could undermine support
for détente. The Stasi's solution was to establish a formal relationship with the intelligence services of the PLO to locate and
prevent the people who wanted to commit terrorist attacks in
West Germany and Western Europe. Conversely, the Stasi was
aware of and supported the PLO, Popular Front for the Liberation of Palestine (PFLP) and the Popular Democratic Front

for the Liberation of Palestine (PDFLP) when they engaged in terrorist attacks on the state of Israel. Hence, I coined the phrase 'Eurocentric definition of counterterrorism'.

Alan Johnson: *Moving on, who were the West German far-leftists also engaged in an undeclared war on Israel?*

Jeffrey Herf: They came from the Baader-Meinhof Group and Revolutionary Cells, two West German terrorist organisations who worked closely with the PFLP in particular. Both groups emerged from the West German new left of the 1960s. One of the most stunning results of that collaboration was the hijacking of an Air France flight to Entebbe in Uganda in 1976. The hijackers included members of the PFLP, and Wilfried Böse and Brigitte Kuhlmann, both members of the Revolutionary Cells organisation based in Frankfurt/Main. At Entebbe these two pointed their machine guns at the hostages and separated the Jews and the Israelis from the non-Jews and non-Israelis. They held on to the Jews and released the non-Jews.

The operation was conducted with the collaboration and cooperation of Idi Amin, the then-president of Uganda. Amin was infamous for celebrating Hitler in the aftermath of the Munich attacks at the 1972 Olympics. He also celebrated the Holocaust. The Entebbe hijacking displayed the absurdity of two young West German leftists claiming to oppose fascism and Nazism at home while pointing automatic rifles at Jews, and collaborating with a man for whom Hitler was a hero.

At the hijacking in Entebbe the distinction between anti-Semitism and anti-Zionism vanished. It was an anti-Semitic act justified in the language of leftist anti-fascism, a discourse that had redefined Israel as a fascist or Nazi-like state.

Alan Johnson: *One of the most interesting things in the book is how you reconstruct – from a multitude of archives – the experiences and the views of the Jewish people who were the targets of this undeclared war.*

Jeffrey Herf: I wanted the Jews to be heard. Sometimes we don't pay attention to what those targeted by antisemitism have to say. For example, Heinz Galinski and his colleagues at the Central Council of Jews in West Germany were receiving death threats whilst ensuring that the children in the kindergartens and day-care centres were safe from attack. The Revolutionary Cells were making public threats to Jewish day care centers. Again, in view of these actions, fine intellectual distinctions between anti-Zionism and anti-Semitism vanished. Galinski and his colleagues wrote a great deal about the turn of the New Left against Israel on West German university campuses. The archives of the Central Council in Heidelberg hold an extensive collection of the leaflets, posters, essays, and manifestos of leftist, and Palestinian leftist agitation in the universities. They document both the propaganda assault on Israel in the universities, as well as the efforts of the small but determined Jewish community to fight back against this form of leftist antisemitism.

Alan Johnson: *You record 'the intensity, voluntarism and passion' with which these young far-left Germans turned against Israel and 'aligned with its enemies'. How did you explain this passion?*

Jeffrey Herf: What amazed me most when reading the East German documents and the far-left West German documents was the absence of reservations, anguish, or doubt, and the sense of absolute moral uprightness of the far-left political leaders. Some scholars have referred to 'secondary antisemitism', that is, antagonism to the Jews not despite but because of the Holocaust. Psychologically, the undeclared war on Israel served to lift the burden of German shame by describing the Israelis as Nazis and the Palestinians as innocent victims, and thus escape from the burdens of German history. The far-left leaders substituted an anti-imperialist, anti-Zionist future for their anti-Semitic past. That sense of liberation from their Nazi past was very important to them, psychologically and emotionally. François Furet warned us in his seminal book *The Passing of an Illusion: The Idea of Communism in the Twentieth Century* that though Communism had indeed collapsed, 'it was not so long ago'. We forget how recently it was that many millions of people believed deeply in international communism and global revolution to destroy capitalism and imperialism. Once you had that conviction – that all the evil in the world came from capitalism and imperialism and that Israel was part of that evil – then you deemed it necessary to justify terrorism to bring about a better world. These political mentalities were the opposite of the views of Communists, leftists, and liberals from 1947 to summer 1949 when they viewed the Zionist project and the new state of Israel as a welcome result of the anti-colonial and anti-Nazi passions the had emerged during World War II and the Holocaust.

Note

1 This chapter was first published in *Fathom* in 2016.

PART 4

Left Antisemitism and the Holocaust

16

HOLOCAUST INVERSION AND CONTEMPORARY ANTISEMITISM

Lesley Klaff

In 2013, the Liberal Democrat MP for Bradford East, David Ward, after signing the Book of Remembrance in the Houses of Parliament on Holocaust Memorial Day, made use of the Holocaust to criticise Israel and 'the Jews' by equating Israel with Nazi Germany, and to characterise the Holocaust as a moral lesson from which 'the Jews' have failed to learn.[1] He wrote, 'Having visited Auschwitz twice – once with my family and once with local schools – I am saddened that the Jews, who suffered unbelievable levels of persecution during the Holocaust, could within a few years of liberation from the death camps be inflicting atrocities on Palestinians in the new state of Israel and continue to do so on a daily basis in the West Bank and Gaza.'

What has been called 'Holocaust Inversion' involves an *inversion of reality* (the Israelis are cast as the 'new' Nazis and the Palestinians as the 'new' Jews) and an *inversion of morality* (the Holocaust is presented as a moral lesson for, or even a moral indictment of 'the Jews'). More: those who object to these inversions are told – as they were by David Ward – that they are acting in bad faith, only being concerned to deflect criticism of Israel. In short, the Holocaust, an event accurately described by Dan Diner as a 'rupture in civilisation', organised by a regime that, as the political philosopher Leo Strauss observed, 'had no other clear principle except murderous hatred of the Jews', is now being used, instrumentally, as a means to express animosity towards the homeland of the Jews. 'The victims have become perpetrators' is being heard more and more. *That* is Holocaust Inversion (see Gerstenfeld 2007, Fine 2009).

The Inversion of Reality and Morality

Clemens Heni, director of the Berlin International Center for the Study of Antisemitism (BICSA), believes that the equation of Israel/the Jews/Zionism

DOI: 10.4324/9781003322320-20

with Nazism amounts to an 'inversion of truth' which is used today as a form of 'extremely aggressive anti-Jewish propaganda' (Heni 2008). Anthony Julius, author of a landmark study of British antisemitism, notes that Holocaust Inversion is becoming part of the iconography of a new antisemitism (Julius 2010). Headlines such as 'The Final Solution to the Palestine Question', references to the 'Holocaust in Gaza', images of IDF soldiers morphing into jackbooted storm troopers, Israeli politicians morphing into Hitler, and the Star of David morphing into the Swastika, are all increasingly common.

The 2009 Report of the European Institute for the Study of Contemporary Antisemitism, *Understanding the 'Nazi' Card: Intervening against Anti-Semitic Discourse*, reported that equating Israel with the Nazis is an important component of incitement and racial aggravation against Jews in the UK today (Iganski and Sweiry 2009). The Report recommended that the Home Office, the Association of Chief Police Officers and the Crown Prosecution Service prepare guidance for the police on whether the use of Holocaust imagery to refer to contemporary Israeli policy amounts to incitement of racial hatred against Jews.

Comparing Israel and the Nazi regime, David Ward said, 'don't forget, long before the death camps were set up, the treatment of the Jews in . . . Nazi Germany was racist . . . nastiness and harassment to begin with, and then escalated. And when you look at it – wherever it may be – the West Bank, and a declared intent by the Israeli forces to harass, often just annoy Palestinians – in terms of a check point that will be open on certain days, and then it will be open but at a later time, and the next day, it will open slightly earlier, so you get there and it's been shut again . . . really just to harass, in many cases to move the Palestinians from land, to just give up and move on.'

Now, whether or not IDF soldiers deliberately change the opening and closing times of checkpoints in the West Bank in order to harass Palestinians, I do not know; but even if they do, no matter how wrong that would be, there is absolutely no equivalence between *that* and the denial of paid work, Jew-baiting, herding into ghettos, incarceration, disease and starvation in labour camps that occurred in Germany and Eastern Europe between 1933 and the Holocaust. Not only is there no historical equivalence between the two; there is no moral equivalence either.

The historian Deborah Lipstadt – author of *Denying the Holocaust: The Growing Assault on Truth and Memory* (1994) and successful defendant in the libel suit brought against her and Penguin Books by the Holocaust denier David Irving – has used the term 'soft-core denial' to highlight the damage done by Holocaust inversion. The false equivalencing of Israel and the Nazis, she says, 'elevates by a factor of a zillion any wrongdoings Israel might have done, and lessens by a factor of a zillion what the Germans did' (Klein 2009). And as Anthony Julius points out, the Zionist–Nazi trope not only says to the world that the 'Zionists are to the Palestinians what Nazis were to the Jews' but also that 'the "Zionists" and Nazis share the same Fascist ideology' and that 'the "Zionists" were complicit with the Nazis in the Holocaust' (2010:507–508).

In 1998, the 'anti-Zionist' writers Hazem Saghiyah and Saleh Bashir published 'Universalizing the Holocaust', which makes clear the moral inversion involved in the Holocaust Inversion. 'The dissociation between the acknowledgment of the Holocaust and what Israel is doing should be the starting point for the development of a discourse which says that the Holocaust does not free the Jewish state or the Jews of accountability. On the contrary, *the Nazi crime compounds their moral responsibility and exposes them to greater answerability.* They are the ones who have escaped the ugliest crime in history, and now they are perpetrating reprehensible deeds against another people' (Saghiyah and Bashir 1998).

Holocaust Inversion, then, involves the abuse of the Holocaust memory to issue a *moral stricture* aimed at Israel and 'the Jews', imposing upon them a *uniquely* onerous moral responsibility and accountability in their treatment of others.

The Accusation of Bad Faith

Criticised for his Holocaust Memorial Day comments, David Ward hit back by accusing his critics of bad faith: 'There is a huge operation out there, a machine almost, which is designed to protect the State of Israel from criticism. And that comes into play very, very quickly and focuses intensely on anyone who's seen to criticise the State of Israel. And so I end up looking at what happened to me, whether I should use this word, whether I should use that word – and that is winning for them.'

This is an example of 'The Livingstone Formulation', a term coined by David Hirsh (2010) to refer to the practice of responding to claims of contemporary antisemitism by alleging that those making the claim are only doing so to prevent Israel from being criticised; in other words, they are 'playing the antisemitism card'. Ward's statement is a perfect illustration of the Livingstone Formulation because while Ward claims that an ad hominem attack is being made on him by a 'huge operation out there, a machine almost', it is, in fact, *he* who is making an ad hominem attack on those who question him. Rather than a 'huge operation' deflecting criticism of Israel, it is actually Ward who is deflecting legitimate concerns about antisemitism in the form of the Holocaust inversion.

By inverting reality and morality, and by recklessly spreading accusations of bad faith, Holocaust Inversion prevents us from identifying the changing nature of contemporary antisemitism and is an obstacle to marshalling active resistance to it.

Note

1 This chapter was first published in *Fathom* in 2014.

References

Fine, Robert (2009) 'Fighting with phantoms: A contribution to the debate on anti-semitism in Europe', *Patterns of Prejudice*, 43 (5): 459–479.

Gerstenfeld, Manfred (2007) 'Holocaust inversion: The portraying of Israel and Jews as Nazis', *Jerusalem Center for Public Affairs*. Available: https://jcpa.org/article/holocaust-inversion-the-portraying-of-israel-and-jews-as-nazis/ (accessed 2 November 2022).

Heni, Clemens (2008) 'Secondary antisemitism: From hard-core to soft-core denial of the Shoah', *Jewish Political Studies Review*, 20 (3–4): 73–92.

Hirsh, David (2010) 'Accusations of malicious intent in debates about the Palestine-Israel conflict and about antisemitism: The Livingstone Formulation, "playing the antisemitism card" and contesting the boundaries of antiracist discourse', *Transversal*, 11: 47–77.

Iganski Paul and Abe Sweiry (2009) *Understanding the 'Nazi Card': Intervening Against Anti-Semitic Discourse*, London: The European Institute for the Study of Contemporary Antisemitism.

Julius, Anthony (2010) *Trials of the Diaspora: A History of Antisemitism in England*, Oxford: Oxford University Press.

Klein, Amy (2009) 'Denying the deniers: Q & A with Deborah Lipstadt', *Jewish Telegraphic Agency*, 19 April. Available: www.jta.org/2009/04/19/lifestyle/denying-the-deniers-q-a-with-deborah-lipstadt (accessed 2 November 2022).

Lipstadt, Deborah (1994) *Denying the Holocaust: The Growing Assault on Truth and Memory*, London: Penguin.

Saghiyah, Hazem and Saleh Bashir (1998) 'Universalizing the Holocaust', *Palestine-Israel Journal*, 5 (3). Available: https://pij.org/articles/382 (accessed 2 November 2010).

17

HITLER AND THE NAZIS' ANTI-ZIONISM

Jeffrey Herf

During the Cold War, the Soviet Union, its Warsaw Pact Allies and the Western far-left spread a variety of lies about the history of Zionism, the most famous of these falsehoods being the assertion that Hitler and the Nazi regime were supporters of Zionism.[1] It was a falsehood that fit well with another big lie of Communist Cold War propaganda, namely that Zionism was itself a form of racism. If the latter were the case, it would make logical sense that racists such as Hitler supported Zionism. The fact is however that Hitler and the Nazis despised Zionism and did all they could to defeat it.

Ken Livingstone, the former Mayor of London and a long-standing prominent figure on the British left, has now repeated the myth of Nazi support for Zionism. However, what was a required and standard slogan of the Communist regimes, parties and the Western far-left during the Cold War now faces opposition from some members of the British Labour Party. That a man as prominent as Livingstone, whom the citizens of London elected as their Mayor for eight years, repeats such rubbish says a great deal about the ideas that have been circulating in the city. At least parts of Britain's left have sunk to the status of a provincial intellectual backwater. Livingstone and those who agree with him are oblivious of the following well-established historical facts.

First, Hitler despised Zionism. In fact, he ridiculed the idea as he was convinced that the Jews would be incapable of establishing and then defending a state. More importantly, he and his government viewed the prospect of a Jewish state in Palestine as part of the broader international Jewish conspiracy which his fevered imagination presented as a dire threat to Germany. While the Nazis did allow some German Jews to leave the country in the 1930s in order to travel to Palestine (after robbing them of most of their

DOI: 10.4324/9781003322320-21

possessions), that policy was primarily driven by a desire to get the Jews out of Germany rather than to build a Jewish state in Palestine. By the late 1930s, the Grand Mufti of Jerusalem, Haj Amin al-Husseini, who later collaborated with the Nazis in wartime Berlin, had informed German diplomats stationed in Jerusalem that the entry of Jews into Palestine from Germany was angering local Arabs. For reasons of their own, the Nazis cut off Jewish emigration in 1941 to pursue their goal of murdering Europe's Jews. This ignorance about the implications of the Holocaust is stunning. As the Israeli historian Anita Shapira has pointed out, it is only a half-truth to say that Israel was founded because of the Holocaust. The other half of the truth is that literally millions of Jews in Europe who might have contributed to the establishment of the Jewish state in Palestine could not do so because the Nazis had murdered them. The Holocaust itself was an enormous blow to the Zionist project.

Second, Livingstone displays an ignorance of the history of World War II in North Africa. In November 1941, Hitler promised the Mufti, then in Berlin, that if and when the German armies were successful in the Caucuses, they would drive South to destroy the Jewish population then living in areas controlled by Britain in North Africa and the Middle East. In the summer and autumn of 1942, German General Erwin Rommel's Afrika Korps drove east from Tunisia to be met by forces from Australia, New Zealand and Britain at the Battle of El Alamein in Egypt. Nazi propaganda in those weeks and months urged Arab listeners to 'kill the Jews', dispensing with any distinctions between Zionists and Jews. As the German historians Martin Cuppers and Klaus Michael Mallman have demonstrated in *Nazi Palestine: The Plans for the Extermination of the Jews of Palestine*, it was only the Allied victory at El Alamein over Rommel's forces that prevented the arrival of SS units eager to carry out mass murders of Jews in North Africa and Mandatory Palestine. Livingstone appears unfamiliar with this glorious page in the history of British anti-Fascism.

While actions speak louder than words, Nazi propaganda aimed both at German audiences and at Arabs in North Africa and the Middle East constantly denounced Britain, the Jews and Zionism. This Nazi flood of anti-Zionist and anti-Jewish hatred is documented in my book *Nazi Propaganda for the Arab World,* which the leaders of the Labour Party really ought to read. Nazi propagandists claimed that a Jewish state in Palestine would be a 'Vatican for the Jews', that is a power centre of an international Jewish conspiracy and thus a threat to Germany. They also argued that an Allied victory would be a victory for the Jews. They repeated lies that a Jewish state in Palestine would be a threat to the religion of Islam in the entire Arab Middle East. Zionism was described as a form of 'Jewish imperialism' that was linked to British and American imperialism, and even to 'Jewish Bolshevism' in Moscow as well. In the post-war years, neo-Nazis and Islamists in the Middle East viewed the establishment of the state of Israel as confirming these Nazi anti-Semitic conspiracy theories. In short, in both word and deed, Nazi Germany did all it could to ensure that a Jewish state in Palestine never would emerge.

Livingstone appears ill-informed about the decisive role that British anti-Fascism in World War II played in defeating Nazi Germany's efforts to murder the almost one million Jews of North Africa and the Middle East. One of the great successes of the Cold War propaganda campaigns waged by the Soviet Union, its Warsaw Pact allies, Arab states most hostile to Israel as well as the Palestine Liberation Organisation was its suppression of the actual history of Nazi anti-Zionism and even the role the Soviet Union played in helping to defeat it. In the immediate post-war years, before Soviet leaders sought to drive out Western influence in the Middle East and gain control over Western Europe's supply of oil from the region, the Soviet Union supported the establishment of the state of Israel. After the 'anti-cosmopolitan purges' of the early 1950s, the history of Soviet Zionism became as embarrassing as the actual history of Nazi anti-Zionism. Neither fit into the dogmas of Communist anti-imperialism which, it appears, have now filtered into some ranks of the Labour Party.

Anti-Semitism, like all forms of racism and religious hatred, is built on lies and distortions about the past and present. Around the world, London stands for worldliness, cosmopolitanism and often for an understanding of history. When the former Mayor of this city reveals how little he knows about World War II and Britain's role in it, one has to wonder what has happened to the qualities we admire in British intellectual life.

Note

1 This chapter was first published in *Fathom* in 2016.

18

HOLOCAUST FALSIFIERS

Blaming 'Zionists' for the Crimes of the Nazis

Paul Bogdanor

Holocaust deniers, typically on the far-right, accuse Jews of inventing the genocide to discredit the Nazis.[1] Certain Holocaust falsifiers, often on the far-left, accuse a group of Jews of *furthering* the genocide in collaboration with the Nazis. Although their ideologies are very different, both sets of extremists mutilate historical facts and evidence to make their case. The activities of the deniers are well known; and the methods of the falsifiers are less familiar.

Today's Holocaust falsifiers did not arise in a vacuum. They are continuing an antisemitic tradition with its origins in totalitarian states. Official Soviet propaganda, especially in the aftermath of Israel's 1967 victory over the Arab armies, accused the Zionist movement of having been Hitler's partner in the murder of six million Holocaust victims. Soviet sources spoke of 'the true role of the Zionists in organising the mass destruction of Jews'. 'Together with the Nazis', they proclaimed, 'the Zionists bear responsibility for the destruction of the Jews in 1941–45 in Europe. The blood of millions is on their hands and on their conscience' (IJA 1978:69).

Antisemitic conspiracy theories have a long life, and the myth of Zionist–Nazi collaboration is a case in point. Outside the Soviet bloc, the myth became embedded in Stalinist and Trotskyist fringe politics in the West. It was stated in canonical form in *Zionism in the Age of the Dictators*, a book published by Lenni Brenner during the 1980s (Brenner 1983). And in recent years, the 'collaboration' charge has provoked a public scandal in Britain.

In Spring 2016, British newspapers reported a stream of antisemitic incidents in the opposition Labour Party. Meanwhile, enthusiasts for Labour leader Jeremy Corbyn insisted, against all evidence, that nothing was amiss.

DOI: 10.4324/9781003322320-22

Among them was one of the country's best-known politicians, Ken Livingstone. Not content with belittling concerns about the resurgence of anti-Jewish bigotry in public life, the former Mayor of London volunteered that Hitler 'was supporting Zionism – this before he went mad and ended up killing six million Jews' (*Independent* 2016). Livingstone was not new to these ideas. As he had written in his memoirs, Brenner's work had, decades earlier, 'helped form my view of Zionism and its history' (Livingstone 2011:223).

In order to befoul the Jewish national movement and its millions of Jewish supporters with moral guilt for the horrors of Nazism, both Brenner and his admirer Livingstone repeatedly misrepresented the historical record. Their methods repay detailed examination.

Part 1: Lenni Brenner and the myth of the Zionist–Nazi conspiracy

Lenni Brenner is an American Trotskyist. Born to an Orthodox Jewish family, as a youth he renounced the traditions of his parents and found his calling as an extreme left-wing activist. Since the 1980s, he has developed a cult following among those convinced that 'Zionists' are to blame for the world's evils.

Antisemitic remarks litter Brenner's writings. 'The Jews', he once claimed, 'were powerful in the emporiums of the world, particularly in two of Germany's biggest markets – Eastern Europe and America' (Brenner 1983:57). Marx, he wrote, was correct to maintain that 'the Jews of Poland are the smeariest of all races', and Zionism was nothing but 'a Shylock operation' (Brenner 1984:11, 38). One of Brenner's books was a savage attack on the American Jewish community, which he denounced as a 'pillar of capitalism' (Brenner 1986:61). He argued: 'The belief that American Jewry, in its majority, will play a progressive role in the future is racist and utopian' (Brenner 1986:358).

Given his animus against many of his fellow Jews, it is unsurprising that this Trotskyist has found admirers at the opposite extreme of the political spectrum: the Institute for Historical Review (IHR) – America's major Holocaust denial outfit – hastened to market Brenner's work to its neo-Nazi followers (Brenner 1986:180).

Brenner's *Zionism in the Age of the Dictators* painted the Jewish national movement as a reactionary cause with many similarities to Fascism and Nazism. In Brenner's version of history, the Zionists were to blame for the collapse of the Weimar Republic; they supported Japanese imperial expansion in Asia; and – worst of all – they contributed to the Holocaust, which some of them welcomed as a step towards the creation of a Jewish state (Brenner 1983:27–37, 183–186, 238, 263–264, 269). Brenner was able to advance these claims only through a prodigious display of propagandist talent. A critical examination of a selection of his manipulations follows.

(i) 'Boycott-scabbing and outright collaboration'

As soon as the Nazi Party came to power in 1933, finding refuge for German Jews became a matter of urgency. Negotiations soon began between the Labour Zionists and the new regime, resulting in the Transfer Agreement. This was meant to facilitate the departure of thousands of German Jews to Palestine, while saving a fraction of their property. The agreement caused intense public controversy within the Zionist movement, as Brenner himself made clear (Brenner 1983:64, 66–67).

Brenner's trump card in his attack on the Transfer Agreement was the fact that two-thirds of German Jews seeking Palestine certificates in the years between 1933 and 1935 were turned down (Brenner 1983:145). However, as his source pointed out, matters were not so simple: Jewish Agency representatives were *forced* to reject these applications because of the British quota, which limited the number of immigrants to Palestine regardless of the plight of Diaspora Jews (Margaliot 1977:253). Brenner concealed this crucial point, the better to accuse the Labour Zionists of the 1930s of 'boycott-scabbing and outright collaboration' with Hitler (Brenner 1983:65).

(ii) Zionists who 'agreed' with Nazi ideology

According to Brenner, 'the German Zionists agreed with two fundamental elements in Nazi ideology', namely 'that the Jews would never be part of the German *volk* and, therefore, they did not belong on German soil' (Brenner 1983:35).

To substantiate these assertions, he invoked the historian Stephen Poppel, who in fact wrote the exact opposite on the very page he cited. In Poppel's words, even though there was a split in German Zionist opinion between those who believed in the existence of 'moderate elements' in the Nazi Party and those who did not, 'Zionists were unanimous in condemning Nazi brutality and racism' (Poppel 1976:161). Poppel proceeded to quote from an official declaration of the German Zionist Federation (ZVfD) in September 1932. The declaration stated in part: 'Zionism condemns a nationalism whose foundations include the conviction of the inferiority of other national groups . . . we demand the protection of full equality and freedom' (Poppel 1976:161–162).

Brenner's fiction about Zionists agreeing with Nazis was rejected by the very scholar he cited, and the evidence against it was available on the very page from which he quoted.

(iii) 'Favoured children' of the Nazis

Brenner attacked the German Zionists of the 1930s as 'mimics of the Nazis', 'confirmed racists' and 'the ideological jackals of Nazism' (Brenner 1983:52, 55). One of the documents he used to establish this was an article by Rabbi

Joachim Prinz, published in 1937 (reprinted in Brenner 2002) after his escape from the Third Reich.

Brenner's quotations from Prinz included the words: 'Solution of the Jewish question? It was our Zionist dream! We never denied the existence of the Jewish question!' (Brenner 1983:47). The passage appeared to suggest a belief on the part of Prinz that Zionists and Nazis had common goals. But Brenner ignored what Prinz wrote next about the real aims of the Zionists: 'We believed in the slim possibility of saving the German Jews.' In contrast, the Nazi government's 'only attitude toward Jews was one of humiliation, degradation, and the spirit of the *Sturmer*' (Prinz 1937). So, Prinz expressly *denied* the existence of any common objectives.

Brenner compounded this distortion with an apparently damning confession by Prinz: the German Zionists appeared to be 'considered as the favoured children of the Nazi Government', which 'asked for a "more Zionist behaviour"' from Germany's Jewish community (Prinz 1937). In Brenner's view, these lines showed that 'The Nazis preferred the Zionists to all other Jews' (Brenner 1983:88). Yet immediately after the words in question, Prinz went on to say: 'But the Nazi attitude toward the Zionists was only a façade. In reality, the Zionists were and are miserably treated. . . . During the years, Zionists have frequently been arrested. . . . Zionist officials were and still are frequently called to the Gestapo. . . . In brief, the seeming pro-Zionist attitude of the German Government is not an expression of, and should not be confused with, cooperation on the part of one side or the other' (Prinz 1937). None of this was divulged in Brenner's book. By selective quotation, Brenner simply reversed the meaning of his source.

(iv) The Haganah's 'offer to spy for the SS'

Brenner accused the Zionists of offering espionage services to the Third Reich before World War II. In his version of events, 'A Haganah agent, Feivel Polkes' reached Berlin in February 1937 and opened negotiations with Adolf Eichmann; the meetings were recorded by the SS; and Polkes invited Eichmann to visit Palestine (Brenner 1983:93–94, 98–99). As Brenner put it, 'Polkes had proposed that the Haganah act as spies for the Nazis', and 'The Labour Zionists were receiving Adolf Eichmann as their guest in Palestine and offering to spy for the SS' (Brenner 1983:99, 176).

According to Brenner, the SS report on the meetings proved that Polkes was acting on behalf of the Haganah when he offered to act as an informer. A review of the report – later republished by Brenner himself – debunks this claim. The SS report included some highly relevant details: '[Polkes] stated that he is ready to serve Germany and supply information as long as this does not oppose his political goal. . . . His standing promises that important information and material will reach us regarding world Jewry's plans' (Six

1937, reprinted in Brenner 2002:113–114). Polkes was offering to become a Nazi spy *against* his fellow Jews, not *for* the Haganah.

As is now known, the Polkes-Eichmann meetings were fiercely denounced within the Haganah when they came to light; Polkes was removed from all positions within the group; and nothing of significance ever emerged from the encounters (Nicosia 2008:126). But the relevant point here is this: Brenner's claims about the Haganah offering to spy for the Nazis and inviting Eichmann to visit Palestine were false, as shown by the very document he was citing.

(v) Lehi's 'collusion with the Fascists and the Nazis'

Brenner devoted a chapter to the 1941 offer to the Nazis by Avraham Stern's group Lehi. Stern proposed to join the war on Germany's side in return for the release of all Jews from Nazi Europe and their evacuation to a Jewish state.

Three points must be kept in mind. First, Lehi was – at the time of this proposal – a minuscule fringe group of no more than a few dozen members, reviled and hunted by the larger Zionist groups in Palestine. Second, no reply ever came from the Nazis, so there was never any actual collaboration. Third – and most important – at the time of the proposal, Stern believed that Hitler's intention was to deport Europe's Jews to Madagascar; he knew nothing of any Nazi plan to exterminate the Jews (Heller 1995:317. n46).

Brenner saw Stern's offer as proof of 'Zionist collusion with the Fascists and the Nazis' (Brenner 1983:269). He quoted from a broadcast made by Lehi in defence of its policies. That broadcast distinguished 'persecutors' from 'enemies', arguing that whereas the Nazis were persecutors, Britain was the real enemy (Brenner 1983:266).

What Brenner did not tell his readers is that the broadcast did *not* advocate collaboration with the Nazis. On the contrary, the broadcast stated that Jewish youth were needed in Palestine 'to guard our brethren here from the Arab terrorists that are awaiting Hitler's victory, as well as the persecutor himself should he invade and set up an oppressive regime' (Sicker 1972:32–33). Far from offering to fight *for* the Nazis, the Lehi broadcast mentioned by Brenner promised to fight *against* them.

According to the article Brenner was quoting, all other Zionist groups were determined to join the anti-Nazi struggle. The official Jewish leadership in Palestine, stated Brenner's source, 'fought vigorously for maximum mobilisation of Palestinian Jews into the British forces' (Sicker 1972:33). Brenner, of course did not mention this: it would have disproved his narrative of Zionist–Nazi conspiracy.

(vi) Ben-Gurion and the Holocaust

David Ben-Gurion's role in rescue efforts during the Holocaust has been much debated. According to Brenner, the Zionist leader was vague and non-committal about his rescue ideas, and uninterested in acting on them (Brenner 1983:232–233). But in Brenner's source, Ben-Gurion is quoted making these demands: '(a) cessation of the slaughter and rescue of the Jews; (b) enabling the Jewish people to fight as Jews against Hitler. It is also our duty to request that the Allies threaten the Nazis with individual and collective retribution for massacres of Jews. . . . We must particularly stress the rescue of children, but we ought not to be satisfied with children alone: every Jew who can possibly be rescued must be saved' (Gelber 1979:195–196).

On reading Ben-Gurion's actual words (which Brenner misleadingly paraphrased), the Zionist leader's concern for Jewish lives is undeniable. And Ben-Gurion's call for a Jewish army to fight Hitler was integral to the Zionist movement's support for the Allied war against Nazism. This is itself sufficient to refute the central claim of Brenner's book about the Zionist movement's 'collaboration' with the Third Reich.

(vii) The Gruenbaum speech

The head of the Jewish Agency's official rescue committee in Palestine during the Holocaust was Yitzhak Gruenbaum. He is remembered both for rejecting Zionist demands to use Zionist funds for rescue operations, and, conversely, for being one of the first to call for Allied bombing to save Jews from Auschwitz.

Gruenbaum's speech to the Zionist Executive in early 1943 is often quoted in antizionist propaganda relating to the Holocaust. His remarks included the words: 'we do not give priority to rescue actions . . . Zionism is above all.' Even though Gruenbaum added that no opportunity for rescue would be missed, his comments were – and still are – the target of justified criticism. Brenner, naturally, reproduced the speech at length (1983:233–235). But he did not tell his readers about the Zionist reaction to Gruenbaum's remarks, as related by one of his own sources: out of 14 members of the Zionist Executive who spoke after Gruenbaum, only one backed him, while eleven rejected his views (Beit-Zvi 1991:130). Gruenbaum's Zionist colleagues overwhelmingly opposed his doctrine of the priority of Zionism over rescue efforts (Beit-Zvi 1991:130–135). Brenner totally ignored this. He reprinted Gruenbaum's speech, but not the hostile Zionist replies to it.

(viii) 'Zionist' collaborators in Nazi Europe

Brenner's attempts to incriminate Zionism included an examination of Jewish leaders in Nazi-occupied Europe. Brenner maintained that the Nazi-imposed Jewish Councils (*Judenräte*) in the Polish ghettos were led by Zionists: 'Upon their arrival in Warsaw the Germans found Adam Czerniakow, a Zionist and President of the Association of Jewish Artisans, as the head of the rump of the Jewish community organisation and they ordered him to set up a *Judenrat*

(Jewish Council). In Lodz, Poland's second city, Chaim Rumkowski, also a minor Zionist politician, was similarly designated' (Brenner 1983:203–204). According to Brenner, the Nazis trusted the Zionists to betray the Jewish masses (Brenner 1983:204–205).

Contrary to Brenner's claims, neither Czerniakow nor Rumkowski had the support of the Zionist movement when appointed by the Nazis. Czerniakow, according to Holocaust historian Israel Gutman, 'was not a member of a Jewish party, nor did he identify with any of the dominant political or socioreligious movements, although at a certain stage he sided with the minority bloc and moved nearer the non-Zionists within the Jewish Agency' (Gutman 1994:54). As for Rumkowski, Brenner suppressed a crucial fact: in early 1941, the Zionist parties in the Lodz Ghetto formed a coalition *against* his leadership (Katz 1970:63).

(ix) The Slovakia and Europa plans

The Nazi drive against the Jews of Slovakia commenced in early 1942. An attempt to halt this campaign was made by the Slovak Jewish 'Working Group' led by Rabbi Michael Weissmandel (an antizionist), and his relative, Gisi Fleischmann (a Zionist). The Working Group tried to bribe the Nazis.

In the first stage of the negotiations, the Working Group approached Dieter Wisliceny, the SS officer in charge of deporting Slovakia's Jews to their deaths, offering money to stop deportations from the country. This was known as the Slovakia Plan. In the second stage, wrongly believing that its bribe had saved Slovakia's Jews, the Working Group offered the Nazis two million dollars to stop the Final Solution throughout Europe. This was named the Europa Plan. Weissmandel was unable to raise the required funds from his Jewish contacts abroad. Both during and after the War, he blamed world Jewry, and specifically the Zionists, for ruining his attempt to end the Holocaust.

Brenner twisted the facts in two ways (1983:235–238). First, he endorsed Weissmandel's claim that there was a genuine opportunity for rescue. The consensus of historians is that there was no such opportunity: the cessation of the deportations from Slovakia had nothing to do with the bribe to Wisliceny, who was actually pressing for their completion; and the Nazis never considered halting the Final Solution in line with the Europa Plan (Rothkirchen 1984, Aronson 2004:170–180).

Second, Brenner quoted Weissmandel's version of a letter supposedly received from Nathan Schwalb, a Zionist rescue activist in Switzerland, who was alleged to have written: 'Only with [Jewish] blood shall we get the land [of Israel].' No version of this letter has ever been found in any archive. Even if such a letter was sent, it surely did not have the sinister connotations given to it by Weissmandel and Brenner. According to Shlomo Aronson, one of the few historians to mention the letter without denying its authenticity, Schwalb 'tried his best to give some future meaning to the deaths of those who could no longer be saved in his correspondence with Weissmandel by making them martyrs' (Aronson 2004:177).

(x) The Brand mission

In March 1944, the Nazis occupied Hungary. Shortly before the beginning of full-scale deportations of Jews from the Hungarian provinces, SS officer Adolf Eichmann summoned Joel Brand, a leading figure in the Jewish Agency's rescue committee in Budapest, and offered to release one million Jews from Europe. In exchange, he wanted goods from the West, including trucks to be used against the Soviets.

Brand was sent to Turkey to pass this 'Goods for Blood' offer to the Jewish Agency and Western governments. But his mission failed: the British authorities arrested him, refused to entertain Eichmann's offer, and later publicly rejected it. Meanwhile Eichmann, with the aid of the Hungarian authorities, deported over 400,000 Hungarian Jews to Auschwitz.

After the war, Brand accused both the Jewish Agency and the British of sabotaging his mission. Brenner quoted from Brand's sensationalised memoirs at length, exploiting them to incriminate Zionist leaders for blocking the rescue of European Jews. As Brenner explained, 'Brand hoped that it would be possible to negotiate for more realistic arrangements or, at least, to decoy the Nazis into thinking that a deal could be made. Possibly the extermination programme would be slowed down or even suspended while an accord was being worked out' (Brenner 1983:254).

What Brenner did not disclose was Brand's subsequent admission that his hopes had been illusory and his mission a blunder. Shortly before his death, Brand testified in a German courtroom: 'I made a terrible mistake in passing this on to the British. It is now clear to me that Himmler sought to sow suspicion among the Allies as a preparation for his much-desired Nazi-Western coalition against Moscow' (*New York Times* 1964).

Brenner never even hinted at the existence of Brand's retraction, which totally discredited the notion that Eichmann's offer was a missed opportunity to halt the Final Solution.

(xi) The Kasztner trial

When Joel Brand left on his mission to Turkey, his colleague Rezső Kasztner remained behind in Budapest and conducted further talks with the Nazis. The result of these contacts was the departure of a trainload of 1,684 Jews to the Bergen-Belsen camp; the passengers were ultimately released to Switzerland. Kasztner was later accused by Holocaust survivors and others of collaborating with the Nazis. The accusations culminated in a famous libel trial in Israel, in which the judge concluded that Kasztner had 'sold his soul to the Devil'. This verdict was partially reversed by Israel's Supreme Court, but not before Kasztner had been assassinated by right-wing extremists.

The question of Kasztner's personal innocence or guilt need not concern us here. As Brenner conceded, 'No movement is responsible for its renegades' (1983:263). What is relevant is Brenner's manipulation of the facts to indict Zionists *collectively* for criminal complicity in the mass murder of Hungary's Jews. To this end, Brenner relied partly on a post-war interview with Eichmann – a transparently worthless source – and partly on the verdict in the Kasztner Trial. He quoted the judge as stating that Kasztner considered his actions 'a great personal success and a success for Zionism' (Brenner 1983:261). In Brenner's eyes, the Kasztner affair exposed 'the working philosophy of the World Zionist Organisation throughout the entire Nazi era: the sanctification of the betrayal of the many in the interest of a selected immigration to Palestine' (1983:263–264).

However, the trial judge, Benjamin Halevi, stated the exact opposite in his verdict, where he referred to repeated efforts by Zionists inside and outside Hungary to prevent the extermination of the Hungarian Jewish masses. For example, 'Calls from leaders of the Yishuv (Yitzhak Ben-Zvi, Moshe Shertok, Yitzhak Gruenbaum) for self-defence and resistance by Diaspora Jews were sent to the rescue committee in Budapest. After the Nazi occupation, the [Zionist] pioneer movements established their own "headquarters" in Budapest and organised information, escape and bunker actions as well as preparations for resistance' (Halevi 1955:section 33). Halevi also noted: 'Experience had taught the Nazis that everywhere the Zionists were the "activist" element in the Jewish population and were able to supply the leadership for resistance and anti-Nazi operations' (Halevi 1955: section 34).

In short, whatever Kasztner's personal role may have been, the Zionist movement opposed the Nazis and tried to save Jews from the Holocaust. Brenner's own source contradicted the conclusion that he wanted to foist on his readers.

(xii) The Zionist paratroopers

Brenner used other misleading tactics to conceal the Zionist rescue efforts in Hungary. He referred to the three paratroopers from Palestine, Hannah Szenes, Joel Palgi, and Peretz Goldstein, who arrived in Budapest during the Nazi occupation hoping to organise Jewish resistance. Szenes was captured, tortured, and executed; Palgi and Goldstein were persuaded by Kasztner to turn themselves in. Through deceptive phrasing, Brenner implied that the paratroopers were sent by the British alone (Brenner 1983:260–261). In fact, the British army sent them at the instigation of the Jewish Agency in Palestine, and it was these Zionist leaders who wanted to arrange Jewish resistance to the Nazis in Hungary. As Judge Halevi explained, the paratroopers had a dual mission: 'The British military mission was to smuggle POWs and send intelligence out of Hungary. The Jewish Agency mission was to organise Hungarian Jews for self-defence against the Nazi destroyer and to assist the underground rescue of Jews' (Halevi 1955: section 82).

Here, again, Brenner manipulated facts to lead readers to his desired conclusion – that Zionists opposed resistance to the Nazis – which was the reverse of the truth.

Part 2: Ken Livingstone on Hitler and the Zionists

Like his 'authority' Brenner, Livingstone had not been shy about offending the Jewish community. Previously, he had accused the Board of Deputies of British Jews of organising 'paramilitary groups which resemble fascist organisations' throughout the country; compared a Jewish journalist to a concentration camp guard; and alleged that the Thatcher government had won votes in Finchley because 'the Jewish community got richer' (Dovkants 2008, Dysch 2014, Hirsh 2018:11–21).

Amplifying Brenner's claims, Livingstone copied his methods. In his statements about Zionist collusion with Nazi Germany, he distorted the historical record and the sources he cited. The following items are representative.

(xiii) The transfer agreement

According to Livingstone, Zionist collaboration with Hitler involved 'a pact with the Nazis to set up a trading company, Ha'avara, to sell Nazi goods, thus undermining the boycott organised by trade unionists and communists' (Livingstone 2011:221).

In truth, the purpose of the Ha'avara or Transfer Agreement was to evacuate German Jews while preserving a fraction of their property from being stolen by the Nazi regime. And the boycott of Germany was not just 'organised by trade unionists and communists', but was championed by Jews in the free world, including many Zionists.

Perhaps aware that his statements were not only false but grossly insensitive to the plight of German Jews in the 1930s, Livingstone insisted that he had never meant to condemn the Transfer Agreement (Livingstone 2017a:11). But his protestations were hardly consistent with promoting Brenner's writings, wherein the agreement was described as a sell-out to Fascism.

(xiv) Medals bearing 'the Swastika and the Poale Zion star'

According to Livingstone, 'medals were printed, were made, which had the Swastika on one side and the Poale Zion star on the other, literally there is such a history of collaboration' (Livingstone 2017c). Poale Zion was a movement advocating Zionism and socialism. Here, Livingstone was accusing Jews who were not only Zionists but also socialists.

In 1933, during the first months after Hitler's takeover, the Zionist Federation of Germany asked Kurt Tuchler to identify moderate Nazi officials and win them over. Tuchler contacted SS official Baron Leopold von Mildenstein and accompanied him to Palestine. Von Mildenstein wrote a 12-part series about the trip for the Goebbels newspaper *Der Angriff*, which ran the series from 26 September to 9 October 1934 (Boas 1980).

Allegedly, *Der Angriff* commemorated von Mildenstein's articles with a coin-shaped medal showing a swastika on one side and a Star of David on the other. The inscription on the medal read: 'Ein Nazi fährt nach Palästina und erzählt davon im *Angriff*' ('A Nazi travels to Palestine and tells about it in *Angriff*') (Boas 1980:38).

All this was, of course, pure propaganda. The Nazis were pretending that they wanted an 'honourable' solution to the 'Jewish Question' and that Jews were their equal partners in finding such a solution. In citing it as proof of 'collaboration', Livingstone was giving credence to the Nazis' own disinformation.

(xv) 'The SS set up training camps' for German Jews

According to Livingstone, 'the SS set up training camps so that German Jews who were going to go there [i.e., Palestine] could be trained to cope with a very different sort of country when they got there' (Livingstone 2017b).

But the SS did not set up the training camps for German Jews. Livingstone was referring to the *hachschara* farms, which Zionists set up even before Hitler's takeover, with the aim of retraining German Jews for life in Palestine.

A thorough study of the *hachschara* farms has been made by historian Francis Nicosia (Nicosia 2005, 2008). Nicosia makes it clear that Zionist and non-Zionist Jews alike, realising the urgency of extricating as many Jews as possible from Nazi Germany, used occupational retraining centres to prepare Jews for a new life abroad. The Zionist centres prepared Jews for Palestine; the non-Zionist centres prepared Jews for other destinations (Nicosia 2005:368, 2008:211, 221, 225–226, 242).

Occupational retraining did gain the support of the SS in the 1930s, but Nicosia explains how the centres were strictly monitored and regulated by the Third Reich (Nicosia 2008:229) When the war began, 'the regime used Jewish trainees to help meet its labor shortage by folding the occupational retraining programs and the young Jews engaged in them into its forced labor programs' (Nicosia 2005:382). Finally, 'As emigration faded from Nazi policy and gave way to genocide, untold thousands of Jewish workers, including those from the Zionist *Hachschara* programmes, would become part of

Nazi Germany's wartime "labor force" prior to their mass murder' (Nicosia 2008:244).

In short, Livingstone's claim that 'the SS set up training camps' for German Jews was false. Jews, not the SS, set up the vocational retraining centres for those hoping to emigrate. The SS initially approved of the Zionist and non-Zionist centres alike, while imposing strict controls on them, but during World War II, the trainees who had not succeeded in escaping from Germany were first exploited by the Nazis as slave labour and then murdered.

(xvi) 'Selling Mauser pistols to the underground Jewish army'

According to Livingstone, the Nazis 'started selling Mauser pistols to the underground Jewish army, so you had right up until the start of World War II, real collaboration' (Livingstone 2017b).

This, apparently, was based on a couple of sentences in an early paper by Nicosia: 'the Hagana had received shipments of Mauser pistols from Germany in 1935 and 1936. The exact source of these weapons within Germany is difficult to determine; it is certain, however, that some agency in Germany did provide the Hagana with Mauser pistols, and that the police authorities were aware of it' (Nicosia 1978:D1266, 1985:63–64).

Whereas Nicosia drew no conclusion about the supplier of these pistols, stating merely that the police were aware of it, Livingstone was certain that the weapons came from the Nazi regime. Since there was no serious evidence that the Nazis supplied these pistols, Livingstone supplied 'facts' consistent with his political agenda.

(xvii) Permission to display the Zionist flag

According to Livingstone, the Nazis 'passed a law that said the Zionist flag and the Swastika were the only flags that could be flown in Germany' (Livingstone 2017b). In his memoirs, he alleged: 'To encourage Zionists, the Nuremberg laws in 1935 allowed only two flags to be flown in Germany, the Swastika and the blue and white Zionist banner' (Livingstone 2011:221).

In September 1935, section 4 of the Law for the Protection of German Blood and German Honour provided: '1. Jews are forbidden to hoist the Reich and national flag and to present the colours of the Reich. 2. On the other hand they are permitted to present the Jewish colours. The exercise of this authority is protected by the State' (Nuremberg Laws 1935).

'The Jewish colours' were not specified. That the Nazis did not have the official Zionist flag in mind is evident from their reaction when a young German Jew, Martin Friedländer, hung a makeshift blue and white banner out of his window in protest against the law. *Der Angriff* labelled it 'the Jewish national flag', which was being displayed 'for the first time', adding: 'This

finally puts an end to the speculation on how the Jewish flag actually looks'
(Berlin Jewish Museum n.d.).

On 31 December, the authorities decreed that until the Jewish community decided what the Jewish colours were, the Zionist flag would suffice,
and would be 'enjoying State protection' (JTA 1936a). But the decree was a
dead letter; 'State protection' was nothing of the kind. The Nazi press openly
threatened Jews who dared to display the Zionist flag (JTA 1936b).

(xviii) Stopping sermons in Yiddish

According to Livingstone, 'When the Zionist movement asked, would the
Nazi Government stop a Jewish rabbi – the rabbis – doing their sermons
in Yiddish and make them do it in Hebrew, he [i.e., Hitler] agreed to that'
(Livingstone 2017b).

A Jewish Telegraphic Agency report filed on 6 December 1936, read in
full: 'The Gestapo (State secret police) today notified synagogues that sermons in connection with the Jewish festival of Chanukah, beginning Dec.
9, must not be in the German language, as had been the custom of Liberal
synagogues' (JTA 1936c). According to this source, the Gestapo banned Chanukah sermons in German, not Yiddish, and the report makes no mention of
any Zionist request.

Livingstone's claim appeared to be drawn from Brenner, who quoted from
a January 1937 report by Abraham Duker in the American Labour Zionist
magazine *Jewish Frontier* (Brenner 1983:86). The passage quoted by Brenner
read: 'The attempts to seclude the Jews in the cultural ghetto have reached
a new height by the prohibition to rabbis to use the German language in
their Chanukah sermons. This is in line with the effort made by the Nazis to
force the German Jews to use the Hebrew language as their cultural medium.
Thus another "proof" of Nazi-Zionist cooperation is seized on eagerly by the
Communist opponents of Zionism' (Duker 1937:28).

Neither Brenner nor *Jewish Frontier* alleged that the Gestapo ban was
imposed at the request of Zionists. Moreover, Brenner had been selective in
his use of the *Jewish Frontier* report, for he had omitted the very next sentences from his quotation: 'A number of leading Zionists including Rabbi
Leo Prinz and the philosopher Martin Buber were deprived of their passports
by the Gestapo. The number of "captives of Zion" in Germany is thus on the
increase. The ransom price is not as yet known' (Duker 1937:28).

In summary, the Gestapo banned German-language Chanukah sermons
in December 1936, but Livingstone's apparent source, Brenner, did not claim
that this was done at the request of Zionists. Brenner himself dealt deceitfully
with the report he quoted, suppressing information in the same report indicating that the Gestapo was taking action against Zionist leaders at the time.

(xix) The July 1937 Nazi conference

According to Livingstone, 'when, in July 1937, many senior Nazis gathered at their foreign office, saying "we should stop sending Jews to Palestine because it could create a Jewish state", in the middle of that meeting a directive comes specifically from Hitler saying "no, we will continue with this policy"' (Livingstone 2017b).

Livingstone was referring to a Nazi ministerial conference held on 29 July 1937. The background was the recent report of the Peel Commission recommending a two-state solution in Palestine. As Nicosia's paper explains, when the conference was under way, 'The representative of the Interior Ministry reported that Hitler . . . had decided that Jewish emigration from Germany was to be promoted by all possible means, and that all destinations, including Palestine were to be utilized to this end' (Nicosia 1978:D1270). Hitler's directive called for Jews to leave Germany for *all* possible destinations, not just for Palestine, as Livingstone implied.

With respect to the charge of Nazi support for Zionism, Nicosia's paper made the facts perfectly clear: on 1 June 1937, Hitler's Foreign Minister, Baron Konstantin von Neurath, stressed the Nazi regime's 'opposition to the creation of an independent Jewish state in Palestine. It was asserted that such a state would serve as a political base for international Jewry' (Nicosia 1978:D1269). Somehow, Livingstone 'overlooked' this passage.

(xx) 'The Gestapo worked with Israeli agents . . . to secretly migrate 10,000 German Jews'

According to Livingstone, 'After Britain banned Jewish migration to Palestine, the Gestapo worked with Israeli agents in Mossad to secretly migrate 10,000 German Jews to Palestine' (Livingstone 2017c).

Livingstone was referring to illegal immigration to Palestine organised by Mossad LeAliyah Bet, a Haganah body operating from 1938. Livingstone's source, once again, was Nicosia's paper. But Nicosia, unlike Livingstone, made it clear that the agreement to send the 10,000 German Jews to Palestine was never carried out: 'The outbreak of war in September forced the cancellation of that scheme' (Nicosia 1978:D1279, see also 1985:161, 2008:275).

Conclusion

Antizionists, and antisemites who want to be laundered as antizionists, have referred to various incidents of Zionist 'collaboration' with the Nazis both before and during the Holocaust. The examples cited by Lenni Brenner and Ken Livingstone turn out to be distorted or even invented. Brenner, a Trotskyist political agitator, is unreliable with facts and evidence. Livingstone, a hard-left politician whose handling of matters involving Jews has been less than ideal, relies partly on Brenner and partly on genuine scholarship that he twists beyond recognition.

The existence of forced contacts between the Nazis and certain Zionists (as well as Jews who were not Zionists) is no secret. At first, the Nazis aimed to terrorise Jews into leaving Germany, and later to annihilate the Jewish people. The Zionist movement hoped to evacuate Jews from Europe so that they could live free from persecution in a Jewish state.

Historians, including those cited by Brenner and Livingstone, dismiss the charge of Zionist 'collaboration' with Nazism (e.g. Laqueur 1972:500–501, Nicosia 2008:291, Schulze 2016, Snyder 2016). The political extremists who peddle such claims are equating victimisers and would-be rescuers, oppressors and the oppressed, the powerful and the powerless. Intent on pursuing their ideological campaigns regardless of the damage they cause, they falsify the history of persecution ending in genocide, while supplying grist to the mill of antisemites.

Note

1 This chapter is based on two essays first published by Paul Bogdanor in *Fathom*. 'An Antisemitic Hoax: Lenni Brenner on Zionist "collaboration" with the Nazis' appeared in Summer 2016, and 'Ken Livingstone and the myth of Zionist collaboration with the Nazis' in Spring 2017.

References

Aronson, Shlomo (2004) *Hitler, the Allies and the Jews*, Cambridge: Cambridge University Press.

Beit-Zvi, S. B. (1991) *Post-Ugandan Zionism on Trial: Volume 1*, Tel Aviv: Privately Printed (the pre-publication synopsis was available for use in Brenner 1983).

Berlin Jewish Museum (n.d.) 'Brave protest against racist laws'. Available: www. jmberlin.de/en/brave-protest-against-racist-laws (accessed 30 November 2022).

Boas, Jacob (1980) 'A Nazi travels to Palestine', *History Today*, January, pp. 33–38.

Brenner, Lenni (1983) *Zionism in the Age of the Dictators*, Westport, CT: Lawrence Hill Books.

Brenner, Lenni (1984) *The Iron Wall: Zionist Revisionism From Jabotinsky to Shamir*, London: Zed Books.

Brenner, Lenni (1986) *Jews in America Today*, London: Al Saqi Books.

Brenner, Lenni (ed.). (2002) *51 Documents: Zionist Collaboration With the Nazis*, Fort Lee, NJ: Barricade Books.

Dovkants, Keith (2008) 'Anti-Semitism – and a timely question for Ken', *Evening Standard*, 17 April. Available: www.standard.co.uk/news/mayor/anti-semitism-and-a-timely-question-for-ken-6626642.html (accessed 30 November 2022).

Duker, Abraham (1937) 'Diaspora', *Jewish Frontier*, January, pp. 27–28.

Dysch, Marcus (2014) 'It's Ken again: Livingstone says "richer" Jews vote Tory', *Jewish Chronicle*, 7 May. Available: www.thejc.com/news/uk-news/it-s-ken-again-livingstone-says-richer-jews-vote-tory-1.54519 (accessed 30 November 2022).

Gelber, Yoav (1979) 'Zionist policy and the fate of European Jewry (1939–1942)', *Yad Vashem Studies*, 13: 169–210.

Gutman, Israel (1994) *Resistance: The Warsaw Ghetto Uprising*, Boston, MA: Houghton Mifflin Harcourt.

Halevi, Judge Benjamin (1955) *Psak Din, 124/53* [Hebrew: *Verdict, Case 124/53*], Jerusalem: District Court of Jerusalem. Available: www.daat.ac.il/daat/vl/kest nerpsak/kestnerpsak00.pdf (accessed 4 December 2022).

Heller, Joseph (1995) *The Stern Gang: Ideology, Politics, and Terror, 1940–1949*, Abingdon: Routledge.

Hirsh, David (2018) *Contemporary Left Antisemitism*, Abingdon: Routledge.

IJA (1978) *Soviet Antisemitic Propaganda: Evidence From Books, Press and Radio*, London: Institute of Jewish Affairs.

Independent (2016) 'Labour antisemitism row: Read the Ken Livingstone interview transcripts in full', *The Independent*, 28 April. Available: www.independent.co.uk/news/uk/politics/labour-anti-semitism-row-full-transcript-of-ken-livingstones-interviews-a7005311.html (accessed 30 November 2022).

JTA (1936a) 'Zionist Banner decreed official Jewish flag by Nazis', *Jewish Telegraphic Agency*, 2 January. Available: www.jta.org/archive/zionist-banner-decreed-official-jewish-flag-by-nazis (accessed 30 November 2022).

JTA (1936b) 'German press advises Jews not to fly Zionist flag', *Jewish Telegraphic Agency*, 23 September. Available: www.jta.org/archive/german-press-advises-jews-not-to-fly-zionist-flag (accessed 30 November 2022).

JTA (1936c) 'Gestapo Bans Chanukah Sermons in German', *Jewish Telegraphic Agency*, 7 December. Available: www.jta.org/archive/gestapo-bans-chanukah-ser mons-in-german (accessed 30 November 2022).

Katz, Alfred (1970) *Poland's Ghettos at War*, New York: Twayne Publishers.

Laqueur, Walter (1972) *A History of Zionism*, New York: MJF Books.

Livingstone, Ken (2011) *You Can't Say That: Memoirs*, London: Faber and Faber.

Livingstone, Ken (2017a) 'Submission to the Labour Party National Constitutional Committee'. Available: http://bit.ly/2oY9DTR (accessed 30 November 2022).

Livingstone, Ken (2017b) *Statement to the Press*, 30 March. Available: www.youtube.com/watch?v=M81xdVZVxhg (accessed 30 November 2022).

Livingstone, Ken (2017c) 'Interview', *Today*, BBC Radio 4, 4 April. Available: https://bit.ly/3ismQlR (accessed 30 November 2022).

Margaliot, Abraham (1977) 'The problem of the rescue of German Jewry during the years 1933–1939: The reasons for the delay in their emigration from the third Reich', in Israel Gutman and Efraim Zuroff (eds.), *Rescue Attempts During the Holocaust*, Jerusalem: Yad Vashem, 247–265.

New York Times (1964) 'Allied rift called aim of 44 Nazi Ransom plan', 21 May.

Nicosia, Francis R. J. (1978) 'Zionism in national socialist Jewish policy in Germany, 1933–39', *Journal of Modern History*, 50 (4), December: 1253–1282.

Nicosia, Francis R. J. (1985) *The Third Reich and the Palestine Question*, Austin, TX: University of Texas Press.

Nicosia, Francis R. J. (2005) 'Jewish farmers in Hitler's Germany: Zionist occupational retraining and Nazi "Jewish policy"', *Holocaust and Genocide Studies*, 19 (3), Winter: 365–389.

Nicosia, Francis R.J. (2008) *Zionism and Anti-Semitism in Nazi Germany*, Cambridge: Cambridge University Press.

Nuremberg Laws (1935) 'Gesetz zum Schutze des deutschen Blutes und der deutschen Ehre', September. Available: https://de.wikisource.org/wiki/Gesetz_zum_Schutze_des_deutschen_Blutes_und_der_deutschen_Ehre (accessed 30 November 2022).

Poppel, Stephen M. (1976) *Zionism in Germany, 1897–1933: The Shaping of a Jewish Identity*, Philadelphia, PA: The Jewish Publication Society of America.

Prinz, Joachim (1937) 'Zionism under the Nazi Government', *The New Palestine*, 17 September (reprinted in Brenner ed. 2002: 98–102).

Rothkirchen, Livia (1984) 'The "Europa plan": A reassessment', in Seymour Maxwell Finger (ed.), *American Jewry During the Holocaust*, New York: American Jewish Commission on the Holocaust, Appendix 4:7.

Schulze, Rainer (2016) 'Hitler and Zionism: Why the Haavara agreement does not mean the Nazis were Zionists', *The Independent*, 2 May. Available: www.independent.co.uk/news/world/world-history/adolf-hitler-zionism-zionist-nazis-haavara-agreement-ken-livingstone-labour-antisemitism-row-a7009981.html (accessed 30 November 2022).

Sicker, Martin (1972) 'Echoes of a poet: A reconsideration of Abraham Stern – yair', *American Zionist*, February, pp. 30–34.

Six, Franz-Albert (1937) 'Report on secret commando matter', 17 June (translation in Brenner ed. 2002: 111–115).

Snyder, Timothy (2016) 'Livingstone Hitler comments "inaccurate"', *BBC News*, 28 April. Available: www.bbc.co.uk/news/uk-36165298 (accessed 30 November 2022).

PART 5

Left Antisemitism in Europe and the United States

19

REFLECTIONS ON CONTEMPORARY ANTISEMITISM IN EUROPE

Kenneth Waltzer

Europe 2014. Authorities in Oslo, Norway, have permanently closed streets to traffic around the Jewish synagogue.[1] In Berlin, Germany, the Jewish community newsletter is sent without any identifiable markings on the envelope, so as not to 'out' recipients as Jews or members. In Amsterdam, police trailers stand before the 17th-century Portuguese Synagogue, the Jewish high school, the Anne Frank Museum, and other institutions. Military police guard the buildings, and Jewish leaders desire that they carry automatic weapons. In Antwerp, an elite army unit patrols the Jewish quarter.

One small group of European Jewish leaders, the European Jewish Association, petitioned the European Union in January to pass new legislation permitting Jewish community members to carry guns 'for the essential protection of their communities'. Observers say that, 70 years after the Holocaust, Jew-hatred is spreading in Europe. Jews are seeing their religious freedom violated, their grave sites vandalised, their synagogues desecrated, and Jewish lives lost.

In Paris, an Islamic extremist tied to the *Charlie Hebdo* killers took over the Hyper Cacher kosher grocery and wantonly killed several Jewish hostages. The *Charlie Hebdo* killers themselves murdered only one woman, a Jewish woman, at the journal's offices, intentionally sparing all others. Soon after the events unfolded in Paris, another jihadist in Copenhagen attacked a free speech gathering, and then murdered a voluntary Jewish community guard outside a bat-mitzvah. In each of these events, Jews were coerced to cower in basement hiding places, as if in a classic Bialik poem, to avoid being massacred.

But such recent events hardly stand alone, following a year during which large public marches in Paris, Brussels, Berlin, and elsewhere included

DOI: 10.4324/9781003322320-24

demonstrators calling on Jews to leave France, Belgium, or Germany, and chanting that Hitler didn't finish the job. 'Jews to the gas, Jews to the gas!', hundreds of demonstrators marching away from the Bastille in Paris called out in mid-July. Mob actions occurred against synagogues and Jewish stores in and around the city, including at the Don Abravanel Synagogue; further mob action came a week later at a synagogue in Sarcelles. Moreover, the events in 2014 came after a rising number of killings since the early 2000s, culminating in jihadi killings of children in Toulouse in 2012 and of tourists at the Brussels Jewish Museum in 2014. The brutal slaying of a Jewish child in 2012 by a jihadist was even celebrated by some French Muslims on social media.

What is going on? How shall we understand the shape and meaning of contemporary anti-Semitism in Europe? How shall we begin to come to terms with the rising danger?

The Scale of the Problem

Historians of Nazi anti-Semitism are quick to assess these events and stress the need for a sense of proportion. David Cesarani, a leading British Holocaust historian, Professor of History in Royal Holloway, University of London, observes that there is not 'a wave of anti-Semitism' – there are no mass movements or significant political parties in Europe that are officially anti-Semitic. Jews are equal citizens with full civil rights in European states with strong claims for protection. Jews are thriving in every walk of life in Europe (Cesarani 2015).

Deborah Lipstadt, a leading American Holocaust historian, and the Dorot Professor of Modern Jewish History at Emory University, who attended the important Organization for Security and Co-operation in Europe (OSCE) Conference on Anti-Semitism in Fall 2014, offers similar advice. 'We are light-years away from the 1930s and 1940s. When anti-Semitism rears its head today, European officials forthrightly deplore and condemn it', she says (Lipstadt 2014a, 2014b, 2015).

Nor are the things we see today, these scholars suggest, entirely new. Arab terrorists attacked Jews in London and Paris during the 1970s and 1980s – and a bomb killed people in the synagogue on the Rue Copernic in Paris; another killed people in Jo Goldenberg's restaurant in the Marais. Personally, when my wife and I visited the Centre de Documentation Juive Contemporaine in the Marais with our young children a few years later in 1985, the building bore signs of having recently been raked by machine gun fire.

And yet, while there is not a 'wave' of anti-Semitism and terrible things have occurred before, and while it is not a matter of centralised political mobilisation or state policy anywhere in Europe, the current upsurge of attacks on Jews and Jewish institutions and the deepening antagonisms directed from specific segments of European society are seriously worrying. The cumulative danger, stress and burden of self-protection threaten lives and communities and also undermine liberal society.

'Seventy years after the Holocaust, many Jews in Europe no longer feel safe', Lipstadt said before the murders in Paris and Copenhagen. 'This is not another Holocaust, but it's bad enough', she observed (2014a). 'Make no mistake – we have a problem', American UN ambassador Samantha Power, speaking forthrightly, told the OSCE conference months before the *Charlie Hebdo* attacks (Smale 2014).

No one writes more pessimistically in Germany than Polish Jewish writer and satirist Henryk Broder, a prominent journalist who is a frequent opponent of anti-Semitism. Broder writes pointedly in *Die Zeit*, and with only slight exaggeration, that Jews barely exist as subjects in their own history in Europe today. Rather, they have become wards of the state, protected Jews, as once they were before emancipation. 'What we are witnessing is not a renaissance of Jewish life in Germany and in Europe, but the end of an experiment. It's over', Broder declares. Things will not get better but will inevitably become worse. 'Toulouse was the prelude to Brussels, Brussels led to Paris, and Copenhagen will not be the last stop' (Broder 2015).

Most recently, American journalist Jeffrey Goldberg – who was in Paris during the *Charlie Hebdo* events – wrote about the crisis in a dramatic cover story in the *Atlantic Magazine*. 'Is It Time For The Jews To Leave Europe?', Goldberg asked. His conclusion was grim: 'European Jewry does not have a bright future' (2015).

The Sources of the New Antisemitism

The new anti-Semitism in Europe appears to come in part from traditional sources on the right side of the political spectrum. Amidst growing economic crisis, there is an intensifying mobilisation of populist responses against immigrants and others and against established elites – in France, Hungary, Greece and elsewhere – which is sharpening antagonisms directed also against Jews. However, the main sources of the new anti-Semitism in most European states are the hard anti-colonial left, which attacks America and Israel as the cornerstones of Western imperialism, and alienated segments of the growing Muslim population, especially marginal youths. French Islamist scholar Olivier Roy talks about the upsurge of a 'globalised Islam' in areas of Muslim concentration on the periphery of French cities – a militant Islamic resentment against Western dominance – along with a serious and rising anti-Semitism (Roy 2004). French sociologist Gilles Kepel writes about the ineffectiveness of French republican ideals in these spaces and, by contrast, the increasing power of an extremist version of Islam (Kepel 2012). Already ten years ago, French philosopher Pierre-Andre Taguieff was writing about a new Judeophobia rising from the muck in France and contributing to increased antagonism towards and rising violence against Jews. Taguieff remarked too – tellingly, at the time, and true ever since – about the absence of anti-racist actions to protest against or blunt the new anti-Semitism (Taguieff 2004). Many on the hard left prefer to think that anti-Semitism is not a real problem, and to insist that claims about anti-Semitism are offered in bad faith to deflect criticisms against Israel. This also appeared as a stock response immediately after *Charlie Hebdo*, when several commentators worried not about the attacks on Jews but about a projected Islamophobic backlash to come against Muslims.

Several recent studies based on extensive interviews carried out with Muslim youths, including *The Lure of Anti-Semitism: Hatred of Jews in Present-Day France*, by French sociologist Michel Wieviorka and his team, report on a Manichean view about Jews that is held by many 'disenfranchised youths' among Muslims of North African origin in France (2007). These elements talk about Jews as powerful, privileged, and evil, as inveterate enemies of Muslims, and as conspirators against humanity. Jews are rich and stingy, these youths say openly; Jews in Europe side with Israel which has stolen Palestinian land and is an unrelievedly evil nation in the world of nations. Jews are treacherous and unscrupulous. The word 'Jew' itself is a negative epithet again – Goldberg heard the neighbourhood parlance of 'Feuj' (a reversal of 'Juif', a street slur) in the Paris outskirts – and many among such youths believe that the Holocaust is a Jewish swindle. 'Jews, and all those who massacre Muslims, I detest them', said the sister of the jihadist who killed Jews in Toulouse.

Brown University historian Maude Mandel has sought to understand this sharpening antagonism between Muslims and Jews by painstakingly retracing the complex history of Muslim-Jewish relations against the backdrop of the North African anti-colonial revolutions and the ongoing Israeli–Palestinian conflict. She also probes the impact of the migration of Jews and Muslims to France, where the two groups underwent divergent integration processes. Still others see such animosity as deriving from a broad anti-colonial resentment against Western hegemony and actions in the Middle East and North Africa, hence not to be considered a base hatred at all but really part of an anti-imperialist resistance outlook (Mandel 2014). But to this writer, it appears that a good deal more than inter-ethnic community political friction and resentment among people of different identities is happening, and that more than a general anti-colonial outlook affects thought and sentiment among the resentful in the *banlieues*. For myself, I see a new anti-Semitism that is growing and metastasising, absorbing earlier forms and themes of Jew-hatred but adding new ones fit for the current age. Jeffrey Goldberg (2015) observes of Europe that 'Traditional Western patterns of anti-Semitic thought have now merged with a potent strain of Muslim Judeophobia.'

Shalom Lappin of Kings College, London, has communicated with this writer that we should comprehend the wider context in order to better comprehend the moment. Lappin argues that European nations have been living through an extended period of economic recession with resultant wrenching social dislocations. These developments have affected living standards and blunted the prospects of large parts of Europe's population, especially the most marginal members among the immigrant minorities. The failure of European states to address the economic causes of the recession and their toleration of deeply misguided austerity policies has extended the stagnation. The failure by social democratic or liberal parties to deal well with the situation has given rise to right-wing xenophobic parties which threaten mainstream politics. At the same time, European Muslim communities have been deeply infected by the rising influence of Islamists who carry on education and recruitment in these communities without much interference from moderates. Dislocated youths without real prospects encounter such people in the mosques, on the streets, in the underground economy, and in the prisons, where such anti-Jewish hatred is clearly communicated. 'The Jews of Europe are [thus] now caught between the anvil of right-wing populism and the hammer of virulent anti-Jewish racism promoted by radical Islamism', Lappin says (2015). (Editor's note. See Lappin's chapter in this collection.)

Mainstream politicians pay lip service to defending Jews from attack and engage in ceremonial hand-wringing and issue proclamations after major violent incidents. However, they are more likely than not to eventually return to more pressing political concerns after the violent events pass. Much of the 'liberal' elite in European countries cannot be counted on, Lappin worries, for the Jews are not a demographically significant population in anyone's electoral calculations, and so – with few exceptions (French Prime Minister Manuel Valls is clearly one) – Jews lack for serious long-term allies. Momentary protection from European leaders and state security forces continues to be highly visible, but Jewish communities are nonetheless increasingly oppressed by the burdens of fear and self-protection, until individual Jews can feel barred from living robust and openly Jewish lives. Others – still a small minority, contrary to recent speeches by self-serving Israeli leaders – contemplate joining in an exodus.

The Breakdown of the Holocaust Dispensation

Jeffrey Goldberg (2015) wrote that a post-Holocaust dispensation has broken down or come to an end in Europe. 'The Shoah served for a while as a sort of inoculation against the return of overt Jew-hatred – but the effects of the inoculation, it is becoming clear, are wearing off. What was once impermissible is again imaginable.' Laws that prevent Holocaust denial, so many Holocaust-related films and books, changes to school curricula, state-of-the-art Holocaust museums and memorials, even the sponsored trips by students for on-site learning to infamous Holocaust sites, serve now mainly as imposed rituals from the past which work to persuade others in the present that the Jews receive too much attention and are over-privileged. Youths whose parents migrated after the war, and who feel strongly the tensions of living still at the periphery in their adopted nations, feel little connection with Europe's dark history during World War II and even less responsibility for internalising past lessons about hate, intolerance, and mass murder.

Moreover, as researchers have indicated, attitudes of Muslim youths in Europe about the Holocaust itself are shaped by widespread and negative views held about Jews. Günther Jikeli of the University of Potsdam and the Centre National de la Recherche Scientifique (GSRL/CNRS) has pointed out that anti-Semitic views of the Jews shape distorted views of the Holocaust by Muslim youths, including minimising the Holocaust, drawing inappropriate comparisons, outright Holocaust denial or even the approval of the Holocaust (Jikeli 2013a). Rather than serving as a prophylactic, then, against future occurrences of ethnic hatred or violence, or even helping cement a pluralist consensus about tolerance, the Holocaust today becomes a brickbat in contemporary intercultural conflicts, abused to create a new claim that the Jews manipulate reality to their advantage and – sliding over to a classic trope – hold unjust, extreme power over others.

This is clearly the message, for example, of Dieudonné M'bala M'bala, the French-Cameroonian demagogue whose anti-establishment and anti-Jewish messages in comedy shows and in various tangles with the French courts stir widespread support among youth in the *banlieues*. French Prime Minister Manual Valls told local authorities even before the *Charlie Hebdo* events they could shut down Dieudonné's miserable performances as potential threats to public order, citing their 'anti-Semitic and defamatory' material and 'virulent and shocking attacks on the memory of Holocaust victims'. After recent events, the French state quickly detained and successfully prosecuted Dieudonné – a man who has been arrested numerous times for violating French hate speech laws – for remarks favouring and inciting to terrorism and for additional outright racist comments. Dieudonné claims openly that France is run by Jewish slave drivers and that 'the big crooks of the planet are all Jews.' He complains that 'the Holocaust has become almost a dominant religion' in France, and attacks Manuel Valls as 'a little Israeli soldier'. His shows turn out thousands of young people from immigrant backgrounds and also from the white lower middle class in the cities, uniting these patrons in anger at the elites that run France. Dieudonné introduces to his audience the ravings of established French Holocaust deniers and activists in the right-wing National Front. His anti-establishment salute, the quenelle, which resembles closely an inverted Hitler salute, is performed at all such shows, making them resemble Nazi mass meetings (see Dave Rich's chapter on the use of the quenelle in this collection). His followers purposefully perform the gesture, photograph themselves in front of prominent Jewish or Holocaust-related institutions and circulate the images on social media (on Dieudonné M'Bala M'Bala, see Ames 2014, Stille 2014, Hussey 2014).

All this suggests that when it comes to anti-Semitism, a post-war, post-Holocaust consensus is coming apart, at least in some quarters and among certain groups. While the state acts to protect Jews and even polices the most radical anti-Jewish speech, a significant anti-Jewish *social movement* spreads in several European societies and retails allegations that Jews exert excessive national power here and abroad, seek nefarious ends, and scheme to impose special burdens on Muslims (Cohen 2014). This movement works to elevate the Palestinians into transcendental victims (like the Jews once were elevated in the aftermath of World War II), and condemns Jews – and friends of Jews – as Israeli auxiliaries. The Jews next door or nearby, or in the next district, are held responsible for events far away in the Middle East, yet are also blamed for events at home, especially those seen to be tied to exercises of supposed 'Jewish power'. Ironically, even the state protection that is offered to Jews and Jewish institutions in the wake of violence is seen as a reflection of Jewish power rather than relative powerlessness.

Even still, the sources of anger among Muslim youth continue to be some-what difficult to pin down precisely, and a healthy discussion continues about the causal factors. Many observers talk about the structural causes behind anti-Jewish violence, like narrowed opportunities and urban ghettos that isolate many youths and bar their integration. Others report on cycles of discrimination and marginalisation, crime, and imprisonment that work in dynamic ways to cumulatively disadvantage such youths. Still other observers, however, including Günther Jikeli, think that cumulative disadvantage is not exactly the case, that many youths are less isolated and better integrated than usually thought and that their anti-Semitism and ripeness for trouble is unconnected with poverty or narrowed chances (Jikeli 2013a, 2013b, 2015). Such youths, including the jihadis in the *Charlie Hebdo* and Hyper Cacher events, appear ripe for what Gilles Kepel calls recruitment in a third wave of international jihad, which is focused on carrying out violent attacks on targets in Europe; at the same time, it is becoming clearer that such youths also include university students who are well integrated in their local settings and pursuing advanced education, and possessing skills, but who are deeply alienated from their French or Belgian identities.

The anthropologist Scott Atran, who conducts field-based approaches to understanding the attraction of Muslim youths to radicalism, testified in 2010 that jihadists are mostly youths in transitional stages of their lives who have been influenced by radical Islamist teachings from the media and influential imams. They seek esteem, fulfilment and glory in the eyes of their friends; they are not religious youths, but are reborn with a new meaning and purpose as Islamic radicals; and they are not necessarily marginal economically (Atran 2010). As Atran concludes, exploring the paths that these youths take to jihad, 'You find it's especially appealing to young people in transitional stages in their lives: immigrants, students, people in search of jobs or mates, or between jobs and mates, and it gives a sense of empowerment that their own societies certainly do not' (Atran 2011). However, Atran's work on pathways to radicalism and violence, which highlights the importance of friendship networks, has not to date focused on those who participate in anti-Semitic mobs or embrace direct violence against Jews. Thus, it is unclear if what he says about recruitment or mobilisation for jihad can also be said about recruitment to purposeful anti-Jewish violence. It is nonetheless tempting to draw similar conclusions.

Historian Robert Wistrich, the Neuberger Professor of European and Jewish History at Hebrew University, suggests that a process began after 2000 in France which, as it reaches maturity, is creating great danger. Echoing Lappin, he argues that a more general European crisis has developed, dividing the country into an 'elite France' well-adjusted to globalisation, and a 'peripheral France' poorly adjusted to the globalising economy. These changes coincide with a cross-breeding of far-left with far-right and Islamic ideas and ideologies, helping spur a resurgent and potent new anti-Semitism. To the question where did young French Muslims acquire their virulent anti-Jewish views, Wistrich argues that it was a component of a militant ethno-religious identity based on hatred of the West and of Jews brought originally from the Maghreb. A Quran-oriented hostility to infidels was then blended with anti-Semitic conspiracy theories drawn from European sources of both the right and the far-left. This deadly brew has been fertilised in recent years by the ongoing currents of global jihad, nourished by media sensationalism and influenced by a cult of heroic violence, which has been aided by the failure of state institutions to fully absorb youths in *les quartiers*, urban anomie, juvenile delinquency and marginalisation (Wistrich 2014).

One must note that there is little which serves to moderate or soften the view of 'the Jew' that now circulates in *les quartiers*, nor is there any deep complexity or nuance in the anti-Jewish portrait. Today, there is little shared experience among Jews and Muslims which might soften the circulated anti-Jewish image. Michael Wieviorka (2007) speaks of '*Un antisemitisme (presque) sans Juifs* [Anti-Semitism (almost) without Jews]' and there are tropes in claims about Jews that begin to approach classic mythic beliefs about Jews with magical powers, Jews as shape-shifters, Jews as satanic, and more. There is nothing at all subtle in the widespread idea of powerful, evil, grasping Jews. In 2014, Sheik Abu Billel Ismail at the Al Nur mosque in Berlin, called on his followers to kill the Zionist Jews 'to the last one', sliding quickly and easily over into calling for the annihilation of all Jews, 'the slayers of the Prophets'. An imam in Copenhagen, speaking the day before the recent anti-Semitic murder, preached that the Prophet did not dialogue with the Jews but identified them as inveterate enemies and made open war on them. This Judeophobia draws together several strands – from left and right, from selective mining of classic Quranic sources and from recirculation of well-known secular texts, like the fraudulent 'Protocols of the Elders of Zion'. Little distinction is made between Israel, Zionists, European Jews, and French or Belgian or German Jews – Jews appear as a unified, organic category. Jikeli, who has studied Muslim youth in Paris, Berlin, and London, observes that there are minimal differences in their attitudes towards Jews despite sharp differences in the respective sizes of the national Jewish communities, the relevant background histories, or in the French case, the shared Maghreb origins. Just as European architecture and art once came to offer an unrelieved portrait of Jewish evil, so now the dominant thought among many Muslim youths on the urban periphery is that Jews are enemies of the good and despicable conspirers against all that is just or holy (Jikeli 2013b, 2015).

What Is to Be Done?

So, in face of resurgent anti-Semitism in Europe in increasingly more dangerous and violent forms and its rise in the mental life of specific segments of society, what is to be done? In February, the Simon Wiesenthal Center warned, 'Paris and Copenhagen are bound to be precedents for a pan-European epidemic. Condemnation is insufficient.' So what might be a sufficient policy agenda to begin to deal with the situation?

First, there is the need for continued state protection and rhetorical support for the equal rights of Jews in Europe. Public pronouncements like those made in recent months by Manuel Valls and others, including the foreign ministers of France and Germany, and the Home Secretary and Prime Minister of the United Kingdom, continue to be important and necessary. They signal concern about the targeted victims and also about anti-Semitism as a barometer of the basic health of their societies. State security agencies have to be bolstered with significant resources, and state intelligence agencies, linked with those in other states, must more efficiently share information and coordinate action against suspects crossing borders to obtain military training and infiltrating back into host European nations.

Surveillance must be stepped up at the borders, in the *banlieues*, and in the prisons. Protection also must continue visibly near Jewish institutions, with the reasons – the universal rights of citizenship – proclaimed to all. The liberal project in Europe is linked with active public embrace of a society of equality before the law for people of all groups. Similar initiative is required at EU level, as well as in individual member states. The adoption of a clear working definition of anti-Semitism similar to the EUMC (European Union Monitoring Centre on Racism and Xenophobia, now the Agency

For Fundamental Rights, FRA) Working Definition adopted in 2005, since unreasonably jettisoned, and the creation of active monitoring institutions tracking and recording onslaughts against Jews and Jewish institutions must be a formal all-European project and a multi-state, trans-national responsibility. Amy Elman, the William Weber Chair in Social Science at Kalamazoo College, has examined the failure of the EU to respond adequately to rising antisemitism even after the *Charlie Hebdo* and Hyper Cacher attacks (The European Union, Antisemitism and the Politics of Denial 2015).

Second, there is the equal necessity for active state support for significant initiatives against unemployment, especially youth unemployment, targeted to creating positive and enduring effects among many hard-hit communities on the urban outskirts. More must be done throughout the EU to create economic growth and ladders of youth opportunity and new possibilities for greater integration into the world of work for youths who are transitioning from school to work and family to maturity. Actions must also be devised to improve services in these immigrant communities, including better policing, special employment agencies, improvements in health care, and better transportation, all to fight against the dominant feeling in such areas that the people there are 'second zone citizens' or outcasts of Europe.

Third, there must be a serious effort undertaken in the schools stressing the relevance and importance of democratic rights to all. How best to carry out such an initiative is debatable – the rigid French approach called *laïcité* continues to be a special problem, pushing away rather than absorbing youths, excluding as well as including – but the bottom line is that many schools have been failing to draw all citizens into a working consensus about the value of the ongoing European liberal project. Central to doing so will be to teach about the current social crisis, discrimination and its effects, and the rights of immigrants. Such relevancy strategies, however, must also be accompanied by courageous teaching about anti-Semitism and its consequences, and about its roots in – amongst other places – radical Islam. There can be no retreat on this. It is already the case that there are very few Jews left in the state schools in most European countries, as Jewish children have been withdrawn for their own safety to private schools, though parallel trends in Jewish and Islamic communities highlight religious as opposed to secular approaches to identity. The failure of the schools reflects multiple problems: failed teaching and curricula, stiff youth resistance, and the radical narrowing of common spaces to learn shared public values.

Fourth, there is a growing need in Europe's social democratic and liberal parties to confront more boldly and effectively the anti-Semitic and anti-Israel currents that course through Europe's hard-left, creating insidious effects in the discussion of Jews and of the Jewish state. These parties must decide strongly to stand against these trends while at the same time supporting international progress towards an agreed two-state solution in Israel/Palestine, and constructive actions to bolster the human rights of Arabs and refugees caught in the dissolution of Middle Eastern state structures, as well as the ongoing Sunni-Shiite internecine wars. Recent events in Paris and Copenhagen must be understood in the context of an international movement to delegitimise the Jewish state through dangerous forms of Judeophobic discourse and actions mainstreamed by hard-left currents. Such talk and actions underwrite damning caricatures of Israel, Zionism, Jews and Jewish politics, and lead into or strengthen claims of Jewish power and evil. The object must be to influence conversation in the public square and, in the process, to remind people in a globalising world where diverse peoples come together in new and challenging ways of the growing threat that anti-Semitism poses to the European liberal project. More than annual commemorations highlighting the liberation of Auschwitz or on-site school visits are required to reach the public. More than stylised, routinised and vague forms of human rights rhetoric are urgently demanded. The issue of anti-Semitism ought not to be the concern of Jews alone but of larger publics. Historically, anti-semitism has not stopped with the Jews.

Finally, to the extent that the motive and energy for hate and violence in Muslim areas comes from international developments in Islam rather than European social realities, rhetorical initiatives, employment efforts, social programmes, schooling campaigns, and aggressive efforts to reclaim the public square may not work fully to change the new reality. There will still be some Muslim youths motivated by rage from currents flowing abroad and influenced by Islamic radicals at home, and there will be marginal youths prone to engage in criminal actions, participate in street mobs, and carry out violence aimed at Jews. So, Jewish communities will also have to work independently – in cooperation with local authorities – to efficiently organise their resources to enhance their self-protection. As in earlier periods of modern Jewish history, Jews must organise self-defence to protect individuals and communities. Already, some rabbis have begun learning simple self-defence tactics, and Jewish youths are being organised in several places into community-based guards. In July 2014, only the Jewish community self-defence force (the SPCJ, or Service de Protection de la Communauté Juivenel) in Paris warded off mob action against the Don Abravanel Synagogue. All such Jewish defence forces will need communications and protective equipment. Jewish groups elsewhere in the diaspora should be organised to support such efforts to strengthen Jewish self-defence, especially when and where state protection begins to wane or weaken.

The second week in April marked the 70th anniversary of the liberation of Buchenwald, and several score survivors made their way back to Weimar, Germany to honour comrades and to share in remembrance. One survivor told of a fellow prisoner in the camp who believed that whoever survived that hell would live in paradise, because when people learned of the Nazi atrocities, they would lose their desire to kill. This sounds hopelessly utopian today and fits poorly with recent terrible events. No one appreciates this better than the survivors. My current scholarship focuses on the rescue of children and youths at Buchenwald, so I continue interacting with a large, if dwindling, group of these survivors. One told me recently how, living in Europe, he feels as if he is reliving, if not the same then certainly a very familiar history. This fellow willingly shares his experiences, believing that his testimony serves as a warning and helps to shape a better world. Such commitment to persistent witness rests on a faith that we can and must do certain things to avoid the worst. This is instructive. Today, we too need to keep on reflecting and talking about what things we and others can and must do to avoid the worst.

Note

1 This chapter was first published in *Fathom* in 2015. The author thanks Alan Johnson, Mark Gardner, Teddy Robertson and Benjamin Waltzer for invaluable assistance, suggestions and encouragement.

References

Ames, Paul (2014) 'Dieudonne M'bala: French anti-Semites' favorite comedian', *Salon*, 14 January. Available: www.salon.com/2014/01/10/dieudonne_mbala_ mbala_anti_semites_favorite_comedian_partner/ (accessed 30 January 2023).

Atran, Scott (2010) 'Pathways to and from violent extremism: The case for science-based research', Statement Before the Senate Armed Services Subcommittee on Emerging Threats and Capabilities, 9 March. Available: www.govinfo.gov/con tent/pkg/CHRG-111shrg63687/html/CHRG-111shrg63687.htm (accessed 14 November 2022).

Atran, Scott (2011) 'Hopes and dreams in a world of fear', *Podcast: On Being With Krista Tippett*, 16 October. Available: https://onbeing.org/programs/scott-atran-hopes-and-dreams-in-a-world-of-fear/ (accessed 14 November 2022).

Broder, Henryk (2015) 'Mehr Schutz für Juden bedeutet weniger Würde [More protection for Jews means less dignity'], *Die Zeit*, 19 February.

Cesarani, David (2015) 'There is no "wave" of anti-Semitism', *Huffington Post*, 26 January. Available: www.huffingtonpost.co.uk/david-cesarani/anti-semitism-char lie-hebdo_b_6542550.html (accessed 30 January 2023).

Cohen, Ben (2014) 'How antisemitism became a social movement', *Mosaic Magazine*, 4 October. Available: https://mosaicmagazine.com/response/uncategorized/ 2014/10/how-anti-semitism-became-a-european-social-movement/ (accessed 30 January 2023).

Elman Amy (2015) *The European Union, Antisemitism and the Politics of Denial*, Omaha: University of Nebraska Press.

Goldberg, Jeffrey (2015) 'Is it time for the Jews to leave Europe?' *Atlantic Magazine*, April. Available: www.theatlantic.com/magazine/archive/2015/04/is-it-time-for-the-jews-to-leave-europe/386279/ (accessed 30 January 2023).

Hussey, Andrew (2014) 'Meet the anti-Semitic French comedian who invented the quenelle', *New Republic*, 31 January. Available: https://newrepublic.com/article/116444/dieudonne-mbala-frances-most-anti-semitic-comedian (accessed 30 January 2023).

Jikeli, Günther (2013a) 'Perceptions of the holocaust among young Muslims in Paris, Berlin, and London', in Günther Jikeli and Joëlle Allouche-Benayoun (eds.), *Perceptions of the Holocaust in Europe and Muslim Communities*, New York: Springer, 105–132.

Jikeli, Günther (2013b) 'Anti-Semitism among Young European Muslims', in Alvin H. Rosenfeld (ed.), *Resurgent Antisemitism: Global Perspectives*, Bloomington: Indiana University Press, 267–307.

Jikeli, Günther (2015) *Antisemitic Attitudes Among Muslims in Europe: A Survey Review*, ISGAP Occasional Paper Series no. 1. Available: https://isgap.org/wp-content/uploads/2015/05/Jikeli_Antisemitic_Attitudes_among_Muslims_in_Europe.pdf (accessed 14 November 2022).

Kepel, Gilles (2012) *Quatre-Vingt-Treize*, Paris: Gallimard.

Lappin, Shalom (2015) Communication to author, 16 March.

Lipstadt, Deborah E. (2014a) 'Why Jews are worried', *New York Times*, 20 August. Available: www.nytimes.com/2014/08/21/opinion/deborah-e-lipstadt-on-the-rising-anti-semitism-in-europe.html (accessed 30 January 2023).

Lipstadt, Deborah E. (2014b) 'Anti-Semitism creeps into Europe's daily routines', *Forward*, 21 November. Available: https://forward.com/opinion/209631/anti-semitism-creeps-into-europes-daily-routines/ (accessed 30 January 2023).

Lipstadt, Deborah E. (2015) 'Hypocrisy after the Charlie Hebdo attacks', *Tablet Magazine*, 16 January. Available: www.tabletmag.com/sections/news/articles/hypocrisy-after-the-paris-terror-attacks (accessed 30 January 2023).

Mandel, Maude S. (2014) *Muslims and Jews in France; History of a Conflict*, Princeton: Princeton University Press.

Roy, Olivier (2004) *Globalized Islam: The Search for a New Ummah*, New York: Columbia University Press.

Smale, Alison (2014) 'Samantha power, U.S. Ambassador, issues warning on anti-Semitism in Europe', *New York Times*, 13 November. Available: www.nytimes.com/2014/11/14/world/europe/samantha-power-warning-on-europe-anti-semitism.html (accessed 30 January 2023).

Stille, Alexander (2014) 'The case of dieudonne: A French comedian's hate', *New Yorker*, 10 January. Available: www.newyorker.com/news/daily-comment/the-case-of-dieudonn-a-french-comedians-hate (accessed 30 January 2023).

Taguieff, Pierre-André (2004) *Rising from the Muck: The New Anti-Semitism in Europe*, Lamham, MD: Ivan R. Dee.

Wieviorka, Michel (2007) *The Lure of Antisemitism: Hatred of Jews in Present-Day France*, Leiden: Brill.

Wistrich. Robert (2014) 'Summer in Paris', *Mosaic Magazine*, 5 October. Available: https://mosaicmagazine.com/essay/uncategorized/2014/10/summer-in-paris/ (accessed 30 January 2023).

20

THE UNWELCOME ARRIVAL OF THE QUENELLE

Dave Rich

The scene is the Zenith de Paris theatre, December 2008.[1] French comedian Dieudonné M'bala is on stage, describing to his audience the genesis of the sketch they are about to watch. It is a response, he explains, to a hostile review by the 'billionaire philosopher' Bernard-Henri Lévy – cue pantomime boos from the crowd – who had described Dieudonné's previous show as 'the biggest antisemitic meeting since the last world war'.

If you really want to 'stick it to them the right way . . . to send them climbing up the wall', he tells his cheering, laughing fans (without ever defining 'them') you will welcome on stage 'the most unfrequentable person in France'. On walks Robert Faurisson, France's best known Holocaust denier, to applause, with Dieudonné shouting 'Louder! Louder!'; and the audience responds to Dieudonné's appeals by greeting Faurisson with cheers and whistles of acclaim.

The punch line to the sketch comes when Dieudonné calls on stage his assistant Jacky, in his 'suit of light', to give Faurisson an award 'for unfrequentability and insolence'. Jacky's 'suit of light' is a mocked-up concentration camp uniform, complete with stitched-on yellow star. 'Photographers, let it rip!' Dieudonné cries, as the three of them stand together on stage. 'Look at the scandal! Let's have an ovation!' And an ovation is what they get. 'I've been treated, in my country, like a Palestinian', Faurisson tells the audience, 'I'm treated like a Palestinian and I can't help making common cause with them.'

The manner in which Dieudonné manoeuvred a Parisian audience into expressing their anti-establishment sentiments by cheering Robert Faurisson (has he ever had such an ovation, even from an exclusively far-right audience?) and laughing at Jacky's 'suit of light', all on the premise of sticking it

DOI: 10.4324/9781003322320-25

to 'them', shows the ease with which raw, old-fashioned antisemitism can be inserted into contemporary radical politics. 'Making common cause' between Holocaust deniers, neo-fascists, the pro-Palestinian left and the revolutionary Islamists of Iran is precisely what Dieudonné has spent the past decade try-ing to achieve. Originally from the political left, he has moved via anti-Israel rhetoric and the fascist Front National (FN) to the establishment of his own Parti Anti Sioniste (Anti-Zionist Party – PAS). Alongside him in PAS is essay-ist and film-maker Alain Soral, who underwent a similar journey from the Marxist left to the FN before finding a political home with Dieudonné.

There are not many political movements that can embrace the neo-fascist right, the anti-capitalist left and Iranian revolutionary Islamism. Dieudonné is close to FN leaders – Jean Marie Le Pen is godfather to one of his children – while also attracting fans who consider themselves to be left-wing radicals. He was a guest in Tehran of Iranian President Mahmoud Ahmadinejad and received Iranian funding for a film project. Historically, movements that suc-cessfully pulled off this kind of balancing act have tended to rely on anti-semitism as their glue, expressed through the *lingua franca* of conspiracist anti-Zionism, and PAS is no different.

Strikingly, for a party that calls itself anti-Zionist, the political programme of PAS makes no direct mention of Israel or Palestine. This is parochial, patriotic anti-Zionism, in which Zionism is portrayed primarily as a subver-sive, corrupting presence in French society. Zionist influence, domination, pressure and advocacy must all be eliminated from 'la Nation', in order to establish a society of justice, progress and tolerance. Only then can French power be restored at home and abroad. In 2009, PAS contested the European Elections on a slogan to 'Keep Europe free from censorship, communalism, speculators and NATO'. In 2010 Dieudonné told Iran's Press TV that France has been taken hostage by 'the Zionist lobby'. Dieudonné's political vision could be mistaken for belonging to Europe's radical right, but for the omis-sion of immigration as a grievance. He could sit easily on the populist left, but for his friendship with the FN. His views carry echoes of the Third Posi-tionist ideas developed by Nick Griffin and Roberto Fiore – who have both sat in the European Parliament – in the 1980s. He is emblematic of the new, post-Cold War, post-9/11 radical politics, described by the journalist David Aaronovitch as 'a loose coalition of impulses: anti-globalisation, broadly anti-modernist and anti-imperialist', and bound together by an 'anti-Israel tinge'.

Dieudonné's ethnicity (he is of French-Cameroon parentage) and origins on the left have lulled some observers into viewing him as an example of a 'new antisemitism', originating in the left and in minority communities, and directed at Israel. This is a category error: Dieudonné's antisemitism is very much of the old variety, blaming Jewish speculators and globalists for the erosion of Europe's moral core and the sapping of the nation's strength.

However, whereas pre-war antisemites portrayed this Jewish influence as a hidden hand, pulling the strings of the elite, nowadays Jews are accused of being the very establishment themselves. Symbolised in France by Bernard-Henri Lévy, they are the new insiders – white, wealthy and influential, accused of using their status to prevent others from achieving their rightful place in society. Thus, neo-fascist antisemitism that sees the 'Big Jew' as the cause of all misfortune merges with the resentments of marginalised minorities, hoovering up the varied grievances of the disenfranchised into one amorphous movement. PAS's programme weaves classical antisemitism, reworked as conspiracist anti-Zionism, with a call for social justice and a lament for France's lost power and purpose, thereby skilfully combining the populist anti-politics of left and right. It's petty nationalism married to Occupy's 99 per cent.

This is the political movement that West Bromwich Albion striker Nicolas Anelka introduced to a British audience when he performed a quenelle salute upon scoring a goal in a Premier League match in December 2013; a salute he later dedicated to Dieudonné (the two are friends). It is claimed by Dieudonné's defenders that the quenelle and what it represents – call it Quenellism – is an anti-system posture and not antisemitic. For example, when the Manchester City footballer Samir Nasri was photographed performing a quenelle he apologised, explaining that it 'symbolises being against the system'. Nasri has in fact done very well out of 'the system': according to media reports he earns over £8 million per year playing football. It may well be the case that not every quenellier is motivated by antisemitism; being 'against the system' is cool and Dieudonné has successfully helped the quenelle to become its signifying meme. For some, it can genuinely represent a more general pose of rebellion against the structures and authorities that influence all of our lives, often not to our benefit. It appeals to some French footballers the way that gangsta rap appeals to some American sports stars. But Dieudonné's association with the quenelle, as its inventor and populariser, means that it can never be completely detached from his antisemitic politics. That Anelka not only performed a quenelle but then dedicated it to Dieudonné is doubly damning.

In France, the quenelle has become both cultural meme and political identifier for Dieudonné's politics and the movement it has spawned. In place of the massed ranks of saluters or marchers that were the political theatre of totalitarianism, we have the viral online spread of quenelle selfies. This may be the first individualist mass movement of the social media age, in which there are no membership cards or party dues, no meetings in pubs or rallies in town centres; nothing more than a user-generated quenelle image is necessary to join, at a time and place and in a style of your choosing. Quenelle at Auschwitz? Fine. Quenelle at Upton Park? Fine. Quenelle in your living room? Fine. As long as you then tweet or post or blog your quenelle, you're in. You don't even need to do anything as collective as clicking 'Like' on a Facebook page to join this mass movement. The power of this meme is demonstrated by its spread: Dieudonné has been much more successful in encouraging quenelliers than he was in attracting votes. However, this is also its political weakness: this is a mass movement of attitude rather than action, which so far has not translated into formal political power.

Now that the quenelle has arrived in Britain, the question arises as to the potential for Dieudonné's politics to take root here. There is a plausible argument that antisemitic mass movements simply lack the potential in Britain that they have in France. Some of the most divisive episodes in the formation of modern France have revolved around Jews – or to be more precise, the Jewish Question. The granting of rights to Jews after the French Revolution; the Dreyfus Affair; the much-belated acknowledgement of Vichy France's record and French collaboration in the Shoah (Holocaust) during the Nazi occupation; are all events that lack parallels in modern British history, in which Jews have, to a certain extent, been protected by their marginality. Furthermore, Holocaust denial has had an association with the left in France, via political activists Paul Rassinier and later Pierre Guillaume, for example, that is lacking in Britain.

Yet it would be complacent to assume that Dieudonné's anti-establishment appeal, expressed through angry, transgressive satire and political stunts, could not find a British audience. The personal followings of Nigel Farage MEP and George Galloway MP demonstrate the appetite in the UK for charismatic, populist anti-politics. The risk is heightened by the introduction of Quenellism to Britain via football, possibly the most culturally powerful and prominent stage of all. British football is a tribal world, where fans support their club against all rationality and young fans will mimic their heroes' goal celebrations in the park the next day. It is also one of the last remaining environments where mass antisemitic chanting is still heard in Britain from time to time, fuelled by the tribal hatreds of inter-club rivalries. A Francophone comic with a taste for the surreal is likely to have trouble finding a mass audience in Britain; but his populist anti-politics, carrying with it a coded antisemitism and transmitted via social media, may have better luck.

Note

1 This chapter was first published in *Fathom* in 2014.

21

A MODERN ORTHODOX-CHRISTIAN RITUAL MURDER LIBEL

St. Philoumenos of Jacob's Well

David Gurevich

A few years ago, a colleague from the UK asked my advice regarding a disturbing story.[1] He showed me a newsletter sent by the Irish Congress of Trade Unions to its subscribers. The publication constituted a report on a solidarity visit of the Northern Ireland Public Service Alliance (NIPSA) to the Palestinian Authority's territories and Jerusalem. One of the sites mentioned in their report was Jacob's Well Church in Nablus, an Orthodox Christian sanctuary, which serves both locals and pilgrims. The Irish mission described a peculiar relic in the church (Robinson 2010:16–17):

> The church is spectacular with exquisite iconography. I noticed it had a tomb for a martyr – Archimandrite Philoumenos Hasapis. I asked which century he had been martyred in. 'This one' was the short answer. He had been murdered with an axe in a 'ritualistic' manner on 29 November 1979 by Zionist settlers who wanted to cleanse the area of any trace of Christianity. Murdered whilst performing vespers, his eyes were plucked out and three of his fingers were cut off – the ones with which he made the sign of the Cross. The attacker was believed to be an American. He was not arrested but merely deported back to America.

I immediately felt that something was very wrong about this report. I was not surprised by a biased account from a group defined as a Palestinian-solidarity mission. However, the story of a helpless Christian victim, who was ritually tortured to death by Zionist Jews in the West Bank, evoked more severe concerns.

Almost at the same time, I received an inquiry from a group of Russian Orthodox pilgrims who asked my help with a visit to Jacob's Well. The

DOI: 10.4324/9781003322320-26

pilgrims planned to worship the relics of St. Philoumenos, the same tomb seen by the Irish mission. I checked in the official records and found that the Greek Orthodox Patriarch of Jerusalem sanctified Philoumenos in 2009. A few years earlier, Philoumenos' body was exhumed from his grave in Jerusalem; the body was claimed to be uncorrupted – a typical phenomenon for saints – and was later moved to the renovated Jacob's Well church in Nablus. The canonisation was adopted in the Russian Moscow Orthodox Patriarchate and in a few other Orthodox churches. The 'ritualistically murdered martyr' thus became an officially recognised saint (Gurevich and Harani 2017).

One can find many instances of the same popular narrative since 1979, including in church-affiliated sources. These accounts deviate around certain details while preserving a broadly similar outline: there was allegedly a group of local 'fanatical' Jews, or 'Zionists', who wished to cleanse Jacob's Well of Christians. After threatening Philoumenos, who served as the Archimandrite (head of the monastery), those Jews secretly broke into the monastery. These sources emphasise that the event took place late at the evening, during heavy rains. As to what supposedly happened next, Orthodox Wiki, a semi-open Internet encyclopedia of Orthodox Christianity, set out the main details on which many accounts agree (OrthodoxWiki 2014):

> They burst into the monastery and with a hatchet butchered Archimandrite Philoumenos in the form of a cross. With one vertical stroke they clove his face, with another horizontal stroke they cut his cheeks as far as his ears. His eyes were plucked out. The fingers of his right hand were cut into pieces and its thumb was hacked off. These were the fingers with which he made the sign of the Cross. The murderers were not content with the butchering of the innocent monk, but proceeded to desecrate the church as well. A crucifix was destroyed, the sacred vessels were scattered and defiled, and the church was in general subjected to sacrilege of the most appalling type.

The 'standard version' of the narrative blames the Israeli authorities for covering up the murder. To emphasise the 'ritualistic' nature of the event, some sources even added that the body of the monk was confiscated by the Israelis, and it was handed back to the Orthodox church only after several days. In other words, nobody knows what the Israelis did with the body.

Blood Libels

These accounts of what happened at Jacob's Well take us back into a dark chapter of the history of medieval Europe: ritual murder accusations and blood libels. Rumours about conspiring Jews capturing a Christian victim, usually a helpless child, to perform religious rites involving torture and the use of victim's body parts (and the extraction of blood) resulted in the massacre of many Jewish communities in Europe. The first accusation of this type relates to Norwich in England in 1144. A body of a child named William was discovered in the woods. A Benedictine monk, Thomas of Monmouth, who arrived in Norwich a few years later, was the person behind institutionalising the new cult based on these common rumours accusing Jews.[2] In his *The Life and Passion of William of Norwich*, he unfolds the circumstances of William's death and his extensive miracles. Thomas depicted Jews as pure evil who attack Christianity itself. Shortly, William's body was moved into the Cathedral and he was acclaimed as a saint. Prior to William's veneration, Norwich was a religious centre which did not possess its own saint. The local church clergy had everything to gain from the new cult – pilgrims, donations, status and influence.

The numerous libellous ritual murder accusations in the next century led to waves of hatred that are (at least, partially) responsible for the expulsion of Jews from England in 1290. Soon, ritual murder cases 'emerged' also on the continent's soil. More details were added to the narratives as the centuries passed. The most prominent motif was that Jews require Christian blood for baking the Passover *matzo* bread.

In the realm of the Eastern Orthodox Christianity, the blood libels arrived a few centuries later. They were still surfacing in the late 19th and early 20th centuries. Probably, the most famous example in the modern era was the Beilis Trial in Czarist Russia in 1913, just a few years before the communist revolution.

One might assume that in the 21st century, humanity would have left this old venomous superstition behind, but the texts about Jacob's Well are quite conclusive. The account of Philoumenos' tragic martyrdom, the torture by 'fanatical Jews', and, furthermore, Philoumenos' post-mortem miracles, leading to his glorification as a saint, all resonate with the medieval-style accusations.

In 2016, I made a professional visit to Cyprus. Philoumenos was born in Cyprus, so I was able to explore how he is venerated in his homeland. In the pilgrimage church of the famous Machairas Monastery in Troodos Mountains, I witnessed a painting which depicts Philomenos' martyrdom – the Christian monk is seen being assaulted by a man who is presented as an Ultra-Orthodox Jew wearing a typical hat, has *payot*, and a long beard. Philoumenos was born in a small, remote village called Orounta. Visiting the village, I discovered a recently established roadside shrine with a public prayer area. Three large icons are placed on its wall: St. Nikolaus, St. Luke, and in the middle – the image of St. Philoumenos! Pilgrims frequent the shrine and leave candles and religious artefacts. Shortly after Philoumenos' canonisation, nuns in the Orounta's St. Nicolaus monastery composed and published the Saint's hagiography – a comprehensive book which elaborates the saint's life story. The nuns travelled around Cyprus and the Holy Land, met with people who personally knew Philoumenos in his life, and claim to collect and record the accounts told of his miracle deeds. The book recounts various miracles performed by St. Philoumenos before and even after his death. One of the miracles is saving Jacob's Well church from the shells of the 'Jewish tanks' which, according to the hagiography, attempted to storm the church in 2005 but were stopped by Saint's supernatural intervention (Hiera Monē Hagiou Nikolaou 2013:148).

Constructing a Modern Ritual Murder Narrative

So what did really happen in Jacob's Well on the night of 29 November 1979? In the last few years, my research partner Yisca Harani and I conducted comprehensive research to answer this question (Gurevich and Harani 2017, 2018). We checked the police investigation files, analysed the local press reports since 1979 and interviewed church officials. Yisca Harani visited Jacob's Well church in the outskirts of Nablus in the Palestinian Authority territory, and I travelled to monasteries in Cyprus. Not surprisingly, the facts we established reject the popular narrative. Today, we know how the myth was constructed, stage by stage.

The Israeli police started an investigation immediately after the murder. The murderer was caught in 1982. He was a serial killer, who murdered several people around the country, Jews and non-Jews alike. He was acting alone and lived in Tel Aviv, far away from Nablus. The murderer was mentally ill. In the investigation protocol, he described hallucinations as well as 'voices' that directed him in committing his criminal acts. Finally, the murderer was hospitalised in a psychiatric institute by the decree of the Court.

The findings from the crime scene and the photographs, which we consulted in the police investigation file are enough to dismiss completely all claims about the 'ritualistic' nature of his criminal act. The murderer threw a stolen hand grenade into the church. It caused significant devastation inside. After the monk ran out, the murderer surprised him with an axe causing his tragic death. There were no cross-form hits on the body and victim's eyes were not plucked out as seen on the police photographic material. The murderer sneaked out quickly, without delay. Philoumenos lost a single finger of each hand when he tried to protect his face from an axe hit; these were not the fingers which he would use in making the sign of the Cross. As for the body, it was submitted by the police for a forensic examination. After the examination, the body was returned to the community and brought to its resting place.

Newspapers confirm that rumours about Philoumenos' death were present shortly after the tragic night in 1979. The 'ritual murder' theme accusing

Jews suited the cultural prejudices that are still not uncommon amongst the Orthodox believers. The two and half years until the murderer was captured were fertile soil for the growth of this narrative. In 1989, an American monk Yeghia Yenovkian, who claims he knew Philoumenos in his life, composed an obituary marking a decade since Philoumenos' death. This obituary, published in the periodical *Orthodox America*, contained the narrative which had been often retold in the oral form. Soon his essay became the basis for countless publications on Philoumenos' martyrdom worldwide. This process intensified after the official canonisation in 2009. For instance, in 2012, the Russian Orthodox Church TV channel (Soyuz TV) aired a programme dedicated to Philoumenos martyrdom in which the interviewer wondered 'what did cause this bright spark of Judaism's fanaticism particularly in this time?' and was answered that it happens occasionally and that 'this bonfire periodically smoulders.'

To understand the framing of the narrative and how its target audience reacts to it, we may refer to the epilogue added to Philoumenos' martyrdom story by a Belorussian Orthodox website 'Odigitria', in an essay published in 2011. Note the use of the antisemitic derogatory term 'Zhids' (Жиды) for Jews.

> We remind that the Russian Orthodox Church has two saints, venerated as 'martyred by the Zhids': the monk martyr Evstratiy of Kiev-Pechersk and the infant Gabriel of Belostok. The martyr Evstratiy lived in the 11th century in Kiev. When in 1096 the Cumans attacked and ravaged Pechersky Monastery in Kiev, exterminating many of the monks, the monk Evstratiy was captured, and with thirty monastic workers and twenty habitants of Kiev was sold into slavery to a Jew, who crucified him on a cross. The holy infant Gabriel was ritually murdered by Jews on 20 April 1690. His body side was pierced to discharge the blood, then the infant martyr was crucified (translated by the author).[3]

In this context, we should remember that contrary to the Catholic church, the Orthodox churches have never abolished the veneration of past sanctified 'victims' of Jewish 'ritual murders'. In the course of the general return to religion in the post-Soviet Orthodox states, more of the cults of those supposedly killed in ritual murders were revived. A well-documented example is the recent restoration of the cult of St. Gabriel of Białystok, who is mentioned in the earlier quote. His relics were translated from Belarus to Bialystok in Poland in 1992. The Patriarch of Russia, Kirill, worshiped Gabriel's relics during his visit to Bialystok in 2012. The Patriarch emphasised his appreciation to the local Orthodox community who cherish this Holy Site in the mostly Catholic Poland. Moreover, in 2017, the Russian Orthodox Church established an official committee of inquiry into whether the last Czar was a victim of ritual murder by Jews (Bennetts 2017).

Why do such events still occur in the 21st century? The answer can be found through an in-depth analysis of St. Philoumenos's case.

Antisemitism as a Tool

The new cult of St. Philoumenos is not solely a product of antisemitic trends nor the geo-political situation in the West Bank. As with the medieval blood libels, material interests have contributed to the myth's distribution. The number of pilgrims to Jacob's Well increased since the body was moved there. In early 2000, the Palestinian Authority gave its permission to expand the church. The fact that the worshipping of this Saint helps to deliver the anti-Israel message to visitors, is probably perceived by the Palestinian Authority as a favourable outcome. On the saint's day of Philoumenos (the date of his death), 29 November, the church is always packed with worshipers and clergy who travel long distances to attend its ceremonies. The Greek Orthodox Patriarch of Jerusalem personally conducts the service. All year round, pilgrims to Jacob's Well are handed an information brochure describing the ritual murder performed by 'fanatical Jews'. The present custodian of the church often shows foreign visitors a tomb that he has already prepared for himself anticipating his future martyrdom in the next assault by the Jewish settlers.

The canonisation of the Cypriot monk indeed played a role in strengthening the ties between Jerusalem's Greek Orthodox Patriarchate and the Cypriot Orthodox Church. In May 2014, a new church was inaugurated at the exarchy of the Jerusalem's Patriarchate in Nicosia, the capital of Cyprus. The new church was dedicated to Jesus' Ascension and St. Philoumenos. It is worth noting that the exarchy was re-established after it was shut down following the Turkish invasion of 1974.

Academics and the Blood Libel

However, the most alarming development is the intrusion of this popular narrative into academic literature. We found several instances in which notable authors and publishers failed to acknowledge the story as a libel. Thus, the myth became a 'well-researched' truth. For example, the *Blackwell Dictionary of Eastern Christianity* (Oxford 1999) states that 'Philoumenos was murdered by Zionist extremists determined to remove Christians entirely from this sacred Jewish site' (Balamoti 1999:380–381). We notified the publisher of the error via one of the dictionary's editors in 2017, but Blackwell refused to modify the online version, nor even to add an explanatory note to it.

More recently, Rupert Shortt's book *Christianophobia: A Faith under Attack* presents the ritual murder narrative as an authentic description of the 1979 events (Shortt 2013:227):

Settlers are violent towards Christians and others from time to time . . . in November 1979, as yet unidentified fanatics murdered Fr Philoumenos

Hasapis, an Orthodox monk, at St Photini's Monastery beside Jacob's Well at Nablus . . ... The killers had already warned Fr Philoumenos to remove Christian symbols from the well, claiming that their presence made it impossible for Jews to pray there. When he refused, they gouged his eyes out and hacked off the fingers of his right hand – the one he used to make the sign of the cross – before ending his life. The current custodian, a veteran of several attacks already, has prepared his tomb for what he senses may be a sudden death.

The importance of these academic works is that they are generally regarded as credible sources. Readers who seek facts might consume classical antisemitic myths without being aware that the authors have dismally failed to challenge the false narrative.

Metropolitan Neophytos of Morphou

Back to Cyprus. Our research encountered a person, who might be the 'living spirit' behind the extensive veneration of the new martyr. Metropolitan Neophytos of Morphou pushed for the writing of the hagiography of Philoumenos. Orounta village, with its roadside shrine and its nuns' monastery, is located in his ecclesiastical district of the Cypriot Orthodox Church. Metropolitan Neophytos does not hesitate to use the ritual murder narrative, enhanced with various antisemitic ideas, in his public sermons. In one of his speeches in 2015, after describing how Philoumenos was murdered by Jews, the bishop delivered a polemic against globalisation and Zionism. He links the martyrdom to what he perceives to be its contemporary context (Metropolitan of Morphou 2021 [2015]):

> All these and even more are contained in the policy of the 'New Order of Things', which we mentioned before, that constitutes the global government that is going to control with secret money all the population economically, politically, and socially. There are many researchers that see behind all these the 'Zionism', which prepares slowly and steadily the ground for claiming the worshiping of a false God, the Antichrist![4]

Tales of blood libels and ritual murders are still present in the historical memory of the Orthodox Christian believers. They remain part of what Hirsh has called the 'cultural reservoir' of antisemitic ideas that can be 'drawn upon and reinvigorated' today (2013:1415). Although the Catholic Church in 1965 during the Second Vatican Council adopted the *Nostra Aetate* document that officially condemned religious hatred against Jews, and has since launched educational work to advance tolerance and dialogue in the spirit of *Nostra Aetate*, the Orthodox Churches have never adopted any similar resolution nor, as an institution, denounced past libels.

The interest of Neophytos in evoking antisemitic speech seems to have a practical reason. With the Turkish occupation of Northern Cyprus in 1974, the Metropolitan of Morphou lost most of his district's territory. The Metropolitanate fled to a non-significant location outside the Turkish territory in Greek-speaking Cyprus. Neophytos is a Metropolitan bishop without a diocese and, as said by scholars of church history, 'Whenever Christianity encountered a frontier, it had a need of martyrs' (Weinstein and Bell 1982:160). In our case, there is a martyr-saint, a story which mobilises feelings of national pride amongst believers by blaming the Jews. Antisemitism was brought to play as a tool in obtaining influence, power and status.

Notes

1 This chapter was first published in *Fathom* in 2019 and revised by the author in 2022.
2 On the history of William of Norwich affair see Miri Rubin's introduction to Rubin 2014.
3 The website was consulted in 2018. It is no longer available in 2022. A copy of the post is found in author's archive. Reference: 'In Memoriam of Philoumenos of the Holy Sepulchre, Fatally Tortured by Jews in 1979', *Odigitria*. Originally available: www.odigitria.by/2011/11/29/pamyat-filumena-svyatogrobca-v-1979-godu-iudeyami-umuchennogo (accessed 30 March 2015).
4 Original text in Greek, translated in Gurevich and Harani (2018:153). The speech was published originally undated but it was available on the Metropolitanate of Morphous's website at the time of the 2015 statements. It was republished online on 12 July 2021.

References

Balamoti, Fani (1999) 'Philoumenos' in Ken Parry et al. (eds.), *Blackwell Dictionary of Eastern Christianity*, Oxford: Blackwell Publishing, 380–381.
Bennetts, Marc (2017) 'Russian church hardliners "believe tsar was victim of Jewish ritual murder"', *The Times*, 28 November. Available: www.thetimes.co.uk/article/russian-church-claims-tsar-was-victim-of-jewish-ritual-murder-rwwv6sctq (accessed 30 January 2023).
Gurevich, David and Yisca Harani (2017) 'Philoumenos of Jacob's Well: The Birth of a Contemporary Ritual Murder Narrative', *Israel Studies*, 21: 26–54.
Gurevich, David and Yisca Harani (2018) 'From the Christian Antisemitism to the new Antisemitism: The case of philoumenos of Jacob's well', in Charles Asher Small (ed.), *Antisemitism in Comparative Perspective: Volume 3*, New York: The Institute for the Study of Global Antisemitism and Policy, 139–170.
Hiera Monē Hagiou Nikolaou (2013) *Ho Hagios Hieromartys Philoumenos ho Kyprios: Bios-Martyrio-Thaumata meta Paraklētikou Kanonos*, Orounta [Greek]: Hiera Monē Hagiou Nikolaou (The Holy Monastery of St. Nicolas).

Hirsh, David (2013) 'Hostility to Israel and Antisemitism: Toward a sociological approach', *Journal for the Study of Antisemitism*, 5: 1401–1422.

Metropolitan of Morphou (2021[2015]) 'The saint new holy martyr of Christ Philoumeno of Cyprus: The beginning of Christ's Martyrs of the New Era'. Available: https://immorfou.org.cy/ὁ-ἅγιος-νέος-ἱερομάρτυς-τοῦ-χριστοῦ/ (accessed 6 December 2022).

OrthodoxWiki (2014) 'Philoumenos (Hasapis) of Jacob's well'. Available: http://orthodoxwiki.org/index.php?title=Philoumenos_(Hasapis)_of_Jacob%27s_Well&oldid=118113 (accessed 5 December 2022).

Robinson, Michael (2010) 'Welcome to the country that doesn't exist'. Available: www.sadaka.ie/Articles/OtherReports/OTHER-Global_Solidarity_Palestine.pdf (accessed 5 December 2022).

Rubin, Miri (ed.) (2014) *Thomas of Monmouth, the Life and Passion of William of Norwich*, London: Penguin.

Shortt, Rupert (2013) *Christianophobia: A Faith Under Attack*, Grand Rapids, MI: William B. Eerdman.

Weinstein, Donald and Rudolph M. Bell (1982) *Saints and Society: The Two Worlds of Western Christendom, 1000–1700*, Chicago: University of Chicago Press.

22

WE SHALL BE AS A CITY ON A HILL

Trump, 'Progressive' Anti-Semitism, and the Loss of American Jewish Exceptionalism

Shalom Lappin

Introduction: From Integration to Crisis

In the approximately 200 years that Jews have lived in the United States in significant numbers, they have enjoyed a level of equality, social integration, and success that is unparalleled in the 2,500 years of Jewish life in the Diaspora.[1] Although previous periods of Jewish history offer instances of relative security and communal flourishing, they have generally involved a clearly defined subordinate status within a stratified host society. The acceptance of Jews in these environments has, for the most part, depended on the goodwill of a ruler. With a change of regime, tolerance often gave way to persecution.[2]

When the Jews of Western Europe were emancipated in the 19th century, they were released from centuries of restriction and exclusion, as well as a history of expulsion and racist violence. It soon became clear that this was a false dawn. The rights granted to them were subsequently withdrawn in the 20th century. The rise of Fascism and Nazism first disenfranchised them, and then systematically slaughtered them.

By contrast, Jewish immigrants to America were never encumbered with these burdens. They arrived to conditions of full citizenship, and previously unimagined opportunities for mobility. To be sure, anti-Semitism was a significant feature of pre-war America. It contributed to the severe restriction of immigration in the 1920s, which prevented Jewish refugees from Nazism from finding sanctuary there in the 1930s. Jews were subjected to quotas at elite universities, barred from certain social environments, and kept out of positions of political power. These constraints were expressions of the anti-immigrant xenophobia that pervaded large swaths of White American society in the interwar period. They quickly disappeared in the post-war era, as second- and third-generation American Jews achieved rapid integration.

DOI: 10.4324/9781003322320-27

The spectacular success of American Jewry has generated perhaps the first post-exile community in the Diaspora. Jews ceased to see themselves as a minority living at the sufferance of a host society and started to regard themselves as an integral component of a pluralised majority. They did not forget Jewish history but began to live outside it. They became a community that had finally escaped the driving forces of insecurity and marginalisation which have shaped life in the Diaspora over many centuries. The position which American Jews came to assume with respect to the rest of the Jewish world is largely that of benefactor, interceding for the oppressed, and curating Jewish cultural and historical memory abroad. They also provide substantial political and moral support to Israel. At home, they embraced the roles of philanthropist and supporter of just causes. They now constitute the world's second largest Jewish community, surpassed only by the Jews of Israel.

Trump's presidency has seriously unsettled some of the assumptions on which American Jewish integration has depended. It unleashed forces that threaten the foundations of democracy and pluralism, whose constancy American Jews had generally assumed to be beyond question. It mobilised segments of opinion that they had always regarded as safely confined to the outer margins of the spectrum, and it transformed them into the mainstream of a powerful political coalition. These forces are acutely dangerous to most ethnic minorities, Jews prominently among them.

Many people breathed a huge sigh of relief when Joe Biden won the last presidential election, and the Democrats obtained effective control of both houses of Congress. It seemed as if normalcy had returned to American public life, at least at the highest levels of government. Events of the past few months suggest that this relief was premature. While Trump may be out of office, the political movement that he orchestrated remains very much in play. It is important to consider the implications of this movement for the continued security of Jewish life in America. It is also necessary to look at how the more radical opposition to the Trumpian Alt-right, relates to these concerns. If the Trump phenomenon has shaken the idea of American Jewish exceptionalism, it is, in no small part, a consequence of the fact that it has exposed some of the broader notions of American exceptionalism as fragile and without foundation.

The Rise of a New Confederacy

Until the 18th century, anti-Semitism in Europe was expressed primarily as a religious prejudice rooted in Christian hostility to Jews. With the emergence of modern nationalism in Western Europe it was reconceived in secular terms as a racist doctrine.[3] Racist anti-Semitism construes the Jews as the Middle Eastern people who are indelibly foreign to European culture. It inherits the conspiracy theories of its Christian antecedents. In these theories, Jews are cast in the role of an international cabal of malefactors plotting the domination and subversion of civilised nations. In its racist variant, these activities are attributed to the intrinsic ethnic character of Jews, rather than to their religious practices. Hence neither conversion nor assimilation offers an escape. This view reached fruition in the eliminationist programme of the Nazi genocide.

In the Muslim world, race was not a primary category of cultural identification. Religious affiliation and language were the criteria for determining one's place in the social hierarchy. Jews were a recognised non-Muslim minority, and so they were generally granted official tolerance. However, their position was immutably subordinate and marginal. As Muslim rule, particularly in the Ottoman Empire, began to decline in the 18th and 19th centuries, European forms of anti-Semitism were imported, and these were incorporated into some strands of the emerging nationalist movements in Arab countries.

When they came to America, Jewish immigrants left behind both types of stigma. They became a non-visible minority. They quickly entered the mainstream of American life in large urban centres. Even in the South during the era of slavery, followed by post-Reconstruction segregation, Jews were exempted from the racial caste system. The White supremacist ideology that supported this system was focused on the repression of African Americans, and it was fashioned to advance the local interests of the ruling White elite. Groups like the Ku Klux Klan, which enforced the roll back of Reconstruction through terror, promoted a generalised racist world view. They targeted Jews and other minorities, as well as Black people. However, southern segregationists were primarily concerned to maintain their subordination of the Black population. Jews were granted the de facto status of honorary Whites. In occupying this precarious role they resembled the Jews in South Africa under apartheid.[4]

In the North, Jews quickly became just another immigrant community. They were perceived (for the most part) as White, and increasingly naturalised, in a highly varied population. In this part of the country, the marginalisation of Black people (as well as other people of colour) was institutionalised through economic and social means, rather than through legal segregation.

Trump has fashioned a coalition of White racial grievance and reaction. His approach has a clear precedent in the career of Pat Buchanan, who came up through the ranks of the Republican Party. Buchanan had been a presidential adviser to both Nixon and Reagan. He then ran in the 1992 and 1996 Republican presidential primaries, before standing as the Reform Party candidate in 2000. He espoused more or less the same positions that carried Trump to victory in 2016. He was a traditional Republican isolationist, who rejected foreign military interventions and international leadership of the Western alliance. He opposed free trade, calling for tariffs on imports to protect American industry. He promoted a vintage nativist attitude. He was hostile to immigration, to immigrants and to ethnic minorities, in particular Jews and African Americans. That he was not successful in his campaigns for office may, at least in part, be due to the fact that the economic and social dislocations precipitated by the financial crash of 2007–2008 had not yet occurred. Moreover, he lacked Trump's perverse talent for demagoguery and media grandstanding.

Amid the chaos and incompetence of his administration Trump consistently cultivated the White supremacist core of his electoral base. The racism that animates this constituency is not an insistence on racial segregation as a local southern caste system. It is a generalised neo-fascist ideology that targets Jews together with people of colour. It was on vivid display in events like the *Unite the Right* march in Charlottesville Virginia, on 11–12 August 2017, during numerous Trump rallies, and in the insurrection at the Capitol Building in Washington on 6 January 2021. Trump has refused to condemn these supporters. Instead, he refers to them as patriots. It is also the force driving a serious rise in deadly acts of far-right terrorism, an increasing number of which are directed at Jews.[5]

America is now dangerously perched on a precipice. The next set of elections will be conducted under conditions that have undermined the institutional foundations of its democracy. Should Republicans regain control of one or both houses of Congress and the Presidency, there is a real possibility that an authoritarian regime will take power (with or without Trump) in which White supremacists determine policy. This could be the beginning of a new Confederacy that discards the achievements of the civil rights movement and entrenches xenophobic nativist practises. Should that happen, it is unlikely to be a Confederacy in which Jews would be honorary Whites. They may well find themselves contending with a government not entirely unlike those that caused their ancestors to flee Europe.

Progressive Anti-Semitism

The period since the 2007–2008 financial crash has seen the revival of the progressive left liberal wing of the Democratic Party as a serious electoral force. The presidential candidacies of Bernie Sanders and Elizabeth Warren attracted widespread support for economic and social policies that continued the tradition of Roosevelt's New Deal and Johnson's Great Society. These policies seek to institute programmes that have been taken for granted in most Western European countries, and Canada, throughout the post-war era, but are considered radical in the American political context. They reflect the reformist class-based politics of mainstream social democracy.

In recent years, a more extreme element has gained force within the progressive movement. This group characterises itself as an anti-colonialist left, and it has made a certain type of identity politics the focus of its agenda. It is the American counterpart of the radical European left. According to the world view that it promotes, most oppression in the world originates in the crimes of Western colonialism. These were driven by White supremacy, which continues to deform the American, and more generally the Western social order. Patriarchy and gender discrimination are also derived from power structures that colonialism created. In this framework, racial and gender identity replace economic class as the primary drivers of repressive social arrangements, and resistance to them. This part of the anti-colonialist left embraces radical Islamists as allies in the struggle against Western colonialism and often replaces class with ethnic identity (see Lappin 2006).

Like the far-right and militant Islamism, it is staunchly anti-globalist in outlook. Variants of these doctrines, packaged in postmodernist language, now constitute orthodoxy in large sectors of American academic life, particularly within the humanities and some of the social sciences. They have become dominant in publishing, the entertainment industry, and significant parts of the media. They are also increasingly influential in the progressive wing of the Democratic party, where their adherents are playing a role not unlike that of the Tea Party insurgency among Republicans in the decades preceding the Trump presidency. In this way, these ideas are beginning to define the terms of discourse on the left in America.

This segment of the left promotes a starkly Manichean view of history and politics. One is either an agent of colonialism and White supremacy, or part of the resistance to them. A virtue metric determines one's objective moral standing in this struggle on the basis of one's ethnic or gender affiliation. Jews do not fare well in this scheme. They are classed as beneficiaries of White privilege. More seriously, they are guilty of association with Israel, the paradigm colonialist enterprise. The American anti-colonialist left views the Israeli–Palestinian conflict as an extension of the US struggle for racial justice. It portrays this conflict as one in which White European Israeli colonialists are dispossessing Palestinians, who are an indigenous people of colour. It also portrays Israel as a collaborator in American racism through its technical assistance to US police forces and security agencies.

The anti-colonialist left is acutely ahistorical. In construing colonialism and racism as specifically European diseases it disregards the existence of numerous non-Western empires that acted in a manner similar to that of their European counterparts. The Mongol Empire (1206–1368), for example, extended from China, through central and southern Asia, and parts of the Middle East, to Northern Europe. The Ottoman empire (1301–1923), based in Turkey, conquered most of the Middle East, North Africa, and the Balkans. Both engaged in slavery, ethnic cleansing, and mass murder of indigenous populations. The Ottomans committed the most serious of the latter two actions at the beginning of the 20th century, in the final years of the

Empire. To recognise facts of this kind in no way diminishes the magnitude of European crimes against native peoples. It does, however, suggest that ethnic and gender categories do not provide a reliable basis for a genuinely progressive politics. In fact, the far-right has shown itself particularly adroit at using these categories for antithetical purposes, with devastating consequences.

The view of Israel as a European settler state is a particularly crude violation of the historical record. Unlike the colonial populations of genuine settler states, such as those of North and South America, Australia, and New Zealand, the Jews of Israel did not come as agents of a mother country in service of its imperial project. They were refugees of pogroms and the Nazi genocide in Europe, and of violent expulsion from Arab countries. Most had nowhere else to go. Over half of Israel's Jews originated in Muslim countries. A significant number also came from India and Ethiopia. A large part of the Jewish population is not White, according to the colour-coding conventions of the American racial caste system. They are neither European nor colonialist. To acknowledge this historical record is not to deny that the Palestinians suffered expulsion and dispossession in the process of Israel's establishment. Nor does it undercut the damage that Israel's continued occupation of Palestinian territory in the West Bank is doing to both the Palestinians and Israeli democracy. But recognising the historical and demographic facts does require that one understand the conflict as a clash between two national movements, each with considerable justice on its side. It obliges one to approach this conflict with nuance, balance, and an awareness of its complexity. Unfortunately, the caricature through which the anti-colonialist left regards history in general, and the Middle East in particular, excludes such a textured understanding of the situation.

Prior to the creation of Israel, left-wing anti-Zionism was one of several political positions in a debate over which strategy offered the best route to Jewish political and social emancipation. Since 1948 it has been an agenda for dismantling Israel as a country. In the hands of the anti-colonialist left, anti-Zionism has become a totalising ideology that promotes Israel to the role of a demonic historical actor. Not only does it exemplify the evils of Western colonialism and racism, but anyone who is associated with it by recognising it as a Jewish homeland, or, increasingly, simply through endorsing its right to exist, inherits its essential criminality. Jews in America (and abroad) who resist this view have become untouchables. As the members of J Street discovered, vigorous criticism of Israel's government from a position of support for the country is not sufficient to secure entry into the anti-colonialist left. Total rejection of Israel's legitimacy as a country is a necessary condition for acceptance. The prevalence of these attitudes in American universities has turned many campuses into hostile environments for Jewish students.

Jewish communities are increasingly affected by this criminalisation of Israel. Radical progressives have followed in the tradition of Soviet propagandists. They are refashioning vintage far-right conspiracy myths of powerful Jewish lobbies controlling international finance, the press, and agencies of government, as leading themes of their anti-Zionist campaign. In 2019 Representative Ilahn Omar was forced to apologise for attributing American support for Israel to the influence of a powerful financial lobby ('It's all about the Benjamins, Baby.'). In a speech to the Democratic Social-ists of America on 1 August 2021 Representative Rashida Tlaib is quoted as stating, 'Cutting people off from water is violence. And they do it from Gaza to Detroit.' She went on to state that 'the structure we've been living under right now is designed by those who exploit the rest of us, for their own profit' (see DeBonis and Bade 2019, Milbank 2021). In this mode, anti-Zionism ceases to be a political view. It becomes an instrument for encrypting hostil-ity to Jews by embedding reference to them in an ideological proxy term. It is a variant of the coding technique that racists have used against people of colour for decades.

Many radical progressives have argued that demonising Trump supporters is counterproductive. They have called for dialogue with them as a necessary part of understanding and addressing their concerns. No such generosity is extended to Jews supportive of Israel, even those on the left. Rather than with constructive discussion, they are greeted instead with boycotts and vilifica-tion. This has recently escalated to violence and widespread abuse directed at Jews in general, particularly in times of active conflict between Israel and the Palestinians, as happened during the recent flare-up with Gaza in May 2021.

There is an interesting historical irony in the career of extreme anti-Zionism. Whenever it becomes government policy, or achieves popular sup-port, it invariably provides strong motivation for the original Zionist thesis concerning the non-viability of Jewish life as an exposed minority in the Diaspora. Three particularly clear instances of this phenomenon stand out. First, when Arab governments launched anti-Zionist campaigns in the period of Israel's creation, 800,000 Middle Eastern and North African Jews were forced out of the countries in which they had lived for millennia, preceding the Arab conquest. The overwhelming majority of them came to Israel as refugees, where they and their descendants now make up the plurality of the population. Second, after decades of Soviet anti-Zionist campaigns, which destroyed organised Jewish life in the Soviet Union, most Soviet Jews left the country at the first opportunity. Over one million of them (the majority) immigrated to Israel. Third, in recent years, the rise of violent anti-Semitism in France, particularly on the far-left, and among radical Islamists, has pro-voked a significant increase in French Jewish immigration to Israel.

One would have thought that reflective anti-Zionists surveying this his-tory might be concerned about the causal role that their ideology has played in generating the opposite effect that they claim to be working for. However, rather than questioning some of their assumptions and methods in light of this evidence, they have persisted in replaying the campaigns of the past. Large-scale radical anti-Zionist agitation serves to marginalise Jews and convince them that they have no place in the society that tolerates it. There is no mystery in this. Contrary to the claims of its advocates, in most cases, it serves as an effective vehicle for mobilising hostility to Jews. In the 19th century, the German social democrat August Bebel described anti-Semitism as the socialism of fools. In the 21st century, it has become the anti-colonialism of illiterates.

The progressive movement is the leading edge of opposition to the Republican far-right. As such, it should be a natural home for American Jews, who are endangered by the rise of White supremacy and the new Confederacy that it seeks to create. Instead, the increasingly pronounced role of the radical component of this movement is turning it into another serious threat to the security and well-being of the Jewish community.[6]

Jewish Responses to the Crisis

American Jews are facing two emerging dangers. On one side Trump's presidency has turned the Republican Party into a far-right ethno-nationalist coalition. Anti-Semitism is one of the strands of racism that figures prominently among its core supporters. On the other side, the anti-colonialist left of the progressive movement is leading a strident anti-Zionist campaign. It has targeted key sections of the Jewish community as the locus of a malign lobby that supports Israeli aggression and forms part of a larger intersectional network of oppression. Its influence within the Democratic Party is growing, and it is now a significant factor on the American left. At this point the threat from the far-right is more immediate and more substantial.[7] However, the attitudes of the radical segment of the progressive movement are also acutely toxic to the safety of organised Jewish life.

The COVID pandemic has greatly exacerbated the political polarisation that has afflicted America over the past two decades. This polarisation is undermining the cohesion and stability that had characterised the post-war American Jewish experience. Jews are now caught in the middle of a major social conflict. This is a situation that is familiar from previous Jewish history in the Diaspora. It is fraught with difficulties and vulnerabilities that American Jews have, for the most part, not encountered before.

Minorities of American Jews, at opposing ends of the political spectrum, have responded to the crisis by embracing one of the forces that threaten the community. Right-wing Zionists and some members of the Orthodox community are active Trump supporters. They point to his pro-Israel actions, like moving the US Embassy to Jerusalem, as evidence that he is a friend of American Jewry. In fact, Trump appears to have done these things as part of a transactional political relationship with Benjamin Netanyahu, and a concern to curry favour with the Christian Evangelical part of his base, rather than from commitment to Israel or American Jews. He has traded in anti-Jewish rhetoric on several occasions. He has described Jews as financially ruthless, and he has suggested that they have dual allegiances by stating that those who vote for the Democrats are disloyal to Israel (see Rubin 2019). He has pointedly refused to condemn the neo-Nazi participants in the 6 January 2020 Washington insurrection, and those attending other pro-Trump events. While right-wing pro-Republican Jewish groups focus on the anti-Semitism of the far-left, they deny its existence in the Trump camp.

Trump follows the pattern of far-right political leaders in Europe, particularly in Poland and Hungary, who combine support for ultra-nationalist movements in Israel with anti-Semitism at home (see Lappin 2019). Netanyahu's willingness to overlook their domestic anti-Semitism was a crucial part of this arrangement. The previous centrist Israeli government appeared to be moving away from it. As foreign minister Yair Lapid sharply criticised Poland's legislation making it virtually impossible for Jews to reclaim property lost during the Nazi occupation, and the subsequent period of Communist rule. This produced a major diplomatic row with the Polish government (Times of Israel 2021).

By contrast, small organisations of radical left-wing Jews, like Jewish Voices for Peace, have joined the anti-colonialist left, adopting its rabidly anti-Zionist views. Like their counterparts on the right, they have no difficulty in identifying the anti-Semitism emanating from the opposing side, but they insist that it is absent from their own. The far-left uses these groups to deflect the charge that they are hostile to the Jewish community. They parade them as the 'good Jews' who represent enlightened Jewish opinion. They construe their critics as agents of the Zionist lobby, who use accusations of anti-Semitism to silence criticism of Israel and other forms of colonialism.

There are clear historical precedents for both types of collaboration. Neither ended well. Prior to the Holocaust the Jews of Italy had been well integrated into Italian society for several centuries. A small minority became active in the Fascist Party in the 1920s and 1930s (see Sarfatti 2017). In his first years in power, Mussolini did not characterise Fascism in racial terms, and anti-Semitism was not part of his ideology. This changed as the ethnic focus of his nationalism became more central, and his alliance with Germany developed. Italy's 1938 race laws targeted all Jews, Fascist, anti-Fascist, and non-affiliated alike. Their political views were irrelevant to their exclusion under these laws, and to their situation during the subsequent Nazi deportations.

The Yevsektsiya, the Jewish wing of the Soviet Communist Party, was established in 1918 to recruit Jewish support for the Bolshevik revolution. It was assigned the task of dismantling the traditional institutions of organised Jewish life, and uprooting Zionism and the study of Hebrew. It was disbanded in 1929, after being largely successful in achieving this mission. Many of its leaders were killed or sent to the Gulag in Stalin's purges during the 1930s. Stalin revived his anti-Zionist campaign in the early 1950s as a pretext for attacking Jewish Communist leaders in the Soviet Union, and in the Eastern European countries under Soviet control. This featured a series of show trials with forced confessions. The Slánský trial of 1953 in Czechoslovakia was among the most infamous of these.

American Jewish Communists and fellow travellers defended this campaign. Harap (1953) is an interesting example. It offers a paradigm of the arguments used by the current anti-colonialist left in their anti-Zionist agitation. In 1953 Harap insisted that anti-Semitism did not exist in the Soviet Union or other Communist countries in Eastern Europe. He identified Zionism as a bourgeois ideology and part of an international network of capitalist oppression. He accused the Western press of misrepresenting the Slánský trial as aimed at Jews, when in fact Slánský and his associates were guilty of crimes against the Czechoslovak Socialist Republic. These involved working with foreign interests to undermine it. He was at pains to stress the distinction between criticism of the Israeli government (at the time headed by Ben-Gurion) and Zionism on one hand, and anti-Semitism on the other. Viewing his apologetics with the advantage of historical perspective, it is at least as remarkable for its apparent innocence as it is for its patent absurdity. It appeared as a pamphlet for the magazine *Jewish Life*, founded in 1946 as a publication associated with the US Communist Party. The magazine broke with the Party in 1956, and it was renamed *Jewish Currents*. It is now a forum for members of the radical anti-Zionist Jewish left. The similarity between some of the diatribes from each period of the publication is striking.

The majority of American Jews belong to neither of these extremes. They occupy positions on the broad continuum that characterises centrist liberal opinion. They are committed to Israel's security and well-being, although many are highly critical of its annexationist policies and its human rights violations. They support strong civil rights legislation, gender equality, and egalitarian social reforms, but they are wary of the more far-reaching initiatives of the progressive movement. They are becoming increasingly alarmed at the rising tide of anti-Jewish racism and attendant hate crime that is coming their way from the two radical groups between which they are caught. For the most part, the community does not seem to have fully processed the depth of the crisis that surrounds it. As a result, serious strategies for responding to this crisis have not yet emerged.[8]

Conclusion: Re-Entering Jewish History

America is going through a period of severe political turmoil which threatens the foundations of its liberal democracy. This turmoil is driven by at least two factors. One is the emergence of sharp economic inequality over many decades, and the serious social dislocations that it has generated. This process has undermined the prosperity of the middle and working classes, and it has created a fertile environment for extremism. The second is a significant regression in civil rights and economic mobility for African Americans. This development has laid bare the extent to which the United States has never overcome its legacy of slavery and racial exclusion. Both phenomena owe much to the conservative economic and social policies of both Republican and centrist Democratic administrations since 1968.

American Jews are caught between a white supremacist threat from the far-right and a hostile anti-Zionist challenge from the far-left. For the first time, they find themselves increasingly at risk from militant forces that are seizing control of the political mainstream. Given their past experience of relative invisibility and integration, they are not well equipped to deal with this situation. Their traditional role of benefactor and advocate for persecuted Jewish communities abroad is of little use in the current context. To fashion a viable set of strategies for coping with the dangers that they now face, it is necessary to recognise that they are no longer outside of the turbulent flow of Jewish history. The crisis of democracy in America is thrusting them into the midst of it.

Notes

1 This chapter was first published in *Fathom* in 2021. I am grateful to Daniel Burston, Eve Gerrard, Jacqueline Gueron, Randy Ingham, Anthony Julius, Matthew Kramer, Elena Lappin, David Lappin, Avishai Margalit, Peter Nicholas, Peter Pagin, Colin Shindler, Richard Sproat, Hillel Steiner, and Kenneth Waltzer for valuable comments on earlier versions of this article. I am solely responsible for the views expressed here, and for any mistakes that the article may contain.

2 Muslim Spain (sometimes described as a Golden Age of religious and cultural pluralism) provides an example of this pattern. Periods of harmony and rich cultural interaction between Jews and the Muslim majority were punctuated by forced conversions, exiles, and pogroms. One such case is the Berber Almohad conquest of parts of North Africa and Spain in the 12th century. This was an extreme Islamic movement, which cancelled dhimmi status, and required Jews to either convert or leave. As a result, Maimonides was forced to flee his native Cordova, eventually settling in Egypt. A second instance is Granada, where Shmuel HaNagid rose to the position of Vizier and general of the army. When Shmuel's son Joseph succeeded him, a popular revolt killed him, and destroyed the Granada Jewish community, in a bloody massacre, in 1066. See Lewis (1986) for a historical survey of Jewish life in Muslim countries.

3 Willhelm Marr formulated this doctrine in his pamphlet *Der Weg zum Siege des Germanenthums über das Judenthum* (The Way to Victory of Germanism over Judaism) in 1879. He had previously supported the democratic revolutions of 1848 as a member of left-wing German nationalist groups. Many graduates of these revolutions went on to careers in far-right ethno-nationalist politics.

4 The 1989 film *Driving Miss Daisy* portrays the fragility of the Jewish position in the segregated Southern social order. Randy Newman's 1988 song *Dixie Flyer* also hints at it.

5 The Tree of Life Synagogue shooting in Pittsburgh on 27 October 2018, in which a neo-Nazi gunman killed 11 people, is one of the most dramatic instances of this pattern. The terrorist who committed the attack claimed that Jewish organisations were promoting immigration. He was responding to the anti-immigrant hysteria that Trump and his associates had generated.

6 Bernie Sanders and Elizabeth Warren, the two most prominent leaders of the progressive wing of the Democratic Party, are not advocates of the anti-colonialist left and its identity politics. They come from the liberal left/social democratic tradition, in which egalitarian economic policies and civil rights initiatives are the primary devices for pursuing social change. They are also not anti-Zionists. While strongly critical of the Israeli government on settlements and human rights violations in the Palestinian territories, they are firmly committed to a two-state solution. Their views align with those of J Street. However, they have sought to deflect criticism of radical members of the House Democratic caucus for extreme statements about Israel and the purported influence of Jewish lobbies that support it. Should current political trends continue, it is reasonable to expect that they will be forced to make a clear decision on the extent to which they are prepared to indulge the anti-colonialist radicalism of this part of their constituency.

7 In this respect the situation in America is distinct from that in Western Europe, particularly Britain and France, where the far-left and its radical Islamist allies constitute the most pressing danger to Jewish communities there. I am grateful to Matthew Kramer for useful discussion on this point.

8 It is difficult to avoid seeing some distant parallels between the situation of American Jews today and that of Jews in Germany and Austria at the turn of the last century. The latter were well integrated and prosperous, but they faced a rising tide of anti-Semitism from the nationalist right, as well as considerable hostility from parts of the left that campaigned against 'Jewish capitalism'. This situation turned deadly in the years following World War I. Lewis (1986) notes the irony in the fact that German and Austrian Jews interceded on behalf of persecuted Jewish communities in the Ottoman Empire and Iran in the 19th and early 20th centuries, only for some of their descendants to seek refuge in those countries when the Nazis came to power.

References

DeBonis Mike and Rachael Bade (2019) 'Rep. Omar apologizes after house democratic leadership condemns her comments as "anti-Semitic tropes"', *Washington Post*, 11 February. Available: www.washingtonpost.com/nation/2019/02/11/its-all-about-benjamins-baby-ilhan-omar-again-accused-anti-semitism-over-tweets/ (accessed 22 November 2022).

Harap, Louis (1953) 'The truth about the Prague trials', *Jewish Life*, January. Available: www.marxists.org/subject/jewish/harap-prague.pdf (accessed 22 November 2022).

Lappin, Shalom (2006) 'How class disappeared from Western politics', *Dissent*, 53 (1): 73–78.

Lappin, Shalom (2019) 'The re-emergence of the Jewish question', *The Journal of Contemporary Antisemitism*, 2 (1): 29–46 (also published in *Fathom*, May 2019. Available: https://fathomjournal.org/the-re-emergence-of-the-jewish-question/ (accessed 22 November 2022).

Lewis, Bernard (1986) *Jews in Islam*, Princeton, NJ: Princeton University Press.

Milbank, Dana (2021) 'Rashida Tlaib's bigotry comes from the MAGA handbook', *Washington Post*, 9 August. Available: www.washingtonpost.com/opinions/2021/08/09/rashida-tlaib-bigotry-antisemitism-trump-maga/ (accessed 22 November 2022).

Rubin, Jennifer (2019) 'Trump's anti-Semitic attacks on American Jews keep coming', *Washington Post,* 9 December. Available: www.washingtonpost.com/opinions/2019/12/09/trumps-anti-semitic-attacks-american-jews-keep-coming/ (accessed 22 November 2022).

Sarfatti, Michele (ed.) (2017) ''Italy's fascist Jews: Insights on an unusual scenario', *Quest: Issues in Contemporary Jewish History,* 11. Available: www.quest-cdec journal.it/?issue=11 (accessed 22 November 2022).

Times of Israel Staff (2021) ''Poland will not pay": Polish PM hits back at Lapid criticism of restitution law', *The Times of Israel,* 27 June. Available: www.timesofisrael.com/poland-will-not-pay-polish-pm-hits-back-at-lapid-criticism-of-restitution-law/ (accessed 22 November 2022).

PART 6

Left Antisemitism and Academia

23

THE MEANING OF DAVID MILLER

David Hirsh

Introduction: David Miller's Amazing World of Zionist Chicken Soup

Professor David Miller, speaking to the Labour Left Alliance in June 2020, warned his audience to be suspicious of interfaith work when it involves Jews. What may appear as contact between faith communities to increase mutual understanding and friendship, working together in an 'apolitical way' to counter racism, might really be something much more menacing. 'No', said Miller, 'Israel have [sic] sent people in' to use interfaith work as 'a Trojan horse'. He gave the example of the East London Mosque, where Jews and Muslims had made chicken soup together. He said that this was really an 'Israel-backed project' whose hidden aim was to make Zionism seem like an ordinary aspect of Jewish identity rather than a racist ideology. This comment from Miller became a running joke amongst Jews, a way of making him seem less frightening. A left-wing Professor of Sociology really did warn that chicken soup is used by Israel as a weapon against British Muslims. It is served up by people who pretend to nurture interfaith friendship but whose real motive is to anaesthetise Muslims to the danger of a global campaign to sow Islamophobia and racism.

Miller says his own Jewish students, if they identify with Israel in any sense, are to be treated as 'Zionist' in his sense, which then makes them, in Miller's story, part of what he has described as an 'enemy' to be 'targeted'. But he remains a Professor at Bristol University and many academics jump to his defence, insisting that he is guilty of nothing more than presenting and evidencing legitimate 'criticism of Zionism'.[1] How did British academia

DOI: 10.4324/9781003322320-29

get here? In this essay, I try to explain, as straightforwardly as possible, the meaning of David Miller and what made him possible.

David Miller Versus the Macpherson Principle

It is often claimed that Jews have trouble telling the difference between criticism of Israel and antisemitism and that they are prone to feel it all as antisemitism. At first sight, this claim feels plausible. Perhaps Jews tend to be so on edge because of their family and communal experiences of antisemitism that they may be a bit prone to seeing it when it is not really there. Yet this scepticism is already a radical departure from how we generally judge, for example, women when they say they have experienced sexual harassment, or black people when they say they have experienced racism.

The High Court Judge who chaired the Stephen Lawrence Inquiry, Sir William Macpherson, sadly died last month. He made two significant contributions to the general acceptance of good practice about racism. First, he cemented the concept of 'institutional racism' into the British mainstream. Racism should not only be recognised as the conscious hatred of those who are designated as being of another 'race'. We should also look out for ways of doing things and ways of thinking which may seem innocent, but which turn out to be contaminated by racism in ways that are not apparent. Racism is part of a larger social phenomenon and is not just an individual moral failing.

His second significant contribution was the *Macpherson Principle*, which asserts that when a person says they have experienced racism, this should be taken in good faith as an honest report of what they have experienced. Any investigation should begin with this assumption and should proceed to look at the evidence objectively.

There is a common principle, derived from identity politics, that the people best qualified to judge when there has been racism, sexism, or homophobia, are the victims of those aggressions themselves. It is not common to question their judgement on the basis that because they have experienced so much bigotry in the past, their clarity is now so blunted as to be generally suspect.

But still, perhaps some Jews, sometimes, see antisemitism in legitimate criticism of Israel. When this happens it can be addressed by a rational discussion of the case, of the evidence, of the intention, of the context, and of the audience's perception. If we agree that some kinds of criticism of Israel are antisemitic while other kinds are not, then we can discuss and agree, or perhaps disagree. That is how freedom of speech and academic freedom work.

But that is not Professor David Miller's position.

He says that 'Britain is in the grip of an assault on its public sphere by the state of Israel and its advocates.' He says that 'Israel's lobby is busily stealing the language of Black liberation to justify ethnic cleansing, racism and apartheid.' (As though Jews do not have their own authentic language to describe the racism they have faced and the liberation for which they yearn.) Miller says that 'Israel and its apologists' employ 'the time-honoured tactic of smearing any critic of Israel or Zionism as an "anti-Semite"' (Miller 2021).

David Miller's description of how the world works is a fantasy of Zionist conspiracy. In form, it is similar to more explicitly anti-Jewish antisemitism. And when he talks about Israel's 'time-honoured tactic', and in another article about an 'age-old Israel lobby tactic', he inadvertently slips into a way of thinking that is much older than antizionism (see Mendel 2021).

David Miller is not articulating a worry that Jews may be oversensitive about antisemitism or about criticism of Israel. His position is that Jews who allege that there is antisemitism on the left, or on campus, are acting as part of a deliberate and collective conspiracy to lie. 'The purpose of all this', (note 'all this' not 'some of this' or even 'most of this') adds Miller, 'is to give cover to Zionist activists, allowing them to present themselves as part of a benighted ethnic minority facing racism' (Miller 2021).

Much may be said about the significance of substituting the word 'Zionist' for the word 'Jew' in the structure of conspiracy fantasy. But Miller's practice is to interpret the mere act of saying that one has experienced or witnessed antisemitism as sufficient evidence to define the person so acting as a member of the Zionist conspiracy. It follows, therefore, for Miller, that people who raise this kind of antisemitism as an issue are necessarily doing it in bad faith. And those people are frequently Jewish.

Antizionism claims that its hostility cannot be antisemitic because it is equally hostile to non-Jews. 'Many Zionists are not Jewish', it says, 'so how can antizionism be antisemitic?' But this does not succeed in setting up a non-antisemitic framework for hostility to Israel; rather, it succeeds in setting up an antisemitic framework into which it ropes non-Jews. Many non-Jewish allies have been relentlessly subjected to the antisemitic thinking and practice of people like David Miller.

It should be noted that over the last five years, through the experience of the rise and fall of Jeremy Corbyn's leadership of the Labour Party, there has been a strong consensus in the Jewish community, and in the institutions of the Jewish community. There is wide agreement that left-wing antisemitism is real and significant. Miller's method, therefore, designates the Jewish community, not just this or that individual, as being part of 'Israel and its apologists' (2021).

The Macpherson Principle tells us that a person who says they have experienced racism should be treated with respect and their experience should be taken seriously. The Miller Principle would seem to tell us that a person who says they have experienced antisemitism, if it is related to rhetoric about Israel, should be assumed to be lying.

This practice of treating Jewish victims of antisemitism as part of a conspiracy to silence criticism of Israel is well documented. It is named 'The

Livingstone Formulation' (Hirsh 2016). It is worth mentioning that rhetoric resembling the Livingstone Formulation long predates antizionist antisemitism. This, for example, from Heinrich von Treitschke's *The Jews are our Misfortune*, published in Germany in 1879:

> Anyone is permitted to say unabashedly the harshest things about the national shortcomings of the Germans, the French, and all the other peoples, but any who dared to speak about the undeniable weaknesses of the Jewish character, no matter how moderately or justly, was immediately branded by almost the entire press as a barbarian and a religious bigot.
>
> *(von Treitschke 2021/1869)*

Wilhelm Marr himself, the inventor of the word 'antisemitism', prefaced his own pamphlet with the expectation that Jews would silence his 'criticism' with a concocted allegation of bigotry: 'I wish two things for this pamphlet. 1.) That Jewish critics will not hush it up, 2.) that it will not be disposed of with the usual, smug commentary' (see Jacobs 2020:85).

Moreover, both writers made it clear – just as contemporary antisemitism does – that the vulgar Jew-hatred that came before them was quite unfair. It is only in our own age, they said, that the Jews have begun to behave in the way that the Jew-haters of old wrongly said they behaved.[2]

The EHRC Restates the Macpherson Principle for Jews

In 2020 the Equalities and Human Rights Commission (EHRC) specifically restated the Macpherson Principle for Jews who say they have experienced antisemitism. The reason the EHRC felt the need to do this was that it had observed the *routine* violation of the principle in the Labour Party during the period in which it was polluted by institutional antisemitism.

The EHRC described the following under the heading 'types of antisemitic conduct that amounted to unlawful harassment':

> Labour Party agents denied antisemitism in the Party and made comments dismissing complaints as 'smears' and 'fake'. This conduct may target Jewish members as deliberately making up antisemitism complaints to undermine the Labour Party, and ignores legitimate and genuine complaints of antisemitism in the party.
>
> *(EHRC 2020:28)*

That is, if you like, 'the EHRC Principle'. And that is why David Miller needs to portray the EHRC itself as a victim of the Israeli assault on Britain. He has to say that the UK's statutory body has been successfully and completely corrupted by the Zionist conspiracy. Miller (2021) writes that

Meaningful conversations about anti-Black racism and Islamophobia have been drowned out by a concerted lobbying campaign targeting universities, political parties, the equalities regulator and public institutions all over the country.

David Miller Versus Sociology

Jean Paul Sartre noted that '[t]he antisemite takes pains to speak to us of secret Jewish organisations, of formidable and clandestine freemasonries' (1970:32). David Miller includes his own Jewish students, anyway those who participate in their Jewish Society or UJS, as part of the Zionist project to prevent anti-Black racism and Islamophobia from being taken seriously, and to subvert UK public institutions on behalf of Israel. He does this by demonstrating that Jewish Societies include 'engagement with Israel' as one of their 'core values' (Miller 2021).

A key principle of the sociological understanding of 'race' is that race is constructed, in the first place by racism. People are certainly free to construct diverse and empowering ways of feeling and living their own identities. But racism constructs people's identities from outside, without their consent, and in hostile ways. A person who is very comfortable being black may feel less comfortable if they are defined as black by a white gang in the street or by an antagonistic employer. That is what racism does.

What David Miller is doing here is defining members of UJS and the Bristol J Soc – that is to say, his own students – as 'Zionist', by which he means racist, imperialist and dishonest. He has imposed the identity onto them without their consent. They may or may not define themselves as 'Zionist', and each may have a unique different understanding of the meaning of the Zionism that they themselves embrace. The Zionism of the Union of Jewish Students and of J Socs has nothing in common with the demonising identity that Miller thrusts upon them. In truth, for the overwhelming majority of Jews, some kind of relationship to Israel, where half of the world's Jews live, is a part of their Jewish identity. But that does not make them racists or unpatriotic to their country, or to whatever other identity Miller thinks they should be loyal.

David Miller's work is reminiscent of the writing of the classic antisemite who sets himself up as an expert on 'the Jews'. Miller warns Muslims at the East London Mosque to beware of Jews doing ostensibly innocent interfaith work with them. He constructs intricate diagrams which illustrate in copious detail the connections, which he claims his work uncovers, between Jewish individuals and institutions which he designates as 'Zionist'.[3] He portrays his work as shining a light into the hidden dark world of the racist and murderous conspiracy.

But sociology is fundamentally an empirical discipline. It starts with a rigorous and structured investigation of the world. Only then does it move on to create concepts and theories which may help to understand and make sense of what has been observed. Conspiracy fantasy works the other way around. It starts with the sense that is to be made, and then it proceeds to find the invented and fantastical patterns in the external world.

This is an account by a student at Bristol of how David Miller teaches sociology:

> I was one of the only Jewish students in David Miller's class. Honestly it was scary because he is a teacher so people believed the anti-Semitism he was spreading. I was scared because I am one voice and felt I couldn't stand up to him or tell him what he was saying was wrong.
>
> In Miller's 'Harms of the Powerful' module he claimed the 'Zionist movement (parts of)' were pillars of islamophobia. He also attempted to link various British Jewish organisations to the state of Israel. As a Jewish student, this conspiratorial spider's web of arrows and organisations was grimly reminiscent of antisemitic tropes where Jews are accused of having unique power and influence over political affairs.
>
> *(See Sabrina Miller 2021a)*

After another Jewish student at Bristol had published this account, 'Electronic Intifada', the same website which published David Miller's piece quoted earlier, posted pictures of her. In what could easily be interpreted as incitement, it called her a representative of the 'Israel lobby' and denounced her as part of the Zionist movement which seeks to punish David Miller. The student recorded some of the abuse she received on Twitter and notified Bristol University (see Sabrina Miller 2021b).

The Jewish Chaplain at Bristol University wrote a letter to the Vice Chancellor:

> One Israeli student has told me that he receives daily abuse on the count of his country of origin, and this is utterly unacceptable. It is clear from Miller's recordings and open statements that he has nothing but contempt for Jewish students and is consciously perpetuating conspiratorial myths about the Jewish state and its power. To read his words is reminiscent of the worst antisemitic propaganda – Jewish students in Bristol are being attacked as fifth columnists.
>
> *(Citron 2021)*

Conspiracy fantasy is necessarily unfalsifiable. *Because* they say there is anti-semitism, both the student and the Jewish Chaplain can be defined as lying lobbyists for Israel. The testimony of their experience is itself *silenced*, by means of an accusation that it is nothing more than a cynical attempt *to silence*. And the individuals are made legitimate targets by defining them as racist supporters of racist Israel.

Sociology itself was invented in the 19th century to offer a scientific account of structures of power in our society. The founders of sociology, a number of whom were Jewish, were aware that one reason why this was so important was because of the attraction of conspiracy fantasy, and specifically antisemitism, as a way of understanding the world (Stoetzler 2010). In my opinion, David Miller does not practice sociology in a way which is in any sense scientific or related to any kind of legitimate methodological framework.

Rather, Miller's work constructs what sociologist Keith Kahn-Harris describes as a kind of 'flatland', a world in which networks of power and influence are so intricately connected that they form a seamless system.

> Take Miller's well-known slide from his presentation on how British Jewish/Zionist/Israel lobby institutions are interconnected. . . . While the nodes on this network are differentiated by type ('Israel institution', 'Key UK individuals' etc) and while the nature of the interconnections are identified ('donor', 'president' etc), these annotations do not in fact tell us anything meaningful, because there isn't any meaningful distinction to be made – and that's the point. That, for example, [two named individuals] Mick Davis and Vivian Wineman have been fiercely criticised from the right of the Jewish community for their dovish views on Israel is of no import. That the Board of Deputies and the Zionist Federation are coalitions constantly riven by tension and dispute is not worth remarking on. Zionism/Israel forms a seamless whole.
>
> *(Kahn-Harris 2021)*

The sociologists in Miller's department at Bristol and the discipline more widely must bear some responsibility for their colleagues. Miller's antisemitic discourse is not that unusual on campus but it sticks out because he likes to say clearly and explicitly the things that other academics prefer to say in more opaque and ambivalent language. Miller resembles Ken Livingstone in this regard. Livingstone was no worse than Corbyn himself, but he enjoyed articulating the logic of their shared antisemitic world view more clearly.

Miller has been given a Chair, the highest position of respect and responsibility in academia; he is a tenured Professor. To be promoted to that status requires the explicit endorsement of a significant number of professors, inside and outside both his department and his discipline. If Sociology is incapable of recognising antisemitic conspiracy fantasy as being outside of its own boundaries, then what does that tell us about the state of Sociology today?

I myself have a significant loyalty to sociology. The sociology that I was taught by Robert Fine and others is keenly aware of the dangers of racist and totalitarian thought. It is also alive to the ways in which human beings exclude each other in hidden, complex, unconscious and unspoken ways and it is vigilant in identifying structures of power that may not be easy to observe. I think that the methods and intellectual frameworks of Sociology have been important to my own work on antisemitism. I spend quite a lot of my working life socialising new students into the discipline and introducing them to some of its very basic ways of thinking. But the fact that David Miller has tenure tells us something about his peers as well as something about himself. It should be part of the very core business of sociology to recognise antisemitism and racism.

Conspiracism and Anti-Democratic Thinking

Miller is not just a random and eccentric individual; he is part of a wider culture on parts of the left and parts of academia. Antisemitism and conspiracy fantasy are forms of appearance of anti-democratic thinking. Some Muslims who have been organising politically against Islamist extremism and terrorism say they have been targeted by Miller as 'neocon' and as pro-imperialist, and thence as part of the global Zionist conspiracy.

And Syrian refugees have also been targeted by Miller as dupes of imperialism because they opposed the Assad regime. According to the Syrian refugee, journalist and campaigner Oz Katerji, Miller has been part of campaigns to support Assad, and his Russian and Iranian backers. They have demonised the genuinely heroic 'White Helmets' as al-Qaeda affiliates (Katerji 2021). According to *The Times*, David Miller has 'provided academic status to a group led by proponents of conspiracy theories'. *The Times* examined the 'Organisation for Propaganda Studies' and found conspiracy fantasies relating to 'the September 11 terrorist attacks, the shooting down of an airliner over Ukraine in 2014, the White Helmets humanitarian rescue group in Syria, the antivax movement and the origins of the coronavirus' (Kennedy 2020).

David Miller Versus the IHRA Definition of Antisemitism

In 2021 there is increasing pressure on Bristol University to fire David Miller. Daniel Finkelstein made the case for Miller's dismissal in *The Times* (2021), the Board of Deputies of British Jews has called for the ending of Miller's tenure (2021) and UJS has raised the slogan 'Get Hate off Campus' (UJS 2021). The most compelling grounds for dismissal are related to his speech about his own Jewish students. If they judge that his work is antisemitic, then he thereby designates them as agents of Israel.

On the other hand, there is significant support for Miller from people who think he is a victim of a Zionist witch hunt, for example, Professor Des Freedman, who designates Miller's work as 'criticism of Zionism' (2021) and Professor Jeffrey Bowers, who asserts that Miller is falsely accused of antisemitism (2021). While many of Miller's allies mobilise the rhetoric of academic freedom and freedom of speech, it is not clear how many of them do so with respect to colleagues who present other kinds of racism or bigotry as academic scholarship.

And then there are many, like Frank Furedi, who fully recognise Miller's work as antisemitic, but who argue for a very strong free speech and academic freedom position whereby even antisemitic professors should be protected (2021). It may be added, however, that this absolutist free speech position puts heavy demands on Jewish students and Jewish scholars. Mirada Fricker (2007) has written about what she calls 'epistemic injustice' and Nora Berenstain has written about 'epistemic exploitation':

> Epistemic exploitation occurs when privileged persons compel marginalized persons to educate them about the nature of their oppression. I argue that epistemic exploitation is marked by unrecognized, uncompensated, emotionally taxing, coerced epistemic labor. The coercive and exploitative aspects of the phenomenon are exemplified by the unpaid nature of the educational labor and its associated opportunity costs, the double bind that marginalized persons must navigate when faced with the demand to educate, and the need for additional labor created by the default skepticism of the privileged.
>
> *(2016)*

It follows that a university which judges David Miller's freedom of speech to be a priority also has a responsibility to employ genuine scholars of antisemitism and to fund scholarly journals about antisemitism, in order to counter his conspiracy fantasy.

How the UCU Prepared the Ground for David Miller

It is impossible to understand David Miller, or the support he has received from other academics, without knowing a little about how Israel, antisemitism and BDS have been debated in the recent history of the lecturers' trade union, the UCU. I have never been in a more hostile and antisemitic space than my union. In the UCU I have been transformed from a loyal member and a fellow scholar into a 'Zionist'. Just as David Miller thrusts 'Zionism', meaning racism, onto his students, this identity has been thrust upon me from outside, in a hostile way, and against my consent, in my union.

Back in 2003, the campaign to boycott our Israeli academic colleagues began to take root in the forerunner of the UCU. The boycott campaign sought to create within our union such a focused anger against Israelis, and only Israelis, that union members would feel ready to single them out and punish them for the crimes, real and imagined, of their state. The crimes of our own state, and those of other states, were sometimes criticised, but nobody proposed to hold the scholars accountable for them simply by virtue of the country in which they work. It did not matter that Israeli academics had been at the forefront of the peace movement nor that universities in Israel were amongst the country's most egalitarian spaces. The boycott campaign designated all Israelis as 'collaborators' with the very worst things done by any Israelis.

You would think that such a campaign would worry about its attractiveness to antisemitism, but this campaign angrily denied even that possibility. The boycotters turned fiercely against their critics within the union. They demonised them as enemies of the Palestinians and then enemies of the principle of solidarity, and so they portrayed their opponents as people who were fundamentally disloyal to the union and its culture. Many of the people within the union who were 'othered' in this way, although significantly by no means all of them, were Jewish.

In 2005, after the union had resolved to boycott academics from specific Israeli universities, we organised and inspired a fight back. We armed opponents of the boycott with information and with arguments. We said that solidarity with Palestinians rather than boycotts of Israelis was the right strategy. We publicised the voices of colleagues who were teaching in Palestinian universities and who opposed boycotting. We highlighted the work of Israeli and other colleagues who were involved in joint academic projects and teaching with colleagues in Palestinian universities. We hoped to do, from the outside, what we could to facilitate solidarity between Israelis and Palestinians, and to support a politics of peace. We opposed the flag-waving posturing which designated one nation to be good and the other bad. We called a huge, special one-day council meeting and we won the day. Our union reversed its position, it disavowed the politics of boycotting Israelis and it resolved to formulate a consistent policy relating to human rights abuses in other countries.

But the boycotters did not accept their defeat in the union. They came back year after year pushing their focused Israel-hatred and spinning a one-sided narrative about the Israel–Palestine conflict. They targeted people within the union and on our campuses in Britain who they regarded as being defenders of Israel. Israel was made symbolic of the whole global evil of capitalism and imperialism. They targeted those Jews who refused to disavow Israel and they isolated those who remained quiet.

The campaign to boycott Israel was wrong in itself for a number of reasons, including its violation of the very meaning of the university, as a global community of scholars. But it was also forged within an authentically left-wing tradition of antisemitic thinking and it normalised, licensed and propagated antisemitism into the future.

In a union of 120,000 people who work in universities, there are quite a few Jewish members. But by 2009 there were no Jews left in the national decision-making structures of the union who were willing or able to oppose the boycott campaign and the antisemitism which fuelled it, and which was in turn fuelled by it. There were some antizionist Jews who played an important role in miseducating people. They taught members to recognise claims of antisemitism, rather than antisemitism itself, as the real threat to the left and to the principles of trade unionism.

The union never actually adopted the boycott. It was afraid of the damage that it would do, it was afraid of legal action, and it knew that such a policy could not be enacted in any way which could even appear coherent. We take that as a victory.

But in the campaign against antisemitism, we were defeated. By 2009, nearly everyone I fought alongside in the union against the boycott campaign and its associated antisemitism, had gone. Many had resigned from the union in protest, many had been bullied out and many had been silenced. Many were just tired and were not prepared to devote their whole energy, forever, to fighting the stubborn Israel-obsessives in the union.

I was bureaucratically excluded from the internal union email 'activist list' because I published some of the antisemitism I witnessed there. Where there is institutional racism, boundaries between 'inside' and 'outside' are always heavily policed because what passes as normal inside an institution is easily recognised as not normal out in the ordinary world. The union leadership protected the space within which antisemitism was allowed as 'free speech' and 'criticism of Israel'. A number of anti-boycotters were excluded from the list but nobody was ever excluded from it explicitly because of antisemitism. I am still, 15 years later, excluded. You get a shorter sentence for murder.

We were told by union colleagues that we opposed the boycott because we thought we were the 'chosen people' and that was why we were racist; we were told our racism originated in the Torah and the Talmud. We were told we were like the Nazis at Theresienstadt, whitewashing Israel's evil; our gay colleagues were told they were 'pinkwashing' Israel's evil. We were told that we only pretended to experience antisemitism as a trick to silence criticism of Israel; we were told that we were apologists for apartheid; we were told that we only pretended to support self-determination for the Palestinians; we were told that we received orders from the Israeli embassy. On and on it went. Some of our very smart and courageous non-Jewish comrades and friends fought bravely alongside us. But I saw people close to me being pushed out, turning to drink, cigarettes and drugs, having breakdowns, losing lifelong friends and being excluded from the community of scholars. This all happened in the University and College Union and in the culture it brought into our university departments.

We failed to defeat antisemitism in UCU and, as we had feared it would, the antisemitism spread into the trade union movement and then into the Labour Party. The story of how it coalesced into the Corbyn movement and came close to 10 Downing Street is now well understood. It has been told in my book and those of Dave Rich, and Matthew Bolton and Harry Pitts; it has been told in the journalism of Gabriel Pogrund and John Ware; it has been told in the testimonies of the victims who were excluded and demonised by Labour antisemitism; not least the women, Luciana Berger, Margaret Hodge, Ruth Smeeth, Joan Ryan and Louise Ellman, who suffered waves of specifically misogynist and sexually violent antisemitic rhetoric.[4]

And, as already mentioned, the story has been told by the EHRC, the statutory body set up by the last Labour Government to defend the principles of the Equality Act. The EHRC focused specifically on the way in which the culture in the Party had 'othered' opponents of antisemitism by accusing them of being involved in a dishonest conspiracy to 'smear', to 'fake'. Opponents of antisemitism were accused of 'weaponising' antisemitism against the left, as though antisemitism itself was not already in essence a weapon forged to hurt Jews. EHRC also said that antisemitism took hold in the institutions and the culture of the Party, that it was not only the antisemitic politics and the hatred that were important, but also the roles played by ordinary loyal members and officials.

Now that antisemitic politics is being driven out of the Labour Party, it is looking to regroup back in its safe space, on campus and in the UCU. Some of the defeated rump of British left-wing antisemitism is trying to disavow the most explicit Jew-hate that it picked up when it went mainstream, and to purify itself again in an academic and respectable discourse of 'criticism of Israel'. If that is the case, the urge to be loyal to David Miller gives it a dilemma.

UCU has never had to face up to what it became or what it did. It incubated and normalised a culture which corrupted the Labour Party to such an extent that it could constitute no electoral threat even to somebody as politically unattractive as Boris Johnson. Ordinary working-class people in Britain sniffed the UCU's antisemitism, as manifested in Corbyn's Labour Party, and they were repelled by it.

But the clever people, the cultured people, the lecturers, the creators of right and good opinion in new generations of journalists, teachers, politicians and the chattering classes, have not been held to account. They are carrying right on. And they're giving an intellectual gloss to the story that between 'us' and 'socialism' stood 'Zionism', which appeared as the institutions and members of the Jewish community.

The danger is that this will inspire a new 'stab in the back myth' to explain the defeat of the Corbyn movement. 'We were never even allowed to fight for socialism', that myth says, 'because we were stabbed in the back by people within our own movement who pretended to be part of us but who were really part of a global, imperial, elite, conspiracy to defend capitalism and Zionism'.

Labour antisemitism is defeated for the moment, but the culture and the common-sense notions it was built out of will outlast it. It was incubated, in part, in academia and the University and College Union, and now it is returning there, looking for a safe place where it can nurture and renew itself. That is the meaning of David Miller.

Notes

1 Editor's note. David Miller was released by the University of Bristol in October 2021 on the grounds that he 'did not meet the standards of behaviour we expect from our staff'.

2 For more on this theme, see David Seymour (2019) 'Disavowal, Distinction and Repetition: Alain Badiou and the Radical Tradition of Antisemitism', in Jonathan Campbell and Lesley Klaff (eds.), *Unity and Diversity in Contemporary Antisemitism: The Bristol-Sheffield Colloquium on Contemporary Antisemitism*. Boston: Academic Studies Press, 203–218.

3 The controversial infographic presented to students by David Miller, ostensibly depicting a spider's web of Jewish and Israeli influence in Britain, can be seen at Simon Rocker, 'CST calls Bristol University "an utter disgrace" for response to complaint about lecture', *The Jewish Chronicle*, 9 September. Available: www.thejc.com/news/uk/cst-condemns-bristol-university-s-response-to-complaint-it-made-about-lecture-linking-it-to-islamoph-1.488385 (accessed 12 November 2022).

4 See David Hirsh (2018) *Contemporary Left Antisemitism*, New York: Routledge; Dave Rich (2016), *The Left's Jewish Problem: Jeremy Corbyn, Israel and Anti-Semitism*, London: Biteback; Matt Bolton and Frederick Harry Pitts (2018) *Corbynism: A Critical Approach*, Emerald Publishing; Alan Johnson (2019), *Institutionally Antisemitic: Contemporary Left Antisemitism and the Crisis in the British Labour Party*, Fathom. Available: https://fathomjournal.org/fathom-report-institutionally-antisemitic-contemporary-left-antisemitism-and-the-crisis-in-the-british-labour-party/ (accessed 15 November 2022).

References

Berenstain, Nora (2016) 'Epistemic exploitation', *Ergo*, 3 (22). Available: https://quod.lib.umich.edu/e/ergo/12405314.0003.022?view=text;rgn=main (accessed 1 March 2021).

Board of Deputies of British Jews (2021) 'It is with regret that we have felt the need to write', *Twitter*. Available: https://twitter.com/BoardofDeputies/status/1362733744453541892 (accessed 24 February 2021).

Bowers, J. (2021) 'Professor David Miller from the University of Bristol', *Twitter*, 20 February. Available: https://twitter.com/jeffrey_bowers/status/13643390681386229979?s=20 (accessed 25 February 2021).

Citron, Y. (2021) 'Letter from the Jewish chaplain to the vice chancellor', *Twimg.com*. Available: https://pbs.twimg.com/media/EumEuCdXUAIue-E?format=jpg&name=medium (accessed 23 February 2021).

EHRC (2020) *Investigation into antisemitism in the Labour Party*, Equality and Human Rights Commission. Available: www.equalityhumanrights.com/sites/default/files/investigation-into-antisemitism-in-the-labour-party.pdf (accessed 15 November 2022).

Finkelstein, Danny (2021) 'Bristol University should sack conspiracist professor', *The Times*, 23 February. Available: www.thetimes.co.uk/article/bristol-should-expel-its-conspiracist-professor-htmgmhvw3 (accessed 24 February 2021).

Freedman, Des (2021) 'When the board of deputies refers to opposition to Zionism', *Twitter*. Available: https://twitter.com/lazebnic/status/1363460169938657282?s= 20 (accessed 25 February 2021).

Fricker, Miranda (2007) *Epistemic Injustice: Power and the Ethics of Knowing*. Oxford University Press. Available: https:/doi.org/10.1093/acprof:oso/978019823 7907.001.0001 (accessed 1 March 2021).

Furedi, Frank (2021) 'Even conspiracy theorists must have freedom of speech', *Spiked-online.com*. Available: www.spiked-online.com/2021/02/23/even-conspiracy-theorists-must-have-freedom-of-speech/ (accessed 24 February 2021).

Hirsh, David (2016) '*The Livingstone Formulation – David Hirsh*'. Engage. Available: https://engageonline.wordpress.com/2016/04/29/the-livingstone-formulation-david-hirsh-2/ (accessed 23 February 2021).

Jacobs, Steven Leonard (2020) *Antisemitism: Exploring the Issues*, Santa Barbara: ABC-CLIO.

Kahn-Harris, Keith (2021) 'Into the flatlands with Professor David Miller', *JewThink*. Available: www.jewthink.org/2021/02/22/into-the-flatlands-with-professor-david-miller/ (accessed 24 February 2021).

Katerji, Oz (2021) 'People on the Labour Left trying desperately to downplay the David Miller stuff', *Twitter*, 22 February. Available: https://twitter.com/OzKaterji/status/1363815469589880832 (accessed 15 November 2022).

Kennedy, Dominic (2020) 'Conspiracy theories spread by academics with university help', *The Times*, 13 June. Available: www.thetimes.co.uk/article/conspiracy-theories-spread-by-academics-with-university-help-9g09xtc73 (accessed 24 February 2021).

Mendel, Jack (2021) 'Pressure mounts on Bristol Uni over academic accused of "antisemitic tropes"', *The Jewish News*, 19 February. Available: https://jewishnews.timesofisrael.com/pressure-mounts-on-bristol-uni-over-academic-accused-of-anti semitic-tropes (accessed 23 February 2021).

Miller, David (2021) 'We must resist Israel's war on British universities', *The Electronic Intifada*. Available: https://electronicintifada.net/content/we-must-resist-israels-war-british-universities/32391 (accessed 23 February 2021).

Miller, Sabrina (2021a) 'I'm tired of waiting for my Uni to act against conspiratorial hatred', *The Jewish News*, 19 February. Available: https://blogs.timesofis rael.com/im-tired-of-waiting-for-my-uni-to-act-against-conspiratorial-hatred/? utm_medium=Social&utm_source=Facebook&fbclid=IwAR1FTf1WwoCC94Tx_x6TIxrxVCSUkR7VW3MXD1YndDbQc6d8_EcWwZyFp5M#Echobox=161 3739481%20%5BAccessed%2023%20Feb.%202021%5D (accessed 15 November 2022).

Miller, Sabrina (2021b) 'Hi @BristolUni. For the past two days I've had to deal with the following', *Twitter*. Available: https://twitter.com/SabriSun_Miller/status/1364 668152630624260?s=20 (accessed 24 February 2021).

Sartre, Jean-Paul (1970) *Literary and Philosophical Essays*, New York: Collier Books.

Stoetzler, Marcel (2010) 'Modern Antisemitism and the emergence of sociology: An introduction', *Patterns of Prejudice*, 44 (2): 107–115.

UJS (2021) 'Bristol – hate off campus', *Union of Jewish Students*, 29 April. Available: www.ujs.org.uk/bristol_hate_off_campus (accessed 15 November 2022).

Von Treitschke, H. (2021/1869) *The Jews Are Our Misfortune*, quoted in GHDI – Document, *Ghi-dc.org*. Available: http://ghdi.ghi-dc.org/sub_document.cfm?docu ment_id=1799 (accessed 24 February 2021).

24

FROM SCHOLARSHIP TO POLEMIC? A CASE STUDY OF THE EMERGING CRISIS IN ACADEMIC PUBLISHING ON ISRAEL

Cary Nelson

Sunaina Maira's book *Boycott! The Academy and Justice for Palestine* would not ordinarily be a publication of special note (Maira 2018).[1] Such a short, poorly documented book attacking Israel and promoting the Boycott, Sanctions, and Divestment (BDS) movement, would typically come from one of the popular political imprints specialising at least partly in disseminating propaganda – among them CounterPunch, Haymarket, Interlink, Pluto, and Verso. Indeed three of the book's blurb writers – Angela Davis, Omar Barghouti, and Steven Salaita – write that sort of book themselves. But *Boycott!* comes to us instead from the University of California Press (UCP), historically one of our more distinguished scholarly publishers. Moreover, it is part of a series, *American Studies Now*, recently founded and edited for UCP by two former presidents of the American Studies Association, Curtis Marez and Lisa Duggan, both themselves leaders of the American Studies Association (ASA) campaign to boycott Israeli universities. Marez and Duggan are praised in the book, but not as a form of toadying to them as series editors. Maira was a leader of the ASA campaign as well. The four, along with additional blurb writer Alex Lubin, speak as one, ideologically.

It is possible for people in political agreement to edit each other's work critically, to demand high standards of debate and proof from an ally. Where bias could be suspected as part of the review process, they might wish to be especially meticulous. But the character of Maira's book suggests that none of this happened. Typically, a university press review identifies readers sympathetic to the author's views or methods who are then charged with deciding whether the project is well executed. The alternative of testing a manuscript against hostile readers is a waste of time and money. Whether Davis, Barghouti, Salaita, and Lubin were among the readers I cannot say, but if so,

DOI: 10.4324/9781003322320-30

they did not successfully apply the standards to be expected in academic publishing. Certainly Marez and Duggan, the series editors with ultimate responsibility, did not. In any case, the book reveals emerging trends in BDS arguments – and says much about the state of academic publishing and about the consequences of an increasingly politicised academy.

Indifference to evidence

Midway through the book, Maira devotes several pages to a celebration of the November 2013 annual meeting of the 5,000-member ASA. That was when the movement to boycott Israeli universities got what remains perhaps its most notable endorsement from a faculty association, though the 2015 anti-Zionist resolution by the National Women's Studies Association gives ASA's substantial competition, given its still wider anti-Zionist focus. In the subsequent vote the following month by the ASA's whole membership the boycott resolution carried the day by a wide margin. Her claim in the book's introduction that 'one major academic association after another' followed by 'endorsing the boycott' (2018:1) is a little harder to demonstrate, given that years later the ASA remains the largest such group to do so, whereas the 10,000-member American Historical Association, the 10,000-member American Anthropological Association, and the 25,000-member Modern Language Association have all defeated efforts to endorse an academic boycott. Maira is not alone among BDS apologists in deciding that the best way to handle defeat is to declare victory.

Contempt for conversation

But that is not the only problem with her account of the sequence of ASA events. The binary model that the American Association of University Professors (AAUP) adopted in its classic *1915 Declaration*, the statement that defined the group's principles and mission, proposed that academic freedom entailed both rights and responsibilities, though most of the responsibilities are defined not within the discourse of academic freedom but by institutions and academic disciplines. Foremost among the responsibilities built into the understanding of academic freedom itself is a commitment to a search for truth. But within the academy that search entails a methodology: approaching the truth through dialogue and debate with the existing scholarship. You do not promote your own views without serious engagement with the opposition. Scholarship is a conversation, not simply a polemic. Sunaina Maira's book, however, is only a polemic.

All she can say about the counterarguments at the ASA is that they constituted 'a pitiful case in defence of Israel' (2018:69). I was not there myself, but I do know several of the boycott opponents who were present, and I have

The weakness of such arguments leads her to compensate by repeatedly claiming that the BDS movement 'expands academic freedom – rather than diminishing it, as anti-BDS critics have claimed' (2018:55). It does so, she says 'for the oppressed population', but she can present no evidence for such an effect, either in the West or in Palestine (2018:62). Indeed the anti-normalisation campaign that BDS promotes, justifies and encourages shutting down all interaction with Israelis and their supporters. It is difficult to see how this '*supports* and enlarges academic freedom' (2018:116). Her more revealing claim is the one asserting 'the dangerous use of academic freedom as a smokescreen for larger struggles over other kinds of freedoms' (2018:114).

We need to talk about BDS academic publishing

The full list of unsupported claims in the book would be very long. High on my list would be her odd fantasy assertion that advocacy for Palestine is at the centre of the academy's widespread exploitation of contingent labour (2018:120–121). The unconscionable exploitation of academic labour has evolved and steadily increased since 1970, driven primarily by administrator commitment to purchasing classroom instruction as cheaply as possible. The pattern has evolved over 50 years and has absolutely nothing to do with Palestinians or the Israeli–Palestinian conflict. That said, it is time to return here to the general concerns I raised at the outset, concerns that are directly related to the Israeli–Palestinian conflict. Berkeley is one of several university presses, including Duke and Minnesota, that have built lists hostile to Israel and now have a warranted reputation as a place receptive only to anti-Zionist manuscripts that tackle the Israeli–Palestinian conflict. Indeed there are academic presses where a surprising number of professional staff members have publicly supported the BDS movement. Duke is one such venue. At least those staff members have been honest about where they stand, giving fair warning that their personal political beliefs may colour their attitude towards manuscripts submitted. A number of presses with lists in Jewish studies or Israel studies, on the other hand, concentrate their acquisitions in historical scholarship, avoiding more politically charged contemporary topics. But that leaves the polemical terrain to Israel's critics, which fails to promote more informed debate.

Maira's and other thinly documented university press books make it starkly clear that the peer review process in a number of subject areas has broken down. That undermines the overall reliability of academic publishing. If *Boycott!* was in fact substantially improved as a consequence of peer review, it is hard to imagine what the original manuscript could have looked like. She does not engage seriously with a single full-length essay or book critical of the boycott movement or supportive of Israel's right to exist as a Jewish state. Except for an op-ed, I cannot find a single such work even cited. The entire peace movement receives only dismissive asides, as in her references to 'tactical resorts to the language of tolerance, peace, dialogue, and coexistence' (2018:107) and to 'interfaith tolerance as the solution to a religious conflict, which elides Zionism and anti-Palestinian racism' (2018:116–117).

Given that Middle East Studies and other academic fields have turned into armed camps, it is not enough to say that a properly executed peer review and editorial process would have prevented a book like Maira's from being published by a major university press. Some faculty already recognise that peer reviewing of job candidates and candidates for tenure and promotion is often flawed for similar reasons, but an assumption that university press reviews are conducted responsibly may still be widespread. Maira insists that Zionist policing of debate has put academic freedom in crisis, but the evidence here suggests instead that existing mechanisms for imposing standards are inadequate, not excessive. While I do not have a clear solution to the problem to offer, a case can be made that the politicisation of scholarship requires better mechanisms for quality control. At the very least, the heightened risks to objectivity entailed need to be highlighted, rather than ignored. One might call for a general statement on the issues to be formulated with faculty assistance and endorsed by academic publishers.

On the UCP website, Curtis Marez points out that books in the series 'are written in an accessible style that will make them useful in classrooms', a standard hope, but one that is worrisome in this context. The Berkeley imprimatur is more likely to encourage course adoption than publication by an officially politicised press. To say the least, significant damage would be done if *Boycott!* were taught as a recommended model for how scholarly debate about Israel and the BDS movement should be conducted.

Notes

1 This chapter was first published in *Fathom* in 2018.
2 Editor's note: see also Nelson 2021 for a fuller treatment of the subject of academic freedom in Palestinian universities.

References

Maira, Sunaina (2018) *Boycott! The Academy and Justice for Palestine (American Studies Now: Critical Histories of the Present)*, Berkeley: University of California Press.
Musher, Sharon Ann (2015) 'The closing of the American Studies Association's mind', in Cary Nelson and Gabriel Noah Brahm (eds.), *The Case Against Academic Boycotts of Israel*. Chicago: MLA Members for Scholars Rights, distributed by Wayne State University Press, 105–118.
Nelson, Cary (2016) 'Academic freedom in Palestinian Universities', *Telos*, 177: 219–239.

Nelson, Cary (2021) *Not in Kansas Anymore: Academic Freedom in Palestinian Universities*, Washington, DC: Academic Engagement Network, distributed by Academic Studies Press.

Nelson, Cary and Gabriel Noah Brahm (eds.) (2015) *The Case Against Academic Boycotts of Israel*. Chicago: MLA Members for Scholars Rights, distributed by Wayne State University Press.

Qumsiyeh, Mazin B. (2010) *Popular Resistance in Palestine: A History of Hope and Empowerment*, London: Pluto Press.

Redden, Elizabeth (2017) 'Breach of duty or legal overreach?' *Inside Higher Ed*, 11 December. Available: www.insidehighered.com/news/2017/12/11/lawsuit-accuses-american-studies-association-officers-concealing-their-plans-boycott (accessed 23 November 2022).

25

PATHOLOGISING 'JEWISH BEING AND THINKING'

Oren Ben-Dor and Academic Antisemitism

Sarah Annes Brown

In 2012 Oren Ben-Dor published an article titled 'Occupied Minds: Philosophical Reflections on Zionism, Anti-Zionism and the Jewish Prison' in the Edinburgh University Press journal *Holy Land Studies*.[1] In the abstract Ben-Dor refers, troublingly, to 'pathologies that pertain to Jewish being and thinking' (2012:33. Future references will be cited parenthetically in the text). Over the course of the article Ben-Dor gradually reveals the nature of these supposed Jewish 'pathologies', and in this piece, I aim to tease out some of the disturbing implications of his analysis. Although framed as an academic piece, 'Occupied Minds' at times reads more like one of H. P. Lovecraft's brooding tales of cosmic horror, continually hinting at a nameless, shapeless, lurking menace which can barely be articulated but which is somehow bound up with Jewish identity. The writing is often opaque, and the argument is heavily dependent on a kind of rhetorical phantasm, built up through a series of mysterious, veiled suggestions.

The essay begins with a comparatively objective discussion of terminology relating to Zionism, but then takes an odd turn: 'Justice can be broadly understood as being about giving back what is due. My concern is with what is the primordial due to be given back in Palestine. Can legal, constitutional, even moral, talk respond to the primordial due that calls for the thinking of Palestine?' (34). The sentences aren't easy to parse. But the repeated use of the word primordial – that is, 'ancient', 'primeval' – already suggests that more than the events of 1948 are at stake here. Ben-Dor goes on to say that in order to work out what is really due to Palestine we need to think about it in a way which is 'still being policed out from thought' (35). He repeatedly warns that 'political correctness' is inhibiting an honest discussion of the issues (35). However, harsh criticisms of Israel and

DOI: 10.4324/9781003322320-31

Zionism are commonplace – so what exactly is he claiming to be unthinkable here?

Ben-Dor goes on to interrogate the nature and root causes of Zionism: 'Is Zionism to be pointed at as the origin of the injustice in Palestine, or should Zionism be approached symptomatically – as an indicator to a more primordial and self-concealed injustice which is itself existential in nature and which is determinative of actuality there?' (35). The reader might first conjecture that this 'primordial and self-concealed injustice' is an allusion to the evil of antisemitism, an important factor in the emergence and development of the Zionist movement. (Sometimes the Palestinians are described as secondary victims of the Holocaust.) But for Ben-Dor the real injustice is in fact enmeshed in something at the core of Jewish identity, 'intimately connected to the existential question that concerns the endemic otherness and exile of Jewish being and thinking'. He insists that anti-Zionism needs to 'overcome its reticence to ask about the Jewish Question in relation to Zionism' (35).

Like Gilad Atzmon, author of *The Wandering Who? A Study of Jewish Identity Politics* (2011), Ben-Dor targets Jewish anti-Zionists as part of the problem. He warns that normal left-wing frames of reference – those of Marxism or Postcolonialism, for example – are inadequate to counter Zionism. In doing so, he implies that some anti-Zionists have a self-serving and secretive agenda: 'Grasped existentially, all these frameworks are conjured up to conceal the possibility that the injustice of Zionism is invoked for the sake of covering up some deeper unfolding that implicates human thoughts more generally' (36). The constructions are passive, but a sinister agency is still strongly suggested. The phrase 'conjured up' implies deceit; 'deeper unfolding' seems to indicate a long-laid plan, carefully concealed.

Ben-Dor then hints further at what motivates Jewish anti-Zionists:

For anti-Zionism to press the moral demand for change according to an egalitarian constitutional rationale and framework – whereby all colonial racist Israeli laws are abrogated and the Jewish state replaced – might not find connective tissue to the mindset of both political Zionists and of those on the left who oppose Zionism as Jews. Nor would it take seriously the mindset of religious Jewish orthodox opposition to Zionism. Anti-Zionism, then, should be able at the very least to articulate and to critically respond to *that in the service of which* both Zionists and their Jewish objectors from the left and the right are existentially united.

(36, emphasis added)

Yes, Orthodox opponents of Zionism have primarily theological motives for their position. But secular Jewish anti-Zionists *do* want the kind of one-state solution he describes in that first sentence. Ben-Dor seems more interested in dark suggestion than in argument or proof; here he hints at a menace which can barely be expressed. There's a kind of ellipsis in the final sentence – we probably expect 'that' to qualify some other word. But it remains simply 'that', the unnamed force which supposedly binds all Jews together, whatever their political differences. This is of course a profoundly conspiratorial, as well as completely unevidenced, perspective. The word 'service' further implies the power of 'that' – whatever 'that' may be – and taps into the trope of Jewish dual loyalties.

On the next page he introduces, via cryptic insinuation, a view which he will develop more openly later in the essay – the idea that Jewish identity is in some way anti-human, and might even be invoked as a key driver of the Holocaust: 'It is thought-provoking that the debt in Palestine that is owed, not only to Palestinians but to humanity as a whole, is not being thought-about' (37). It would seem that the whole world, not just the Palestinians, is a victim of that elusive 'that', discussed earlier. He continues: 'The very persistent use of the Jewish Question by Zionists should have provoked the contemplation of whether Zionism is not itself a historical manifestation, as well as a means for the uncanny regeneration and preservation of that Jewish being and thinking that keeps re-igniting that Jewish Question. But it does not, or rather is not allowed to' (37).

Thus, rather than seeing Zionism as, in part, a response to antisemitism, Ben-Dor seems to view it as a manifestation of a mysteriously potent force, something which inevitably prompts the 'Jewish Question', that is, prompts antisemitism – later he refers, startlingly, to the 'self-provoked hatred against Jews' (39). 'Uncanny regeneration' is another charged phrase, echoing images of the Jew as a blood-sucking vampire. These intimations of something supernatural at work are congruent with a pervasive tendency to couch criticism of the Jewish Other in mystical or theological terms, crediting Jews with more than human powers. Susan Shapiro explains the origins of this trope in Christian antisemitism and the legend of the Wandering Jew: 'The Jewish Uncanny represents the Jew(s) as spectral, disembodied spirits lacking a national home and, thus, as unwelcome guests or aliens wandering into and within other peoples' homes, disrupting and haunting them, making them "Unheimliche," unhomey' (1997:65).

Ben-Dor quickly returns to that suggestion of something supernatural at work: 'We must connect to what *is*, but not the "is" of the unjust *acts* but the "is", the deepest "is" that connects to the "how" of the people who perpetrate, justify and rationalise these acts. That which stealthily causes such perpetration and rationalisation has already unfolded in a way that representations of the acts themselves do not perturb' (37). The final sentence is typically opaque, but once again the subject is a 'That' which is 'unfolded', and which acts 'stealthily'. As elsewhere, it is not clear whether Ben-Dor is describing consciously underhand moves from individuals, or simply personifying a mysterious underlying cause. But the latter interpretation is equally troubling, as it reinforces that uncanny suggestion of something more (or less) than human, the combination of power and secrecy promoted by the idea of the *Ewige Jude*, the Eternal Jew.

He then characterises what is wrong with Jews, inexplicably but ominously, as a 'gap' (38), before yet again hinting that Jews caused or even in some sense sought the Holocaust because of their 'paradoxical nature of being and thinking that persists and is strengthened by the success of generating hatred and violence against itself' (38). On the following page Jewish anti-Zionism is described as a 'camouflaging vehicle' for what Ben-Dor sees as the true evil, and the loaded word 'camouflage' is used twice more in the article (39). The idea of a 'gap' recurs also. Later we are told of the 'self-imposed forgetfulness of a hole in their own being' (44). This suggests some strange inherent moral defect or twist.

Ben-Dor continues with this dehumanising theme, a staple of antisemitism of course:

> The Zionist victim and supremacist mentality – that living force and unity which is nourished by the desire to be hated – stems, before all else, from sublimated hatred of, and supremacy towards, all 'others'. It is a mentality that forces separation from the essential, mysterious togetherness that is bestowed on all others. . . . Hatred of all others is a manifestation of self-hatred which is itself symptomatic of an unresolved trauma and separation from some basic human ability, some basic response-ability of humans to mirror, to be responsible and first and foremost to dwell together, accepting ultimately the interconnectedness of, and compassion between, all beings.
>
> *(44)*

One feature of Ben-Dor's article is that, just when one feels it cannot get any more abhorrent, new depths are plumbed. It is a commonplace for anti-Israel discourse to make taunting comparisons between Jews and Nazis, to draw a parallel, for example, between the Warsaw Ghetto and Gaza. Here, this trope is intensified into a more twisted suggestion that antisemitism is a function of becoming 'Jewified' (46). Rather than suggesting that Jews are turning into Nazis, Ben-Dor suggests that Nazis in fact turned into Jews:

> Those assimilated into this kind of thinking desire to do [to] the assimilator that which would nourish the assimilator's desire to be hated. In other words, when those assimilated, unconsciously, do not like what is being done to them in a self-concealing way, they too start to hate themselves for being so assimilated they turn into 'Jews', or become Jewified, and in return hate the assimilator in what superficially lends itself to a simple racist discourse and which, in turn, serves the assimilator's pathology.
>
> *(46)*

And here the same idea is hinted at: 'The philosophical and existential inquiry asks how enlightened existence has nevertheless managed to attract so much hatred and violence whether in Palestine as the "paragon of democracy in the Middle East" or as a central pillar of German culture before "the Holocaust". What is that which gets stronger in generating so much hatred against itself again and again wherever it is?' (52). Yet again the root of the problem (whatever precisely it is) is referred to simply as 'that'.

The current situation in Israel/Palestine and the context of 1930s Germany are forced together in order to suggest that there is something inherent in the Jewish mindset or condition which inspires hatred and perversely feeds on that hate. Here the point is made still more explicit – the Jews, or Jewishness, were the cause of the Holocaust: 'liberal Zionists grasp somewhere in their unconscious . . . that the Holocaust occurred because of something that haunts Jewish being and thinking, something that cannot be tamed' (53). Again, the rhetoric works to indicate that this destructiveness is essentially uncanny, something which cannot be pinned down or controlled.

This sense of something uncanny at work, something which haunts, is reinforced by Ben-Dor's almost hypnotic compulsion to repeat certain words and ideas, for example, in this sentence which asserts that Jewish anti-Zionism is part of 'that' problem, shielding Jewishness from criticism through cunning subterfuge: 'Furthermore, could it be Jewish precisely because cloaking the well-concealed Jewish pathology of Zionism behind comforting ethical and universal Jewish ethics creates the existential camouflage that enables pathology to survive and to unfold so successfully?' (48). 'Pathology' (or related words) is used 40 times, the verb 'unfold' 15 times and words relating to 'concealment' 29 times.

Towards the end of the essay we return to the word 'due', used oddly in the opening sentences in relation to the rights of Palestinians: 'Left Jews who oppose Zionism would sing in one voice with liberal Zionists by being the first ones to condemn as anti-Semitic any person who dares to claim that "the Holocaust" might have been provoked by Jewish being and thinking and that some due has been given back in the form of one of the most horrible of genocides.' Ben-Dor goes on: 'Anti-Zionist Jews would be the first to condemn as anti-Semitic anyone who says that Jewish being and thinking brought, as its Being demands, violence and hatred upon itself, and that the same being and thinking preserves itself in the realisation of Zionism, the result of a successful concealment of the Holocaust's origin' (54). Ben-Dor offers no apology for claiming that the Holocaust was 'provoked' and his use of the word 'due' suggests the idea of a just retribution for Jewish culpability. The suggestion that Jewish 'Being' inevitably attracts violence and hatred resonates with earlier discussions of such issues, for example, this passage from the Nazi journalist Dietrich Eckart: 'If he is not commanded to stop he will annihilate all humanity. His nature compels him to that goal, even though he dimly realizes that he must therefore destroy himself . . . To be obliged to try

26

ON MISREPRESENTATIONS OF THE IHRA DEFINITION OF ANTISEMITISM

Dave Rich

The campaign against the International Holocaust Remembrance Alliance (IHRA) working definition of antisemitism (2016) has been running for long enough that it is now possible to identify its common themes.[1] These include repeated misrepresentation of what the definition does, and does not, say about Israel and antisemitism; unevidenced claims about the definition's alleged impact on free speech; confusion over its legal status and power; and an appeal to authority by quoting others from within this same campaign.

Case Study: Eight Lawyers and the IHRA

A letter published in the *Guardian* on 7 January 2021, signed by eight experienced lawyers, is a helpful example of how this works. It opens with the claim that '[t]he legally entrenched right to free expression is being undermined by an internally incoherent "non-legally binding working definition" of antisemitism.' The letter then cites the Universal Declaration of Human Rights, the Human Rights Act 1998 and the Education Act 1986 before noting that the IHRA definition 'has no legislative or other authority in international or domestic law'.

Given that this is the case, it is hard to see how a non-legal definition with no legal authority could undermine legally guaranteed rights to free expression and academic freedom. Most universities understand this, even if these eight lawyers don't: the University of Oxford, in announcing its recent adoption of the IHRA definition, stated, 'The IHRA definition does not affect the legal definition of racial discrimination, so does not change our approach to meeting our legal duties and responsibilities.'

DOI: 10.4324/9781003322320-33

There are other legal restrictions on free expression which these lawyers did not mention in their letter, including the Public Order Act, the Equality Act, the Protection from Harassment Act, the Malicious Communications Act, and so on. These Acts all limit free speech, including at universities, but the letter's signatories do not seem troubled by this. Instead, a definition that even they concede is 'non-legally binding' is, apparently, such a grave threat to free expression that it is worth a letter to the *Guardian*. Why is this the case?

The answer lies in their misrepresentation of what the definition says and does. They claim, as others have before them, that 'the majority' of the IHRA definition's 'illustrative examples' of potentially antisemitic speech 'do not refer to Jews as such, but to Israel. They have been widely used to suppress or avoid criticism of the state of Israel.' The implication is that the IHRA definition is more concerned with, or directed against, anti-Israel speech than anti-Jewish speech.

This is simply not true: of the 11 'illustrative examples' of potentially antisemitic speech listed in the IHRA definition, nine explicitly mention Jews or the Jewish people (seven mention Israel, of which five mention both Jews and Israel). Given that this is the case, the claim that 'The majority of these examples do not refer to Jews as such, but to Israel' is so obviously untrue that it is difficult to understand how a group of such experienced lawyers can put their names to it. Either they did not read the definition before writing to the *Guardian* about it, or they read it but decided to ignore what it actually says. Perhaps they hoped that the qualifier 'as such' would magically change the meaning of the word 'Jews' that precedes it. I'm not sure which of those three explanations would be the most damning.

The examples that mention both Jews and Israel include 'Accusing the Jews as a people, or Israel as a state, of inventing or exaggerating the Holocaust'; 'Holding Jews collectively responsible for actions of the state of Israel'; 'Using the symbols and images associated with classic antisemitism (e.g. claims of Jews killing Jesus or blood libel) to characterize Israel or Israelis'; or 'Accusing Jewish citizens of being more loyal to Israel, or to the alleged priorities of Jews worldwide, than to the interests of their own nations'. Do the signatories of this letter really intend to claim that these examples suppress legitimate, non-antisemitic criticism of the State of Israel? If that is the case, let them try. They will struggle to persuade many people of their argument.

More likely is that they object to the examples stating that it 'could' be antisemitic to deny 'the Jewish people their right to self-determination, e.g., by claiming that the existence of a State of Israel is a racist endeavour'; and 'Applying double standards by requiring of it a behaviour not expected or demanded of any other democratic nation'; and perhaps the one that says 'Drawing comparisons of contemporary Israeli policy to that of the Nazis' is antisemitic. The IHRA definition says that these examples 'could' be antisemitic; implying that sometimes they could not be. Perhaps the lawyers who the IHRA Definition' (January 2020); David Hirsh, 'Jews are asking for protection from their universities from antisemitism. David Feldman's "All Lives Matter" response is not helpful' (December 2020); Eve Garrard, 'The IHRA Definition, Institutional Antisemitism, and Wittgenstein' (December 2020); David Hirsh, 'It was the new phenomenon of Israel-focused antisemitism that required the new definition. David Hirsh responds to a recent "call to reject" the IHRA' (January 2021); Dave Rich, 'The IHRA: A Reply to the Guardian Letter signed by Sir Stephen Sedley et al.' (January 2021); Lesley Klaff and Derek Spitz, 'Why the 2010 Equality Act does not make the IHRA definition of antisemitism redundant' (February 2021); John Hyman and Anthony Julius, 'Calling a truce with left-wing antisemitism: The Case Against the Jerusalem Declaration on Antisemitism' (May 2021); Cary Nelson, 'Accommodating the New Antisemitism: a Critique of "The Jerusalem Declaration"' (April 2021); Gerald Izenberg, 'The Jerusalem Declaration on Antisemitism may inadvertently give cover to antisemites' (April 2021); Michael Walzer, 'The Jerusalem Declaration: A Response to Cary Nelson' (April 2021); Derek Penslar, 'Why I Signed the Jerusalem Declaration: A Response to Cary Nelson' (April 2021); Cary Nelson, 'Once Again on the Jerusalem Declaration: A Rejoinder to Derek Penslar and Michael Walzer' (April 2021); Richard Landes, '"A Remarkably Aggressive Naïveté": A Response to Derek Penslar and Michael Walzer' (April 2021); Jeffrey Herf, 'IHRA and JDA: Examining Definitions of Antisemitism in 2021' (April 2021); Dave Rich, 'Read it again. Read better. Dave Rich on Derek Penslar's serial misrepresentations of the IHRA' (May 2021); Michael Walzer, 'I hope that UCL faculty and staff will defend IHRA, as I would do were I with them' (May 2021); Cary Nelson, 'Antisemitism and the IHRA at University College London' (May 2021); and David Matas and Aurel Braun, 'Rejecting IHRA: The Avoidable Debacle at the University of Toronto' (February 2022).

References

Community Security Trust (2020) *Campus Antisemitism in Britain 2018–2020*, London: CST. Available: https://cst.org.uk/public/data/file/b/2/Antisemitism%20 on%20University%20Campuses.pdf (accessed 23 November 2022).

European Commission (2020) *Handbook for the Practical Use of the IHRA Working Definition of Antisemitism*, Luxemburg: European Commission and International Holocaust Remembrance Alliance. Available: https://report-antisemitism.de/ documents/IHRADefinition_Handbook.pdf (accessed 23 November 2022).

Feldman, David (2020) 'The government should not impose a faulty definition of antisemitism on universities', *The Guardian*, 2 December. Available: www.the guardian.com/commentisfree/2020/dec/02/the-government-should-not-impose-a-faulty-definition-of-antisemitism-on-universities (accessed 23 November 2022).

International Holocaust Remembrance Alliance (2016) *What is Antisemitism? Non-Legally Binding Working Definition of Antisemitism*, International Holocaust Remembrance Alliance. Available: www.holocaustremembrance.com/resources/ working-definitions-charters/working-definition-antisemitism (accessed 23 November 2022).

Jerusalem Declaration on Antisemitism (2021) Available: https://jerusalemdeclaration. org (accessed 23 November 2022).

Penslar, Derek (2021) 'Why I signed the Jerusalem declaration: A response to Cary Nelson', *Fathom*, April. Available: https://fathomjournal.org/why-i-signed-the-jda-a-response-to-cary-nelson-2/ (accessed 23 November 2022).

27

POLITICAL ANTISEMITISM

A Defence of the IHRA Definition

Bernard Harrison and Lesley Klaff

Introduction

The 'IHRA Definition of Antisemitism' is frequently cited in current political debate as the key to recognising and combating antisemitism.[1] But it has also been widely criticised, on two main grounds: the first, that it is useless as a legal tool; the second, that it illegitimately restricts freedom of speech.

The second of these criticisms is the fundamental one, on which the case for the first depends. It is that the Definition illegitimately conflates antisemitism and political criticism of Israel. Critics who pursue this line argue that antisemitism is best defined – in the phrase of Sir Stephen Sedley, writing recently in the *London Review of Books* – as 'hostility towards Jews as Jews' (2017:8).

If that is what antisemitism is – and *all* it is – then it would appear to follow that no criticism of Israel, however 'hostile' or 'extreme', can be *antisemitic*. For criticism of Israel, even 'hostility' towards Israel, is criticism directed not towards 'Jews as Jews' but towards a *political entity*: a state. The IHRA Definition, however, expressly characterises certain criticisms of Israel (describing it as a Nazi state, or denying the right of the Jewish people to political self-determination, for instance), as antisemitic. Hence, so the argument goes, the IHRA Definition represents (perhaps not in intention but in effect) an attempt to restrict political debate by stigmatising certain political views as racist, when the views in question can in logic be nothing of the kind.

The first line of criticism that we mentioned earlier follows very simply from the success – *if* it succeeds – of the second one. The IHRA Definition consists of two main parts: first, a preamble, which offers a general

DOI: 10.4324/9781003322320-34

characterisation of antisemitism, and second, a series of 11 putative 'examples', or instances, of antisemitic speech or conduct. The brief characterisation of antisemitism offered in the preamble reads in part, 'Antisemitism is a certain perception of Jews, which may be expressed as hatred toward Jews.' Legal critics have argued that this characterisation must necessarily *constrain the legal interpretation* of the 'examples' which occupy the bulk of the remaining text of the Definition (Robertson 2018, Tomlinson 2017). The wording of the preamble in their view must entail the legal consequence that nothing can be considered antisemitic unless it can be shown to manifest 'hatred towards Jews as Jews'. Thus, claiming that Israel is a Nazi state, or that Jews are more loyal to Israel than to their countries of citizenship, could be shown to be antisemitic, by the terms of the IHRA Definition, only if such claims could be shown to arise from *hatred towards Jews in general* on the part of those making them.

If this criticism stands, what it shows is that, legally speaking, the utility of the IHRA Definition is vitiated by a requirement to prove *intent* (in this case, intent to express hatred of Jews in general). Such requirements are in practice very difficult to meet and, indeed, make it difficult to devise legal restraints, not merely upon antisemitic speech and action, but upon racist speech and action of any kind. It was for this very reason that the MacPherson Report 1999, which reported on the racist killing of teenager Stephen Lawrence in 1993, emphasised 'outcomes' rather than 'intention'.

These arguments no doubt seem powerful enough at first sight. But they depend for their validity on a single premise: that antisemitism is 'hostility towards Jews as Jews' – and *is never anything else but that.*

Antisemitism is also a pseudo-explanatory political theory

That premise is highly contestable. In effect, it identifies antisemitism as a *mental state*: an emotional disposition to feel hostility towards any Jew merely because he or she is a Jew. Certainly, that is one of the things covered by the term 'antisemitism'. But is it the only thing covered by that term? We also use the word, surely, to describe something altogether different in nature – not a mental disposition at all, in fact but, rather, a cultural artefact: *a body of pseudo-explanatory political theory.* Antisemitism as a political theory is designed to explain why national or world politics are failing to move in ways congenial to the antisemite and his friends. That failure (whatever form it may take, in the minds of this or that group of antisemites) is, according to the theory, the fault of the Jews, a people united in the pursuit of evil, who secretly control the world, and whose vast powers of conspiratorial organisation have allowed them to take control of institutions – the banks, Hollywood, International Finance, the State Department, the US Presidency, etc. – which, though they may appear to be reassuringly Gentile to the core, are in reality entirely Jewish concerns, secretly managed from behind the scenes, entirely for the benefit of the Chosen People.

Whereas antisemitism as an *emotional disposition* is rooted in contempt, antisemitism as a *political doctrine* is rooted in fear, not to say panic. It is this kind of antisemitism that led, in the hands of the Nazis, to the mass murder of the bulk of European Jewry between 1933 and 1945. One does not commit vast resources of manpower and militarily valuable material to the murder of extraordinary numbers of civilians – many of them being one's own fellow citizens and the vast majority of them of no political significance whatsoever – because one happens to *despise* them. One does it because one *fears* them; regards them as constituting a serious, collectively motivated enemy force, albeit one working in secret, and disposing, through its quasi-demonic powers, of modes of operation beyond the power of the simple Gentile mind to unravel.

That all of this nonsense is evident merely from its content. Jews – of all people – are certainly not up to running the World Conspiracy attributed to them by the night terrors of the political antisemite. But nobody could be 'up to' such a thing. 'The world' is simply too big, too complex, and too diverse to be 'run from behind the scenes' by anyone. The world we live in is no doubt, at all times and in many ways, a mess. But there is nothing 'behind' that mess; and if you want to know who is 'responsible' for it, go look in the mirror.

Nonsense as it is, however, political antisemitism has demonstrated its profound attractions for minds attuned to conspiracy theory by repeatedly reinventing itself as a strand in European politics over the past two millennia. In this process, it has shown itself as attractive to minds of that type on the left of politics as to their homologues on the right. Most recently it has resurfaced, in connection with Israel, as a way of 'making sense' of the strained relationship between the West and the Islamic world. From the standpoint of many minds on the left and centre-left of Western politics, these strains are entirely the fault of the Jews, and originate in the foundation of the State of Israel. It is commonplace for people who would like to believe that without the presence of Israel in the region all would be sweetness and light between the Islamic world and the West, to commit themselves to the view that Israel is in some sense an 'illegitimate state', which should never have been allowed to come into existence in the first place. Once on the table, such a claim requires reasons to back it up. The easiest and most obvious way of backing up the contention that Israel – alone among the nation states of the world – has *no right to exist as a state* is to claim that its conduct as a state *outdoes in evil* that of any other state in the world. Given the remarkable levels of evil-doing achieved by a wide range of 20th- and 21st-century regimes, from the Third Reich in Germany to the Pol Pot regime in Cambodia, or more recently the Assad regime in Syria, a detailed case for putting Israel, of all countries, at the head of the list would be difficult to assemble. Rather than making out a detailed case, therefore, those anxious to brand Israel as a 'pariah state' tend to choose the easier option of attempting to associate it as widely as possible, in suitably receptive minds, with things *already* widely considered to represent the nadir of evil. Such things include Nazism, the Apartheid regime in South Africa, racism, colonialism and war. Hence the frequently heard claims that Israel is a 'Nazi State', a 'racist state', an 'Apartheid state', or a 'settler-colonial state', or that it is 'the main threat to peace' in the region, or possibly in the world.

These more specific claims, however, cut no nearer the truth than the more general claim they attempt to substantiate, that Israel is an illegitimate state. Considered as a candidate for any of these descriptions, Israel falls at the first hurdle. Israel is not a 'Nazi state', because its government (unlike that of the late Saddam Hussein in Iraq, for instance, or for that matter that of Bashar al-Assad in Syria) is not in the hands of a single political party obedient to an inspired leader and committed to enforcing policies in broad alignment with those of the former *Nationalsozialistische Deutsche Arbeiterpartei*. It is not an 'Apartheid state' because it altogether lacks the legal and social apparatus of racial separation that characterised the Apartheid regime in South Africa. It is not a 'racist state' because its Jewish population embraces Jews of all racial origins and colours, and for that matter because its citizens are only about 74 per cent Jewish, the remainder being Arab, including Muslim and Christian, Druze, Circassian and others. There are Arab Israeli Members of the Knesset and Arab Ministers of Government, as well as Arab Israeli Supreme Court Justices. Many Druze, some Christian Arabs and a few Muslims choose to serve in the IDF. It is not a 'settler-colonial state' because it did not come into being as a result of any European project of colonialism, but as the result of the Jewish population of Palestine establishing its right to political autonomy in the face of an attempt, from which the European powers stood aloof, to exterminate it or drive it from the land by military force. It has manifestly proved in practice a far lesser threat to peace, even in the region, than great-power rivalries between Iran, Turkey and Saudi Arabia, or for that matter, than the so-called Arab Spring.

These accusations, in short, make no contribution to serious political debate. Rather, they are sonorous but empty phrases, good only for hurling during demonstrations or the rowdier kind of meeting. Moreover, they clearly reanimate central elements of the type of antisemitism that takes the form of a pseudo-explanatory political theory; notably the thesis that the collective goals of the Jewish community are both profoundly evil and profoundly inimical to non-Jewish interests.

The factual baselessness of the earlier claims, that Israel is a 'Nazi state', a 'racist state', and so on, evidently vitiates their claim to articulate 'political criticism' of Israel deserving the protection of the law guaranteeing political freedom of speech. In the absence of serious factual grounding, 'anti-Zionist' slogan-mongering of this type lapses from the category of political discourse into that of politically motivated defamation. It is defamatory in the legal sense of falsehoods calculated to undermine the reputation of the victim and to expose him or her to hatred and contempt: the 'victim' in this case being any Jew (or for that matter non-Jew) supportive of Israel who finds herself or himself publicly labelled, with consequences ranging from reputational damage to risk of personal assault, as a putative supporter of Nazism, racism, colonialism, Apartheid and war.[2]

If we now examine the claims concerning Israel characterised as antisemitic by the IHRA Definition, we find that they correspond very closely to those we have just identified as defamatory. The list of things identified as *prima facie* antisemitic by the Definition via its 'examples' is in fact a very short one: denying the right of the Jewish people to exercise political autonomy; describing Israel as an essentially racist or Nazi state; asserting the existence of a Jewish Conspiracy; asserting support for Israel on the part of non-Israeli Jews to argue disloyalty to their actual nations of citizenship; and the singling out of Israel for condemnation in respect of conduct passed over or condoned in other nations. These are all contemporary versions of claims regarding Jews central to *political* antisemitism of the type disseminated by the Nazis: antisemitism manifesting itself in the form of a delusive pseudo-explanatory political theory.

That would seem to set the second ground of criticism of the Definition in a rather less flattering light. It would appear that the 'examples' section of the Definition in no way restricts critical political debate concerning Israel; it merely restricts, by characterising them correctly as antisemitic, certain lines of mendacious defamation, primarily of Israel, and secondarily of its supporters, Jewish and non-Jewish.[3]

Defamation

In the light of that conclusion, what are we to say about criticism one, that the IHRA Definition is useless as a legal tool? The main ground of this objection is that the presence of the sentence of the preamble reading 'Antisemitism is a certain perception of Jews, which may be expressed as hatred toward Jews' entails in law that the acts stigmatised as antisemitic in the examples can be so regarded only if they can be shown to express hatred of Jews in general. It is true that the Definition in its present form does not distinguish explicitly between antisemitism as an emotional disposition and antisemitism as a delusive pseudo-explanatory theory. But at certain points, it certainly presumes the validity of that distinction. In the passage of further elucidation immediately following the preamble, for example, we find the following: 'Antisemitism frequently charges Jews with conspiring to harm humanity, and it is often used to blame Jews for "why things go wrong".' This is a sentence that efficiently captures in outline the main contentions of antisemitism in its mode as a body of delusive political theory.

In any case, once this (fairly evident) distinction between the two types of antisemitism is above the table, it seems clear, for the reasons offered earlier, that what is morally and legally objectionable about the claims regarding Israel characterised as antisemitic in the 'examples' section of the Definition, is not that they offer instances of 'hatred of Jews as Jews', but rather that they offer instances of defamation. This changes the legal landscape in two important respects. Firstly, in proving an allegation of defamation there is no need to prove intent. A defamatory statement regarding X, whether X is an individual or a collectivity, may be published without any intention of harming X, but is not rendered any the less defamatory by that fact. By the same token, the publication of an antisemitic and defamatory false statement by someone innocent of 'hatred of Jews as Jews' does not cease to be antisemitic in virtue of that fact. The antisemitism here resides not in the intention but in the content of the act. And finally, returning briefly to the ground of criticism two, there is no freedom of expression defense to a charge of defamation.

The second change to the legal landscape introduced by placing defamation, rather than simply the expression of hatred, at the heart of antisemitic discourse, is that abundant resources *already* exist in British law for prosecuting the circulation of statements likely to attract hatred towards, or provoke actual assaults against, minority groups. Part III of the Public Order Act 1986, for instance, criminalises acts involving 'words', 'behaviour', or 'material' of a 'threatening, abusive or insulting character', that are merely *likely*, given all the circumstances, to stir up racial hatred. No freedom of expression defense is available in such cases.

The Equality Act of 2010 similarly proscribes antisemitic acts of the sort stigmatised as such by the IHRA Definition, in virtue of its recognition that the word 'Jewish' refers to 'a race', 'a religion', or 'belief'. The Act protects Jews and others from 'hostile environmental harassment'. Section 26 defines 'harassment' in a way that does not require 'intent'. It provides that 'a person A harasses another B if (a) he engages in unwanted conduct relative to a protected characteristic, and (b) the conduct has the purpose *or effect* [our italics] of (i) violating B's dignity, or (ii) creating an intimidating, hostile, degrading, humiliating or offensive environment for B.' Where such harassment is found to occur, there is no freedom of expression defense.

Online antisemitism may be actionable under both the Malicious Communications Act 1988 and the Communications Act 2003. The former makes it an offense to send indecent, grossly offensive, threatening *or false* [our italics] electronic communications, if the purpose (or one of the purposes) of the sender is to cause the recipient distress or anxiety. The latter criminalises the use of a public electronic communications network to send a message (or other matter) that is grossly offensive or of an indecent, obscene or menacing character; or to send a false message 'for the purpose of causing annoyance, inconvenience or needless anxiety to another'. Again, where such an offense takes place, there is no freedom of expression defense.

It seems, then, that criticism one – that the IHRA definition is useless as a legal tool – treads on ice as thin and infirm as that trodden by criticism two – that the definition illegitimately restricts freedom of speech. The IHRA Definition was not designed as a legal instrument, and in no jurisdiction has it been adopted in that role. It remains what it was designed to be: a means of clarifying, for the benefit of governments and administrators at all levels, what kinds of activity are to be considered antisemitic and why. It is possible – but this is a longer story – that some kinds of antisemitism are not caught by the Definition. But there seems little doubt, for the reasons offered earlier, that what it does characterise as antisemitic is indeed so. And there seems little doubt, either, that ample means already exist in British statute law for giving legal effect to the clarifications it offers.

Notes

1 This chapter was first published in *Fathom* in 2020. It summarises the main argument of a longer paper, 'The IHRA Definition and its Critics', presented to the 23–27 March 2019 conference of the University of Indiana Institute for the Study of Contemporary antisemitism, and published in Alvin H. Rosenfeld, ed., *Contending With Antisemitism in a Rapidly Changing Political Climate*, Bloomington: Indiana University Press, 2021. *Fathom* platformed an extensive debate about the merits of the IHRA between 2020 and 2022. See Bernard Harrison and Lesley Klaff, 'In Defence of the IHRA Definition' (January 2020); David Hirsh, 'Jews are asking for protection from their universities from antisemitism. David Feldman's "All Lives Matter" response is not helpful' (December 2020); Eve Garrard, 'The IHRA Definition, Institutional Antisemitism, and Wittgenstein' (December 2020); David Hirsh, 'It was the new phenomenon of Israel-focused antisemitism that required the new definition. David Hirsh responds to a recent "call to reject" the IHRA' (January 2021); Dave Rich, 'The IHRA: A Reply to the Guardian Letter signed by Sir Stephen Sedley et al.' (January 2021); Lesley Klaff and Derek Spitz, 'Why the 2010 Equality Act does not make the IHRA definition of antisemitism redundant' (February 2021); John Hyman and Anthony Julius, 'Calling a truce with left-wing antisemitism: The Case Against the Jerusalem Declaration on Antisemitism' (May 2021); Cary Nelson, 'Accommodating the New Antisemitism: a Critique of "The Jerusalem Declaration"' (April 2021); Gerald Izenberg, 'The Jerusalem Declaration on Antisemitism may inadvertently give cover to antisemites' (April 2021); Michael Walzer, 'The Jerusalem Declaration: A Response to Cary Nelson' (April 2021); Derek Penslar, 'Why I Signed the Jerusalem Declaration: A Response to Cary Nelson' (April 2021); Cary Nelson, 'Once Again on the Jerusalem Declaration: A Rejoinder to Derek Penslar and Michael Walzer' (April 2021); Richard Landes, '"A Remarkably Aggressive Naïveté": A Response to Derek Penslar and Michael Walzer' (April 2021); Jeffrey Herf, 'IHRA and JDA: Examining Definitions of Antisemitism in 2021' (April 2021); Dave Rich, 'Read it again. Read better. Dave Rich on Derek Penslar's serial misrepresentations of the IHRA' (May 2021); Michael Walzer, 'I hope that UCL faculty and staff will

28

MISREADING HANNAH ARENDT

Judith Butler's Anti-Zionism and the Eichmann Trial

Russell A. Berman

On Hannah Arendt

In 1961 Adolf Eichmann, one of the architects of the Shoah, was appre-
hended in Argentina by Israeli agents and brought to Jerusalem where he was
put on trial, convicted and executed.[1] The trial was a turning point in the history of Holocaust jurisprudence and the judicial treatment of human rights
crimes more generally. Hannah Arendt reported on the trial for *The New
Yorker*, and her accounts, published as the book *Eichmann in Jerusalem* in
1963, provoked an enormous controversy, not the least because its subti-
tle, *A Report on the Banality of Evil*, was understood (or misunderstood) to
trivialise the crimes. Yet there were many other dimensions to the criticism
of the book, driven in part by the fact that Arendt had taken the occasion of
the trial to express her own antagonism towards David Ben-Gurion and her
reservations about the shape the Zionist project had assumed. Was it Eichmann who was on trial or did Arendt treat the State of Israel as the ultimate
defendant?

Much of this debate is well known and is in any case too extensive to
treat exhaustively here. However, posing the question today is appropriate
because the contemporary American scholar, Judith Butler, draws specifically
on Arendt's account in *Eichmann in Jerusalem* to support her own emphatically anti-Zionist conclusions in her 2014 volume *Parting Ways: Jewishness
and the Critique of Zionism*. While Arendt raised doubts about the character
of the Eichmann trial, especially the prosecutor, Butler magnifies Arendt's
position into a fundamental rejection of the state, not merely the single judicial act. For both, however, the problem of reaching and representing justice
is central to their respective and very different arguments.

DOI: 10.4324/9781003322320-36

I will trace aspects of the transformed representation of justice from Arendt's reading of Eichmann to Butler's reading of Arendt, from the critique of the trial to the rejection of the state. The story spans half a century and therefore can be thought of as a kind of reception history of the trial. It is also an object lesson in the indeterminacy of the political values of ideas, insofar as Arendt, an ultimately conservative political theoretician, curiously turns into a source for Butler who understands herself unambiguously as a thinker of the left.

This conceptual journey from right to left is intertwined with another trajectory, from Arendt's early Zionism to a more distanced relationship to Israel. The significance of the anti-Zionist overtones in *Eichmann in Jerusalem* become all the more pronounced against the backdrop of Arendt's enthusiastic embrace of Zionism during the 1940s. This is not the place to trace the complexities of the competing Zionist political programmes that were debated during the darkest days of war and genocide. Suffice it to say that Arendt, during her first years in the United States, appeared to live up to a primary tenet of her philosophy, an advocacy for politics as public action. She participated in and identified with the Zionist movement, thus, for example, insisting at one point on the need to raise a Jewish army to fight the Germans, and she celebrated the Warsaw uprising by placing it in the context of a long Jewish national history: 'Honor and glory are new words in the political vocabulary of our people. We should perhaps have to go back to the days of the Maccabees to hear such language' (Arendt 2007:199). Referring to the novelty of the terminology, Arendt implies the emergence of a new Jew, akin to the 'new man' of modernism and socialism, now casting off the subaltern degradation of the past and achieving a genuine political nationality: 'To the extent that *the* Jew is disappearing, Jews have come to life: organising, fighting, proud of their flag and deeds, suffering and hoping for a better future – a nationality like the other nationalities who sprang from the fostering soil of Western history' (2007:256). It is important to parse the political language here. The terminology of Jews as 'a nationality like the other nationalities' reveals her core secular Zionism. The shift from the disappearance of 'the Jew', in the singular, to the plurality of 'Jews' is consistent with her emphasis on politics as action in concert with others, and resonates with the Heideggerean notion of *Mitsein*. No doubt, the birth of the 'new Jew' can be read as a progressive vision, but her values and points of reference – honour, glory and the legacy of antiquity – echo a conservative rhetoric, as does the invocation of 'Western history'.[2]

Despite this momentary enthusiasm for the political ambitions of the Jewish nation, Arendt rapidly distanced herself from the Zionist movement after the 1942 Biltmore Conference, which established the focus on state formation. As committed as she was, in theory, to the public sphere and political action, she developed an animosity towards popular nationhood and any nationalism, combined with a general disdain for party politics, especially when politics merged with variants of ethnic identity. The rejection of ethno-national politics is a key theme in her *Origins of Totalitarianism* of 1951, reflecting an anxiety that what we would today call identity politics can disrupt the proper functioning of civic life, including the pursuit of justice, and this argument ultimately paves the way to her core critique of modernity, in which the political sphere is subverted by what she labels 'the rise of the social', as developed in *The Human Condition* (1958). Her sharply binary distinction between public and private spheres formed the categorical basis for her critique of American school desegregation in 'Reflections on Little Rock', which originally appeared in *Dissent,* where she asserted that the education of children belongs fundamentally to the private sphere of family life and that it should therefore not be subject to political or judicial mandates. While she would ultimately express public regret for her resistance to desegregation, it is noteworthy that she did not retract a side argument in the same essay defending the practice of restrictions in clubs and resorts that excluded Jews.[3] On this point too, the rigid distinction between private and public led her to argue that the private facts of ethnicity or nationality should not belong to the sphere of civil rights or public equality. Moreover, one sees here an indication of a certain reluctance to criticise anti-Semitism, one end of a long arc that leads decades later to her reader Butler's efforts to shield anti-Zionism from allegations of anti-Semitism; I will return to this point.

The scandal of 'Reflections on Little Rock' in 1958 anticipated key aspects of the provocation of *Eichmann in Jerusalem* in 1963: Arendt would again show herself fundamentally unsympathetic to political agenda with ethnic or national dimensions, while continuing to insist on an uncompromising separation of private and public. Private matters, she would argue, do not belong in the public sphere. Yet paradoxically her core contention in the book relied on a very private matter: not the objective substance of Eichmann's deeds but her conjectures about his personality. Her insistence on his 'banality', which provoked so much anger, may have been intended to mean that he was not a diabolical genius, not a monster, not an ideological Jew-hater, but ultimately it suggested that he was merely an uninteresting personality, always mechanically following someone else's orders. But is personality a criminal matter?

In fact, considerable scholarship, most recently by Bettina Stangneth, demonstrates that Arendt misjudged Eichmann who likely feigned his own blandness in a failed effort to avoid the death sentence, but the point here is that Arendt based her primary argument on a (probably wrong) claim about Eichmann's personality, rather than on his crimes (Stangneth 2015). While by the end of the book, she affirms the conviction on the basis of his acts, her main argument treats his character, not his crimes. Nonetheless, she would condemn the prosecution, as we will see, for not limiting itself to the criminal acts and instead addressing material she deemed irrelevant to the pursuit of justice. While she was prepared to criticise others for introducing private matters into the public sphere, she clearly failed to hold herself to the same norm by emphasising the banality of the personality over the egregiousness of the deeds.

This background is necessary to appreciate why her criticism of the prosecutor's case is the key point relevant to the representation of justice in *Eichmann in Jerusalem*. Arendt claims repeatedly that the mandate of the court is to 'do justice', which she understands exclusively in terms of determining the culpability of the defendant. All that should matter was Eichmann and the law: the wider context, the sort of historicist framing that in other circumstances a liberal sensibility might introduce to suggest some exculpatory relativisation, was not fair game. In the case of the Eichmann trial, however, discussions of the wider context could only mean explaining how his actions contributed to genocide and therefore strengthen the case against him. This is the wider context she opposed including in the trial's deliberations.

Instead, Arendt argued for a tunnel vision focus on the defendant, betraying a preference for a modality of justice that excludes victims and their suffering as fundamentally irrelevant. Hence her repeated criticism of what she regards as the excessive expansiveness of the prosecutor's case and the introduction of survivor testimony regarding what, from the standpoint of her understanding of justice, had no place in the courtroom. Thus she resented 'this atmosphere, not of a show trial but of a mass meeting, at which speaker after speaker does his best to arouse the audience [which] was especially noticeable when the prosecution called witness after witness to testify to the rising in the Warsaw ghetto and to similar attempts in Vilna and Kovno – matters that had no connection whatever with the crimes of the accused' (Arendt 2006:121). Further references to this volume are included in parentheses in the main text.). Her repetitive phrasing – 'speaker after speaker', and 'witness after witness' – signals an annoyed impatience with the voices of victims. To do justice for Arendt means pursuing a restrictive judgement on the defendant; it does not involve providing any platform for victims. On the contrary, to achieve justice, she implies, requires the exclusion of victims whose testimony might prejudice the court against the defendant: hers is not an empathetic or liberal jurisprudence.

There was however more at stake here than a legalistic resistance to 'an endless procession of witnesses' (207). As Elhanan Yakira has pointed out, 'Arendt was not a historian, and what she had to say about the trial, Eichmann, and the Holocaust was not based on scholarly research. . . . she relies mainly on the works of Hilberg and Reitlinger, that is, on scholars who investigated the Holocaust from the point of view of the perpetrators' (Yakira 2009:291). This emphasis on the machinery of the killing reflects her own existentialist critique of modernity defined as bureaucracy plus technology. At stake are the deeds of the perpetrators, not the sufferings of the victims.

Thus she delays any substantive discussion of witness testimonies until the next to last chapter, selects only a few examples and subjects most of them to dismissive comments. Arendt thereby overlooked the truly innovative aspect of the Jerusalem trial, the turn towards victim experience, a development that sharply distinguished the Eichmann hearings from Nuremberg and which would eventually lead, decades later, to the South African Truth and Reconciliation Commissions and its very different representation of justice.

The complaint against the use of victim testimony reflects the philosophical insistence on a categorical distinction between public and private: victim suffering is a private matter that does not belong in a court of law. Meanwhile, *Eichmann in Jerusalem* documents an additional, symmetrical contamination of legal space in its initial setting of the stage, as the curtain rises with the opening lines: ' "*Beth Hamishpath*" – the House of Justice: these words shouted by the court usher at the top of his voice make us jump to our feet as they announce the arrival of the three judges, who, bareheaded, in black robes, walk in to the courtroom from a side entrance to take their seats on the highest tier of the raised platform' (2006:3). What follows immediately is a vertical scenario: below the judges sit the translators; below the translators, the accused and the witness box; and below them the prosecutor and the counsel for the defense. Such is the hierarchy of the law, but curiously, Arendt devotes most of this opening paragraph to the question of translation and her complaint of the 'frequently incomprehensible' quality of the German-language renderings, which she does not attribute to 'the old prejudice against German Jews' but rather to the 'powerful "Vitamin P", as the Israelis call protection [i.e. patronage – RB] in government circles and the bureaucracy'. Thus, the initial scene of the law becomes a site of contamination, the inappropriate intrusion of private interests, as powerful political forces distribute sinecures, such as legal translation jobs. The language of the law has, Arendt suggests, been corrupted by the client politics of a socialist state, and this insinuation anticipates the subsequent argument that the prosecutor is himself merely a creature of a manipulative government: 'And Ben-Gurion, rightly called the "architect of the state", remains the invisible stage manager of the proceedings. Not once does he attend a session; in the courtroom he speaks with the voice of Gideon Hausner, the Attorney General, who, representing the government, does his best, his very best, to obey his master' (2006:5). That the trial ultimately succeeds, and that justice is done, takes place, for Arendt, despite the prosecutor's political subservience. The positive outcome is due instead to the judges and their integrity. Yet by confounding Hausner and Ben-Gurion, Arendt turns the trial into a judgement on the State, especially the quasi-socialist state, at least as much as it was a judgement on Eichmann, the National Socialist, and this argument makes Arendt's book available for Butler's anti-Zionist reading.

Before proceeding to Butler's account, however, I want to confront Arendt's published description of the courtroom scene in the book with another version she provided, in private, in a letter to her teacher and friend, Karl Jaspers, on 13 April 1961. In it, she offers him her own personal view of the trial, with the same vertical architecture albeit with more revealing characterisations. 'My first impression [of the court room in Jerusalem – RB]. On top, the judges, the best of German Jewry. Below them, the prosecuting attorneys, Galicians, but still Europeans. Everything is organised by a police force that gives me the creeps, [die mir unheimlich ist] speaks only Hebrew and looks Arabic. Some downright brutal types among them. They would follow any order. And outside, the oriental mob, as if one were in Istanbul or some other half-Asiatic country. In addition, and very visible in Jerusalem, the peies and caftan Jews, who make life impossible for all reasonable people' (see Arendt and Jaspers 1992:434–436, Letter 285).[4]

The description reads as an unexpurgated draft for the opening description of the courtroom in the book, and it provides us with important insights into Arendt in Jerusalem and the prejudices she brought to her evaluation of the judicial apparatus. The admiration for the German Jewish judges and the contempt for the Galician prosecutor are terribly stereotypical, as is the hostility to the orthodox Jews. Of particular interest however is her judgement on the presumably Mizrahi Jewish police force that 'speaks only Hebrew and looks Arabic', and to whom she attributes brutality – evidently on the basis of physiognomy – and a willingness to 'follow any order'. With that suggestion of unlimited obedience, she builds a conceptual bridge between the Israeli police force and the Nazi defendant who would become the iconic representation of following orders, regardless of their content. For Arendt, the police force of the state of the erstwhile victims shares the defining characteristic of the perpetrator now on trial, and this opens a rhetorical door for the polemical inversion that would come to inform later anti-Zionist polemics in general and Butler's work in particular. Still, we should avoid conflating the two thinkers, and not only because of the political distance between Arendt's conservatism and Butler's progressivism. Ultimately, as far as the Eichmann trial goes, Arendt admires the Israeli judges, accepts the legitimacy of the court, and affirms the legality of the verdict and the sentence. Measured against Butler in 2014, Arendt in 1963 appears to be still almost a Zionist who appreciates the importance of states, and in particular the State of Israel, as the necessary framework for a judicial system that has the capacity to achieve justice. There is no justice without a state, and in 1961, so Arendt suggests, despite her own doubts regarding Zionism, there could be no justice for the Jewish people without a Jewish state.

On Judith Butler

In *Parting Ways*, Butler attempts to rebut claims that anti-Zionism is anti-Semitic by appealing to a group of Jewish thinkers – in addition to Arendt,

Walter Benjamin, Emanuel Levinas, and Primo Levi – (as well as to Edward Said and Mahmoud Darwish) in order demonstrate the viability of a Jewish critique of Zionism (2014).[5] If these Jews can oppose Zionism (as she claims, not necessarily convincingly, that they do), then anti-Zionism cannot be anti-Semitic. The argument, which has some strategic importance in contemporary academic radicalism, is symptomatic of the debates around the anti-Israel boycott movement, although it tells us little about the thinkers themselves; we will see how Butler significantly distorts Arendt in particular.

Regarding the substantive matter, anti-Zionism and anti-Semitism, much could be said that would go far beyond the scope of this chapter. No doubt, the two terms reference different semantic fields and therefore should not be conflated: generalised Jew-hatred is not the same as opposition to the political movement to establish a Jewish state. Yet neither are the terms mutually exclusive, they can certainly overlap, and really existing anti-Zionism in the contemporary world has demonstrably and often crossed the border to anti-Semitism, for example, when, instead of protesting outside of Israeli embassies, anti-Zionist activists attempt to storm synagogues, as in Paris, deface them as in England or demonstrate in front of them as in the United States. Nor to my knowledge have anti-Zionists ever demonstrated outside of the churches of Christian Zionists who, in the United States, are much more numerous than Jews and in any case much more supportive of current Israeli government policies than are the typically liberal American Jewish communities. Nonetheless, Butler tries to shield anti-Zionism from the allegation of anti-Semitism – she certainly has her work cut out. Yet she goes beyond a merely defensive posture by mounting the much more ambitious argument that any genuine Judaism must be emphatically anti-Zionist, so she demands, setting herself up as the arbiter of Jewish authenticity, and effectively excommunicating those who disagree. She develops this argument especially in the two chapters in *Parting Ways* devoted to Arendt which focus above all on *Eichmann in Jerusalem*: Butler reads Arendt reading Eichmann.

For Arendt, it is the duty of a court to pursue justice, and it is equipped to do so because of an authority grounded in the political community that finds expression in the state and its laws. To be sure, she qualifies the standing of the state in several ways: by locating any single state within an international system, that is, a state among a plurality of states; by limiting the reach of the state to public matters, narrowly defined and excluding it from the private sphere, a strangely extra-judicial space; and by otherwise expressing the preference for the sort of dispersal of sovereignty she admired in the American constitutional system of separated powers and – as in 'Reflections on Little Rock' – the federalism of the so-called 'states' rights'. Within this restrictive framework, however, justice can be pursued, in its proper terrain, thanks to the authority of the state.

In contrast, Butler treats justice and law as mutually exclusive. Positive law as an expression of the state is only an exercise in power (here one sees the indelible influence of Michel Foucault) while justice, akin to Walter Benjamin's understanding of divine violence, has a messianic status and dwells somewhere beyond rational scrutiny, outside of normal politics. Therefore, in the Arendt chapters, aside from a few passing remarks, Butler refrains from addressing justice per se, but focuses instead on the necessary corruption of the law of the state, which is always and constitutively incapable of rendering justice. State power, for Butler, is *a priori* suspect because of its association with the state, and any positive law therefore necessarily an expression of malice. In contrast, for Arendt, power is viewed positively as the capacity of individuals to act in concert as a political community that can articulate laws and establish courts capable of pursuing justice.

In effect, Arendt's qualified suspicion of centralised sovereignty becomes for Butler an unqualified rejection of any sovereignty, including even that popular sovereignty which, in democratic modernity, is the source of the legitimacy of the state and the foundation of any system of legality. However, 'the people', whose political expression is the democratic state, and on whom democratic legitimacy depends, is more than a statistical accumulation of strangers. At stake instead are forms of historical community and shared identity, whether one understands the 'people' in a phenomenological sense as the empirical inhabitants of a shared life world or, more romantically, as the folk participants in national traditions. Butler's rejection of sovereignty altogether applies necessarily to popular sovereignty as well and therefore to democratic political formations. While Arendt objects to the intrusion of ethno-nationality into politics, she does not erase it altogether: she treats it instead as a merely private matter. In contrast, and in particular for Jewish identity, Butler radicalises Arendt's apprehensions concerning ethnicity into an uncompromising imperative of dispersion: the only permissible community, for Butler, is the dispersed community. 'Jewishness can and must be understood as an anti-identitarian project insofar as we might even say that being a Jew implies taking up an ethical relation to the non-Jew, and this follows from the diasporic condition of Jewishness' (2014:117). It follows then that the only authentic Jewish condition is exile because Jewishness requires that we 'affirm the displacement of identity', and she continues: 'The point is not simply to scatter geographically, but to derive a set of principles from scattered existence' (2014:117–118). Hence the eleventh commandment: thou shalt disperse. Genuine Jewishness is, for Butler, necessarily diasporic: the true Jew is the wandering Jew, with the surely intended implication that the adoption of, for example, a Balfourian homeland objectively represents a forced political conversion into a gentile normalcy, or what we saw Arendt call 'a nationality like the other nationalities', which is exactly what Butler rejects.

Butler's refusal of an identitarian Jewishness does not only pertain to the formation of a territorial state – although that is her primary target – but goes much further to a rejection of any 'solidaristic' community (2014:148), including in diaspora. Butler calls for a 'departing from a communitarian basis for political judgment and responsibility alike', that is, Jews must never be responsible for other Jews, nor should Jews as Jews engage in the exercise of political power. That claim in particular goes far beyond her consistent anti-Zionism to proscribe any Jewish politics altogether, which amounts to a retraction of Enlightenment and civil emancipation as the right to participate in political processes: 'if Jewishness mandates this departure from communitarian belonging, then "to belong" is to undergo a dispossession from the category of Jewishness' (2014:127). It is difficult to read this as anything other than a rejection of any possible Jewish community organisation, even in diaspora. Butler's prohibition of Jewish political practice, arguably consistent with a broader anarchist inclination to oppose states as such, is however profoundly incompatible with Arendt's positive evaluation of politics and political power. Arendt harboured doubts about Israeli politics, and perhaps about the wisdom of the Zionist foundation altogether; unlike Butler however, she did not reject the notion of the state – any state – altogether.

The question of the state is relevant here because, even in *Eichmann in Jerusalem*, it is the state that is the source of the authority of the court to render justice. Not so for Butler with her anti-political inclinations that lead to the conclusion that no possible court can ever succeed in representing justice. To reach this position, she wrongly appeals to Arendt's authority, via two distinct misreadings, one concerning the problem of the nation state, the other the significance of sovereignty. In each case she mischaracterises Arendt in order to provide her own anti-Zionism with a false genealogy.

Misreading Arendt on the Nation State

In *Origins of Totalitarianism*, Arendt works with the ideal type of an early modern state as the guarantor of the rule of law and the possibility of rights. She describes how various historical processes ensue that undermined this civil order, including the emergence of nationalism and the aspiration for nation states, key components of 'the rise of the social' mentioned earlier. While Arendt's narrative eventually leads to the totalitarianism of Nazi Germany and Stalinist Russia, she hardly equates 19th-century nationalism with the 20th-century catastrophes: Bismarck's Germany was not already the Third Reich. Yet Butler blurs this distinction and wrongly claims to be following Arendt in doing so. For Butler the liberal nation state and the totalitarian racial state are effectively indistinguishable from each other, a very un-Arendtian assertion, but one that allows Butler to denounce the Zionist agenda of nation state building.

This distance between the two thinkers becomes particularly salient in Butler's manipulative rephrasing of Arendt's conclusion. The epilogue to *Eichmann in Jerusalem* finishes with Arendt's memorable rearticulation of the judgement of the Jerusalem court in her own terms. She purports to speak with the voice of the judges, as she concurs with their verdict but provides what she regards as her own better arguments. Hence Arendt's final sentences, addressed to the defendant: 'And just as you supported and carried out a policy of not wanting to share the earth with the Jewish people and the people of a number of other nations – as though you and your superiors had any right to determine who should and who should not inhabit the world – we find that no one, that is, no member of the human race, can be expected to want to share the earth with you. This is the reason, and the only reason, you must hang' (279).

Arendt's argument clearly references Nazi genocidal policies that presumed the right to decide who may 'inhabit the world'. Butler confuses the matter, transforming it into an exhortation to 'cohabitation' (2014:125). This shift from Arendt's question of inhabiting the world – the critique of mass murder – to Butler's imperative of cohabitation dilutes Arendt's value of the plurality of human life, turning it into a plea for our contemporary multiculturalism. Butler wrongly enlists Arendt in her own campaign against any communitarian identity, but especially Jewish identity. To do so, she has to transform Arendt's condemnation of genocide into a criticism of any possible community. This in turn leads her to the bizarre conclusion that the judicial system of any nation state is constitutively incapable of ever rendering justice because it is predicated on restrictive cohabitation. A state that engages in the biopolitical practice of managing immigration in any way can by definition never be just. Butler does however leave room for a non-statist Jewish (ethical or religious but not political) 'pursuit of justice – different [however] from the one that would of necessity find its representation in the Israeli courts' (2014:150). Here is Butler's clear accusation that Israeli courts, including the Eichmann court, by necessity cannot represent justice because they are the expression of the authority of a nation state. One should note that on this point, the legitimacy of Israeli courts, Butler's rejectionism contrasts fully with Arendt's explicit endorsement of the court and its verdict, as she made clear in her response to Gershom Scholem's harsh criticisms of her book.

Misreading Arendt on Sovereignty

Yet – and here I come to Butler's second misreading of Arendt – Butler's anti-judiciary account is not only a matter of Jewishness or Israeli courts or even the nation state in general. Instead, she suggests that no possible human court of law that is charged with the adjudication of legality derived from legitimate political authority can ever achieve justice. In other words, positive law, the staple of any court decision, can never lead to genuine justice. In Butler's terms: 'Arendt is not only taking issue with the way the Israeli courts arrived at the decision to sentence Eichmann to death. Her book finds fault with every existing legal code brought to bear upon the scene' (2014:155). This claim that Arendt, in *Eichmann in Jerusalem*, rejects 'every existing legal code' is not supported by the intratextual evidence: there are no philologically tenable grounds for Butler's colonisation of Arendt for her own antinomianism. It is rather Butler's own rejection of all positive law that defines her own understanding of justice, even if she wrongly believes that Arendt writes 'at some distance from positive law' in order to stake out a 'prelegal' perspective (2014:155). On the contrary, it is exclusively Butler, and not Arendt, who endeavours to define a pre-legal or extralegal space as the exclusive home of justice. Hence the difference between the two in the understanding of Eichmann's culpability: For Arendt, as we have seen, the court rightly and justly condemned him for certain deeds, supporting and carrying out genocidal policies, while Butler, extrapolating from Arendt's characterisation of Eichmann's personality, emphasises his obedience to the law, rather than the substantive acts, as the ultimate crime. In *Origins of Totalitarianism*, Arendt had described the fundamentally lawless character of the murderous regimes in Germany and Russia, far from any *Rechtsstaat*, with no rule of law; for Butler, by way of contrast, it is the rule of law itself that is the problem. For her, the obedience that law necessarily expects stands opposed to justice.

Following Butler, it is the rule of law that demands that we obey the law, and any such obedience leads us quickly down the slippery slope to complicity. The *Rechtsstaat* is always already the *Unrechtsstaat*, in the shadow of which good citizens are likely to become mass murderers. One recalls on this score Ward Churchill's notorious characterisation of the 9/11 victims as 'little Eichmanns'. Yet we need not go so far afield to find similar claims. In her letter to Jaspers, cited earlier, Arendt expressed concern with the Israeli policemen that looked like they would carry out any order, an echo of the common characterisation of Eichmann. Nonetheless, for Arendt, that anxiety about the Israeli police contrasted sharply with her trust and admiration for the Jerusalem judges. On this point, Butler differs. For Butler, the ultimate source of injustice is any assertion of sovereignty, that is, state power expressed in positive law, compliance with which describes the failing of both the court and the defendant because 'certain kinds of norms are already operative in both crime and judgment even if judge and criminal do not know what they are' (2014:161). Butler's Hegelianism is unmistakable: a common spirit operates behind the backs of court and defendant, unbeknownst to either: judge and criminal are found to be cut from the same cloth. Buried in Butler's prose is the scandalous equation of Nazi bureaucrat and Israeli judges, understood equally as functionaries of state sovereignty, which is the real crime. Even if elsewhere Butler rejects the propagandistic equation of Zionism and Nazism (2014:121), the logic of her argument draws them inexorably together along with any state formation, as if all sovereignty, any state anywhere, can only be understood in the terms of Carl Schmitt at his most ruthless.

Yet she is inconsistent in this critique of sovereignty since, when all is said and done, it is only or primarily Israeli sovereignty that she denounces: regarding the Jews she is an anarchist, but she is a statist for the Palestinians. Similarly, she develops the critique of 'solidaristic' community exclusively with regard to Jews, as if she has internalised the anti-Semitic trope of Jewish clannishness, which she attempts to erase with her injunctions. But an alternative argument concerning her bias against Jewish community is more likely: by insisting on the critical capacity of an exilic or diasporic condition to Jewishness, she effectively stakes out her own claim for privilege as a Jewish thinker. Her own condition of displacement, so she suggests, tends to elevate her above other scholars who are not (in her view) fortunate enough to live outside of a community of solidarity. At the end of the day, we find another case of an intellectual arguing for the priority of intellectuals over and against the benighted participants in shared identity structures.

Epilogue

There is a left-wing adage, derived from a letter of the American labour organiser Joe Hill, executed in Utah in 1915: 'Don't mourn. Organise.' The phrase has circulated widely in radical movements, thanks to its powerfully binary opposition of past and future, affect and practice, indolence and politics. It is a useful point of concluding orientation for our discussion on representing justice. Should the organisation of justice be blind to the suffering of mourners? Must we segregate the emotion of mourning from the organisation of legality? Hill's imperative may convey the wisdom that we refrain from unproductively irrational responses, such as crimes of passion or vengeance, as well as any debilitating melancholy. Nonetheless is there no room for affect and grief in the public, and in what relation do they stand to justice? Why can't we mourn *and* organise?

Arendt's response is clear: personal suffering is a private matter that has no claim on the court's attention. Justice should be blind and deaf as well and make its case solely on the basis of the law. The guarantor of the law is the state, and the success of the state depends on the rational intelligence of its judges and the reflectiveness of its citizens, not their emotions. The intrusion of emotions into the public only paves the way for the corruption of civil life. To return to Hill's phrase: mourning is antithetical to political organisation and stands outside the law.

Butler's approach is different, we have seen, based on a fundamentalist suspicion of any state and its law, an emphatic anti-politics that may be symptomatic – and not only in its anti-Zionism – of contemporary academic radicalism. The state cannot represent justice as long as it is the state. This conclusion became particularly clear in Butler's commentary on the ISIS attacks in Paris in November 2015.[6] Her short essay bears the title 'Mourning Becomes the Law', a recycling of a book title by Gillian Rose. Observing the responses to the terror attacks, Butler chides the French public, arguing that the expressions of grief served only to legitimate the transition to a police state under the mantle of the declared state of emergency. In effect, mourning turns into the source of organisation or, rather, the reorganisation of the state and the establishment of a new regime of power marked by diminished civil liberties expectations. Yet precisely this outcome was already inherent in Butler's evaluation of any sovereignty in *Parting Ways*.

The distance between Arendt and Butler testifies to the contemporary delegitimation of the state and transformations in estimations of political community. While Arendt, for all of her criticism of ethno-nationalism, nonetheless prized nothing more than politics as the capacity to act in concert, Butler directs us to dissolve any 'solidaristic' allegiances. Without solidarity or community or loyalty, however, no politics are possible. Regarding Butler's response to Paris, two final comments follow that shed light on the question of justice.

First, in her Paris text, 'mourning' is exclusively a matter of manipulated affect. The security state incites mourning in order to amplify its power. This instrumentalist account of mourning is antithetical to Benjamin's account, which Butler otherwise invokes, the *Trauerspiel* as the portal to a messianic justice via the extra-legal decisionism of the sovereign. Yet facing the French state of emergency, Butler abruptly renounces Benjamin's mystic radicalism and reverts to a conventionally liberal concern about infringements on civil rights as a result of the state of emergency. That her liberal concern is conventional hardly makes it wrong. The point, however, is that in the face of a dictatorship – I would say an imaginary dictatorship under Francois Hollande – Butler appeals to the conventional understanding of that same rule of law which she otherwise treats as inimical to genuine justice.

Secondly, Butler views the French mourning as fundamentally unjust because it addresses the victims of the Paris attacks exclusively. This is a standard internationalist response: the French mourning the Parisians is judged to be hypocritical because it ignores so much suffering elsewhere. 'Mourning seems fully restricted within the national frame. The nearly 50 dead in Beirut from the day before are barely mentioned, and neither are the 111 in Palestine killed in the last weeks alone, or the scores in Ankara' (see Shin 2015). Her mention of 111 Palestinians most likely refers to a newspaper account published just days before her text appeared that reported on 111 injuries, which she however turns into 111 deaths: evidently for her a minor discrepancy she felt compelled to gloss over for the sake of her narrative (Ma'an News Agency 2015). Be that as it may, her list exposes her to the same accusation of exclusion: if the Parisians forget the 'scores in Ankara' then Butler has herself forgotten the Israeli stabbing victims, or the Iranian executions or the extensive list of other deaths that one could easily compile. Indeed, only an infinite list of all those who have died or ever will die would be sufficient.

The appropriate question instead is whether the suffering that I witness directly has any special significance for me, any special claim on my empathy, that is, whether one can distinguish between suffering that is close, spatially or metaphorically, and suffering that is distant. Such proximity, however, is a marker of the community solidarity that Butler explicitly rejects as identitarian. For her, only a world populated by non-solidaristic strangers could achieve justice because only its absolute randomness could eliminate any grounds for discrimination. The death of my loved one before my eyes must not touch me more than the death of a stranger on the other side of the world. Critical Theory, which began as a critique of alienation, comes full circle with Butler's endorsement of infinite estrangement. What she cannot envision is a political community that despite its community character could nevertheless build institutions, a judicial system, capable of treating everyone, even strangers, with equality: for her, because a state is a state it cannot be just. The contrast between Arendt and Butler marks a half century in the withering away of the state as a location of trust and inclusion. The neoliberal assault on the welfare state is only a small piece in a much larger secular retreat from the state in general and an endemic cynicism towards politics. There is some irony perhaps to discover that Butler's anarchism is heir to neoliberalism and its congenital animus against state power. To pursue justice today requires addressing this legitimacy crisis of the law.

Notes

1 This chapter was first published in *Fathom* in 2016.
2 Ruth Starkman (2013:196) describes the transformation of Arendt's usage from this moment of militant Jewish patriotism to a still public but less assertive value in her later account of Greek antiquity. 'In *The Human Condition* she asserts that *action* was always bound to ideas of "honor" and "glory," since the Greeks and all the way to Machiavelli. Honor and glory derive from appearing publicly and participating in the theatrical nature of politics . . .. That she includes the Jews in this human plurality with honor and glory is already apparent in her wartime writings. It seems, then, that for Arendt honor and glory shifted, after the War, to other kinds of experience besides fighting under a people's flag and publically demonstrating national passions.'
3 Her comments on minority students in *On Violence* a decade later suggest that she had not moved far away from her predispositions in 'Reflections on Little Rock'. See Gines (2014).
4 Arendt's animosity towards the prosecutor and the public is quite emphatic throughout the letter to Jaspers. Regarding the prosecutor: 'a typical Galician Jew, very unsympathetic, is constantly making mistakes [in German – RB]. Probably one of those people who don't know any language' (p. 434). Regarding the public: 'An oriental mob that would hang around any place where something is going on is hanging around in front of the courthouse' (p. 435). The translation softens the

German phrasing: 'Vor dem Gerichtssaal lungert ein orientalisher Mob, der überall lungern würde, wo was vorgeht' (pp. 471–472).

5 For a critique, see Cary Nelson, 'The Problem With Judith Butler: The Philosophy of the Movement to Boycott Israel', in *The Case Against Academic Boycotts of Israel*, edited by Cary Nelson and Gabriel Noah Brahm (2015) Chicago: MLA Members for Scholars Rights, distributed by Wayne State University Press, pp. 164–201.

6 On the evening of 13 November 2015, Paris was struck by an unprecedented series of terrorist attacks claimed by the Islamic State group (also known as ISIS, ISIL or Daesh). At least 130 people died and hundreds were wounded.

References

Arendt, Hannah (1958) *The Human Condition*, Chicago: The University of Chicago Press.

Arendt, Hannah (2006) *Eichmann in Jerusalem: A Report on the Banality of Evil*, New York: Penguin.

Arendt, Hannah (2007) 'The political organization of the Jewish people', in Jerome Kohn and Ron H. Feldman (eds.), *The Jewish Writings*, New York: Schocken Books, 199–240.

Arendt, Hannah and Karl Jaspers (1992) *Correspondence, 1925–1969*, edited by Lott Kohler and Hans Saner, translated by Robert Kimber and Rita Kimber, New York: Harcourt Brace Jovanovich. Cf. the original in: Hannah Arendt and Karl Jaspers (1985) *Briefwechstel 1926–1969*, edited by Lotte Köhler and Hans Saner, Munich: Piper, 472.

Butler, Judith (2014) *Parting Ways: Jewishness and the Critique of Zionism*, New York: Columbia University Press.

Gines, Kathryn T. (2014) *Hannah Arendt and the Negro Question*, Bloomington: Indiana University Press.

Ma'an News Agency (2015) '111 Palestinians shot, injured during West Bank, Gaza demonstrations', *Ma'an News Agency*, 13 November. Available: www.maannews.com/Content.aspx?id=768807 (accessed 27 November 27).

Shin, Sarah (2015) 'Mourning becomes the law; Judith Butler from Paris', *Verso Blog*, 16 November. Available: http://webcache.googleusercontent.com/search?q=cache:imemmrnJr5EJ:www.versobooks.com/blogs/2337-mourning-becomes-the-law-judith-butler-from-paris+&cd=1&hl=en&ct=clnk&gl=us (accessed 27 November 2015) (The *Verso Blog* byline attributes the piece to Sarah Shin, but it is identified as a text by Butler).

Stangneth, Bettina (2015) *Eichmann Before Jerusalem: The Unexamined Life of a Mass Murderer*, New York: Vintage.

Starkman, Ruth (2013) '"For the honor and glory of the Jewish People": Arendt's ambivalent Jewish Nationhood', *The European Legacy*, 18 (2): 185–196.

Yakira, Elhanan (2009) *Post-Zionism, Post-Holocaust: Three Essays on Denial, Forgetting and the Delegitimation of Israel*, Cambridge: Cambridge University Press.

29

THE PLEASURES OF ANTISEMITISM

Eve Garrard

There is something strangely ineffective about many of our attempts to combat antisemitism.[1] We treat it as involving various cognitive errors – false beliefs about Jews or about Israel, the application of double standards to the assessment of Jewish activities, the one-sided focus on things which can be criticised and the neglect of things which might be praiseworthy. We try to combat these cognitive failures (of which there certainly are plenty) by pointing out the errors involved, listing the relevant facts which correct those errors, and revealing the logical inconsistencies involved in, for example, the use of double standards. And when these attempts prove to be totally fruitless, as they so often do, we're puzzled and dismayed. Don't people want truths which would enable them to abandon their hostilities to various aspects of Jewish existence?

The answer, of course, is very often that no, they really don't want these truths. They prefer the errors, with all their dramatic fears and hatreds, and the excitement of conspiracy stories, to the unremarkable truth that Jews are on the whole just like everyone else, a mixture of good and bad, strong and weak, but with a history which has very real and terrible implications for the present. Why is this? We can't explain it just in terms of cognitive error, since part of what we want to know is why the cognitive errors are so immune to alteration and why they appear and reappear so very persistently. We have to look outside the cognitive domain to the realm of the emotions, and ask: what are the pleasures, what are the emotional rewards which antisemitism has to offer to its adherents?

Antisemitism is fun, there's no doubt about it. You can't miss the relish with which some people compare Jews to the Nazis, or the fake sorrow, imperfectly masking deep satisfaction, with which they bemoan the supposed

DOI: 10.4324/9781003322320-37

fact that Jews have brought hatred on themselves, especially by the actions of Israel and its Zionist supporters, and that they have inexplicably failed to learn the lessons of the Holocaust. (The Holocaust was not, of course, an educational exercise; and if there are lessons to be learned from it, we might think that the weakest pupils are those who once again wish to single out Jews above all others for hostile attention.) Like other forms of racism, antisemitism provides a variety of satisfactions for those who endorse it, and it's worth trying to analyse these pleasures, so that we may better understand and combat the whole phenomenon. In what follows I will be mentioning and briefly describing various antisemitic attitudes, all of which I believe to be deeply and often culpably misguided. But I won't be discussing their errors, nor will I be distinguishing the circumstances in which criticism of Jews and Israel is legitimate and accurate, and circumstances in which it is not. Much has been written on just those topics; here I will simply take it for granted that some such criticisms are accurate, but that others, often many others, are false, and constitute a form of racist discrimination against Jews – in short, antisemitism. My concern here is not with the falsity of antisemitic discourse, but with the pleasures which it offers to those who engage in it.

There are (at least) three principal sources of pleasure which antisemitism provides: first, the pleasure of hatred; second, the pleasure of tradition, and third, the pleasure of displaying moral purity. Each of these is an independent source of satisfaction, but the three interact in various ways, which often strengthens their effects. No doubt the different sources of pleasure appeal to different individuals and groups, so that the appeal of tradition may resonate most strongly with those who are politically on the Right, and the attraction of displaying moral purity may be most strongly felt by those on the political left, but both varieties can be detected in most political groupings, and the pleasures of hatred are well-nigh universal.

The Pleasures of Hatred

The satisfactions which hatred has to offer us are regrettably familiar to most people. Most of us know only too well the surge of self-righteousness, the thrill of condemning others and the intense bonding with a like-minded hater, which we feel when a good jolt of vicious hostility has risen within us. Of course, there are some situations in which hatred is justified – there are some actions and attitudes to which hatred is the proper response, and anyone who is broad-minded and tolerant at the building of an Auschwitz needs to clean up his moral compass. But the pleasures which hatred provides are just as available when the hatred is entirely unjustified, as most of us also know, at least in retrospect. Hatred and its cognates – contempt, rancour, and detestation – offer the seductive satisfaction of feeling our own superiority to the hated object, and feeling also a sense of deep justification and indeed righteousness in taking steps to punish or otherwise hurt him (or her, or them). Hurting others is also fun, for more people than we would normally like to believe (see, e.g. the notorious Zimbardo experiments, and the evidence from those involved in the genocidal killing in Rwanda; but also the ubiquitous phenomenon of playground bullying, and its various adult analogues such as workplace bullying and the kind of political hostilities that sometimes break out in small ideologically overheated groups). So where antisemitism takes the form of Jew-hatred, it's not hard to understand that it offers psychological rewards which are nothing to do with the truth or falsehood of people's beliefs about Jews. Nor is it hard to see that people would prefer not to be deprived of these pleasures, especially if, as is often the case with those who are formally committed to anti-racism, they don't recognise themselves to be antisemitic, and hence pay no inner price in damage to their own self-esteem.

The Pleasures of Tradition

Since the pleasures of hatred are universal, why, we must ask, do they get realised in Jew-hating in particular, here and now? At this point, we can turn to the second main source of the pleasures of antisemitism: tradition. There is a Jew-shaped space in Western culture, and the shape is not a pleasant one. Long centuries of tradition have constructed the Jew as a being who is both contemptible and dangerous, the purveyor and transmitter of evil; and various tropes have been deployed to flesh out this picture – in particular the blood libel, according to which Jews use the blood of Christian children for their terrible ceremonies of machination and control, but also tropes about uncanny power, in which Jews are depicted as the puppet masters of the rest of the helpless non-Jewish world. (There's a version of this trope in which tentacles, rather than puppet strings, figure most prominently. Being classified as killer octopi rather than as puppet masters isn't noticeably an improvement for the Jews.)

As has often been pointed out, the tradition of antisemitism is very flexible, and it generally gets expressed in terms of the preoccupations of the period: so mediaeval Jew-hatred was religiously based; 19th and, even more 20th, century hostility was given a scientific top-dressing in terms of the now discredited theories of 'race science'; and late 20th-century and early 21st-century prejudice are generally cast in terms of human rights violations. (I speak here primarily of antisemitism in the West. Antisemitism in other parts of the world, while undoubtedly deriving large parts of its force from Western examples, is an even more complicated matter.) Although an antisemitism which was proud to speak its name became unfashionable on the liberal left after World War II, for reasons which are too obvious to mention, it's a remarkable feature of the persistence of antisemitic tropes that they have survived relatively unaltered through these cultural changes. Recent cartoons expressing profound hostility to the Jewish state, on the grounds of supposedly outstanding human rights violations, reproduce fantasies of sinister control and bloodthirstiness which earlier antisemites would have recognised without difficulty.

The weight of tradition, which makes it feel comfortable, perhaps even natural, to fit living Jews into the space created for them by so many centuries of hostility, may help to explain one of the many failures of logic infecting contemporary antisemitic discourse: where the Jewish state does bad things, these are taken to reveal its true inner nature; where it does good things, these are interpreted as deceitful, as mere propaganda designed to cover up its vile motives and actions. (The relative freedom which is afforded to gay and bisexual people in Israel, as witnessed by the Gay Pride marches there, has been described as 'pinkwashing' – that is, as a mendacious attempt to persuade people that Israel is a tolerant respecter of human rights, instead of the colonial imperialist baby-killing oppressor which many anti-Zionists declare her to be. It will be interesting to see whether the selection of a very beautiful black woman of Ethiopian descent to be Miss Israel gets described as 'black-washing'.) The suggestion by the Liberal Democrat peer, Baroness Jenny Tonge, that Israeli medical aid to Haiti was a cover for organ stealing by Israeli medics was perhaps the crudest and most egregious of such examples, though people trying to defend Israel against such criticisms have become accustomed to being told again and again that they only mount these defences as a way of covering up Israel's crimes.

Why are people so ready to make these hostile moves, in a way which they wouldn't tolerate with respect to other forms of racism? Anyone who announced that the political and economic troubles of African countries were the result of low intelligence in black Africans, or who drew a cartoon of President Obama as an ape, would be committing social and political suicide among those members of the bien-pensant classes who so often display the forms of prejudice against Jews and the Jewish state with which we're here concerned. The availability of the traditional picture of the Jew as sinister and controlling and duplicitous may make these moves against living Jews, right now, seem comfortably familiar, and perhaps even freshly revealing of an age-old wisdom. There has been a distinctive tradition on the left, going back to the 19th century and beyond, of what might be called rich-Jew antisemitism, where the basis of the objection to Jews was that they were rich, and hence exploitative and oppressive. It is easy to see how that can be picked up today. To that we might add the consideration that Jews have intermittently been treated appallingly, and sometimes genocidally, in the West; and as Tolstoy and others have noticed, we often hate people in proportion to the injustices which we have done them. It's very hard for Europe to forgive the Jews for the Holocaust, and seeing Jews as hateful makes life easier – people needn't worry about whether they're treating Jews quite fairly if they believe them to be lying, bloodthirsty and oppressive. But the main difference between resurgent hostility to Jews on the part of sections of the left and the absence of any such resurgence towards people of colour is probably the result of the rise of imperialism as the political hate object of the post-Marxist left. Israel can be cast, though only at the expense of an enormous distortion of historical facts, into the role of imperial coloniser, and hence hostility towards Israel and the Jews who support her existence can be legitimised as part, sometimes a leading part, of the global fight against imperialism. This construal of Israel's geo-political position permits those people who are hostile to her to see themselves as warriors against the great evil of colonialism, a role which many on the left find very gratifying to contemplate themselves as occupying.

The Pleasures of Moral Purity

This takes us to the third source of satisfaction which antisemitism provides: the desire for moral purity, especially a purity which is readily visible to others, and can count as a ticket of entry to socially and politically desirable circles. This source of satisfaction is in many ways the most interesting of them all, partly because it seems to be the motive du jour of antisemitism coming from sections of the left, which might have been expected to be hostile to all forms of racism and sadly isn't; and partly because it's so supple and flexible, it can accommodate and explain away a very wide range of facts which tell against it. (I say that these things are interesting to contemplate and analyse, which indeed they are. But in no way do I want to underestimate the extent to which meeting them in the flesh, so to speak, is primarily disgusting, and also in many cases exhausting and sometimes frightening.)

Moral goodness and purity are of course genuinely desirable and admirable – it's good if people have deep moral insight, and the ability to judge correctly what's the right thing to do in complicated circumstances, and the strength of character and will to carry out their decisions, and the understanding and factual knowledge and courage and kindness and sympathy to judge others fairly, and to fight for justice where need be. But one look at that list is enough to remind us of how hard it is to be good, and how much easier it is to pursue the appearance rather than the reality. Israel as the Jewish state is a real opportunity for people who want to display their supposed moral purity, and harvest a suitable quantity of admiration from like-minded others, without having to deliver on the exacting demands of genuine moral probity. So we find people declaring that Israel is an apartheid state, thus allying themselves to the righteous fight against apartheid half a century ago, but omitting to notice the huge moral, social and political differences between Israel and apartheid South Africa; they declare that Israel is a colonial settler state, thus displaying their hostility to colonialism without having to ask who the colonising power is, and where else the survivors of the mid-century horrors should have gone, and why the UN decided that the Jews of the world should have the opportunity for self-determination, and why they were so clearly in need of it; we have people publishing in the broadsheet press complaints about how their hostile views about Israel have been silenced by powerful unnamed forces, without noticing the performative contradiction in what they say; we have people explaining that they do of course completely condemn the Holocaust, and this shows that they can't be antisemitic, but, they go on to declare, it's appalling to find Jews behaving in the same way against the Palestinians of Gaza and the West Bank that the Nazis did in the Warsaw ghetto. And so on, and on.

However, my concern here is not with the factual and logical errors in these various charges; I want rather to point out the emotional dividend they provide to those who deploy them. Such people can present themselves as the champions of the weak against the strong, of the colonised against the supposedly imperialist colonisers, and of wholly innocent Palestinian victims against bloody and heartless Jewish oppressors. They can also present themselves as being victimised, both by the way in which powerful forces have imposed silence on them (albeit one of the noisiest silences ever heard) and also by the charge, deeply offensive to their moral purity, that their extraordinarily selective hostility towards Israel and its supporters might constitute discrimination against Jews. Indeed so offensive is this charge that it amounts, so it is claimed, to a further victimisation, of a kind which can only be explained by the deceitful and manipulative nature of those who raise the concerns about alleged antisemitism. So people who deploy these tactics against Jews can see themselves, and can hope to be seen by others, as being not only on the side of morally pure victims against morally vicious villains, but also as having the coveted status of victims themselves, slandered by people who are determined to exploit their own past sufferings in order to oppress others. Furthermore, since in this narrative Jews are cast as the powerful oppressors, those who single them out for hostile attention can see themselves as 'speaking truth to power'. And paradoxically, focusing on Jews for singular criticism can also be presented as subversive and transgressive, flouting the conventions of polite discourse, and thus conferring on the hostile critic the accolade of being untrammelled by convention, excitingly edgy, possibly even outrageous. All in all, that's an awful lot of moral bang for your antisemitic buck.

The reason that it's plausible to construe these various claims and attitudes as being driven by a concern to display moral purity, rather than simply as showing honest moral commitments, is that the hostile attitudes displayed towards Israel and Zionists are rarely directed against other malefactors, including those who have committed far more, and far more serious, violations of human rights than any that Israel has managed. Furthermore, the charges made against Israel are often simply false, and demonstrably so. These two considerations together suggest that what's in play is not a serious moral concern, but rather an easy simulacrum of it, along with a conviction of moral rectitude which, though misplaced, offers distinctive pleasures of its own.

The various sources of pleasure which antisemitism provides interact in diverse ways. Sometimes the effect of this interaction is simply to reinforce the rewards on offer: tradition plus hatred is a natural pairing, as is tradition plus the desire for moral purity – these relations are simply multipliers. But other relations look at first sight as if they might involve a certain tension: tradition plus transgressiveness, or hatred and condemnation plus the desire for moral purity. However, these tensions can be and often are resolved in antisemitic discourse in ways which leave the discriminatory drive undisturbed. The claim of transgressiveness can be asserted with respect to the post-war convention of being polite about Jews, arising understandably from their sufferings at the hands of Nazi Germany, but now, it is suggested, exploited by Jews to cover up their wrongdoings. And in the description of such alleged wrongdoings, the rich seam of traditional Jew-hatred can be drawn on without embarrassment, indeed with a delicious frisson, because the transgressiveness defuses in advance any objections based on more conventional concerns about racism. The defusing of such concerns is expedited where the transgressor uses the device of claiming that he himself is not antisemitic, but he can understand those who are, since the Jews bring hostility on themselves by their behaviour. The tension between the pleasures of hatred and those of moral purity can also be reconciled, allowing them to coexist and even reinforce each other. Hatred, it can be suggested, is an excusable and perhaps even appropriate response to the bloodthirsty acts of Israel; the hatred supposedly arises out of an overwhelming sensitivity to injustice, and is a sign of the extreme moral purity of the hater, who selflessly struggles for justice for the innocent victims of a tyrannical state and its supporters. It's easy to see the attractions of this self-serving self-image to one who wishes to claim moral rectitude, and also to enjoy the pleasures of hatred. It's a terrific opportunity both to have your moral cake and to eat it up in huge and satisfying gulps.

Conclusion

The factual, logical and moral errors in the various forms of antisemitism under consideration are legion, and have been discussed extensively elsewhere (e.g. in the work of David Hirsh and Norman Geras, both in their contributions to previous issues of *Fathom* and in many other places). In trying to account for the prevalence of these errors, and also to combat them, we shouldn't overlook the pleasures, sometimes very intense ones, which they provide. With the increasing normalisation of antisemitic hostility in many parts of the left as well as the far-right, we can expect these pleasures to be more widely disseminated and enjoyed. What can be done about this state of affairs isn't immediately obvious – the fact that some pleasures are vile doesn't stop them from being pleasurable, or prevent some people from wanting to taste them again and again. In order to do so, these people must bolster up their image of the Jewish state as oppressive and illegitimate, and the Zionists who support her as lying, manipulative, and hostile to human solidarity and justice. Here the devil frequently does have the best tunes, and the thin and reedy voice of rational argument is often quite drowned out by their brassy insistence. But we'll do better in the combat, however we conduct it, if we realise that the views which we're struggling against provide deep emotional satisfactions to those who hold them, satisfactions not easy either to overcome or to replace.

Note

1 This chapter was first published in *Fathom* in 2013.

30

INTERSECTIONALITY AND ANTISEMITISM

A New Approach

Karin Stögner

Intersectionality is an analytical instrument for critically understanding the multidimensionality of power relations.[1] It emerged first in the 1970s, in debates on Black Feminism and signalled an intersectional struggle, that is, a struggle on two fronts: against (hetero-)sexism within the Civil Rights Movement and against racism within the Women's Movement (Combahee River Collective 1977). In this respect, intersectionality has always been both an analytical concept *and* a political practice. Currently, global antisemitism is only rarely included in the intersectional paradigm, and Jews are often excluded from feminist anti-racist social movements that claim to be guided by intersectionality. The vehement antizionist orientation of some of these movements, be it *Women's March on Washington*, *Chicago Dyke March* or parts of the *Black Lives Matter* platform, poses the question: why does the intersectionality framework routinely exclude the critical focus on antisemitism? In this chapter, I will first contrast antisemitism and racism, before showing that antisemitism research and intersectionality need not necessarily exclude each other. I will go on to develop a specific approach to intersectionality that views ideologies in relation to each other, reads antisemitism itself *as* an intersectional ideology, and reads those forms of intersectional theory and practice that exclude Jews as themselves invoking antisemitism.

Antisemitism and racism: a complex relationship of similarity *and difference*

The difficulties in analysing antisemitism within the intersectionality paradigm arise to a large extent from a widespread misunderstanding about the

DOI: 10.4324/9781003322320-38

relationship between antisemitism and racism. Antisemitism is not merely a form of racism, to be analysed with the tools provided by research on racism. Rather, antisemitism is a distinctive ideology that cannot be reduced to racism, any more than homophobia can be reduced to sexism. We have here a variation of the feminist paradox that we cannot understand the circumstances and living conditions of women and men if we *only* look at them through the category of gender, but nor will we understand them *without* the category of gender. In regard to antisemitism as a phenomenon, we can say that we will fail to grasp its complexity if we see it *only* as a form of racism; but we will not understand it if we do not *also* recognise it as a form of racism.

In order to prevent competitive victimhood, and to facilitate alliances in the fight against antisemitism *and* racism, Glynis Cousin and Robert Fine (2012) proposed that we think of antisemitism and racism as *related* ideologies. They warned against the complete subsumption of antisemitism under the abstract umbrella term of 'racism', arguing that such conceptual fuzziness would only make the respective *specificities* of antisemitism and racism disappear.

There is no doubt that antisemitism operates with numerous racist elements, as well as with nationalist, sexist, and homophobic ones. Racism is evident already in the very concept of antisemitism, a linguistic invention of Wilhelm Marr in the 19th century, when a political and social hostility towards Jews, with a secular and pseudo-scientific concept of 'race' to the fore, replaced a pre-modern, religious form of anti-Judaism. As I have discussed elsewhere (Stögner 2014, 2017), this shift became evident particularly in antisemitic body images that depicted Jews as having a distorted relationship with nature.

Capitalism and 'the greedy Jew'

Racism is unquestionably an important moment for the functioning of antisemitism as a modern ideology, but it is not the only one. *Modern* antisemitism operates substantially on the basis of a distorted perception of *capitalist* relations of production and their logic of exploitation. Antisemitism, in the figure of the 'greedy Jew', introduces a personalisation of what are in reality supra-individual, abstract, social processes. This is combined with an anti-intellectualism that sees Jews as a subversive and disintegrating spirit, 'too clever by half'. Antisemitism is essentially about the rejection of 'money and mind, the exponents of circulation' (Horkheimer and Adorno 2002:141; see also Postone 1980), expressing a deep unease and discontent in civilisation and an inability to understand abstract power relations and their institutions.

The *differences* between antisemitism and racism are clear. Both colonial and apartheid racism are based on the hierarchical construction of supposedly superior and inferior races (Balibar 2005). The enemy, constructed as primitive and inferior, represents a lack of civilisation and modernity, while racists consider themselves representatives of civilisation. Absent are conspiracy myths presuming People of Colour and colonised people secretly rule the world, control the media and finance, and accelerate the processes of modernisation, globalisation and cosmopolitanism. These are *not* usually part of racist ideology. Such conspiracy myths, however, *are* an essential feature of antisemitism, which suspects an intangible power resides among Jews, one that is ubiquitous and to which antisemites do not feel superior but rather *inferior*. While racism is very much about legitimising the economic exploitation and social discrimination of racialised and colonised people, antisemitism is largely about projecting the responsibility for exploitation and inequality onto the Jews.

A current example of the idea of the all-powerful Jew that sits at the heart of antisemitic ideology is the conspiracy myth that Jews control migration flows and are thus responsible for what the extreme right-wing calls 'foreign infiltration and domination', that is, for the immigration of people regarded as ethnically or culturally inferior, which result in the destruction of 'native' identity. The portrayal of Jews as an abstract, intangible *elite* who secretly rule the world and oppress peoples and nations can be observed also on the left. In this version, antisemitism can even claim to be oppositional and on the side of the oppressed worldwide.

Whiteness and Jews

Many intersectional feminist movements that stand up against racism have great difficulty in grasping how antisemitism works. They understand antisemitism as only a form of racism, while they reduce racism itself to the dichotomy of White and Black, with Jews implicitly or explicitly identified with 'Whiteness'. This is analytically disabling because antisemitism does *not* run along the colour line, and consequently not along the binary divide 'privileged/non-privileged'. Jews are not 'Whites'. However, both 'whiteness' and 'privileged/non-privileged' are central to the concept of racism that is prevalent today in academic discourse and in the discourse of intersectional political practice.

The Whiteness frame, as a tool for making visible structural racism, not only proves to be completely unsuitable for antisemitism, but can even confirm antisemitism, as David Schraub (2019) has pointed out. The privileges associated with Whiteness include power, influence, money, property, education, dominance, participation, being heard and having a voice, cliques and networks, and positions inherited over generations. If this frame is applied to the White majority society, ingrained power structures can be made visible. If, on the other hand, it is applied to the Jewish minority, this frame can actually result in *the confirmation of antisemitic stereotypes* such as the excessive influence of Jews in business, politics and the media. Jews appear as the super-Whites. Schraub observes that 'The hope in applying the Whiteness frame to a gentile White is to unsettle received understandings of the White experience – to make people see things they had not seen before. By contrast, the effect of applying Whiteness to Jewishness is confirmatory: "I always thought that Jews had all this power and privilege – and see how right I was!" ' (2019:393).

The exclusion of global antisemitism from anti-racist intersectional analyses and practices means that Jews are increasingly not recognised as a minority that has been racially persecuted and murdered for centuries, and Israel is not recognised as a refuge for Jews worldwide after the Shoah. Instead, Jews appear as representatives of an exploitative, structurally racist group and Israel appears as a bastion of Western imperialism in the Middle East, as an artificial and alien element in the midst of supposedly autochthonous Arab peoples (Hirsh 2018, Nelson 2019).

By completely subsuming antisemitism under the category of 'racism' it appears to be the problem of bygone times. In fact, while antisemitism and racism are historically closely related, they have developed *in different directions* after the Shoah and in postcolonial contexts. Contemporary antisemitism no longer primarily operates as a racism but has changed into postnational forms, in which Israel is utilised as a universal scapegoat for wars and crises worldwide. The discrimination against Jews today is different from that of People of Colour. If this difference is not recognised, current forms of antisemitism that differ from racism, such as antisemitism related to Israel, not only disappear from view but can also mask themselves as anti-racist and oppositional. Thus, *over*-inclusion (treating antisemitism, simply, as racism) necessarily leads to the problem of *under*-inclusion: contemporary antisemitism is *not* viewed as racism at all and the fight against it is less and less recognised as part of the anti-racist struggle, and can even be considered to be *itself* conservative, reactionary, even racist.

Lost in translation: 'intersectionality' across contexts

Kimberlé Crenshaw defines intersectionality as 'a way of seeing, thinking and acting' (cf. Maan 2019), thus raising the problem of the *transferability* of the concept to other oppressions. If intersectionality does not want to be merely a buzzword – or be mentioned purely doxographically according to the motto: 'don't use that concept, only mention it' (Derrida 1990) – then clear thinking about its *translation* from one context into another is necessary. To that end, Gudrun-Axeli Knapp (2005) advises us to conceive of intersectionality as a 'travelling concept', one that brings pieces of luggage on its journey, some of which may be inappropriate in a changed context.

If this 'baggage' means that antisemitism cannot be adequately grasped, then the analytical value of the concept of intersectionality must come under question. The concept of intersectionality actually functions today to *underpin* some of the assumptions of contemporary antisemitism. For example, in the political practice of certain queer and feminist activists – the so-called *Queer International* – Israelis *en masse* are considered to be on the privileged side of global power relations, and so antisemitism is no longer perceived as a concrete danger. There is a great deal of ingenuity in interpreting Israel as a depravity for doing what activists are actually advocating elsewhere: women's and LGBTIQ rights. For Israel, however, all is reversed, making possible the accusation of 'pinkwashing' and 'homonationalism' (Schulman 2012, Puar 2013). There has arisen resistance to the exclusion of Jews from queer and feminist initiatives such as *Women's March on Washington*, *Chicago Dyke March* or *Black Lives Matter*. The journalist and LGBTIQ activist Gretchen Hammond lost her job at the *Windy City Times* after she made public the antisemitism of the *Chicago Dyke March* organisers. Feminists such as Emily Shire (2017) refuse to accept the argument of Linda Sarsour, the former organiser of the *Women's March on Washington*, that Zionism and feminism would exclude and contradict each other, while Anna Isaacs (2016) elaborated on the complexity of the *Black Lives Matter* movement, which in the beginning did not exclude Jewish experiences and also included a focus on antisemitism. Likewise, former Jewish comrades of *Women's March on Washington* have been forced to withdraw or to launch their own feminist intersectional campaigns that are dedicated to educating the public about antisemitism, such as *Women For All* or *Zioness*.

Bringing antisemitism back in: reclaiming intersectionality for the Jews

In the face of this growing political abuse of the concept of intersectionality in many feminist and anti-racist movements, and the opening it has offered to antisemitism, some reject it completely. I argue for a critical reclaiming of the approach. Suitably reformed in ways I will go on to suggest, informed by certain advances made by the Frankfurt School, I believe the concept can strengthen our analysis of contemporary societies and be particularly fruitful for ideology critique.

Learning from the Frankfurt School

A closer look at the history of sociological and social-psychological thought shows that the treatment of antisemitism in the early critical theory of the Frankfurt School anticipated later concepts of intersectionality. The broad empirical studies on the *Authoritarian Personality* conducted by Theodor

Adorno, Else Frenkel-Brunswick and colleagues at Columbia University in the 1940s had the aim of measuring the authoritarian-fascist potential across the American population. One of its most prominent discoveries was that ideologies such as antisemitism, racism, sexism, homophobia, ethnocentrism, nationalism and the legitimation of class inequality rarely occur as isolated phenomena but develop within *a broader framework* – the authoritarian ideological attitudinal syndrome (Adorno et al [1950] 2019). Ideologies, then, are certainly intersectional: they permeate and reinforce each other, constantly reforming and reactivating themselves in this process. Moreover, depending on political expediency, one ideology can come to the fore at any one time, while the others continue to operate in the background able to be called up.

The intersectionality of ideologies

This insight from Adorno et al. helps us to pose the question of how the ideology of antisemitism intersects with the ideologies of sexism, racism, nationalism and class inequality. How do antisemitic motives shine through in anti-feminism? How does nationalism or anti-genderism – as a particular variation of antifeminism – cover up latent antisemitism? To address such questions I have developed the concept of the *intersectionality of ideologies* (Stögner 2014, 2017, 2019). I do not mean that ideologies are interchangeable or should be equated. Rather, I believe we need to view ideologies within a relationship of difference and affinity, in order to understand that ideologies gain their respective specificity precisely *from their interaction with other ideologies*. Such an approach has radical implications for our understanding of the functioning not only of antisemitism, but also of antifeminism, sexism, homophobia, racism, and nationalism.

I am proposing a change in perspective in intersectionality research. My ideology critical approach would shift our attention from the level of identity formation, which is often in the foreground today, to the level of *the ideological concealment of social contradictions*. Furthermore, this approach also focuses on the question of why repressive social categorisation and identification take place *at all*. This further shift in focus, by making visible our compulsion to categorise and identify as a ruling practice, also helps us grasp why and when this compulsion may sometimes permeate identity politics itself, with bad consequences.

Ideologies are best understood as being interdependent. They not only usually appear in a bundle, but each ideology also carries moments of the other ideologies within themselves and they thus merge together. Due to its complexity, antisemitism is particularly suitable for an understanding of this kind, which we can call an intersectional ideology critique. Antisemitism is permeated by sexism, racism, and nationalism, while reflecting the economic class relationship and the corresponding inequalities in a completely delusory and distorted way, masquerading as a critique of capitalism. Antisemitism can be understood as *the* example par excellence of an ideology shot through with the marks of other ideologies.

Antisemitism pushes the Jews beyond the stable categories of intersectionality

Most societies are organised along binary markers such as bottom-up, inside-out, White-Black, male-female, and hetero-lesbian/gay. Accordingly, ideologies such as racism, sexism, homophobia, nationalism, and ethnocentrism position People of Colour, women, gays and lesbians, foreigners, and strangers more or less unambiguously along these binary codes. Antisemitism, by contrast, is characterised by *ambivalence* with regard to these markers. It does not position Jews unambiguously on one or the other side of these markers, but rather attributes to Jews a position *beyond* binary categorisation. The history of antisemitism shows that Jews are regarded as unclassifiable in the three dimensions that are central to the classical intersectionality approach: gender/sexuality, class and race/ethnicity/nation. This can be seen in the 19th-century figure of the anti-national Jew, who questioned the principle of nationhood, no less than in the image of the Jew as a 'gender bender' who thwarts gender binarity. In antisemitism, Jews are not clearly assigned to classes either, but identified simultaneously with communism *and* capitalism, especially with financial capital. Jews do not so much represent a foreign, hostile identity, but rather a non-identity, in other words, the threat of the *dissolution* of identity itself, of unity itself.

The anti-categorical character of antisemitic stereotypes makes it hard to grasp for dominant intersectional approaches that assume the interdependence of stable categories. Antisemitism denies Jews any clear categorisation and derives its effectiveness and efficiency from an almost 'queer' thwarting of familiar binaries and from undermining clear categorisations. Antisemitism itself blurs the categories and portrays the Jew as not belonging to any identity criteria.

Antisemitism is a particular fear that the unity and identity of the nation, religion, community, etc., might be infiltrated and decomposed. Conspiracy myths are a manifestation of this fear. They secretly manifest that the fixed boundaries of collective, cultural identities are already dissolved. Here, a difference to newer forms of racism like cultural racism and 'racism without races' becomes clear. For example, anti-Muslim resentment ascribes to Muslims a hermetically sealed and fixed identity. In antisemitism, by contrast, Jews are characterised as *lacking* identity or roots. The National Socialist mania saw Jews not as an 'alien race' that was to be subjugated and exploited, but 'the antirace, the negative principle as such; on their extermination the world's happiness depends' (Horkheimer and Adorno 2002:137). The mania of redemption through exterminatory antisemitism emerged from a view of Jews as settled in a non-place beyond the authoritative categorical order of the world. Let us review the various non-places to which the Jew is consigned by antisemitism.

The 'anti-national Jew'

Antisemitism depicts Jews as not loyal to any nation and incapable of establishing true statehood. It dates back to the time of the European nation state formation in the late 18th and 19th centuries and inverted the fact that Jews as a people had no nation state of their own into the stereotype that they would infiltrate other nations and undermine the national principle from within. They were considered international, cosmopolitan, free-floating, rootless, inauthentic and untrustworthy in terms of their national identification. Nationalism and the construction of a homogeneous national community were not only directed against external enemies but also developed through the explicit exclusion of 'foreign' and 'non-belonging' elements within the national borders.

The figure of the anti-national Jew served thereby as a projection screen for unacknowledged uncertainties and antagonisms within the modern nation state, as well as for the legitimation of nationalistic exclusions: Ethnic (and to a lesser degree also civic) nationalism effectively covers up the division of society according to economic classes and pretends a unity that is in reality highly fragile. The break in the unity is projected onto the 'anti-national Jew'. This motif recurs in extreme antizionism, which rejects Jewish statehood as an 'artificial entity' and today ranges from neo-Nazi to Islamist and 'anti-imperialist' discourses.

The 'Jewish gender bender'

Countless are the images, especially in the late 19th and early 20th centuries, which ascribed an ambiguous gender and sexuality to Jews. Antisemitism traditionally considered Jewish men to be effeminate and Jewish women to be masculinised. They were said to blur the clearly drawn boundaries between the genders, to dissolve gender identity, reversing gender roles and the gender-specific division of labour. Consequently, women's emancipation was also interpreted as Jewish machination against the unity of the people. Due to the intermediate position regarding gender and sexuality attributed to them, Jews were seen as an essential threat to the unity of the cultural community, which is still inseparably linked to the heteronormative order today.

Emancipated women who claimed autonomous subjectivity and sexuality were considered part of a Jewish conspiracy: the 'Jewish democratic feminist mammon spirit', as the Nazi mastermind Ludwig Langemann formulated it in 1919. This is by no means overcome today, as we can see in the right-wing anti-gender ideologies across Europe and America, in which feminism functions as the new scapegoat of current identity crises. Islamists express the close connection between antisemitism and antigenderism more explicitly: for example, the supreme spiritual leader of Iran, Ali Khamenei, sees in the 'objectification of women' in the West and 'concepts like gender justice' a 'Zionist plot to destroy human community' (Magid 2017). Or take the Algerian Islamist Malek Bennabi, who in the 1960s swaggered about the 'century of the woman, the Jew and the dollar' and thus summarised the threats to the Islamic Umma that were central to him (Bensoussan 2019).

In left wing postcolonial contexts, the narrative is widespread that the Israelis force on the Arab other a Western notion of homosexuality and feminism in order to denigrate purportedly authentic Arab sexuality and gender relations (cf. Puar 2007; Massad 2007).

The Jew as 'misfit bourgeois'

One major characteristic of antisemitism's classical inventory is that Jews are identified with the intermediary economic sphere of circulation, that is, with trade, banking and money transactions, and so are primarily seen as speculators and financial capitalists. In feudal, traditional societies, Jews were denied access to landed property and to craft guilds, just as in modern, functionally differentiated, capitalist societies, they were excluded from ownership of the means of production, and the source of surplus value, for a very long period. They were therefore increasingly forced into the intermediary spheres of circulation.

That *all* bankers were Jews and all Jews were engaged in money transactions, on the other hand, has always been an antisemitic cliché, closely linked to the antisemitic idea that Jews will not work. This in turn announces the ideological division of the capital relationship into 'productive' and 'rapacious'. The position of the trader is an intermediate one that makes the class position appear ambiguous and vague: Jews were neither masters nor servants. If they attributed themselves to the class of the bourgeois, they encountered the cliché of the 'misfit bourgeois' (Adorno et al. [1950] 2019), who would only imitate the capitalist business while lacking any feeling for real and sincere entrepreneurship and therefore representing the negative effects of capitalism in its purest form. As the voice of the working class, they were seen as hypocrites, speaking from a position alienated from all physical labour, about things they knew nothing about.

Conclusion: intersectionality cannot be an emancipatory theory while excluding antisemitism

Inconsistency, ambiguity and comprehensive unclassifiability; fluid boundaries and manifold overlap with other ideologies; these are the reasons why antisemitism has developed into a comprehensive and delusional world view in the course of the rapid and disruptive modernisation process. It has helped to stabilise a system of values and norms that appeared to be under threat. More than other ideologies, antisemitism helps to maintain the traditional rules of capitalism, patriarchy, and nation state order by always being sexist, homophobic, nationalist, and racist and in addition by posing as anti-capitalist and anti-imperialist. The consistently anti-categorical moment, by positioning Jews *beyond* the categories, distinguishes antisemitism from other ideologies, which are much less ambiguous.

This insight challenges those approaches that assume there must be a critical potential in an anti-categorical view. Antisemitism *itself* transgresses categorisation effectively, positioning Jews beyond gender, sexuality, class, race, ethnicity and nation. Antisemitism gains its effectiveness from exactly this characteristic. We have to understand the banality that in antisemitism *everything* can be interpreted against the Jews – particularly that they allegedly do not correspond to the socially prescribed categories.

An intersectional approach must not be limited to the insight that society is structured by certain categories, but must, in a radical critique of power, uncover the social reasons and conditions of these categories. The process of perennial categorisation of people in society and the underlying traditional identity logics must also be criticised. The approach of intersectionality of ideologies proposed here is therefore critical of approaches that support an identitarian and cultural-relativist discourse and can tip in the direction of antisemitism and homophobia under the guise of anti-racism. The critique of intersectionality presented here is intended to open the approach to a dialectical feminist theory that does not blind out antisemitism, and which is *therefore* connected to truly emancipatory practice. Such a truly inclusive critical approach to intersectionality also enables alliances in theory and practice against antisemitism, sexism, *and* racism.

Note

1 This chapter was first published in *Fathom* in 2020.

References

Adorno, Theodor, Else Frenkel-Brunswik, Daniel J. Levinson and R. Nevitt Sanford ([1950] 2019) *The Authoritarian Personality*, London: Verso.

Balibar, Étienne (2005) 'The construction of racism', *Actual Marx*, 38 (2): 11–28. Available: www.cairn-int.info/article-E_AMX_038_0011–the-construction-of-racism. htm (accessed 24 November 2022).

Bensoussan, Georges (2019) *Jews in Arab Countries. The Great Uprooting*, Bloomington: Indiana University Press.

Combahee River Collective (1977) 'The Combahee River Collective Statement'. Available: https://www.blackpast.org/african-american-history/combahee-river-collec tive-statement-1977/ (accessed 30 November 2022).

Cousin, Glynis and Robert Fine (2012) 'A common cause. Reconnecting the study of racism and antisemitism', *European Societies*, 14 (2): 166–185.

Derrida, Jacques (1990) 'Some Statements and Truisms about Neologisms, Newisms, Postisms, Parasitisms and other Small Seismisms', in David Carroll (ed.) *The States of 'Theory': History, Art, and Critical Discourse*, Stanford, CA: Stanford University Press.

Hirsh, David (2018) *Contemporary Left Antisemitism*, London and New York: Routledge.

Horkheimer, Max and Theodor W. Adorno (2002) *Dialectic of Enlightenment. Philosophical Fragments*, Stanford, CA: Stanford University Press.

Isaacs, Anna (2016) 'How The Black Lives Matter and Palestinian Movements Converged', *Moment*, 14 March. Available: https://momentmag.com/how-the-black-lives-matter-and-palestinian-movements-converged/ (accessed 16 June 2023).

Knapp, Gudrun-Axeli (2005) 'Race, class, gender. Reclaiming baggage in fast travelling theories', *European Journal of Women's Studies*, 12 (3): 249–265.

Maan, Noura (2019) '30 Jahre Intersektionalität: Gegenrede als Strategie'. *Der Standard*, 30 April 2019. Available: https://www.derstandard.de/story/2000102288080/30-jahre-intersektionalitaet-gegenrede-als-strategie (accessed: 30 November 2022).

Magid, Jacob (2017) 'Iran leader says of women Zionist plot'. *Times of Israel*, 19 March 2017. Available: https://www.timesofisrael.com/iran-leader-blasts-objectification-of-women-as-zionist-plot/ (accessed 30 November 2022).

Massad, Joseph (2007) *Desiring Arabs*, Chicago: University of Chicago Press.

Nelson, Cary (2019) *Israel Denial. Anti-Zionism, Anti-Semitism, and the Faculty Campaign Against the Jewish State*, Bloomington: Indiana University Press.

Postone, Moishe (1980) 'Anti-Semitism and national socialism: Notes on the German reactions to "holocaust"', *New German Critique* 19 (1): 97–115.

Puar, Jasbir (2007) *Terrorist Assemblages: Homonationalism in Queer Times*, Durham: Duke University Press.

Puar, Jasbir (2013) 'Rethinking homonationalism', *International Journal of Middle East Studies*, 45: 336–339.

Schraub, David (2019) 'White Jews: An intersectional approach', *AJS Review*, 43 (2): 379–407.

Schulman, Sarah (2012) *Israel/Palestine and the Queer International*, Durham and London: Duke University Press.

Shire, Emily (2017) 'Does feminism have room for Zionists?' *New York Times*, 7 March 2017. Available: www.nytimes.com/2017/03/07/opinion/does-feminism-have-room-for-zionists.html (accessed 24 November 2022).

Stögner, Karin (2014) *Antisemitismus und Sexismus. Historisch-gesellschaftliche Konstellationen*, Baden: Nomos.

Stögner, Karin (2017) 'Nature and Anti-Nature: Constellations of Antisemitism and Sexism', in Ulrike Brunotte, Jürgen Mohn and Christina Späti (eds.) *Internal Outsiders: Imagined Orientals? Antisemitism, Colonialism and Modern Constructions of Jewish Identity*, Würzburg: Ergon Verlag.

Stögner, Karin (2019) 'Intersectionality and anti-Zionism. New challenges in feminism', in Alvin Rosenfeld (ed.), *Anti-Zionism and Antisemitism. The Dynamics of Delegitimization*, Bloomington: Indiana University Press.

31

LEFT ALTERNATIVES TO LEFT ANTISEMITISM

A Conversation Between Alan Johnson and Philip Spencer

Alan Johnson and Philip Spencer

Part 1: The Equivocations of Enlightenment Universalism and the Two Souls of the Left

AJ: In *Antisemitism and the Left*, the book you co-authored with the late Robert Fine, you point out that 'Historically, there has been no shortage either of antisemitism or of opposition to antisemitism within the left tradition' (Fine and Spencer 2017:4). Let's conclude this collection of *Fathom* essays, which has been all about the former, by looking more closely at the latter, and at some of the exemplary figures who offer resources for a specifically left-wing opposition to contemporary left antisemitism.

Let's begin with the Enlightenment. You and Robert argued that left antisemitism has its roots in that version of 18th century Enlightenment universalism which cast the Jews as the bad 'other' to universalism, hence as 'reactionary'. As you put it, the Jews were framed as the 'personification of a particularism opposed to the universal' and/ or as 'the personification of a false universalism concealing Jewish self-interest' (2017:2). I think the key insight of your book is that only when today's left-wingers break from that framing, seeing plain how it has mis-shaped the left itself, can they recognise and settle accounts with left antisemitism.

PS: Indeed. Two main forms of universalism emerged in the Enlightenment. One was inclusionary and gave more and more people recognition as fellow human beings, entitled to the same rights as everyone else. The other defined the universal in opposition to various designated groups that were identified as somehow not deserving. The Jews were one such

DOI: 10.4324/9781003322320-39

group, told to change their (purported) behaviour if they wanted to become full members of enlightened society. Antisemitic tropes rooted in an older Christian and Islamic antisemitism were rearticulated within a universalist frame of reference, constructing a supposed 'Jewish Question' which has persisted in various forms to this day for a significant section of the left.[1]

In the latter part of the 19th century in the Socialist 'Second International', it was assumed by many that holding on to a Jewish identity was incompatible with adherence to the socialist version of universalism. In the Communist 'Third International' that emerged after the Russian Revolution, you can see a similar approach – only now the universalism was seen as being embodied in the Soviet state. A section of the left, to put at its simplest, believed that Jews failed the test of emancipation if they did not abandon their loyalties to their fellow Jews, reject their traditions and beliefs, and forget the injustices inflicted upon them. These injustices were, crucially, all now deemed to be in the past. If antisemitism did continue to threaten from time to time, it could only be from those seeking to turn back the clock, i.e. from the reactionary right, never the left.

So we see certain tropes recur repeatedly in the articulation of antisemitic discourse in the 19th and 20th century left: that Jews are only loyal to each other, that they place their own interests in opposition to those of the wider society, that they hate and despise non-Jews, that they cheat and exploit them whenever they can, that they exaggerate their misfortunes for their own advantage and cling to outworn beliefs and practices. In the Soviet Union, and in the wider communist movement that was in thrall to it for decades, Jews were attacked for being disloyal, albeit on two quite contradictory grounds – either they were 'rootless cosmopolitans' and so not proper patriots or they were exactly the opposite, nationalists (Zionists) loyal to another country, a reprise of the catch-22 the Enlightenment had often imposed on Jews.

Fortunately, this understanding of universalism has never been the only one on the left. There have always been those who have not singled out Jews in this negative way but instead proposed a universalism which includes Jews and Jewish peoplehood, recognised the contributions that Jews make to society, and to humanity, and who have viewed an attack on Jews as an attack on society and on humanity itself.

Part 2: The Ambivalences of Karl Marx and Their Consequences

AJ: I think we disagree about Karl Marx. You have argued Marx is 'a key resource for recovering a tradition of critical thought that repudiates "left antisemitism"' (Fine and Spencer 2017:41). I don't agree, holding to what you call in your book the 'disparaging view' of Marx. Apart from the slew of antisemitic statements in his private letters and journalism, I read his 1844 essay 'On The Jewish Question' as a communist version of that bad Enlightenment universalism which excludes disfavoured groups. In pages that antisemites have quoted ever since, Marx identified the Jews' haggling, huckstering, greed, unspiritual materialism, and contempt for man, as the basis for identifying his 'solution' to 'the Jewish Question': communism. Here is the worst of it:

> What is the secular basis of Judaism? Practical need, self-interest. What is the worldly religion of the Jew? Huckstering. What is his worldly God? Money. . . . An organisation of society which would abolish the preconditions for huckstering, and therefore the possibility of huckstering, would make the Jew impossible. . . . The Jew has emancipated himself in a Jewish manner, not only because he has acquired financial power, but also because, through him and also apart from him, money has become a world power and the practical Jewish spirit has become the practical spirit of the Christian nations. The Jews have emancipated themselves insofar as the Christians have become Jews. . . . Money is the jealous god of Israel, in face of which no other god may exist. Money degrades all the gods of man – and turns them into commodities. . . . The bill of exchange is the real god of the Jew. His god is only an illusory bill of exchange. . . . The chimerical nationality of the Jew is the nationality of the merchant, of the man of money in general.
>
> *(Marx 1975 [1843]:236–237)*

I think one has to work really hard not to see this as a combination of crass antisemitic stereotyping and a communist version of bad Enlightenment universalism: Judaism, Jewishness and Jewish peoplehood, which are granted no positive value at all, are to be dissolved in the solvent of the universal-communist-proletariat. This idea – that the disappearance of Jewishness and Jewish peoplehood is a condition for and a marker of human progress – has been one key driver of left antisemitism ever since. As Norman Geras highlighted in his *Fathom* essay 'Alibi Antisemitism' (2013), it has been one reason so much of the left has been willing to offer Jewish people only individual rights as individual citizens, not collective recognition as a people or acceptance of their statehood. Because *as a collective* Jews are always seen as *suspect*.

PS: I don't think there is any point in denying the unpleasantness of some of Marx's language or to put Marx on a pedestal. He was an heir to precisely the ambivalences of Enlightenment universalism, so it should be no surprise that a hostile attitude to Jews can be found in the way he sometimes writes. That essay, however, was written before Marx had discovered the idea of capitalism itself. He talks a lot about money and haggling but not about accumulation or exploitation. This matters because it is one of the features of leftist antisemitism that it too is based on a superficial view of economy and society, and then, from this distorted perspective, makes Jews responsible for all that is supposedly going wrong.

The key question is: what contribution did Marx make to thinking about antisemitism and universalism on the left? His essay was a critical *response* to an antisemite on the left, Bruno Bauer. Bauer was one of those who believed that 'the' Jews had failed the conditions of emancipation. What was distinctive about Marx's response was his insistence that singling out Jews was absolutely wrong. There were no grounds whatsoever for attributing any of the grave flaws of modern society to Jews. All the comments he makes about Jews (however ugly the phrasing) are about features of contemporary society which need to be changed, but those features are not there *because* of the Jews and they will not be solved by the exclusion of Jews. On the contrary, Marx insists repeatedly that Jews should have the *same* rights as everyone else. What is really needed, he thinks, is something much more fundamental, a radical change in how society itself is organised.

Crucially, from Marx's perspective there is no 'Jewish Question' to be solved, no problem posed by the presence or activity of Jews as such. But there is an *antisemitism* question, which is exactly the opposite. If Marx does not explicitly point this out, that is because political antisemitism had not yet emerged as a significant political force, although it was stirring. Those who came after cannot hide behind this as an excuse. Marx's effective demolition of the notion of a 'Jewish Question' seems to me to be a fundamental step forward for the left, but not a path that everyone has followed. Far too often there has been a disturbing tendency to go back to exactly the argument that Bauer put forward and Marx demolished. Lars Fischer has shown how this was a very strong temptation for very many Marxists almost immediately after Marx's death (Fischer 2007).

AJ: Let's move on. I think useful resources for today's left can also be found in a tradition that runs from Friedrich Engels and Eleanor Marx through to Eduard Bernstein. Robert Wistrich's book *From Ambivalence to Betrayal: The Left, the Jews and Israel* is the best overview of the history of left antisemitism. He claims that Engels overcame his personal prejudices when faced with the rising tide of political antisemitism in late 19th century Europe, including on the left, and so produced 'one of the most unequivocal repudiations of antisemitism to be found in modern socialist journalism' (Wistrich 2012:135). Famously, when the socialist and antisemite Eugen Dühring became influential over German social democracy, Engels entered the lists against him with his book *Anti-Dühring*. Less famously, that book was sharply critical of pseudo-progressive antisemitism.

Marx's daughter Eleanor was very close to Engels. She was also the only Marx to embrace Jewish peoplehood and particularism and to balance it with her universalist commitments, a balance that seems to be found in every left-wing refusal of left antisemitism. 'I am a Jewess', she would proclaim in the face of antisemitism. (Sidney Hook thought those four words were the perfect riposte to her father's 1844 essay.) The German social democrat Eduard Bernstein – who rowed out from Beachy Head together with Eleanor to scatter Engels' ashes in the sea – praised her for exactly this quality, noting that she 'did not allow herself to be led astray by her deep-rooted proletarian class feeling whenever the Jew was oppressed as a Jew, but declared herself for the oppressed, irrespective of class affiliation' (Wistrich 2012:145).

According to Wistrich, Bernstein 'stands out as a maverick among the leading German Jewish socialists of his generation' because he refused to 'expunge, deny, or repudiate his Jewishness' and because 'he rejected any simplistic identification of Jews with capitalism'. Wistrich went on: 'One cannot find in his writings any residue of the Schacher (huckster) stereotype popularised by the young Karl Marx' and he 'never called on his co-religionists to abandon their Jewish affiliations in order to become "humanly emancipated" or to benefit from progress and enlightenment' (2012:140–141). I think this is what the left needs today, an understanding of universalism that has space for, indeed respect for, Jewishness and Jewish peoplehood, affiliations, identities, and traditions. For me, that has to mean support for 'two states for two peoples' as the democratic programme for the Israeli-Palestinian conflict; not chanting 'from the River to the Sea, Palestine will be free' which, for those who know the code, is a call for a genocide.

In 1898 Bernstein wrote that 'it is a categorical imperative for me to be a "philosemite" in the face of all antisemitism'. Never a Zionist as such – 'I feel myself too German to become one', he said – he became convinced that a Jewish national home in Palestine was desperately needed. He insisted that 'cosmopolitan sentiment is not identical with anti-national or anti-patriotic conviction. It is compatible with recognition of individual nations as legitimate members of the great organism of civilised mankind, with their own needs and interests'. In 1928 the left-wing Jewish movement in Palestine, Poale-Zion, sent Bernstein a telegram, addressed to 'a true friend of the Jewish worker in Palestine'. I think we can – and must – be critical of Bernstein's views on imperialism while agreeing with Wistrich's conclusion that Bernstein gave us a glimpse of what a synthesis of 'the Jewish cultural heritage with neo-Kantian German philosophy and the socialist vision of human brotherhood' might look like as a response to rising antisemitism (Wistrich 2012:145–150).

PS: I certainly think it is important to recall all this. It is a crucial part of the history of the left that Engels and Eleanor Marx and Bernstein were quite explicit at times in their opposition to antisemitism. It has to be remembered that in Eleanor Marx's case she was directly combatting antisemitism on the left too, in her fury with those who refused to support Dreyfus (and quite a lot of people on the left refused, a fact which is often forgotten).

The case of Bernstein raises important issues about revising one's ideas in the face of new evidence. When he was developing his main revisionist ideas and being attacked for supposedly betraying Marx, it does not seem to me that the question of antisemitism was particularly significant for him. But he began to think much more seriously during the war, when the antisemitism of the German state began to become much more ominous (with the so-called 'Jews Census') and especially afterwards.[2] Of course, Bernstein did not live to see the Nazis come to power but seeing what they were already threatening he had come, as you say, to revise his opposition to the idea that Jews needed their own national homeland.

Rosa Luxemburg and German Socialism

AJ: In your view, we should add Rosa Luxemburg to this better left-wing tradition. Can you say why? Wistrich complained of an 'unpleasant streak of contempt for Jewry' in Luxemburg, pointing to her 1917 response, when told of the pogroms in Russia: 'Why do you come to me with your special Jewish sorrows?' Are there not weaknesses, as well as undoubted strengths, in her view that 'for the followers of Marx, as for the working class, the Jewish question as such does not exist, just as the "negro question" or the "yellow Peril" does not exist. From the standing of the working class, the Jewish Question . . . is a question of racial hatred as a symptom of social reaction, which to a certain extent is an indivisible part of all societies based on class antagonism'. And especially in her statement that Marx had 'for the first time removed the Jewish Question from the religious and racial sphere and given it a *social* foundation, proving that what is usually described and persecuted as "Judaism" is nothing but *the spirit of huckstering and swindle*, which appears in *every* society where *exploitation* reigns' (quoted in

Wistrich 2012:363). Is this not, alongside her rejection of antisemitism, an example of the very stereotyping and bad Enlightenment universalism that was helping to generate antisemitism in the first place?

PS: Luxemburg is important at a number of levels. One is that, like Marx, she did not accept there was a 'Jewish Question' to be answered (I am indebted to Lars Fischer for this insight). The crucial part of her quote above says this explicitly, even if she seems to half go back on this. I would say this is an example of a struggle going on inside her, as we saw with earlier Enlightenment thinkers. But even in this moment of regression, she says that what is supposed to be 'Judaism' is actually to do with exploitation, which is what Marx was also saying. Like Marx, she is giving a hostage to fortune in even using the term 'Judaism' so I am not holding her up as perfect. What we need to do here, as with Marx, is to build on what she was saying, and go further down the path he and she laid out.

In her case, far more so than Marx, she had to deal directly with a growing and serious antisemitic threat which she experienced herself, not only from the right in Germany but from a section (the dominant section) of the Polish left. Her response to it had nothing in common with those who thought philosemitism was a more serious problem or that there might be some kind of rational kernel to antisemitic 'thinking' (see Fischer 2007:224–225).

I think her position was not, at that time, so different to Bernstein's. But Luxemburg's cosmopolitanism had a more fundamental aspect than his which set her apart from the rest of the left in a way that has serious import for our own thinking about the left and antisemitism. She did not think that *any* forms of nationalism were progressive, so she did not single out Jewish nationalism for opprobrium. Again, this has contemporary echoes, given how much of the antizionist left today has adopted the obviously antisemitic position that *only* Jewish nationalism is illegitimate. Her cosmopolitanism provides the basis for a principled response to those who I think only masquerade as cosmopolitans in order to mount their attack on Zionism.

It can certainly be argued that even Luxemburg's cosmopolitanism does not offer enough solidarity to Jews, and I think, as Norman Geras pointed out (and he was very sympathetic to her, as I am), that there is something missing in her seemingly dismissive comment you cite about special Jewish sorrows. But remember when she said this – before those sorrows became not so much special as unprecedently acute. I do not think it is a stance she would have continued to adopt had she lived as long as Bernstein and certainly not had she witnessed the Holocaust. I say this because there is another facet of Luxemburg's thought which in my view offers the contemporary left important resources to improve its (often threadbare) thinking about the Holocaust and antisemitism.

Part 3: The Holocaust: Barbarism and the Left

PS: Let me put it this way: Luxemburg was aware that things can go cata-strophically wrong. In the so-called 'Junius Pamphlet', a quite brilliant piece written during the slaughter of the First World War (Luxemburg 1970:269), she went back to Engels' suggestion that if socialism did not replace capitalism, then society might regress to a state of barba-rism. The terms she used to describe the incipient barbarism of the First World War – *destruction of culture*; *depopulation*; *desolation*; *degen-eration*; the *construction of a vast cemetery* – seem to me actually to be much better applied to the Holocaust. I am not arguing that Luxem-burg foresaw the Holocaust as such. She was not a prophet. But she, like Trotsky, had an acute sense that something really dreadful was on the horizon for humanity as a whole.

While Trotsky is distinguished by his awareness that barbarism was highly likely to be visited on Jews specifically, predicting the Holocaust in 1938, there was a profound and widespread reluctance on the part of many on the left to respond to the threat posed to Jews by the Nazis, as they were mobilising in the late 1920s and early 1930s, when they began to use the state power they had acquired to attack Jews, and then when the extermination began. At each stage, a significant section of the left downplayed antisemitism, fearing it would lose the left support. And this is something that few on the radical left today are prepared to acknowledge (see Bankier 2000, Herf 1995). Rather than facing the dismal reality of this experience, many take refuge in the claim that the radical left (by which I mean primarily the Communists but not only them) has always been 'anti-fascist'. Well, first, that is not even true as the Nazi-Soviet pact forcibly delivered many Jews to Hitler.

AJ: Stalin even forcibly deported German communist Jews who had taken refuge in the Soviet Union. He sent them to their deaths in the hands of Hitler. Until Hitler's invasion of the Soviet Union in 1941, Communist Parties around the world denounced the war of the Allies as 'Imperial-ist' and refused to support it (Bornstein and Richardson 1982:57–74).[3] They were very selective 'anti-fascists'. The needs of Stalin's foreign policy always came first.

PS: Indeed. But the other point I want to make is that anti-fascism and solidarity with Jews when they are attacked *are not the same thing*. The Holocaust was more than a question of fascism, which is of course always racist and intrinsically violent. It was a radical *genocide*, in which the aim was to kill all the Jews wherever the Nazis could find them, as an end in itself, not as a means to another end. It involved the transformation of a process for producing commodities (the factory system) into one (in the death camps) that produced only ashes. Previous antisemites may have had fantasies about getting rid of Jews in a particular place, but not globally and not forever. If this project had been successful, it would have fundamentally altered humanity itself.

For a post-Holocaust and universalist left, solidarity with Jews in the face of this threat is an *existential* question, just as the genocidal assault is for Jews themselves. The Holocaust posed very sharply the question of the place Jews have in the version of universalism the left adopts. If the Jews are the 'other' of the universal, if they have no secure place in the universal, then a lack of solidarity is probably inevitable.

Later, there was the Soviet regime's insistence that the 'Great Patriotic War' was not fought to save Jews, a stance adopted right across the resistance in Europe too, even in France (Blatman and Poznanski 2011:201).[4] In each case, it was claimed that defending Jews would not be popular. Sometimes this went beyond being an excuse for inaction into something much more sinister: the instrumental adoption of antisemitism itself. Antisemitism was in Stalinism all the way through: from its origins in the initial campaign against Trotsky in 1923 through to the purges of the 1930s; from the brutal suppression of the Jewish anti-fascist committee and the murder of its leading activists very soon after the war through to the appallingly antisemitic show trials across Eastern Europe, some of which resulted in executions, and then on to the near-genocidal assault begun on Jews in the Soviet Union in Stalin's last years with the sustained assault on 'cosmopolitanism' and so-called 'Doctor's Plot' (Rubenstein and Naumov 2001, Brent and Naumov 2003).

Why did the Holocaust, at the centre of which was a radicalised antisemitism, not make many on the left rethink? There remains to this day no sustained study of the Holocaust as what Marxists used to call a *world historic event*, something which fundamentally altered the course of human history.

To think about antisemitism in and after the Holocaust, you have to think about it not as a secondary question, but as a primary one for socialists. As Hannah Arendt put it, the Holocaust was 'an attack on humanity carried out on the body of the Jewish people' (Arendt 1965:269). If you eliminate a group, humanity would no longer be what it was. So, from an inclusionary universalist point of view, the protection of Jews is not only a theoretical question: it is existential, to do with the existence of humanity itself. It is of course also existential for Jews, for whom what happened in the Holocaust changed everything. It made Zionism, which had not previously been the dominant political ideology among Jews globally, now unarguable. If no one could protect the Jews, then they would have to do it themselves.

The better section of the left has, to its great credit and to our considerable benefit, recognised this, albeit in different ways and at different levels, and it is crucial that we remind ourselves repeatedly of this other and continuing tradition.

Part 4: Excavating a Better Left

AJ: Let's do that, then. Four exemplary left-wing thinkers illustrate many of the qualities of that other, better left-wing tradition. Let's look more closely at Leon Trotsky, Theodor Adorno, Moishe Postone and Norman Geras.

Leon Trotsky: 'The Jewish Nation Will Maintain Itself for an Entire Epoch to Come'

AJ: Whatever criticisms can be made of the Bolsheviks during the early years of the revolution, and I think there are a great many, the decision to appoint a Jew, Jacob Sverdlov, as the first president of the new Soviet republic has rightly been described as 'an act of courage' and 'a declaration of war against antisemitism, now identified with the counter-revolution'. In July 1918 a decree was passed outlawing antisemitism, promising harsh measures against pogromists and declaring antisemitism 'a mortal danger for the entire revolution'. The result was that 'the party's leadership was widely identified as a Jewish gang' (Johnson 2019).

Trotsky already knew about, and had fought against, Christian antisemitism and the Tsar-licensed Black Hundred pogroms, about which he wrote powerfully in his book *1905* (Trotsky 1971). And he had written movingly about the antisemitic Beilis 'blood libel' trial in 1913. The 1917 revolution taught him that antisemitism was present among the revolutionary as well as the counter-revolutionary armies. He suffered right-wing antisemitic abuse from the White counter-revolutionaries and then, soon enough, left antisemitic abuse from the Stalinist counter-revolutionaries. About the latter he said this in 1937: 'Of course we can close our eyes to the facts and limit ourselves to vague generalities about the equality and brotherhood of all races. But an ostrich policy will not advance us a single step. . . . All serious and honest observers bear witness to the existence of antisemitism, not only of the old and hereditary, but also of the new "Soviet" variety' (in Trotsky 1937).

In the 1930s, in the face of Nazism and Stalinism, in that awful midnight of the century, when Trotsky was in exile and 'on the planet without a visa', he managed to carry out a 'global revision' of the classical Marxist approach to antisemitism that was so radical that he alone on the left predicted the Shoah and embraced a kind of proto-Zionism before his death in 1940. This notion of a 'global revision' I take from Enzo Traverso, whose intellectual history *The Marxists and the Jewish Question* argued that Trotsky's was, though not systematic, 'the most profound analysis of antisemitism that Marxist thought produced in the interwar period' (1994:202, 204).

Three inter-related qualities of Trotsky's thought made this global revision possible. First, his life-long *political practice* of solidarity with persecuted Jews. Second, his serious *intellectual engagement* with the phenomenon of antisemitism, tracing its long history and changing forms (religious, secular, right and left), as well as its utility for political leaders of right and left, and its sometimes *utterly irrational and radically violent* character. He wrote in *1905* of how the anti-Jewish pogroms of that year satisfied perpetrators 'drunk on the smell of blood' (which as Norman Geras observed, is not a well-known Marxist category) who he thought were 'capable of everything' (Geras 1998:158). Third, Trotsky had a preference (often) for a flexible, *non-linear* approach to theory, attuned to the complex ways in which specific political situations had been shaped by the combined and uneven character of historical development.

I think these three qualities enabled Trotsky's 'global revision', which we can see as a series of radical shifts:

- from the depiction of antisemitism as a feudal hangover to locating it at the very heart of modernity itself;
- from the uncritical celebration of assimilationism as the only acceptable answer to 'the Jewish Question' to a chastened assessment of assimilationism as historically bankrupt;
- from the rationalist and vulgar-evolutionary form of Marxism that underpinned a remarkable complacency in the face of antisemitism, to a non-linear Marxism able to grasp all that was specific to the emergency facing the Jews at mid-century;
- from the acceptance of the merely civic rights of the Jews – what Norman Geras called Marxism's 'spurious universalism' – to the embrace of the national rights of the Jewish people;
- from a reluctant acquiescence in the merely cultural expression of Jewish peoplehood to the blunt acceptance of the necessity of the 'territorial' settlement of the Jewish nation in their own 'spot in the sun', as a 'compact mass'.

The revolutionary Marxist Ernest Mandel gave a qualified endorsement to Trotsky's global revision. 'Among all the prominent Marxists of the second and third international', he wrote, 'it was Trotsky alone who developed the positive aspects of Rosa Luxemburg's and Engels's ideas into a less simplistic and less mechanical approach to the Jewish Question'. He went on: 'Trotsky's analysis of contemporary antisemitism and his recognition of the right of self-contained Jewish populations to a territorially and politically secure national existence constitute a coherent unity and a decisive step forwards in the Marxist attitude to the Jewish Question' (1995:148, 152).

Although Trotsky never thought of himself as a Zionist – he had a fierce faith in the capacity of a 'World Socialist Revolution' to solve 'the Jewish Question' – he became convinced of the necessity of a national solution to the problem of radicalising antisemitism. Traverso notes Trotsky's always 'original attitude to the national question' captured in his 1915 statement that nations 'constitute an active and permanent factor of human culture', and his prediction that 'The nation will not only survive the current war, but also capitalism itself' (quoted in Traverso 1994:139–140). In his later writings we find him arguing that the Jews had every right to live in a 'compact mass', as a nation, in their own 'spot in the sun'. In 1937 he predicted that 'The Jewish nation will maintain itself for an entire epoch to come' (see Trotsky 1937–1940).

For Trotsky's biographer, the brilliant Polish socialist Isaac Deutscher, the Jewish state was a necessity. Though he opposed many of its *policies*, Deutscher supported its *existence* as, literally, a matter of Jewish life and death. He famously confessed that 'I have, of course, long since abandoned my anti-Zionism, which was based on a confidence in the European labour movement, or, more broadly, in European society and civilisation, which that society and civilisation have not justified. If, instead of arguing against Zionism in the 1920s and 1930s I had urged European Jews to go to Palestine, I might have helped to save some of the lives that were later extinguished in Hitler's gas chambers'. Deutscher went on: 'For the remnants of European Jewry – is it only for them? – the Jewish State has become an historic necessity. It is also a living reality' (1968:111–112).

I think the other, better, post-Holocaust left has always allowed its thinking about antisemitism, Zionism and the Jewish state to be radically impacted by that eruption of world history of which the Holocaust was the dark centre – the socialist revolution in Europe failed; the revolutionary movement degenerated into Stalinism and antisemitism; the Nazis took power; European antisemitism culminated in the Holocaust, a rupture in world history, while the wider world closed its doors; the Jews from the Arab and Muslim lands were brutally expelled in the 1940s and early 1950s (after millennia of presence); Israel was created with international (and Soviet) approval as a refuge state and as an expression of the Jewish people's right to self-determination. After that climacteric, the left should have made a major reassessment. That much of it has not, blithely carrying on as before, preaching assimilation-only and opposing the existence of Zionism and the Jewish State, I do find remarkable.

PS: I am in full agreement with what you say about Trotsky, so I will only make a couple of additional observations. We need to say very clearly that there has been a widespread failure of many on the Trotskyist left to pay attention to what Trotsky was actually arguing and the way he developed his thinking. This is not a wholly new phenomenon in the history of the left: we saw it this earlier in the way many Marxists after Marx regressed to exactly the position that Marx had come to criticise in his response to Bauer. It is true that Mandel and Traverso did recognise something of Trotsky's contribution to taking antisemitism seriously but they were both pulled back to what we could call a pre-Trotsky position. In Mandel's case, this takes the form of a desperate attempt to claim that antisemitism is only one example of a much broader racism used to justify Western imperialism. This is, at best, a half-truth and like other half-truths, when taken for the whole, can all too easily be deployed for antisemitic purposes. In this case, it is a claim which can be used (as it now very often is) to provide a framework and excuse for many on the left to downgrade the significance of the Holocaust and the specificity of antisemitism. In Traverso's case, a recent book of his, which I reviewed critically in *Fathom*, represents a serious regression from his own early work. He now claims, echoing themes we first encountered in the Enlightenment, that antisemitism was a problem before but is no longer, with the obvious implication that Jews who go on about it now are being dishonest, engaging in special pleading and setting their own interests against others who are far more deserving (see Traverso 2016, Spencer 2017).

Max Horkheimer and Theodor Adorno: Universalism Can 'Compress the Particular Like a Torture Instrument'

AJ: You have praised the Frankfurt School critical theorists Max Horkheimer and Theodor Adorno for making 'the most significant contribution to our understanding of antisemitism from within the Marxist tradition' and – here is this theme again – you suggest one reason was their willingness to critique the economistic Marxist orthodoxy about antisemitism and, like Trotsky, grasp that the eruption of Nazi eliminationist antisemitism into the world demanded 'a major reassessment, not only of antisemitism but also of the Marxist tradition itself' (Fine and Spencer 2017:53–54, 56). In reappraising the legacy of the Enlightenment, I have always been struck by the power of Adorno's insight that universalism can 'compress the particular like a torture instrument'. What can we learn from Adorno and Horkheimer?

PS: First of all, their willingness to *rethink*. They accepted that they might have been seriously wrong on an issue of major importance, with significant implications for their thinking as a whole. This is quite a rare phenomenon. The temptation for many of us on the left is to hold fast to an opinion, in some ways especially as we get older. A fairly awful piece by Horkheimer appeared in 1938. 'The Jews and Europe' viewed Nazi antisemitism as a temporary, secondary phenomenon; a 'safety valve', its violence being 'aimed more at the spectators than the Jews'. If antisemitism had any deeper significance, it had to do with the Jews' supposed role as 'agents of circulation'. The analysis was reductionist, and hopelessly inaccurate (Horkheimer 1989). (This kind of reductionism is very common on the left even today). Other members of the Frankfurt School were equally dismissive, notably Franz Neumann, their acknowledged expert on Nazism. In his major work, *Behemoth* (which came out as late as 1942) he assured his readers that the Nazis had no intention and would 'never allow a complete extermination of the Jews' (2009:125). He assured Adorno on 14August 1940 that one could quite properly 'represent National Socialism without attributing to the Jewish problem [sic] a central role' (cited in Rabinbach 2001:184).

Like Neumann, Horkheimer and Adorno were by now in exile in the United States, but reading their correspondence (and this was an eye-opener for me), you get a very clear sense of how shaken they were by what they were beginning to hear. In 1940 Adorno wrote to Horkheimer to tell him, 'I cannot stop thinking about the Jews any more. It often seems to me that everything we used to see from the point of view of the proletariat has been concentrated with frightful force upon the Jews'. Horkheimer was afraid that 'nothing more remains for the Jews' (see translation in Wiggersaus 1994:275).

So they fundamentally revised their approach to an extent that seems to me to be indispensable for all of us on the left who come after the Holocaust. They now saw antisemitism as *fundamental*. Horkheimer wrote to the English socialist Harold Laski on 10 March 1941, 'Just as it is true that one can only understand antisemitism by examining society, it seems to me that it is becoming equally true that society itself can only be understood through antisemitism' (Wiggersaus 1994:690). To Adorno, in October 1941, he wrote, it is 'the focal point of injustice . . . where the world shows its most horrible face' and 'the central injustice' (Wiggersaus 1994:346, 309). From a universalist perspective, antisemitism is of decisive significance because 'whoever accuses the Jews today aims straight at humanity itself', and so, wrote Horkheimer to Isaac Rosengarten, 'To protect the Jews has come to be a symbol of everything mankind stands for . . . the Jews have been made what the Nazis always pretended they were – the focal point of world history'. 'The Jews have become the martyrs of civilisation' (Horkheimer 1996:223).

Adorno and Horkheimer also teach us that if we are to understand civilisation itself, we have to trace antisemitism back to its origins. This did not mean that antisemitism is eternal and invariant but that it has had many different aspects that have been articulated in different ways over time. In the final chapter of their major revision of Critical Theory, *The Dialectic of Enlightenment*, they essentially produced a template for us to follow (1973 [1943]). Antisemitism is 'much more complicated than I thought', Horkheimer told Adorno. They realised that a host of factors had played a part in its rise – economic, sociological, political, cultural, anthropological, psychological – and so it is necessary to study each not in isolation but in 'their constant interaction' (Horkheimer 1996:463–464).

Of course, all injustices should matter to socialists. We are (or should be) universalists. If you care about antisemitism, it does not mean you do not or cannot care about anything else. (That itself is an antisemitic charge, and part of the framework of the 'Jewish Question'.) All forms of racism, for example, are abhorrent. But antisemitism is not only a form of racism, or, if it seen as such it has very distinct features, in that Jews are seen as not only inferior and sub-human but also – unlike other racisms – *all-powerful, demonic and super-human.*

Horkheimer and Adorno get us thinking about the depth and complexity of antisemitism; how hopeless (even dangerous) it is to reduce it to an 'effect' of something else, or to imagine it is of only passing significance, or to assume that it must have finally disappeared. Even after it had been radicalised to an unprecedented extent by the Nazis, it was unlikely to just vanish. Indeed, Adorno's research after the Holocaust showed how a new variant was emerging, in which guilt about what the Germans had done to the Jews was so unbearable that many projected that guilt back on to the Jews. What Adorno was pointing to here ('secondary antisemitism') has a significance which goes far beyond post-war Germany.

AJ: How important was Adorno's willingness to use the conceptual resources of psychoanalysis – paranoia, repression, projection, delusion, aggression – to explain antisemitism?

PS: Psychoanalysis was a very important resource for both Adorno and Horkheimer. It helped them understand the irrationality of antisemitism, and the unconscious (though not always unconscious) drives within the antisemite. What the Nazis feared (and they were not alone in this) was the supposedly immense power of Jews, not just in Germany but globally. Since this was nonsense, and was contradicted by the idea, held simultaneously, that Jews were weak and pathetic, Adorno and Horkheimer realised the source of the fear must lie not in external reality but in the minds of the antisemites. The hatred and aggression that are attributed to Jews, actually reside *within* the antisemite. These (and other) feelings are so intolerable that they have to be repressed, but they also have to find an outlet, so are projected onto Jews. Of course, there is a level at which this is not always so unconscious. The Nazis claimed that the Jews were going to commit genocide against them, when they were of course planning to do this themselves. This is quite a common strategy in the history of antisemitism by the way. Islamists today – and in this they are often excused or even supported by some on the left – claim that Israel is committing genocide against the Palestinians when it is obvious from their own words that Islamists themselves are the ones who harbour the genocidal ambitions.

Adorno and Horkheimer are telling us that the Nazis were *delusional*. This is something that many (not just on the left) find difficult to deal with, because they think it somehow 'demonises' the Nazis and is the opposite of a materialist explanation that roots Nazism (and antisemitism more generally) in objective circumstances, such as the fact that Germany lost the war, or that the reparations demanded at Versailles were extortionate, or that inflation and mass unemployment helped the Nazis come to power. These are not unimportant factors, but they do not explain why the Nazis explained them as they did – as the fault of the Jews. They also do not explain the madness of the Nazis and how that madness came to be shared by large numbers of people. So, you need to *combine* these ideas with other explanatory factors, as Horkheimer insisted.

Moishe Postone: Left Antisemitism Is 'A Fetishised Form of Anti-Capitalist Consciousness'

AJ: Many of us have been influenced by Moishe Postone's insights into the ways in which certain kinds of left-wing (mis)understandings of 'capitalism' and 'anti-capitalism' can lead to left antisemitism. Anti-semites, from right and left, often have a picture of capitalism as 'Jewish'. Both frame Jews as the *personification* of what's wrong with capitalism, rendering what is really an abstract and authorless system graspable-because-embodied; because 'Jewish'. The way some today rail against 'Rothschild Capitalism' would be a contemporary example of this. The internet has made this problem much worse. But it's really only an updating of the German communist Ruth Fischer instructing the German workers in the 1920s to 'Hang the Jewish capitalists from the lamp posts!' Postone has much to tell us about how left antisemitism can take the form of what he calls a 'fetishised form of oppositional consciousness' (Postone 2006).

PS: Postone is a very important resource for a left that wants to take antisemitism seriously (see Postone 2003). He was one of the first to identify the widespread failure of the New Left in Germany to place antisemitism at the heart of its understanding of Nazism (Postone 1980). It wasn't just that many saw antisemitism only as an epiphenomenon but that they then engaged in what he called a 'psychological reversal' (updating in a way Adorno's earlier analysis of German guilt) to portray Jews as the new Nazis. Shockingly, this has become a quite common trope, not just in Germany but more widely in the antizionist world. His own analysis, in sharp contrast, anchored an explanation of antisemitism in his understanding of Marx, going back to the distinction the latter made right at the beginning of *Capital* between the two aspects of a commodity – its use value (as something usable and tangible) and its exchange value (very roughly speaking, and this is a shorthand, its price in the marketplace). Postone said antisemites tend to see capitalism not as what it is, an abstract *system*; instead they personify it as 'Jewish'. They make the abstract qualities of capitalism intelligible by personifying them. Capitalism is certainly intangible, its decisions always seem to be hidden (but that's because 'they' are hiding them, says the antisemite). Capitalism is mobile, universal and global (but that is because 'they' are everywhere, alien to every place, nation, and state, says the antisemite). This process of personification is, according to Postone, a prime example of what Marx identified as reification and fetishism. By attributing every bad consequence of capitalism to the wicked intentions and actions of a particular and tiny set of people, 'the' Jews, who are viewed as having astounding, superhuman, even demonic powers, the antisemite thinks they have 'explained' what is in reality a very confusing *system*, with no centre, but with an impersonal logic by which we are all constrained. Postone then explained different articulations of antisemitism in the modern world in relation to shifts in the capitalist mode of production. Antisemitism, in each case, presents itself as an explanation for everything that is going wrong. But as a purportedly anti-hegemonic resistance it is at best a 'pseudo-emancipatory' politics which is in fact not remotely progressive.

Contemporary left antisemitism is arguably making an even worse mistake. What we have now is antisemitism as 'the anti-imperialism of fools' in which a section of the left supports and condones a host of appallingly reactionary regimes and movements, many of them Islamists such as Hamas, Hezbollah and Iran, but also other tyrannical regimes that are oppressive of their own peoples – and antisemitic.

AJ: Judith Butler infamously said that 'Understanding Hamas and Hezbollah as social movements that are progressive, that are on the left, that are part of a global left, is extremely important'. She looks at the fascistic, but somehow sees something progressive, part of the left. You can't really get more politically disorientated than that (Johnson 2013, Nelson 2014, Berman 2016).

PS: During the Cold War, a large part of the anti-capitalist left destroyed itself by uncritically supporting the Stalinist 'camp', condoning and excusing the misery and injustice it too inflicted. Postone argues rightly that today's idiotic form of anti-imperialism is even worse because back then at least there was *some* connection, for a brief period, between the Soviet Union as the object of left-wing dreams and delusions and the goals of the left. Today the regimes and movements making up the anti-Western camp, have always slaughtered the left in their own societies, and always engaged in their own violent imperialist projects of annexation, conquest and exploitation. Antisemitism is often the glue that holds these contemporary 'anti-imperialist' alliances together. Behind the US, and within the US, lurks, for this section of the left and for their allies, the greatest enemy of all – the Jews.

Norman Geras: On Israel, 'Alibi Antisemitism' and the Holocaust

AJ: Norman Geras was my tutor at university in the early 1980s and has been a major influence since then; though we disagreed about the Iraq War, which I opposed (Johnson 2017). In 2006 we both worked with him and others to create the Euston Manifesto, a statement of left principles, which Norman pretty much wrote (see Euston Manifesto Group 2006). He once told an interviewer that 'I think of myself in the category of the "non-Jewish Jew" discussed by Isaac Deutscher' but added that he ascribed to himself a quality often lacking in those listed by Deutscher: 'a more particularistic concern for the future of the Jews'. He was a supporter of the two-state solution: 'Israeli Jews and

Palestinians alike have a right to national self-determination' (2002-3:213, 214).

One contribution of his, made in an essay in *Dissent* in 2005, and regularly at his blog, was to identify those post-9/11 'reductions of the left' which contributed to contemporary left antisemitism (Geras 2005). Parts of the left, he argued, had reduced world politics to a crude two-camp world view which meant that they had stopped attending to the nature of the perpetrators of terrorism if it was aimed at America or its allies: 'the weight and specificity of their religious outlook, of their political project, of the social values they represent' were excluded from left analyses. If included, it was only in passing – he called it 'throat-clearing' – and was allowed no *political weight*. Geras believed these outlooks, projects and values, should have made clear to the left that these perpetrators were comparable not to revolutionary freedom fighters but to *fascists* (2002–3:208). 'It is worrying' he observed, that the left did not register 'blatant moral criminality, fuelled by religious certainty' as being 'a menace far beyond the cities of America, and – emergent out of whatever conditions – one antithetical to every ideal of its own' (2002–3:209). These reductions led parts of the left to believe that Israel has no right to self-defence against Hezbollah, Hamas, and Palestinian Islamic Jihad. Instead, there was a quite ludicrous romanticisation of such forces, who were credulously praised for 'bringing about long-term peace and social justice and political justice in the whole region', as Jeremy Corbyn did (Corbyn 2009). Geras indicted a segment of left and liberal opinion with routinely failing to oppose the 'indiscriminate murder of Israeli civilians' and failing to see that such violence was 'directed against the existence of Israel as such' and 'against Jews' (Geras 2002-3:214).

Another contribution was his essay 'Alibi Antisemitism' which argued that the relationship between Jews and the left was being undermined by a new climate of antisemitic opinion within parts of the left, but 'Israel' was being invoked, he thought, as an *alibi* to deflect the charge that there was anything of antisemitism at work. He gave examples of four types of 'alibi antisemitism' found on parts of the left. First, the breezy dismissal of antisemitism as an 'understandable' epiphenomenon of the Israel-Palestine conflict. Second, as non-existent in the absence of clear and deliberate subjective antisemitic intent. Third, as mere programmatic rhetoric, also understandable and 'so not to be treated as in earnest'. Lastly, as something one is politically obliged to turn a blind eye to (Geras 2013).

Parts of the left, he argued, were espousing a *spurious* type of universalism for the Jews, who were held to be 'special amongst other groups in being obliged to settle for forms of political freedom in which their identity may not be asserted collectively' (Geras 2013). So while he was a sharp critic of several Israeli policies – he believed that 'the absolute, and principal, precondition for a just solution of the conflict is the abandonment of the Israeli occupation of the West Bank and Gaza and the dismantling of Jewish settlements there' and that 'the major responsibility for an initiative towards finding a solution lies with Israel' (2002–3:214) – he distinguished legitimate criticism of that kind (whatever its fairness or accuracy in any particular instance) from the demonising and dehumanising animus directed at Israel by the parts of the left today, which he thought was often of a plainly antisemitic character, relying on modern refits of old anti-Jewish stereotypes.

When left-wingers protested that because they didn't hate Jews as Jews, as the Nazis did, nothing they said about Israel, Israelis, Zionism and Zionists could be antisemitic, Geras was especially impatient. At Normblog he argued again and again that intention isn't everything. Sometimes, he pointed out, it's not much at all. 'It is constantly surprising how stuck people can be over the view that racist prejudice is *simply* a matter of what one intends; and how stubbornly they resist the obvious truth that words and symbols carry meanings associated with their history and which cannot simply be disowned by declarations of good will'. The absence of subjectively malicious intent is not decisive because 'language doesn't fully belong to any individual user or even small group of users. Words acquire meanings and associations as part of a whole structure of usage, and you can't simply legislate away hateful connotations by declarations of intent'. He gave the example of Steve Bell, the *Guardian* cartoonist, who drew Israeli PM Benjamin Netanyahu as a huge, looming puppet-master, towering over and manipulating Tony Blair and William Hague, depicted as his glove puppets, a classic antisemitic trope of the all powerful string-pulling Jew. Bell angrily rejected the criticism, saying 'I can't be held responsible for whatever cultural precepts and misapprehensions people choose to bring to my cartoon'. Geras pointed out what was wrong with this response: 'He *can* be held responsible for the meanings widely attached to symbols he chooses to use. Where words, pictures, meanings are concerned, it isn't just up to him what these must signify for the rest of the world. He can confirm this for himself by drawing some other racist stereotypes (than anti-Jewish ones) in the weeks ahead to see what happens. It is, however, entirely common these days for anti-Semitism to be thought of as being in people's heads and nowhere else' (All quotes from Normblog).

His anger at the *Guardian* newspaper went deep. 'This once great paper of British liberalism now provides space on its opinion pages for the spokesman of Hamas, the contents of its programmatic charter notwithstanding; provides space on its letters page for philosophers justifying the murder of Jews; and provides space on its website for people who deploy well-known antisemitic themes even while professing that they have nothing whatever against Jews'. The result of all this, Geras argued, amounted to a moral scandal: the return to respectability of antisemitic themes and ruses 'within polite society, and within the perimeters of a self-flattering liberal and left opinion' (Geras 2013).

PS: Norman Geras was probably the most important influence on me over a long period of time, especially his book on the Holocaust, *The Contract of Mutual Indifference* (1998). The central thesis of the first half of the book has to do with the indifference of so many to the Jews in the Holocaust and what that tells us about the limits of and need for solidarity, and about our responsibility to others not just in our own society but to others beyond the borders of the nation state. Its conclusion is clear – and stark: if you do not come to the aid of others when they need your solidarity, you cannot expect them to come your aid when you need theirs. That would be what he calls a 'contract of mutual indifference'. If you are a socialist, that is fundamentally unacceptable of course. But why then was there so much indifference, even on the left, to what was done to the Jews?

He then goes on to address two closely related questions. The first concerns our political horizons, i.e. what we can reasonably hope for, as socialists, *after* the Holocaust. He argues that the occurrence of catastrophe means we have to *rethink* what is possible and desirable. We now live with the possibility of a catastrophic regression and so 'a shadow stretches across the vision at the heart of the socialist project' (1998:113). We now know more about the capacity of human beings for evil, so we have to guard against it, and struggle to secure some basic minimum of security, freedoms and rights for all citizens. This 'minimum utopia' should be the ground from which socialist efforts to go further than capitalism must take off (Geras 2000).

This is not an abstract question at all. There are states, largely in the capitalist West (for all the criticisms that socialists rightly make of them) that have accorded these rights since the Holocaust. A simplistic and malign anti-Westernism, aimed primarily at the United States and Israel as its supposed tool (or vice versa), he argued, could have grave consequences when it led sections of the left as it has done, especially since 9/11, to condone or even support those movements and states which actually aimed to destroy precisely those states where those rights had been won.

The second question has to do with the extent to which the attempt not just to take those rights away from, but to kill every Jewish person on earth, seems to have been unimaginable to so many on the left. I think it still is today, even though (or, to go back to Adorno, precisely because) it has been attempted. Until I read Norman's book, I had taken for granted that there was a coherent and convincing Marxist account of and response to the Holocaust. To my great surprise I found hardly anything – and what I did find was often dismaying, not least because so few on the left actually saw antisemitism as central to the Holocaust. (Postone had already pointed this out but I hadn't properly read him at that point). If you cannot see antisemitism in the Holocaust, you are not likely to see it anywhere. If you cannot see how the Holocaust changed everything for Jews, you cannot recognise how they are acutely sensitive to its reappearance and feel the need for a protection that wasn't there then: their own state – Israel. From Geras's perspective, we could say this is a form or aspect of the 'minimum' that is needed after catastrophe.

Final Thoughts

PS: For me, all the thinkers we have been discussing provide support for a universalist (I would say cosmopolitan) politics, grounded in solidarity with all suffering injustice across the globe, including Jews. The universalism of some of the left today is both highly selective and toxic, because it excludes Jews and casts them out as its criminal other. One of its most serious consequences is that it legitimates a particularly revolting argument, that Jews are now the perpetrators of the very crime committed against them – genocide. The latter has, along with the issue of antisemitism, been the focus of my own work in recent years, and I see them as closely connected, in at least two respects. The first is that genocide as the crime of crimes was first identified after and because of the Holocaust (Spencer 2012). It was the event that lit up the sky as it were. So, what happened to Jews did affect everyone, or at least everyone who was shocked by it. The second is that genocide is committed both against a particular group and against humanity. It has two sides – the particular and the universal. A universalism that only sees the latter is seriously flawed. It invariably downplays antisemitism and what was done to the Jews. It typically claims that too much is made of the suffering of the Jews, and that now, after the Holocaust, antisemitism no longer matters. This line of argument essentially rearticulates antisemitic tropes first visible in the Enlightenment – that Jews make too much of their suffering, that Jews going on about antisemitism is more special pleading, seeking to privilege Jews at the expense of far more deserving others, when antisemitism belongs only to the past, with the clear implication that if there is any antisemitism today it must be because Jews provoke it.

But the particularist converse, that only the Holocaust and antisemitism matter, is also seriously flawed, and can lead to the refusal of solidarity with those facing genocide, although as a matter of fact this has rarely been the case. But to the extent that anyone does think like this, it does a disservice to the struggle against antisemitism itself, as well as to the victims of other genocides, who all need solidarity, because none can survive without the help of others.

None of this means that I do not see the necessity today for the state of Israel, after the Holocaust, in a world of nation states. But I do not think the nation state is the last word in political organisation, and I think nationalism always has a powerful exclusionary dynamic (Spencer and Wollman 2002, Fine 2007). It always has the problem of who is to be included in the nation and on what grounds. All nation states have problems with this, so we have to find a way to go beyond nationalism and the nation state, sooner or later.

Doing so must start from insisting that we are part of one inherently diverse humanity, that we owe solidarity to any group within it which suffers injustice. But the history of humanity, and of solidarity on the left, is not a story of linear progression and we need to think critically about how and why we have gone forward at times and backwards at others, above all with the Holocaust in whose shadow we all now live. After that catastrophe, socialist hope cannot be the same. But if we do not hold on to the hope, then all we are left with is the shadow.

AJ: I am pessimistic about the future of the radical left and so of its capacity to be the repository of that hope. Social democracy once thought the task of the left was not to *trash* the civilisational gains of the twin revolutions, industrial and democratic, but to preserve them, regulate and humanise them, and struggle to *extend* their best fruits to all: in the first instance to workers, women and colonised subjects. And it looked not to middle class 'activists', tenured radicals or the churn of 'revolutionary' students, but to popular movements, trades unions and mass workers' parties to be the core of a great international movement of rational reform. But since the disastrous anti-liberal and anti-democratic detours of Bolshevism, Stalinism, Maoism, Authoritarian New Left Third Worldism, and since the dubious innovations of postmodern 'Theory' and middle-class identity politics, I am not sure how much of that rational, serious, social democratic left remains. As for the social neoliberalism of the 'Third Way', it has proved to be more of an exit from social democratic politics than its renewal.

Today, I see a radical left that supports or apologises for violence against the West and its allies, including violence from some of the most reactionary forces on the planet. So we get the radical left marching under the banner 'We Are All Hezbollah Now!' or calling Hamas 'progressive' or acting as lawyers for Putin or the CCP.

I see a radical left that is in retreat to a time before social democratic mass politics, when middle-class utopian socialist sects dreamt of using an 'Enlightened Dictatorship' to impose from above their vision of utopia on the poor beknighted plebs below. I think we have that mindset, and those sects, in new forms today. The older social democratic preference for reasoned critique, mass movements and popular reforms is being replaced by a mostly worthless postmodern 'cynical theory', middle class activism, and the fundamentally dishonest politics of institutional capture-and-control-by-minorities rich in time and cultural capital.

I see a rational materialist outlook giving way on the radical left to the extravagant belief that everything is 'culturally and socially constructed'. The materialist left-wing philosopher Sebastiano Timpanaro warned us back in the early 1970s, a half century ago, that the left's war on materialism, its 'contempt for . . . the ground floor' of our existence, i.e. its refusal to accept that the human being is a 'biological being' not 'an abstract construction', was becoming 'increasingly pronounced' and this would not sustain a rational politics (Timpanaro 1975:45). How right he was! But who talks of Timpanaro today?

Instead, I see the rise and rise of three kinds of relativism on the left, each socially and intellectually disintegrative: epistemological relativism ('there is no Truth'); moral relativism ('there is no Right'); and cultural relativism ('there are no cultural values or practices that are better than any others'). Of course, each of these relativisms is strictly *faux*: the truths, values and cultural commitments of the West are not granted equal, or indeed *any* billing; they are trashed ('Debate is Hate!', 'Objectivity is a cover for Western Subjectivity!' and so on), or they are imprisoned in sneering inverted commas. The universities are being turned by the left into sites of dull conformism, in which intellectual pluralism is cast aside in favour of a new Left Orthodoxy. Dissidents are hounded. I just don't recognise any of this as leading to a just and free society.

As for Israel, this new radical left treats it as an abomination; a 'white', 'western', 'racist', 'imperialist' or 'Nazi-like' oppressor; part of, or even the dark centre of 'Empire', with no right to continue existing. It either supports, or will not raise its hand to oppose, the many murderous antisemitic enemies of the world's only Jewish state (see Hirsh 2018). So if we want our course to be set on hope, we will need a very different map than that being offered by the radical left today.

Notes

1 David Nirenberg's *Anti-Judaism* (2013) showed conclusively how, at times, certain versions of each religion (both of which saw themselves as universalist) cast Jews as their essential and denigrated other.

2 In 1916, the Prussian army ordered a census of Jews serving in the army. The implication was that Jews were not doing their bit for the war effort – the exact opposite
of the case. Approximately 100,000 German Jews fought, 18,000 died, and 12,000
won the Iron Cross during World War I.
3 Bornstein and Richardson note the behaviour of the CPGB leader Rajani Palme
Dutt during the Nazi-Soviet Pact. 'By laying all the blame for the continuation
of the war on the shoulders of the British government, [he] had converted the
Communist Party into an instrument of Hitler's propaganda in the country.' When
Hitler invaded the low countries, the CPGB ran the headline, 'Britain spreads the
War to Holland'. School students took to greeting known communist teachers with
mock Nazi salutes (1982:68). Only when Hitler turned on Stalin on 22 June 1941,
did the supposedly 'anti-fascist' British Stalinists turn on Hitler and support the
Allied war effort.
4 Blatman and Poznanski tell us that the Communist underground press effectively
organised a 'total silence . . . even when an antisemitic propaganda campaign was
launched and even when it directly targeted the resistance . . . [T]hroughout the
occupation, the resistance spared no effort to prove that its members had not signed
up to the goal of defending the Jews' (2011:201).

References

Arendt, Hannah (1965) *Eichmann in Jerusalem: A Report on the Banality of Evil*,
New York: Viking Press.
Bankier, David (2000) 'Ethos versus expediency: German social democrats and the
Jewish question', in D. Bankier (ed.), *Probing the Depths of German Antisemitism:
German Society and the Persecution of the Jews 1933–1941*, Oxford: Berghahn,
511–532.
Berman, Russell (2016) 'Misrepresenting the Trial: Judith Butler Reads Hannah Arendt
Reading Adolf Eichmann', *Fathom*, Spring. Available: https://fathomjournal.
org/representing-the-trial-judith-butler-reads-hannah-arendt-reading-adolf-
eichmann/?highlight=JUdith%20Butler (accessed 28 February 2023).
Blatman, Daniel and Renée Poznanski (2011) 'Jews and their social environment:
Perspectives from the underground press in Poland and France', in Beata Kosmala
and Georgi Verbeeck (eds.) *Facing the Catastrophe: Jews and Non-Jews in Europe
During World War Two*, Oxford: Berg.
Bornstein, Sam and Al Richardson (1982) *Two Steps Back. Communists and the
Wider Labour Movement, 1939–1945. A Study in the Relations Between Van-
guard and Class*, Ilford: Socialist Platform.
Brent, Jonathan and Vladimir P. Naumov (2003) *Stalin's Last Crime. The Plot Against
the Jewish Doctors, 1948–1953*, New York: Harper Collins.
Corbyn, Jeremy (2009) 'Stop the war coalition – Meet the resistance – Jeremy
Corbyn MP London 3 March 2009', *YouTube*. Available: www.youtube.com/
watch?v=FQLKpY3NdeA (accessed 28 February 2023).
Deutscher, Isaac (1968) *The Non-Jewish Jew and Other Essays*, London: Oxford
University Press.
Euston Manifesto Group (2006) 'The Euston Manifesto', *Democratiya*, 5. Avail-
able: www.dissentmagazine.org/wp-content/files_mf/1390330362d5Euston.pdf
(accessed 28 February 2023).
Fine, Robert (2007) *Cosmopolitanism*, London and New York: Routledge.
Fine. Robert and Philip Spencer (2017) *Antisemitism and the Left: On the Return of
the Jewish Question*, Manchester: Manchester University Press.

Fischer, Lars (2007) *The Socialist Response to Antisemitism in Imperial Germany*, Cambridge: Cambridge University Press.

Geras, Norman (1998) *The Contract of Mutual Indifference: Political Philosophy After the Holocaust*, London and New York: Verso.

Geras, Norman (2000) 'Minimum Utopia: Ten theses', in *Socialist Register 2000: Necessary and Unnecessary Utopias*, London: The Merlin Press. Available: www.marxists.org/reference/subject/philosophy/works/us/geras1.htm (accessed 28 February 2023).

Geras, Norman (2002-3) 'Marxism, the Holocaust and September 11: An interview with Norman Geras', *Imprints: A Journal of Analytical Socialism*, 6 (3): 194–214.

Geras, Norman (2005) 'The Reductions of the Left', *Dissent*, 52 (1): 55–60.

Geras, Norman (2013) 'Alibi Antisemitism', *Fathom*, Spring. Available: https://fathomjournal.org/alibi-antisemitism/?highlight=Alibi%20Antisemitism (accessed 28 February 2023).

Herf, Jeffrey (1995) 'German communism, the discourse of "anti-fascist resistance" and the Jewish catastrophe', in Michael Geyer and John W. Boyer (eds.), *Resistance in the Third Reich*, Chicago: Chicago University Press, 257–294.

Hirsh, David (2018) *Contemporary Left-Antisemitism*, London and New York: Routledge.

Horkheimer, Max (1989) [1938]) 'The Jews in Europe', in Stephen Eric Bronner and Douglas Kellner (eds.) *Critical Theory and Society*, London and New York: Routledge, 77–94.

Horkheimer, Max (1996) *Gesammelte Schriften Vol. 17 Briefwechsel 1941–1948*, edited by Gunzelin Schmid Noerr, Frankfurt am Main: Fischer.

Horkheimer, Max and Theodor W. Adorno (1973 [1943]) *Dialectic of Enlightenment*, London: Allen Lane.

Johnson, Alan (2013) 'Book review. Parting ways: Jewishness and the critique of Zionism', *Fathom*, Spring. Available: https://fathomjournal.org/book-review-parting-ways-jewishness-and-the-critique-of-zionism/?highlight=JUdith%20Butler (accessed 28 February 2023).

Johnson, Alan (2017) 'On Geras's Marxism', in Ben Cohen and Eve Garrard (eds.), *The Norman Geras Reader: 'What's There Is There'*, Manchester: Manchester University Press, 9–13.

Johnson, Alan (2019) 'Leon Trotsky's long war against antisemitism', *Fathom*, March. Available: https://fathomjournal.org/the-fathom-long-read-leon-trotskys-long-war-against-antisemitism/ (accessed 28 February 2023).

Luxemburg, Rosa (1970 [1915]) 'The Junius Pamphlet: The crisis in German social democracy', in Mary-Alice Waters (ed.), *Rosa Luxemburg Speaks*, New York: Pathfinder.

Mandel, Ernest (1995) *Trotsky as Alternative*, London and New York: Verso.

Marx, Karl (1975 [1843]) 'On the Jewish question', *Early Writings*, Harmondsworth: Pelican, 211–241.

Nelson, Cary (2014) 'The problem with Judith Butler: The political philosophy of the movement to boycott Israel', *Los Angeles Review of Books*, 16 March. Available: https://lareviewofbooks.org/article/problem-judith-butler-political-philosophy-movement-boycott-israel/ (accessed 28 February 2023).

Neumann, Franz (2009 [1942]) *Behemoth: The Structure and Practice of National Socialism*, London and Chicago, IL: Ivan R. Dee.

Nirenberg, David (2013) *Anti-Judaism: The History of a Way of Thinking*, London: Head of Zeus.

Postone, Moishe (1980) 'Anti-Semitism and national socialism. Notes on the German reaction to "holocaust"', *New German Critique*, 19: 97–115.

Postone, Moishe (2003) 'The holocaust and the trajectory of the twentieth century', in Moishe Postone and Eric Santner (eds.), *Catastrophe and Meaning*, Chicago: University of Chicago Press, 81–116.

Postone, Moishe (2006) 'History and helplessness: Mass mobilization and contemporary forms of anticapitalism', *Public Culture*, 18 (1): 93–110. Available: https://platypus1917.org/wp-content/uploads/readings/postonemoishe_historyhelplessness.pdf (accessed 28 February 2023).

Rabinbach, Anson (2001) 'The cunning of unreason: Mimesis and the construction of antisemitism in Horkheimer and Adorno's *dialectic of enlightenment*', in *His in the Shadow of Catastrophe: German Intellectuals Between Apocalypse and Enlightenment*, Berkeley: University of California Press.

Rubenstein, Joshua and Vladimir P. Naumov (2001) *Stalin's Secret Pogrom: The Postwar Inquisition of the Jewish Anti-Fascist Committee*, New Haven and London: Yale University Press.

Spencer, Philip (2012) *Genocide Since 1945*, London and New York: Routledge.

Spencer, Philip (2017) 'Book review. The end of Jewish modernity', *Fathom*, Autumn. Available: https://fathomjournal.org/book-review-the-end-of-jewish-modernity/?highlight=Philip%20Spencer (accessed 28 February 2023).

Spencer, Philip and Howard Wollman (2002) *Nationalism: A Critical Introduction*, London: Sage.

Timpanaro, Sebastiano (1975) *On Materialism*, London: NLB.

Traverso, Enzo (1994 [1990]) *The Marxists and the Jewish Question: The History of a Debate 1843–1943*, Atlantic Highlands, NJ: Humanities Press.

Traverso, Enzo (2016) *The End of Jewish Modernity*, London: Pluto.

Trotsky, Leon (1937) 'Thermidor and antisemitism'. Available: www.marxists.org/archive/trotsky/1937/02/therm.htm (accessed 28 February 2023).

Trotsky, Leon (1937–1940) *On the Jewish Problem* (Excerpts from four statements). Available: www.marxists.org/archive/trotsky/1940/xx/jewish.htm (accessed 28 February 2023).

Trotsky, Leon (1971) *1905*, London: Pelican.

Wiggershaus, Ralf (1994) *The Frankfurt School: Its History, Theories, and Political Significance*, Cambridge: Polity Press.

Wistrich, Robert (2012) *From Ambivalence to Betrayal: The Left, the Jews and Israel*, Nebraska: University of Nebraska Press.

INDEX